Designs on the Past

Neil

Happy Christmas

lots of love

David xx

Pete
x

Screening Antiquity
Series Editors: Monica S. Cyrino and Lloyd Llewellyn-Jones
Screening Antiquity is a cutting-edge and provocative series of academic monographs and edited volumes focusing on new research on the reception of the ancient world in film and television. Screening Antiquity showcases the work of the best-established and up-and-coming specialists in the field. It provides an important synergy of the latest international scholarly ideas about the conception of antiquity in popular culture and is the only series that focuses exclusively on screened representations of the ancient world.

Editorial Advisory Board
Antony Augoustakis, Alastair Blanshard, Robert Burgoyne, Lisa Maurice, Gideon Nisbet, Joanna Paul, Jon Solomon

Titles available in the series
Rome *Season Two: Trial and Triumph*
Edited by Monica S. Cyrino
Ben-Hur: *The Original Blockbuster*
Jon Solomon
Cowboy Classics: The Roots of the American Western in the Epic Tradition
Kirsten Day
STARZ Spartacus: *Reimagining an Icon on Screen*
Edited by Antony Augoustakis and Monica S. Cyrino
Ancient Greece on British Television
Edited by Fiona Hobden and Amanda Wrigley
Epic Heroes on Screen
Edited by Antony Augoustakis and Stacie Raucci
Designs on the Past: How Hollywood Created the Ancient World
Lloyd Llewellyn-Jones

Forthcoming Titles
Screening the Golden Ages
Edited by Meredith Safran
Pontius Pilate on Screen: Soldier, Sinner, Superstar
Christopher McDonough
Screening Divinity
Lisa Maurice
Screening Antiquity in the War on Terror
Alex McAuley

Designs on the Past

How Hollywood Created the Ancient World

Lloyd Llewellyn-Jones

EDINBURGH
University Press

Edinburgh University Press is one of the leading university presses in the UK. We publish academic books and journals in our selected subject areas across the humanities and social sciences, combining cutting-edge scholarship with high editorial and production values to produce academic works of lasting importance. For more information visit our website: edinburghuniversitypress.com

© Lloyd Llewellyn-Jones, 2018

Edinburgh University Press Ltd
The Tun – Holyrood Road, 12(2f) Jackson's Entry, Edinburgh EH8 8PJ

Typeset in 10/12 Palatino by
Servis Filmsetting Ltd, Stockport, Cheshire
and printed and bound in Great Britain.

A CIP record for this book is available from the British Library

ISBN 978 0 7486 7563 0 (hardback)
ISBN 978 0 7486 7565 4 (webready PDF)
ISBN 978 0 7486 7564 7 (paperback)
ISBN 978 0 7486 7566 1 (epub)

The right of Lloyd Llewellyn-Jones to be identified as the author of this work has been asserted in accordance with the Copyright, Designs and Patents Act 1988, and the Copyright and Related Rights Regulations 2003 (SI No. 2498).

CONTENTS

Cartoon sketch: Cecil B. DeMille directs *The Sign of the Cross*. Magazine cutting, 1932.

SERIES EDITORS' PREFACE

Screening Antiquity is a new series of cutting-edge academic monographs and edited volumes that present exciting and original research on the reception of the ancient world in film and television. It provides an important synergy of the latest international scholarly ideas about the on-screen conception of antiquity in popular culture and is the only book series to focus exclusively on screened representations of the ancient world.

The interactions between cinema, television and historical representation is a growing field of scholarship and student engagement; many Classics and Ancient History departments in universities worldwide teach cinematic representations of the past as part of their programmes in Reception Studies. Scholars are now questioning how historical films and television series reflect the societies in which they were made and speculate on how attitudes towards the past have been moulded in the popular imagination by their depiction in the movies. Screening Antiquity explores how these constructions came about and offers scope to analyse how and why the ancient past is filtered through on-screen representations in specific ways. The series highlights exciting and original publications that explore the representation of antiquity on-screen, and that employ modern theoretical and cultural perspectives to examine screened antiquity, including: stars and star text, directors and auteurs, cinematography, design and art direction, marketing, fans and the online presence of the ancient world.

The series aims to present original research focused exclusively on the reception of the ancient world in film and television. In itself this is an exciting and original approach. There is no other book series that engages head-on with both big-screen and small-screen recreations of the past, yet their integral interactivity is clear to see: film popularity has a major impact on television productions and, for its part, television regularly influences cinema (including film spin-offs of popular television series). This is the first academic series to identify and encourage the holistic interactivity of these two major media institutions, and the first to promote interdisciplinary research in all the fields of Cinema Studies, Media Studies, Classics and Ancient History.

Screening Antiquity explores the various facets of on-screen creations of the past, exploring the theme from multiple angles. Some volumes will foreground a Classics 'reading' of the subject, analysing the nuances of film and television productions against a background of ancient literature, art, history or culture; others will focus more on Media 'readings', by privileging the on-screen creation of the past or positioning the film or television representation within the context of modern popular culture. A third 'reading' will allow for a more fluid interaction between both the Classics and Media approaches. All three methods are valuable, since Reception Studies demands a flexible approach whereby individual scholars, or groups of researchers, foster a reading of an on-screen 'text' particular to their angle of viewing.

Screening Antiquity represents a major turning point in that it signals a better appreciation and understanding of the rich and complex interaction between the past and contemporary culture, and also of the lasting significance of antiquity in today's world.

Monica S. Cyrino and Lloyd Llewellyn-Jones
Series Editors

To Monica

Who 'was already eminent when my eminence was merely imminent'.
And who has brought so much learning, insight, fun and humanity to
film reception studies.

MOVIE TRAILER

One of the reasons I became an ancient historian was because, as a child, I overdosed on Hollywood epics. I saw a lot of them, although I particularly remember watching *Solomon and Sheba* on a wet Saturday afternoon in my grandparent's house in Cefn Cribwr, south Wales. (In those pre video, DVD, Blu-ray, downloadable days the BBC would always run a good, long movie to counteract the sport which was shown on the two other channels.) I vividly recall the film's opening credits: to a soundtrack of heavenly choirs and set against a pale pink stone carved with (what I later learned were) Assyrian reliefs, gilded lettering spelled out the film's title and the exotic names of the movie stars. I knew of King Solomon of course from my Sunday School lessons (again remember that this was Wales in the 1970s and I was chapel all the way) and I also knew that the Queen of Sheba had visited him, but I knew little else about them. I was willing to learn though and so I settled in to watch the film. By the time the movie had ended I knew all about Solomon's illicit love for Sheba, the wickedness of his brother Adonijah, the Egyptian pharaoh's invasion of Israel and the destruction of Jerusalem's temple, and I had followed with puzzled enthusiasm the orgiastic sex rites in celebration of the god Ragon, the Sheban god of love. In three hours my knowledge of biblical history had expanded considerably and I hadn't needed to open a single book (let alone the Bible). In the following years I developed a distinct penchant for the Hollywood epic and each Easter would find me sitting reverentially through the various Jesus movies shown on TV over the holiday. The Golgotha scenes always impressed me the most. I remember being struck that *Ben-Hur*, my favourite Easter movie, never showed Jesus' face and that he only appeared with his back to the camera. But I certainly loved the Valley of the Lepers and I recall being intrigued by the Judah-Messala 'thing'. Christmas meant that the BBC would broadcast epics with a different feel: *Cleopatra*, *The Fall of the Roman Empire* and *Spartacus*. I was infatuated – overawed – by Elizabeth Taylor the very first time I saw her wearing the Egyptian-style eyeliner and I recall sitting with a sketch-pad hurriedly trying to capture her costumes in coloured pencils as a way of remembering the look of the film movie. This became a tradition for me and I realised early on that the sets and costumes were the most memorable and exciting part of my watching experience. I recall thinking that the scenes were often over-long and the dialogue was usually a bit too biblical.

It was while watching *Solomon and Sheba* that something else began to stir in me and which later began to define who I would be. I recall *very* clearly Gina Lollobrigida's costumes – all that gold, all those fleshy bosoms (she seemed to have a bigger share than most women), all those sequined veils, and bangles, and necklaces, and bling upon bling. I loved it all. Of course I did. I loved too the way Lollobrigida moved and the style in which she spoke in an alluring (not Welsh) accent (persuading her parrot to 'Come . . . come . . . come . . .') and how – in the aforementioned sex rites of Ragon – she shimmied, shook and rotated her hips. I realised even at that young age that I did not desire Gina Lollobrogida, but *perhaps* I desired to be her. I do remember thinking her fabulous though, a thing of great beauty but also sort of . . . Well I didn't have a word for it then. But later the word I would use was 'camp'. Gina Lollobrigida was camp. The love-rites of Ragon were certainly camp. Hell, *Solomon and Sheba* was camp. From that point camp came to define the epic genre for me. It still does. As I see it, camp is not necessarily gay (although of course it can be a strong queer aesthetic). No, camp is an artifice that masquerades as the truth and so, in that respect, epic films tend to be more camp than any other film genre because they try to take themselves seriously while giving themselves over to an outrageous Hollywoodian flamboyancy. Incidentally, *Solomon and Sheba* did not make me gay, although Yul Brynner sort of did. But not the Solomon Yul Brynner, but the King of Siam Yul Brynner. When I first saw him dance that vigorously sexy polka with Deborah Kerr in *The King and I* and I gawped at how the hoops of her huge crinoline skirt flew around behind her, *that's* when I knew I was gay.

My mother was a movie fan and she could roll off the names of Hollywood stars and the films they made with the casual abandon of a real fan. I used to enjoy talking to her about her cinema-going experiences in Wales in the 1950s and the excitement and glamour the movie stars brought to the lives of her and her girl-friends in rural Glamorgan. She would walk four miles with them, a gaggle of teenagers in full petticoat frocks and bobby-socks, to catch the local bus to Bridgend, the nearest town some ten miles away, to go to the 'pictures' (the Embassy Cinema). This was not a casual night out, it was a weekly pilgrimage. My father too was (and is) a huge fan of films – Westerns are his favourites – and in the 1930s and 1940s he would spend hours in the Welfare Hall, Pyle with his sister watching the gun-slinging as well as the usual programme of cartoons, shorts and newsreels. My dad also liked Errol Flynn movies where, either as Robin Hood or Captain Blood, he would end up rescuing the long-suffering Olivia de Havilland; he has no patience for Margaret O'Brian movies though ('She was always crying because nobody believed in fairies'). Even my grandmother, no great fan of 'the pictures', had her favourite actor: Robert Taylor.

With my family life and family memories truly bound up in films and film-going, as well as my own formative experiences of self-recognition, needless to say cinema has retained a central place in my life. I especially love the experience of watching films of the 1930s, the 1940s and 1950s maybe because they coincided with my parents' cinema-going heyday which I enjoyed hearing about so much and probably because they give me an insight into the manners, morals and dreams of a generation lost. My working life too has always nodded towards my formative experiences with epic films: I worked for many years as a costume designer in the theatre and in television and then as a theatre director for a decade before the call of academia became too powerful. And now I get to indulge my love of film in different and ever-changing ways. This book is a product then of years of film-watching, of family histories, of scholarly endeavour (I hope), and of happily teaching film reception courses to enthusiastic students, as well as a personal fascination with 'old Hollywood'.

Over the years I have put together a sizeable collection of original materials relating to the creation of Hollywood epics. These include pressbooks, still images, advertising materials and tie-ins. All the images in this book are taken from my private collection.

I've run up a lot of debts in writing this book and I'd like to cash in something of what I owe by thanking the following people who have contributed in so many ways to the process of getting this book written: Sandra Bingham, Tony Keen, Joanna Paul, Kim Shahabudin, Emma Stafford, Graham Sumner, James Robson and Shaun Tougher. A particular kind of thanks – deeply heartfelt – goes to Monica Cyrino and Alex McAuley who helped mould the final manuscript into shape. Sincere thanks goes to Carol Macdonald, James Dale and the team at Edinburgh University Press. A very special thanks, as always, goes to David Pineau who has helped me keep it real and who made the tea.

In her leopard-skin-lined coat, Elizabeth Taylor shoots an outdoor scene; *Cleopatra*. Candid shot, 1963.

OPENING CREDITS

EPIC, HISTORY AND HOLLYWOOD

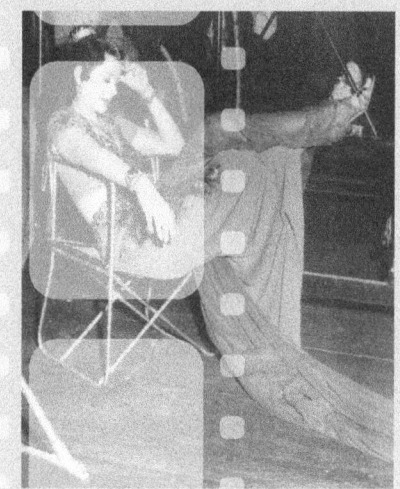

The epic film is surely the most difficult to make well. Charlton Heston

This book is about movie-making in Hollywood and movie-watching in twentieth-century America (and beyond) in the period 1916–66 – a Golden Age of cinema. The movies explored in this work are classified as 'epics' – a distinct and popular cinematic genre which played a central role in twentieth-century filmmaking and defined the ancient world for generations of spectators. The titles of the epic greats resonate in our consciousness: *Ben-Hur, Cleopatra, Spartacus, The Ten Commandments, Samson and Delilah* and *Quo Vadis*; so do the movie stars who performed in them and the directors who crafted them. Less familiar though are the names of the designers who visualised them and the teams of workers who and brought them into being. In fact, it is the uncovering of the work of the forgotten designers and craftspeople and marketing teams that has been my motivation and consequently the Hollywood visualisation of the past through (and on) film is the focus of this study.

This book illustrates how the visual elements of the creation of epic films – posters and graphics, set designs, costumes, as well as the visual on-screen performances of actors – interacted with common images and popular perceptions of the ancient world to promote and make visible a time long gone. There is something about the medium of film after all that enables it to implant images in the mind that are somehow more real than the real world; film images stage manage our perception of the facts of real life: how we should kiss, fight or walk in the rain are images encoded in our minds through filmic reflections. Our perception of the lived world of history is similarly coded by cinematic constructions and we know how Chicago gangsters, Viking warriors, harem girls and

Apache look like because the movies tell us. Romans, we know, wore white togas and enjoyed orgies; Egyptians wore eyeliner and liked religious ceremonial; Hebrews wore homespun headcloths and liked piety. For millions of movie-goers, epic cinema has been their chief access point to antiquity and for most individuals Hollywood's ancient past was (and is) accepted as being more real than the shattered archaeological ruins of the genuine ancient world. Why try to understand the rubble of an archaeological site when film reconstructs the past as it was lived, in marble and burnished gold?

Movies are something we watch. In film, the image dominates. When one thinks of a movie, one sees an image in the mind: a woman swimming by moonlight jerked underwater by an unseen force (*Jaws*; dir. Spielberg, 1975); a pair of ruby red slippers on a yellow brick road (*The Wizard of Oz*; dir. Flemming, 1939); two charioteers racing side by side as their horses thunder around the Roman arena (*Ben-Hur*; dir. Wyler, 1959). Think of a favourite movie. What happens? An image from the film emerges. But it is important to realise that every image in every film is an artificial construction, the products of the collaborative effort of a production team: a director, producer, production designer, costume designer, director of photography, film editor and distribution manager. Very little appears on the screen that is not manufactured to be seen and to encode and solicit meaning.

In films set in a historical period – in our case the ancient world – the development of a visual concept must encompass a sensibility of place and time. This might be manifest in a small detail like an oil lamp on a marble-topped table or the design of a woven stripe on a toga; it might be made manifest in sets of vast proportions – the Forum Romanum, Cleopatra's barge or King Solomon's temple – or in elaborate costumes of shiny silk and gold lamé. Whether large or small, plain or opulent, the visual word of Hollywood's antiquity was constructed by a team of designers intent on creating a coherent (but not necessarily reliable) sense of the past.

Epic films of the period 1916–66 were rich in visuals. They were spectacles. In fact, they turned history into a spectacle. The 'Tarsus Barge sequence' in Cecil B. DeMille's *Cleopatra* of 1934, for example, in which the Egyptian queen (Claudette Colbert) seduces Marc Antony (Henry Wilcoxon) manifests great narrative attention, taking twenty minutes (about one-fifth of the film's running time) to play out. During this time the screen is packed with lavish decor and the spectacle of performance as troops of dancing girls dressed as leopards, nymphs and sirens gyrate, leap and shimmy in a Busby Berkeleyesque musical of overt artifice. And yet the surface artifice of the scene is grounded by the rhetoric of historical research, given that the head of Paramount's Special Effects Department claimed that, 'the barge was painstakingly constructed from historical records.'[1] The truth though is that epic films used historical research and inventive design to create an original 'look' – we might label it the 'decor of history' – which conveyed the spirit of antiquity through the aesthetics of the present; a creative interpretation of antiquity dominated filmmaking of this era. By their nature, films set in antiquity tended to draw more attention to their visuals than films set in contemporary periods with corresponding contemporary designs. Consider, for instance, Bosley Crowther's enthusiastic 1951 *New York Times* review of *Quo Vadis* and note how it focuses on the visuals:

> Centurions in gleaming Roman costumes march with arrogance and power, shackled slaves groan and grovel by the hundreds and chanting Christians die in hordes while thousands cheer . . . Huge orgies of drinking and love-making are staged with intoxicating mass, and the splendour of the retinue of courtiers that hangs around Nero and his wife, the evil and voluptuous Poppaea, is utterly dazzling to the eye.

Due to the compelling nature of period design, epic films were often marketed to audiences based on these types of visual aesthetics and much of the thrill of the genre was in gazing overawed at the set designs and costumes as about enjoying the performances. Indeed, the visuals were the facets of epic film production which tended to be recognised in award ceremonies, like the Oscars, because of the important impact they had on box-office success and critical acclaim.

The promotion and marketing of epic films frequently included stories of their lavish budgets, the number of extras and the time, effort and money spent on the creation of sets, costumes and props. The *Los Angeles Times* (4 October 1925) heralded the MGM *Ben-Hur* with the headline, 'History of Stupendous *Ben-Hur* Screen Production Brings New Triumphs to Hollywood as Film Capital: Theatre Industry Gasps at Picture's Prodigal Expense' – an outlay which was exaggerated to be ten million dollars, although it was actually completed for four million. At Paramount Studios, Cecil B. DeMille loved quoting statistics and in the 1956 promotional pamphlet 'Why I Made *The Ten Commandments*', he exaggerated his budget to almost twice the original eight million dollars he had first requested for the film. He justified his expenditure as an expression of his Christian belief: 'In the great age of faith men built magnificent, soaring cathedrals to express their love of God. [Paramount's producers] gave me the means to produce in another form of art, on twenty-one thousand feet of celluloid, a modern expression of faith in the same God.'

The message behind these statistics is simple: no expense was too great when it came to presenting antiquity on-screen. It went without saying that the lofty nobility of antiquity, especially 'biblical' events, warranted lavish budgets and the promotion of spectacle. In fact, Bruce Babington and Peter Evans have suggested that epic movies all include, to varying degrees, a set of eleven spectacular sub-genres: architecture, geography, the body, presentations, costumes, forbidden gods, warfare, slavery, sadism and the Act of God.[2] For me, each of these categories solicits a visual response:

1. *The spectacle of architecture.* This is meant to overwhelm. The long-shots of Rome in *The Fall of the Roman Empire* and the panorama of Alexandria in the 1963 *Cleopatra* are both impressive and intimidating. Indeed, sometimes the spectacle of architecture bears negative moral connotations, for instance the Roman arena in *The Sign of the Cross* and *Quo Vadis* or the temple of Dagon in *Samson and Delilah.*
2. *The spectacle of geography.* The vast expanses of desert in *Cleopatra* (1934), *Ben-Hur* (1959) and *Solomon and Sheba*, or the outré but brilliant Colorado backdrop masquerading as Judaea in *The Greatest Story Ever Told.*
3. *The spectacle of the body.* Absolute maleness and femaleness.
4. *The spectacle of the orgy.* Roman, Egyptian, Babylonian or Sheban, these are much the same.
5. *The spectacle of presentations.* Ceremonies, gift-giving – such as the presentation of Nubian tribute in the 1956 *The Ten Commandments* and the gifts of the Queen of Sheba to the court of Jerusalem in *Solomon and Sheba* – emphasise the wealth of the ancient world. Military parades and triumphal entries – *Quo Vadis, Cleopatra* – show its power.
6. *The spectacle of costumes.* Fabrics, jewels, push-up bras and Brylcreemed hair.
7. *The spectacle of forbidden gods.* Invoking the powers of pagan deities through ritual; for instance, Ragon god of Love in *Solomon and Sheba*, or the pantheon of Rome's gods in *Quo Vadis*, is thrilling and wrong.
8. *The spectacle of ancient warfare.* Land battles, sea battles, chariots, sling-shots, sieges and arson.
9. *The spectacle of slavery.* A ubiquitous vision of antiquity.
10. *The spectacle of sadism.* Whips, torture, Christians and lions, gladiators and masochistic emperors with their 'thumbs down'.
11. *The spectacle of the Act of God.* That is, the visual manifestation of the Judaeo-Christian God (pagan gods do not exist and are therefore redundant); the parting of the Red Sea, the destruction of Sodom, and the collapsing of the temple of Dagon through God's agent, Samson.

In spite of the fact that epic films are dominated by visuals, acknowledgement of the fundamentality of the subject is too often underplayed (and often ignored) in contemporary studies of the epic genre. Alarmingly little attention has been paid to the on-screen visualisation of the ancient world and even less focus has been given to the process whereby the on-screen 'look' of antiquity was created. This book aims to explore and explain the processes of, and rationale behind, the visual creation of the ancient world in Hollywood filmmaking. In doing so we will encounter the many skilled artists – the directors, production designers, costumiers, marketing experts and movie stars – whose talents merged, converged and clashed in creating the ancient world on-screen and who brought to life Hollywood's idiosyncratic version of antiquity and made the past a more of a reality than the remains of the genuine thing.

We must keep in mind, however, that in Hollywood movies of the Golden Age, 'reality' (whether the 'reality' of the past, the present or, for that matter, the future) was different from the image of the real that prevails in movies today. 'Back then' audiences were more willing to accept (and in all probability didn't even notice) a greater degree of stylisation in sets, costumes and performances. Many Golden Age movies were overlaid with a sentimental innocence which today's audience would find overly saccharine. Foster Hirsch sums up the development in audience expectations clearly:

> Films still construct a parallel world, a place necessarily different from the real world, but if in the past the movie world tended to be finer, prettier, more artful and ennobling, than the world outside the theatre, today's movies frequently confront audiences with settings that are harsher, more brutal and dangerous than the ones spectators are likely to live in. The fantasies movies supply have changed, inevitably, as have the actors who . . . embody them.[3]

In what has become known as 'classical Hollywood style', films were subject to rules for creating a narrative cinematic form which was supposed to mimic real life. As Alastair Blanshard and Kim Shahabudin have noted:

> The need to artificially disguise the artifice of cinema dictated the way that shots were staged, lit and edited. For example, key characters in a scene [were] centred in the foreground, in focus, and clearly lit. Dialogue between two characters [was] often edited in a shot/reverse-shot sequence . . . mimicking the way we might look at each speaker in turn. The purpose of editing [was] to promote continuity . . . This imperative for naturalism also promoted the use of more colloquial dialogue and accents, contributing, in the case of cine-antiquity of the period, to the notion that the ancient world was just the same as the modern world, but in fancy dress.[4]

In the period of our study, epic films had a profound impact upon American filmmakers and cinema audiences. Their creation of the visuals of the antique past had a crucial role in determining the essence of the epic genre itself and, as we will discover, the central aspects of the epic *mise-en-scène* were aesthetically predetermined and codified. How can we estimate that impact? I think that, in fact, this can best be seen in the way in which *other* film genres were able to reflect on, pastiche and even capitalise upon the conventions of the movie epic.

The Epic World of Norma Desmond

Sunset Boulevard (dir. Wilder, 1950) is the greatest Hollywood movie about Hollywood movies.[5] As an Academy Award-winning *film noir* classic, the movie is a darkly humorous, pessimistic and caustic indictment of the business of making Hollywood movies; no other film better represents Hollywood's vision of itself.[6]

It might seem odd, then, that this study of the visual world of Hollywood's epic films should begin with reference to the archetypal *film noir* masterpiece. After all, the term *film noir* denotes a motion picture of omnipresent darkness, both literally and figuratively, a film style employing a unique cinematography and lighting which deliberately enhanced the dramatic mood and the contrast of black and white photography and was, in all aspects, the very antithesis of the colourful, loud, brash and lavish movies of the epic genre.[7] So why do I start this book with *Sunset Boulevard*? It begins this way because not only do I love *Sunset Boulevard* and consider it to be one of cinema's finest works, but also because I think that it has at its core an intrinsic understanding of how the epic films of Hollywood's Golden Age worked. This *film noir*-great functions so well because its director, the visionary Billy Wilder, understood, used and toyed with the conventions of the kind of epic movies which Hollywood was making at the time of its release in 1950 – and had been successfully producing since the 1910s. Wilder not only understood these conventions, he went on to frame them within *film noir* aesthetics. *Sunset Boulevard* is (at least in part) Wilder's wry comment on the Hollywood epic.[8] Let's explore this further: take a look at Text Box OC.1 for an outline of the plot.

With the plot in mind, let's now think about how this movie is cast and what resonances emerged from the casting process.

The casting of *Sunset Boulevard* was central to Wilder's vision for the film. Norma Desmond is played by the real-life silent-screen movie star Gloria Swanson and her real-life one-time director Erich von Stroheim plays a supporting role as Max, Norma's former director and husband now turned butler and confidant. Film critics have long speculated about which actress Norma Desmond was based upon (in fact she was probably an amalgamation of the tragic Mabel Normand, the egocentric Pola Negri and the stir-crazy Mae Murray), but in casting Swanson in the role of Norma, Wilder gave the film a credibility which transcended the plot; Swanson's presence in *Sunset Boulevard* encouraged fact and fiction to merge. As the film historian Jeanine Basinger explains:

> [Swanson is] magnificent. Who could know better than she how to play an exotic diva from that era? Everything about her, from her leopard trim, her cigarette holders, her bangle bracelets, to her bed shaped like a golden swan and her outré open-air automobile seems completely authentic – because it is. And when Norma goes to the lot, to Swanson's old studio Paramount Pictures, and meets her old

Text Box OC.1 *Sunset Boulevard*: The Plot

Joe Gillis (William Holden), a young penniless screenwriter, stumbles into an old mansion on Sunset Boulevard in Los Angeles, California; it is the home of Norma Desmond (Gloria Swanson), an aging actress and one-time movie star who lives there with her butler and caretaker, Max (Eric von Stroheim). Unsure of who she is at first, Gillis then recognises the former film diva:

GILLIS: You're Norma Desmond. You used to be in silent pictures. You used to be big.

NORMA: I *am* big! It's the *pictures* that got small!

When Norma realises that Joe is a writer, she hires him to edit a script she is composing that will provide a vehicle for her screen comeback:

NORMA: This is to be a very important picture. I have written it myself . . . It's the story of Salome. I think I'll have DeMille direct it. We've made a lot of pictures together . . . Salome! What a woman! What a part! The Princess in love with a Holy Man. She dances the Dance of the Seven Veils. He rejects her, so she demands his head on a golden tray, kissing his cold, dead lips.

GILLIS: They'll love it in Pomona!

NORMA: They'll love it everywhere!

Joe moves in with Norma and becomes dependent on her for money, essentially becoming her gigolo, although he acknowledges that his relationship with Norma is emotionally disturbing. When Joe begins a healthier relationship with a young woman, Norma finds out and threatens suicide but Joe decides to leave her anyway. Unhinged and utterly desperate, Norma shoots him dead and descends into further mental chaos.

director, Cecil B. DeMille playing himself, everything rings true. For many people in the audience, it was an extraordinary blurring of fact and fiction, since for them it had been less than twenty-five years since it had all been real. Swanson herself was just past fifty years old, yet she and the world of the movie seemed to come from a time and a place so remote that few could remember it . . . This was heady stuff . . . a masterpiece.[9]

Sunset Boulevard plays with time and genre and catapults the viewer between the 1920s and the 1950s, between a world of opulent Hollywood fantasy and a world of harsh filmmaking reality. Completely immersed within *film noir* aesthetic, it somehow nonetheless engages with other, earlier, filmmaking styles, as the introduction of Cecil B. DeMille (at the cost of $10,000) into the picture makes clear. DeMille (who will go on to figure prominently throughout this book) was one of the few

Hollywood producer-directors to capitalise upon his silent-film-era successes to make the transition into talking pictures. In his long and illustrious career of seventy movies created between 1913 and 1956, DeMille earned a reputation as both a formidable taskmaster and as Hollywood's 'Great Showman'.[10] As we will go on to explore, in his religious epics like *The King of Kings* (1927) and *The Sign of the Cross* (1932), DeMille promoted American Christian values while titillating his audiences with scenes of ancient debauchery and material excesses, and by the time of the cinematic release of *Sunset Boulevard* DeMille had established himself as one of the most significant figures in American cinema. His appearance as himself in the movie added immeasurable prestige to the picture's aim of creating 'Hollywood authenticity'.

DeMille had directed Gloria Swanson on numerous occasions during the silent era, and in Wilder's film, Swanson, now morphed into Norma Desmond, visits DeMille on the Paramount back-lot in order to discuss her new movie project: the story of the biblical vamp, Salome (which, in theory, was indeed perfect DeMillian material). In filming the scene Billy Wilder added another layer of 'Hollywood authenticity' to his movie as it takes place on the Paramount soundstage where DeMille is filming one of his Biblical spectacles, *Samson and Delilah* – a variant of the *Salome* script Norma is writing with Gillis – and Wyler used the actual lavish sets and costumes of DeMille's epic film within his *film noir* frame (see Colour Plate 1). In other words, an epic movie-classic plays a cameo role in a *film noir* masterpiece.

DeMille, who liked to promote and publish candid photographs of himself on-set in full directorial mode (instructing actors or cameramen or crew (Figure OC.1)), appears in *Sunset Boulevard* in a similar vein; it was a self-made role he was happy to recreate on-screen (Figure OC.2). Kind, and sympathetic to Norma, DeMille is compelling and convincing in the role of 'himself' and 'under Wilder's direction, he gives a more subtle performance by far than any actor did in one of DeMille's own pictures.'[11]

But Wilder's cross-referencing of earlier times and previous films is subtly played out in other aspects of the scene set in DeMille's studio; for instance, Edith Head, who designed the costumes for Heddy Lamarr's Delilah in DeMille's movie, was also responsible for Swanson's Norma costumes, and she cleverly linked the two films which she designed by using peacock feathers in both actresses' wardrobes – a lavish feather cape for Delilah (Colour Plate 1) and a white plume for Norma's hat (Figure OC.2). But the resonances went deeper, as Swanson recalls:

> Edith Head and I together created perfect clothes for my character – a trifle exotic, a trifle exaggerated, a trifle out of date. For my scene with Mr DeMille, I [wore] a hat with a single white peacock feather, remembering the peacock-feather headdress [I wore] when Mr DeMille and I made *Male and Female* [in 1919 – see Figure OC.3].[12]

Figure OC.1
Cecil B. DeMille on set with Hedy Lamarr. *Samson and Delilah* (1949). Candid shot.

Sunset Boulevard is a film saturated in allusions to an earlier age of Hollywood filmmaking, but it is in the film's extraordinary final scene that the blurring of time, space and genre (*film noir* and epic) comes to the fore. The bleak, brilliant but despairing end of *Sunset Boulevard* sees the mad and murderous faded movie star made to believe that she is finally shooting *Salome*, the film she has been so desperate to make; she is compelled to believe it so that she can be taken away to prison or, more likely, an asylum (see Text Box OC.2).

In his films, including other classics like *Some Like it Hot* (1959) and *The Apartment* (1960), Billy Wilder generally demanded a 'naturalistic' approach to acting and his directing style was of the same mode, but nonetheless, as a master at creating a subtle *mise-en-scène*, Wilder was also able to transcend, as need demanded, the naturalism that framed his form of cinema. He employed artificial devices in his films, especially at moments of death or madness, and the ending of *Sunset Boulevard* exemplifies perfectly his ability to switch style.[13] The last scene is designed as the (bogus) realisation of Norma's dream of appearing as Salome before the cameras; she has no idea that her crime means that cameras will indeed be rolling, but for a very different reason.

Figure OC.2
DeMille the actor: on set with Gloria Swanson ready to film *Sunset Boulevard* (1949).
Candid shot.

Norma's gloomy old mansion, vast, echoing and empty throughout the film, now becomes crowded with newspaper journalists, newsreel cameramen and police officers; even the real Hedda Hopper, Hollywood's premiere newshound, is there, adding another level of verisimilitude to the scene. They pack onto the grand staircase hoping to get a photograph of Norma or to snatch a squalid scoop for a gossip column. Max, loyal slave, joins forces with the police and psychiatrists to get Norma to leave the house and he tells her that she's going to shoot the climactic scene in *Salome*. It is *as* Salome that she begins to walk down the staircase.

As she does so, Wilder does an extraordinary thing: suddenly, he switches style from *film noir* to epic, and for a brief moment we, the audience, are inside Norma's imagination. We are back in Paramount Pictures of the 1920s, filming DeMille's *Salome*. The newsreel cameras become DeMille's studio cameras and they roll to capture Norma's vampish performance. As Norma-Salome makes her stately descent of the palace staircase (Figure OC.4), the film score (brilliantly composed by Franz Waxman) takes on epic proportions too: steady orientalist rhythms (lifted by Waxman from 'The Dance of the Seven Veils' from Richard Strauss's *Salome*) merge with a distorted sultry habanera previously associated in the film with Norma's hedonism.[14] Norma finally hears the music of the *Salome* she wanted DeMille to direct for her come-

Figure OC.3
Gloria Swanson as the 'Princess of Babylon'. *Male and Female* (1919). Studio portrait.

back (Figure OC.5). Then, at the foot of the stairs, ready for her close-up, Norma forgets everything around her, walks towards the camera and breaks all on-screen conventions by looking straight into the lens at us, the audience, as she disappears into a haze of her own madness.

Text Box OC.2   The Final Scene of *Sunset Boulevard*

From the original script:

[Max makes his way down the stairs through the crowd of newsmen to the
   newsreel cameras, which are being set up in the hall below.]

MAX: Is everything set up, gentlemen? Are the lights ready?

[From the stairway comes a murmur. They look up. Norma has emerged
   from the bedroom and comes to the head of the stairs. There are golden
   spangles in her hair and in her hand she carries a golden scarf. The police
   clear a path for her to descend. Press cameras flash at her every step. Max
   stands at the cameras.]

MAX: Is everything set up, gentlemen?

CAMERAMAN: Just about.

[The portable lights flare up and illuminate the staircase.]

MAX: Are the lights ready?

2ND CAMERAMAN: All set.

MAX: Quiet, everybody! Lights! Are you ready, Norma?

NORMA: [From the top of the stairs] What is the scene? Where am I?

MAX: This is the staircase of the palace.

NORMA: Oh, yes, yes. They're below, waiting for the Princess . . . I'm ready.

MAX: All right. [To cameramen] Camera! [To Norma] Action!

[Norma arranges the golden scarf about her and proudly starts to descend
   the staircase. The cameras grind. Everyone watches in awe.

GILLIS' VOICE: So they were grinding after all, those cameras. Life, which
   can be strangely merciful, had taken pity on Norma Desmond. The dream
   she had clung to so desperately had enfolded her . . .

[At the foot of the stairs Norma stops, moved.]

NORMA: I can't go on with the scene. I'm too happy. Do you mind, Mr.
   DeMille, if I say a few words? Thank you. I just want to tell you how
   happy I am to be back in the studio making a picture again. You don't
   know how much I've missed all of you. And I promise you I'll never desert
   you again, because after *Salome* we'll make another picture, and another
   and another. You see, this is my life. It always will be. There's nothing
   else – just us and the cameras and those wonderful people out there in the
   dark . . . All right, Mr. DeMille, I'm ready for my closeup.

FADE OUT. THE END.

This scene works so well because Wilder completely understands the
conventions of epic cinema: he gives us visual spectacle, with an emphasis on a packed *mis-en-scène*, costume, scale and movement; he provides
too a certain lofty visual campness to the overall style of the sequence.
Wilder knew that these individual factors when combined together
made up an epic because such films had been one of the most dominant
genres in Hollywood filmmaking since the birth of cinema. The epic had

Figure OC.4
Gloria Swanson as Norma Desmond, descending the stairs of her mansion in the final scene of *Sunset Boulevard* (1950). Production shot.

been a permanent feature of the Hollywood landscape since the 1910s, and by 1950 (thanks to DeMille's *Samson and Delilah*) the genre was all set for a major revival. Wilder was aware of this legacy of epic film, and so his *Sunset Boulevard* was able to play with epic conventions because he, his actors, his designers and, subsequently, his audiences already knew precisely what those conventions were.

Figure OC.5
Gloria Swanson as Norma Desmond as Salome in a make-shift costume described by Staggs (2002: 128) as 'a drag queen's version of the Queen of Sheba'. *Sunset Boulevard* (1950). Production shot.

The Ancient World and the Epic Screen

From its earliest inception, Hollywood cinema has been fascinated with the ancient world. Antiquity has always offered a natural vehicle to filmmakers, perhaps because the stories of larger-than-life characters and events were generally familiar to cinema-goers. But Hollywood epics were not overly reverential towards the antique past, and directors ploughed the history books with abandon, often shattering the fragments of factual information in favour of spectacle, eroticism, sensuality, weighty morality or pure fantasy.

While epic movies are products of film studios across the globe, nothing has come close to the American Hollywood studios' identification of the epic movie as the quintessential spectacular experience. This book will concentrate, therefore, on the Hollywood epic genre alone, although in using the term 'Hollywood epic' we might think about a conceptual framework rather than a strict geographical one. Take a look at Text Box OC.3 to discover more about the nuances of the term 'epic movie'.

Derek Elley in his 1984 study *The Epic Film* focuses on epics beginning with biblical history and ending with the Late Antique era, thereby defining the historical epic by the distance of its temporal content from the present. We too will concentrate on the same period, although it must be emphasised that the Hollywood epic genre also encompasses films set in historical periods post CE 1000 (like *El Cid*, dir. Mann, 1961; and *Marie Antoinette*, dir. van Dyke, 1938) as well as epics of the American West and Civil War (like the sweeping *Gone With The Wind*, dir. Fleming, 1939). Recent work on the Hollywood 'history films' of the 1950s has revealed that ancient history received notable attention from the filmmakers throughout the decade and that between 1950 and 1959 some sixteen films were set in the BCE period, with another eleven set in the era CE 1–500, and a further sixteen set between CE 500 and 1000.[15] When compared with only twenty-nine movies set between 1865 and 1890 (the American Civil War and Reconstruction era), the forty-three films set in antiquity (if we extend the term to encompass the very early Middle Ages) were a testimony to the mass appeal of the ancient world during the Cold War period.

History of the Epic Genre

The two great ancient world epic cycles in Hollywood films occurred during the silent period (1915–27) and into the 'talkies' era of the early 1930s and, later, throughout the 1950s and early 1960s, two periods in which epics were produced as self-conscious demonstrations of Hollywood's capabilities in cinematic virtuosity.[16] This was a time when the American film industry was controlled by the great Hollywood studios (see Text Box OC.4) and throughout this book we will explore how these influential production companies created an identifiable

Text Box OC.3   What Is an Epic Movie?

Defining an epic is only slightly less complicated than making one.

Charlton Heston

Joanna Paul begins her important study, *Film and the Classical Epic Tradition*, with a question: 'What is at stake in describing a film as an epic?' to which she offers a sensible answer:

> Most of us use the term [epic] quite casually, comfortable in the knowledge that whatever else it might be, it will be big. As a label for the kinds of films that have been fundamental to the cinema industry since its birth, 'epic' has enjoyed widespread and seemingly straightforward use. Audiences assume that it will be a film with a cast of thousands, a gigantic budget, lengthy running time, and (hopefully) high box-office takings. Whatever else it may contain – a historical setting or a heroic narrative, for example – a grandiosity of scale and a variety of spectacle is central to expectations. (Paul 2013: 1)

So, an epic is:

- a film that attempts to deal with real or fictional events in a grand and sweeping style;
- a film which includes action on a massive scale, with large casts set in spectacular surroundings;
- a film which deals with weighty, heroic issues: fate of empires, politics, religion and beliefs, struggles between individuals;
- a film with larger-than-life (charismatic or despotic) characters;
- a long film (sometimes approaching four hours; sometimes with even an interval);
- a film that nonetheless entertains its audience in its use of technology, music, set and costume design, and star actors

In our case, the term 'epic movie' applies to films set in antiquity and actually includes two categories with several distinct subtypes (with some room for cross-over):

Category 1: RELIGIOUS EPIC

Old Testament Epic – stories based on or around heroes and heroines of ancient Hebrew scripture: *The Bible: In the Beginning . . .* (dir. Huston, 1966); *David and Bathsheba* (dir. King, 1951); *Esther and the King* (dir.

Walsh, 1960); *Joseph and his Brethren* (dir. Dieterle, 1955 – not completed); *Judith of Bethulia* (dir. Griffith, 1914); *Noah's Ark* (dir. Curtiz, 1929); *The Queen of Sheba* (dir. Gordon Edwards, 1921); *Samson and Delilah* (dir. DeMille, 1949); *Sodom and Gomorrah* (dir. Aldrich, 1962); *Solomon and Sheba* (dir. Vidor, 1959); *The Story of Ruth* (dir. Koster, 1960); *The Ten Commandments* (dir. DeMille, 1923); *The Ten Commandments* (dir. DeMille, 1956).

The Jesus Movie (or Christ Film) – based on the New Testament Gospels: *The Big Fisherman* (dir. Borzage, 1959); *The Greatest Story Ever Told* (dir. Stevens, 1965); *King of Kings* (dir. Ray, 1961); *The King of Kings* (dir. DeMille, 1927).

The Proto-Christian Movie – where a protagonist, while not a Christian, is nonetheless touched by Christian mores – even centuries before the birth of Christianity – or comes into direct contact with Christ or converts to Christianity: *Barabbas* (dir. Fleischer, 1962); *Ben-Hur* (dir. Niblo, 1925); *Ben-Hur* (dir. Wyler, 1959); *The Prodigal* (dir. Thorpe, 1955); *The Robe* (dir. Koster, 1953); *Salome* (dir. Dieterle, 1953); *The Silver Chalice* (dir. Saville, 1955).

Rome versus Christianity – the struggles of early Christians set against the pagan excesses of the Roman Empire: *Androcles and the Lion* (dir. Erskine, 1952); *Demetrius and the Gladiators* (dir. Daves, 1954); *Salome* (dir. Dieterle, 1953); *The Sign of the Cross* (dir. DeMille, 1932); *Quo Vadis* (dir. LeRoy, 1951).

Category 2: HISTORICAL EPIC

Ancient World Bio-epic – based on real events revolving around an individual: *Alexander the Great* (dir. Rosen, 1956); *Cleopatra* (dir. Gordon Edwards, 1917); *Cleopatra* (dir. DeMille, 1934); *Cleopatra* (dir. Mankiewicz, 1963); *Julius Caesar* (dir. Mankiewicz, 1953); *Serpent of the Nile* (dir. Castle, 1953); *Spartacus* (dir. Kubrick, 1960).

Ancient World Historical Epic – plots incorporating moments of historical crisis; historical characters are cameo roles: *The Egyptian* (dir. Curtiz, 1954); *The Fall of the Roman Empire* (dir. Mann, 1964); *Intolerance* (dir. Griffith, 1916); *Land of the Pharaohs* (dir. Hawks, 1955); *The Last Days of Pompeii* (dir. Schoedsack, 1935); *The 300 Spartans* (dir. Mate, 1962).

Mythical Epic – based on literary or mythic subjects, supposedly rooted in the past: *Helen of Troy* (dir. Wise, 1956).

Text Box OC.4   The Hollywood Studio System

Referred to as the 'Dream Factory' by its fans and as 'the most beautiful slave quarters in the world' by many of its employees, Hollywood dominated filmmaking throughout the twentieth century. In fact, by 1920 the Hollywood studios were producing up to ninety per cent of all American movies and they exported their films abroad so extensively that Hollywood practically became a worldwide industry. Due to its unique production techniques, the strict division of labour and mass-marketing techniques, during the height of its powers in the 1930s Hollywood was producing around six hundred films a year. Not surprisingly, the Hollywood studio system has been likened to a factory, and it is important to recall that the studios were indeed industrial money-makers first and artistic institutions only second. The main Hollywood studios not only made and distributed movies, but since they owned the majority of the movie houses in which the films were screened (between them, the eight most influential studios controlled ninety-five per cent of the theatres in the USA), they had a complete monopoly over the film industry and brooked no competition from independent producers.

During the Golden Age, the studios benefitted from the long-term management of the studio heads – the infamous 'movie moguls' – who ruled over their companies with absolute, unquestioned authority. The studio system hinged on the moguls' abilities to contract, market and control star actors and actresses who were carefully constructed and exploited by the studios as money-making commodities. Moreover, each of the major Hollywood studios had a distinct 'house style' and specialised in manufacturing certain 'types' of films. Paramount, for instance, excelled in comedy films (having under contract actors like Mae West, W. C. Fields and the Marx Brothers), while Warner Bros produced films of social realism, gangster pictures, war movies and Westerns. Universal cornered the market in horror films and Twentieth Century Fox was famed for its opulent biopics, musicals and epics. (For further discussions of the Hollywood studios see Mordden 1988; Schatz 1988; Gomery 2005. For the exhibition side of the industry see discussions in Hark 2002.)

By the late 1950s, however, the five main studios were in crisis. Unable (and unwilling) to change or develop their working methods, the big studios came into direct competition with vibrant new production companies and youthful, vigorous new producers. Moreover, the decline in cinema audiences, thanks to the popularity of television, saw thousands of movie theatres close, and the increased union power (such as the creation of the Screen Actors Guild) within the workplace which gave actors and musicians more rights, all conspired to curb the powers of the studios. All the large studios, with the exception of RKO, survived the difficult years of the late

1950s, and struggled through into the opening years of the 1960s, but it is fair to say that by 1965, the studio system was well and truly finished. (For a comprehensive discussion see Lev (2003: 197–216).)

The Major Studios ('The Big Five')

Fox Film Corporation (Later Twentieth Century Fox) was founded by William Fox in 1914 who built up an empire buying up chains of movie theatres. His production strategy emphasised scale and spectacle but this led to financial crisis and so in 1935 the studio merged with 20th Century Pictures to become Twentieth Century Fox, under the authoritarian leadership of Darryl Zanuck, a former producer at Warner Bros. With the Chase National Bank as its major investor and with child-star Shirley Temple as its primary asset, unsurprisingly Zanuck promoted big-budget, wholesome family films with strong pro-Republican sentiments as well as family-orientated musicals.

- Leading films included: *How Green Was My Valley, All About Eve, The King and I*
- Leading stars included: Jane Russell, Richard Burton, Marilyn Monroe, Tyrone Power, Elizabeth Taylor
- Twentieth Century Fox epics: *The Bible: In the Beginning . . .* (dir. Huston, 1966); *Cleopatra* (dir. Gordon Edwards, 1917); *Cleopatra* (dir. Mankiewicz, 1963); *David and Bathsheba* (dir. King, 1951); *Demetrius and the Gladiators* (dir. Daves, 1954); *The Egyptian* (dir. Curtiz, 1954); *Esther and the King* (dir. Walsh, 1960); *The Queen of Sheba* (dir. Gordon Edwards, 1921); *The Robe* (dir. Koster, 1953); *Sodom and Gomorrah* (dir. Aldrich, 1962); *The Story of Ruth* (dir. Koster, 1960); *The 300 Spartans* (dir. Mate, 1962).

Paramount Pictures Corporation was at first only a distribution company but in 1917 it was acquired by Adolph Zukor, who merged it with his own production company to create a studio-style which was unique in Hollywood. By the early 1930s Paramount chiefly employed Austrian and German exiles (fleeing from the Nazi regime) as its leading directors and technicians (such as the German-born master-director Ernst Lubitsch), and consequently the studio developed a distinctly 'European' look of dramatic lighting design, elaborate set designs and sophisticated costume design. One of Paramount's main directors was Cecil B. DeMille who, in his epic movies, was keen to promote Paramount's theme of sophisticated European glamour.

- Leading films included: *Duck Soup, The Palm Beach Story, Sunset Boulevard*
- Leading stars included: Marlene Dietrich, Bing Crosby, Gloria Swanson, Claudette Colbert, Susan Hayward, Rudolph Valentino

- Paramount epics: *Cleopatra* (dir. DeMille, 1934); *The Fall of the Roman Empire* (dir. Mann, 1964); *Samson and Delilah* (dir. DeMille, 1949); *The Sign of the Cross* (dir. DeMille, 1932); *The Ten Commandments* (dir. DeMille, 1923); *The Ten Commandments* (dir. DeMille, 1956).

Warner Brothers was established in 1924 by Harry, Jack and Albert Warner and was known, from its inception, for its technical innovations. In 1925 Warner Bros partnered with Western Electric to pioneer a sound system which involved a massive investment in new equipment which paid off handsomely when the studio released *The Jazz Singer*, the first ever 'talking picture' (eventually grossing $3 million). Famous for its production-line creation of movies, the studio was best known for its gritty real-life dramas and gangster films. Warner Bros also hired ex-Disney animators to create the *Loony Tunes* cartoons which had scenarios that were more risqué or 'adult' than Disney films.

- Leading films included: *Little Caesar, The Public Enemy, Casablanca*
- Leading stars included: Humphrey Bogart, Ingrid Bergman, James Cagney, Errol Flynn, John Barrymore, Edward G. Robinson, Gary Cooper, Cary Grant
- Warner Bros epics: *Helen of Troy* (dir. Wise, 1956); *Land of the Pharaohs* (dir. Hawks, 1955); *Noah's Ark* (dir. Curtiz, 1929); *The Silver Chalice* (dir. Saville, 1955); *Hannibal* (1959).

Metro-Goldwyn-Mayer (MGM) was established in 1924 from its parent company, Loew's Inc., and became the biggest and most prolific of the studios, releasing by the 1930s a staggering average of one movie every week. MGM was run by the powerful and unscrupulous Louis B. Mayer, a ruthless but gifted businessman, and under his leadership MGM developed the biggest exhibition and distribution network in Hollywood. There was no film or star too big for MGM and the studio contracted many of the leading film stars and marketed glamour and glitz, especially through big-budget musicals.

- Leading films included: *Grand Hotel, The Wizard of Oz*
- Leading stars included: Judy Garland, Spencer Tracey, Jean Harlow, Bette Davis, Lana Turner, Joan Crawford, Hedy Lamarr, Robert Taylor, Katharine Hepburn
- MGM epics: *Ben-Hur* (dir. Niblo, 1925); *Ben-Hur* (dir. Wyler, 1959); *Julius Caesar* (dir. Mankiewicz, 1953); *King of Kings* (dir. Ray, 1961); *The Prodigal* (dir. Thorpe, 1955); *Quo Vadis* (dir. LeRoy, 1951).

RKO Radio Pictures Incorporated was founded in 1928 as an offshoot of RCA (the Radio Corporation of America), which was headed by the tycoon J. D. Rockefeller. RKO was largely responsible for streamlining Hollywood film by creating the 'unit production' mode of filmmaking. RKO contracted

independent producers to be in charge of different genres; they took responsibility for making an agreed number of films in a specific style or with a set
storyline (all of RKO's musicals, for instance, were made by a single crew
on just one sound stage).

- Leading films included: *Top Hat, Bringing Up Baby, King Kong, Citizen Kane*
- Leading stars included: Fred Astaire, Ginger Rodgers, Irene Dunn, Cary Grant, Robert Mitchum
- RKO epics: *Androcles and the Lion* (dir. Erskine, 1952); *The Last Days of Pompeii* (dir. Schoedsack, 1935).

The Three Minor Studios

Universal Pictures was founded in the early 1930s and had an immedi-
ate success with a series of sound films. It produced classic horror films
as well as emotionally restrained melodramas and satirical romantic
comedies.

- Leading films included: *Frankenstein, Imitation of Life, Pillow Talk*
- Leading stars included: Boris Karloff, Doris Day, Kirk Douglas, Rock Hudson
- Universal Epic: *Spartacus* (dir. Kubrick, 1960).

United Artists was founded in 1919 by D. W. Griffith, Charlie Chaplin,
Mary Pickford and Douglas Fairbanks. The company did not own a studio
lot and therefore did not have the overheads, maintenance or the expensive
production staff that ran up costs at other studios. In the mid-1930s, UA was
reporting profits of over a million dollars a year.

- Leading films included: *12 Angry Men, The Great Dictator, Stagecoach*
- Leading stars included: Charlie Chaplin, John Wayne, Buster Keaton, Gary Cooper
- United Artists Epics: *Alexander the Great* (dir. Rosen, 1956); *The Greatest Story Ever Told* (dir. Stevens, 1965); *Solomon and Sheba* (dir. Vidor, 1959).

Columbia Pictures earned a reputation for crafting witty and urbane
screwball comedies and glamorous 'night-life' movies. Columbia also
sponsored and encouraged fine craftsmanship both in front of and behind
the camera.

- Leading films included: *It Happened One Night, His Girl Friday, Gilda*
- Leading stars included: William Holden, Rita Hayworth, Judy Holliday
- Columbia Epics: *Barabbas* (dir. Fleischer, 1962); *Joseph and his Brethren* (dir. Dieterle, 1955, not completed); *Salome* (dir. Dieterle, 1953); *Serpent of the Nile* (dir. Castle, 1953).

Figure OC.6
Biblical glamour, DeMille style. Jaqueline Logan as Mary Magdalene – compare Figure
OC.5. *The King of Kings* (1927). Studio portrait on set.

'style' in the way in which the narrative, design, casting and publicity of
epic movies were produced and controlled.

The first full-length motion picture in the American repertoire was
an Old Testament story, *Judith of Bethulia* (dir. Griffith, 1913), which
thrust the actress Blanche Sweet into the limelight, made her one of
Hollywood's first superstars and established the movies as a new art
form.[17] As elaborate as it was, Griffith's *Judith of Bethulia* was overshadowed by a twelve-reel Italian screen adaptation of the very popular novel
Quo Vadis (dir. Guazoni, 1912), released in America at the same time
Griffith was filming *Judith*.[18] But it was D. W. Griffith's film *Intolerance*
(1916) which proved that, in terms of the treatment of space, time and
spectacle, the cinema was capable of producing grander subject matter
than the physical limitations of the theatre which, up to that time, had
been the dominant form of popular entertainment.[19] It is no coincidence

that the word 'epic' first found used in a cinematic context in 1916; it occurs in a letter written by Aldous Huxley in which he enthuses about another film of D. W. Griffith, *Birth of a Nation*: '[it is] a really great film, an epic in pictures . . . a new epoch in cinematographic art.'[20]

In 1914 the Italians topped their production of *Quo Vadis* with *Cabiria*, directed by Giovanni Pastrone and written by Gabriele D'Annunzio. *Cabiria* is often regarded as the pinnacle of the early Italian spectacle, and the film helped push cinema into the age of feature-length pictures. It cost some $210,000 to make and was a huge financial success, although due to the Great War it was not as successful as *Quo Vadis* of 1912. Set in Carthage, *Cabiria* established the visual vocabulary of the epic film and contains generous amounts of spectacle: Hannibal's elephant army crossing the Alps in the snow, Scipio's battle against the Carthaginians, an erupting volcano and, most influentially, the temple of Moloch where little children are sacrificed to a hungry god. The camera shots are somewhat static, opting in the battle sequence, for instance, for one high angle long shot, but the set designs contain real imagination, especially the hell-mouth entrance to the temple of Moloch and the elephant columns of the royal place.[21] *Cabiria* had a profound influence on D. W. Griffith's production of *Intolerance*.[22] In fact Griffith attempted to outdo the Italian film in all respects and with *Intolerance* he set a standard for screen spectacle that has seldom been equalled.

Prior to the release of *Birth of a Nation* (1915), D. W. Griffith had begun filming a piece he had blandly titled *The Mother and the Law*; it dealt with the exploitation of workers. Griffith felt the story lacked bite and so he elaborated on the theme of social morality by exploring how badly the human race treats one another. The First World War was raging and Griffith decided to tackle the long, unending history of human hatred by weaving together four tales: the modern-day episode, one set in France on the eve of the St Bartholomew Day's massacre, another in Roman Judaea (the crucifixion of Jesus) and the last, most spectacular and memorable of the tales: the fall of the city of Babylon ('the mother of harlots') to the forces of the invading Persians. The four stories are intercut, connected always by a haunting image of the 'eternal mother' (Lilian Gish) rocking a cradle.

Today *Intolerance* is rightly regarded as an early film masterpiece of cinematic sophistication, and as its layers of storylines develop and converge, so too the editor's skill gets brought to the fore. The final fifteen minutes of the film whizzes along at a breakneck pace, the whole thing composed of short scenes spliced together with a breathless sense of drama. Griffith's vision is masterful; the technical acumen that brought such a montage to fruition is bewildering. For all its romantic clichés and moralising, *Intolerance* has a visual energy that rooted the epic at the bedrock of early cinema.[23] For all his bravado and boasting of his mastery of cinema spectacle, Cecil B. DeMille never matched D. W. Griffith for his sense of scale or for his understanding of the technical potentials of film. *Intolerance* is an epic movie with cinematic intelligence and verve – rare features in the history of this weighty and often cumbersome genre. None of the epics of the 1950s come close to challenging the technical and visual superiority of *Intolerance*.

However, at the time of its release, at the height of the atrocities of the Great War, *Intolerance* proved unpopular with audiences which resulted in a financial disaster for Griffith. His career would never fully recover from this blow, although his problems did not deter other directors from making their contributions to the epic genre. The following years (Norma Desmond's Golden Age, as it were) brought such notable productions as *Cleopatra* (dir. J. Gordon Edwards, 1917), *The Queen of Sheba* (dir. J. Gordon Edwards, 1921),[24] another imported *Quo Vadis* (dir. D'Annunzio, 1925) and MGM's enormously successful and influential *Ben-Hur* (dir. Niblo, 1925).

But it was Cecil B. DeMille who best realised the potential of the epic with his productions of *The Ten Commandments* (1923) and *The King of Kings* (1927), for DeMille had hit on the perfect epic formula with his mixtures of sex, splendour and sanctity, and with these two films he became the undisputed 'King of the Spectacle', a title he would retain up to his death in 1959.[25] Michael Curtiz's mammoth retelling of *Noah's Ark* (1929) was the last of the great silent spectaculars, but by the time it was released to theatres the advent of sound had already destroyed any chances for box-office success. The last-minute addition of some sound sequences did little to improve the situation and the days of the silent movies – and of Norma Desmond – were over.[26]

During the early 1930s, DeMille almost singlehandedly kept the ancient-world epic alive with his films *The Sign of the Cross* (1932) and *Cleopatra* (1934). Most of the major Hollywood directors were tempted to tackle the epic at least once in their careers, but only DeMille built his reputation on filming spectaculars. The one film which might have threatened DeMille's eminence was RKO's *The Last Days of Pompeii* (dir. Schoedsack, 1935), which certainly helped satisfy the Great Depression's taste for spectacle. The film fancifully rearranges history by linking Christ to the apocalyptic eruption of Vesuvius as it weaves together the tale of a gruff pagan who converts to Christianity in a morality drama closely modelled on the types of films made successful by DeMille.

The emergence of *film noir* in the 1940s heralded an especially lean period for epics and even DeMille temporarily abandoned ancient history for Americana. The Second World War had audiences much more interested in the present than the past, although *The Sign of the Cross* was reissued during this time, with a modern prologue linking ancient Rome to fascist Europe and an epilogue showing American bombers flying over Rome while an army chaplain compares Mussolini to Nero. Late in the decade, in 1949, DeMille returned to the Bible for inspiration, and the result was *Samson and Delilah*, the biggest film of his career up to that time (and the movie which makes a cameo appearance in *Sunset Boulevard*). It also turned out to be one of the most successful movies of the 1940s, and upon its release, *Samson and Delilah* broke all box-office records for Paramount studios (grossing $9 million on its release). As lavish as it was vacuous, *Samson and Delilah* was the precursor to the major revival of the Hollywood epic, for during the early 1950s the epic film flourished as never before as extravagance increased with each new production.[27] In 1951 *David and Bathsheba* (dir. King) became the most successful box-office film of the year and after a year of runs *Quo Vadis* (dir. LeRoy, 1951) brought in a cool $11 million dollars for its producers.

In 1953, as Hollywood began to realise that large-scale historical spectaculars might be the way to lure audiences away from their television sets, Twentieth Century Fox added further inducement by introducing the CinemaScope widescreen process in the Roman epic *The Robe* (dir. Koster). CinemaScope turned out to be the perfect medium for this type of film and most of the major studios quickly adopted the new technology for their new films or else invented their own widescreen processes. Eventually, DeMille outdid them all with his VistaVision and Technicolor remake of *The Ten Commandments* (1956).

The popularity of *The Robe* quickly prompted Fox to release a sequel, *Demetrius and the Gladiators* (dir. Daves, 1954), a crude potboiler which nonetheless convinced the Studio to release an epic cycle, beginning with an adaptation of Mika Waltari's best-selling novel *The Egyptian* (dir. Curtiz, 1954) and concluding, by the end of the decade, with threadbare films like *The Story of Ruth* (dir. Koster, 1960) and the dismal *Esther and the King* (dir. Walsh and Bava, 1960).[28]

Following the lead set by Twentieth Century Fox, other studios transported cinema-goers into the ancient world: MGM produced *The Prodigal* (dir. Thorpe, 1955), *Ben-Hur* (dir. Wyler, 1959) and *King of Kings* (dir. Ray, 1961); Warner Brothers produced *The Silver Chalice* (dir. Saville, 1954), *Land of the Pharaohs* (dir. Hawks, 1955) and *Helen of Troy* (dir. Wise, 1956); Paramount offered *The Ten Commandments* (dir. DeMille 1956); Columbia produced *Salome* (dir. Dieterle, 1953) and *Barabbas* (dir. Fleischer, 1962); Universal, *Spartacus* (dir. Kubrick, 1960); even Walt Disney entered into the spirit of the age with a production of *The Big Fisherman* (dir. Borzage, 1959, distributed through Buena-Vista International).

It is clear to see that screenplays set in ancient Greece, Rome, Egypt and the Near East with subjects taken from the Bible or adapted from best-selling novels became hot commercial properties throughout the 1950s. Christ-films were especially popular and any film that touched in some way on the life of Jesus (*Ben-Hur, The Robe, Barabbas*) was almost guaranteed box-office success.[29] Each major studio had its own contender in the epic sweepstake and epic movies were manufactured as vehicles for major movie stars such as Richard Burton, Charlton Heston and Victor Mature. Even screen goddesses were utilised in the genre, hence the inappropriate displays of Rita Hayworth as Salome and Lana Turner as the pagan high priestess of Astarte. The movie stars, as well as the directors, wanted to prove themselves in the epic revival.[30]

In 1963 the notorious production problems and the $44 million dollar cost of *Cleopatra* (dir. Mankiewicz) nearly destroyed Twentieth Century Fox studios and the epic genre (the sum equates to $320 million dollars in today's money). Escalating production costs indicated that the heyday of this type of film was drawing to a close. Big-budget box-office failures like *The Fall of the Roman Empire* (dir. Mann, 1964), *The Greatest Story Ever Told* (dir. Stevens, 1965) and *The Bible: In the Beginning . . .* (dir. Huston, 1966) dealt the final death blows to the epic genre and provides an end point for the period of our current study.[31]

The Genre and History: Defining the 'Epic'

An 'epic' can be qualified as a work of elevated, if lengthy, character, describing the exploits of heroes and composed in a lofty, linear narrative style. As a literary genre, epics like the *Iliad*, the *Odyssey*, the *Aeneid* and, it has been claimed, even certain books of the Hebrew Bible, centre on a hero (or, rarely, a heroine) and involve him in an event or series of events – a battle, journey or quest – connected to a bigger theme, such as the destiny of a people or a nation. Epics are action-filled historical or legendary stories which enforce fundamental moral, religious, cultural or political norms and as such epics are among the oldest narrative forms in world history. Epics are the national ballads that publicly celebrate the heroic aspects of a historical society; the protagonists of these exhilarating sagas have little time (or use) for tormented inner-lives of self-doubt and inertia, which is why Aeneas and not Hamlet represents the quintessential epic hero.[32]

With its broad movements through time and space and its emphasis on action and external characterisation, the epic is ideally suited for film. Whether produced on a shoestring budget like *The Silver Chalice* or at a cost of millions like the 1963 version of *Cleopatra*, all movie epics are concerned with momentous events and larger-than-life characters. The ancient world has always held a strong fascination for both filmmakers and movie-goers, since they permit modern audiences a glimpse into the (perceived) historic or historical-mythic past. The vastness and scale that define the epic literary genre are directly realised in the medium of epic film. The vastness of the length of the average literary epic is also inherited by its cinematic successor, which is not necessarily considered a good thing; take as an example this review of *Quo Vadis*: 'The colour is magnificent, the crowd scenes stupendous, the taste poor and the length appalling' (*The Spectator*, 1951).

The epic 'mythic' elements of history are as important an aspect of the filmic take on the past as 'conventional' history, and Hollywood's ancient world is therefore a temporal space in which mythology and history converge, unite and interweave. This is certainly true of Hollywood's treatment of Homeric epic as authentic history in *Helen of Troy* and to the validity accredited to biblical stories such as the plagues on Egypt and the Hebrew Exodus in *The Ten Commandments* or the destruction of the Jewish temple in *Solomon and Sheba*.

Hollywood's conception of antiquity incorporates a distinctly Herodotean approach to history by mixing together myth, legend and fact; it can, therefore, easily encompass legendary figures like Helen of Troy, Moses and the Queen of Sheba alongside historical individuals such as Alexander the Great, Julius Caesar and Marcus Aurelius. The Trojan Horse and the Tower of Babel are as real to Hollywood as are the pyramids, the Golden Age of Athens, the reign of Cleopatra and the birth of Christianity (Figure OC.7). Yet despite its close association with oral epic, as a film genre, the epic has not enjoyed the same high cultural kudos bestowed on its literary cousin. Epic movies are customarily dismissed by critics as vulgar and garish burlesque spectacles which trade on a crude sensationalism that is usually masked beneath turgid religious morality, a facet of the genre self-consciously explored by Cecil B. DeMille.

Biblical sex and biblical spectacle were DeMille's trademarks and when it came to filming equal loads of moralising and debauchery he was the unquestioned master. Audiences, safe in their understanding that they were going to see a film of high religious morality, actually flocked to his epics specifically for the sex and violence. 'I am sometimes accused', he said, 'of gingering up the Bible with lavish infusions of sex and violence but I wish my accusers would read their Bible more closely, for in those pages are more violence and sex than I could ever portray on the screen' (Figure OC.8).[33] Nevertheless, after watching *Samson and Delilah*, John Steinbeck recorded that he: 'Saw the picture. Loved the book.'[34] At the release of Robert Aldrich's *Sodom and Gomorrah* (1962) the satirist Dougald B. MacEachen mocked the pseudo-morality of the biblical epic in his pseudo-epic verse *The Hollywood Bible*:

The Bible's one huge girlie show,
As now all moviegoers know.
Of course it had some muscle men,
Whose strength is as the strength of ten,
Mobs and battles by the score,
And rivers running red with gore.
The Book of God in Filmland means
Pretty starlets, violent scenes.
Today we've *Sodom and Gomorrah* –
But wait and see what gives tomorrah!

The derogatory way in which the epic movie has traditionally been regarded by critics and theorists still persists. The cultural historian of cinema Robert Rosenstone, for example, has argued that 'film is a disturbing symbol of an increasingly post-literate world in which people can read but won't' and for many film critics and film historians alike, the epic film falls at the nadir of the cinematic experience. The genre is condemned for its overtly elaborate decor and its impoverished imagination and in its presentation of history that is both contemporary and

Figure OC.7
Epic rhetoric: Marlowe meets Madison Avenue. *Helen of Troy* (1956). Advertising poster.

provincial.[35] Hollywood's history films are often regarded as perverting history to the point that it becomes unrecognisable to the historian, a concern that has led Rosenstone to complain that:

> The Hollywood historical drama . . . like all genres . . . locks both film-maker and audience into a series of conventions whose demands – for a love interest, physical action, personal confrontation, movement

Figure OC.8
The ubiquitous orgy, including DeMillian foot-fetish. *The Ten Commandments* (1923).
Production shot.

towards a climax and denouement – are almost guaranteed to leave
the historian of the period crying foul.[36]

Duncan Cooper goes further and fears for the safety of proper academic
history connoisseurship, suggesting that:

> If there were a Memorial Society for the Preservation of the Historical
> Truth About Spartacus and the Servile War, then its members
> would be demanding that Universal Pictures include in all adver-
> tising for [the film] *Spartacus* a sort of Cinematic Surgeon-General's
> label – CAUTION: Viewing This Film May Be Hazardous To Your
> Understanding of the Actual Historical Events.[37]

But does Hollywood have a responsibility, or a duty, to educate? 'There
is nothing duller on the screen than being accurate but not dramatic,'
maintains Stephen Ambrose.[38] As far as I am concerned, watching

history through film changes the rules for approaching history itself, since cinema insists on its own sort of 'historical truths' which arise from a visual and an aural realm that is difficult to capture adequately in the written word. Our engagement with the past on film is potentially much more complex and hazardous than it is via any written text. After all, on the screen many 'historical' things can occur simultaneously – images, sound, speech, even text: the fundamentals that support or contradict each other to create a realm of engagement and understanding which are as different from written history as written history is from oral history. So different and so complete is our engagement with history on film that it forces us to acknowledge that cinematic history constitutes a seismic shift in our perceptions and interpretations of the past.[39]

I do not regard this as necessarily negative and, indeed, some critics have suggested that Hollywood, 'by providing splendid entertainment, has sent people to the history shelves in their millions', a comment which can be endorsed not only by the meteoric rise of reception studies as a significant academic focus among historians, but by the number of students regularly enrolled on cinema-and-history courses in colleges and universities worldwide.[40] For the director Oliver Stone (no stranger to history films), '[There's] only [one] answer to people who say that movies brainwash young minds: Movies are just the first draft. They raise questions and inspire students to find out more.'[41] Perhaps the most temperate approach to the thorny problem of film's relationship to academic history though is that which is offered by Frederico Fellini:

> The essential question must be: what is the director trying to do, and is he succeeding? If historical authenticity is part of what he is trying to achieve, then it must be brought into question; if not, then in all fairness dramatic criteria alone must be used.[42]

It must be conceded that in most reviews of the epic genre, historical veracity is of little consequence and that most of the enthusiasm (should it exist at all) is reserved for the epic's extravagant excess – in terms of sets, costumes, extras, stars and spectacle, as well as the millions of dollars spent on making such lavish entertainment. Take, for example, a review of a recent re-release of *Quo Vadis*:

> Colossal is just one of the many superlatives trumpeting the size and scope of this mammoth drama about Romans, Christians, lions, pagan rites, rituals, and Nero. Roman soldier Robert Taylor loves and pursues Christian maiden Deborah Kerr. It's Christians versus Nero and the lions in the eternal fight between good and evil. The sets, scenery, and crowd scenes are nearly overwhelming. Peter Ustinov as Nero is priceless.[43]

What makes Ustinov's Nero so 'priceless'? For me that is easily answered: it is his sense of camp. There is something in the epic film

Figure OC.9
'The Chicks of Cleopatra': ultra-femaleness in epic cinema. Studio portrait on set for
Playboy magazine, 1962.

genre's 'relish for the exaggeration of sexual characteristics and personality mannerisms',[44] as Susan Sontag put it, that is allied to the notion of
camp – that hard-to-pin-down concept of artifice, fun, elegance, kitsch,
and of lies that tell the truth. When Sontag wrote that 'Camp is a woman
walking around in a dress made of three million feathers' she must have
been thinking of Hedy Lamarr's Delilah peacock gown (Colour Plate 1),
for camp lies at the core of the epic genre where everything on-screen
(and off) is pretending to be more worthwhile, lofty and serious than it
really is or even deserves to be.[45] The corny flamboyant femaleness of
Claudette Colbert, Liz Taylor, Gina Lollobrigida, Lana Turner, Susan
Haywood and a myriad of dancing-girls (Figure OC.9) and the over-
the-top he-man-ness of Victor Mature, Chuck Heston and Yul Brynner
(Figure OC.10) somehow ensure that the hyper-gendered performances
take on a quality of camp. These performances are so female and so
male that they characterise notions of gender and suggest almost the
opposite of female or male. An anecdote that illustrates the point can be
drawn from the premiere of *Samson and Delilah*: when asked by DeMille
what he thought about the film, Groucho Marx infamously quipped,
'No picture can hold my interest where the leading man's tits are bigger

than the leading lady's.'[46] Therefore 'cinematic excesses' – campness – in appearance (sets, costumes, locale), in subject matter (rise and fall, redemption) and in on-screen performances (flamboyant, dramatic, scenery-chewing) give the epic its substance.

By and large the epic film submerges the director's voice beneath this rich panoply of the film's visual needs (although some directors have managed to preserve something of their *auteur* voice in the melee: Cecil B. DeMille himself even represents the personification of the epic movie in the public perception). Unlike other popular Hollywood movie genres – the Western, the gangster film, the horror movie and the musical – however, the epic has proved to be less than congenial in its attitude towards directorial idiosyncrasy, mainly due to the size and cost of mounting the vastness of the epic project. While most movie genres were elastic enough to accommodate the offbeat styles of even the most subversive directors, the epic's need to reach a wide audience so that it could reap some profit over the huge costs of the production budget called for restraint on originality. As a result the epic is the most conservative of all Hollywood genres and the flavourless high tone of lofty nobility that often classifies the epic in terms of storyline, characterisation, dialogue and design spurns novelty and innovation and positively encourages self-referencing and repetition. Thus Gore Vidal, the one-time scriptwriter on *Ben-Hur*, noted that the director 'William Wyler studied not Roman history but other Roman movies in preparation for *Ben-Hur*', although Wyler himself regarded his work on *Ben-Hur* as bringing history to life and wanted to explore the characters in the film as real people with needs, foibles and anxieties: 'The Romans had real problems too', he noted, 'and history is no fairy tale.'[47]

Nonetheless, the self-referencing inherent in the epic genre has had a major cultural impact on how people have envisaged the ancient past. Commenting on the popular conception of ancient Rome, for example, it has been noted that

> most Americans and Europeans ... receive their principle contact with the ancient world through popular culture in its diverse manifestations: films and television programmes, historical novels and plays, comic books and toys, advertising and computer games. The Romes created in popular culture are so pervasive and entrenched in the contemporary imagination that television programmes purporting to present the real Rome use clips from Hollywood's historical epics to bring ancient Rome to life.[48]

Robert Toplin agrees, suggesting that

> for many Americans, and for people around the world, visions of the past emerge from scenes in Hollywood productions. When imagining conditions in ancient Rome ... individuals often conjure up images and words from the movies ... Audiences remember Hollywood's

productions for their style, not their statistics; for their flair, not for their facts. Many of the great motion pictures of recent decades give audiences only limited information about historic events, yet they leave viewers with memorable portraits of the past.[49]

The interaction between cinema and historical representation is a growing field of scholarship. Scholars now question how historical films reflect the societies in which they were made and speculate on how attitudes towards the past have been moulded in the popular imagination by its depiction in movies. Recent scholarship has rightly been concerned with pointing out that there is more to the epic than glitz and spectacle; epics are political allegories, reinforcing, by and large, the conservative Christian values of American society or acting as warnings that America, like the ancient empires of the past (particularly Rome), might succumb to hubris and corruption.[50] Hollywood's epic films overlay questions of faith and paganism with the theme of freedom versus tyranny: DeMille's re-working of *The Ten Commandments* is explicit in this respect, pitting the noble (proto-Christian) Hebrew lawgiver Moses against the evil Pharaoh-cum-dictator Ramses, who enslaves God's chosen people while worshipping pagan idols. In 1956 Ramses' catch phrase, 'So let it be written, so let it be done,' came to stand, in the public imagination, for all that was perceived to be oppressive and totalitarian in the atheist Soviet state under the dictators Stalin and Khruschev.[51] This basic conflict narrative is repeated in numerous Rome *v.* Christianity movies – such as *Quo Vadis*, *The Robe*, *Demetrius and the Gladiators* and *Androcles and the Lion* – in which early Christians are persecuted by despotic Roman emperors (usually Caligula or Nero) who see themselves as living gods.

The influence of this conception of polarisation extends well beyond the Old Testament and Rome *v.* Christians films. *The Egyptian*, set *c.*1300 BCE, takes as its source the Middle Kingdom Egyptian literary classic *The Tale of Sinuhe* and interweaves it with the historical evidence for the reign of the New Kingdom 'heretic' pharaoh Akhenaten. The film presents the monotheistic beliefs of Akhenaten as a pre-vision of a Christian-like deity.[52] Horemheb, the army general who overthrows Akhenaten and massacres his disciples, becomes associated with the ungodly beliefs of the pagan priests (and hence Soviet tyrants) who fear that Akhenaten's new religion of all-embracing love and tolerance will overthrow the old order and their hold over the populace. Even Robert Rossen's *Alexander the Great* holds onto this mindset, playing up Alexander's insistence that his Greek and Persian subjects worship him as a god. When, late in the film, Alexander's attitude changes to a realisation that 'We are all alike under God, the Father of all,' his expansionist policy of conquest is tempered and his tyrannical rule over his subjects ceases.

There have been, of course, attempts to present a different perspective. William Wyler and Stanley Kubrick sought out new ground with *Ben-Hur* and *Spartacus*, both of which can be classified as 'the thinking

Figure OC.10
Hyper-masculinity in the form of Yul Brynner's Ramses II. *The Ten Commandments* (1956).
Studio portrait.

person's epics', and both of which reacted against the melodramatics of DeMille's take on the past.[53] Audiences were not short-changed of spectacle, however: in *Ben-Hur*'s chariot race and great sea skirmish, or in *Spartacus*' gladiatorial fights and battle scenes, surge and splendour were still dominant. In both *Ben-Hur* and *Spartacus* though, the theme is not really the struggle between faith and paganism, but the personal and political differences between Judah Ben-Hur and Messala and between Spartacus and General Crassus. Both protagonists challenge the power of Rome not for spiritual ends, but for a personal vision of social equality and freedom, and in doing so they asked cinema audiences of McCarthy-era America to question their own accessibility to free speech and free action at a time of national and international crisis.[54]

But what about the visuals? How far were movie audiences convinced that they were seeing the past as it was lived? And how far were they aware of political subtexts and social comments within the epic films they were watching? These questions are impossible to answer definitively, but it is feasible to believe that filmmakers and audiences of the epic genre were (and are) *always* conscious that the notion of 'experiencing the past' through film is a deception, albeit one that can be indulged. Filmmakers know what to include in the production of an ancient-world history film and they understand the compromises they have to make with the historical truth; all filmmakers, whether they choose to publicly acknowledge it or not, are aware that their historical filmic representation is merely one construction of many possible pasts. After all, unlike this book, a movie has no endnotes.

Most directors are also conscious that their intentions in making a historical film differ from that of an academic historian. Hollywood directors make history films to make money at the box office and in tie-in merchandise and to make an impact upon contemporary popular culture. The academic historian has a different agenda (it is presumed): to reflect accurately on the past and to enter into and open up debate with peers. There can be no debate in a Hollywood film; there is only one take on history as it is projected onto the screen, and while the projected picture may be sharp, the focus between historical fiction and historical reality will always be blurred.

Using This Book

To a certain extent, this book bucks the scholarly trend for reading epic movies as allegories for the American socio-political or religious experience. Instead it concentrates on the real American socio-cultural experience. It examines the numerous creative elements that went into *making* the movie epics themselves – the producers' demands, the directors' decisions, the designers' visions, the actors' interpretations, the publicists' inspiration and the audiences' expectations and reactions – and the way in which epics were received by movie-goers. In other words, this book explores how and why, in the period 1916–66, the Hollywood film industry created, promoted and distributed ancient-world epics; it aims to give an introduction to the subject of cinema and ancient history by offering an exploration of how we can identify the epic genre in terms of narrative, visualisation, marketing, casting of actors and spectatorship.

This book is not about how Hollywood got its ancient history wrong. That book would be easy to write but ultimately pointless. If, as Alastair Blanshard and Kim Shahabudin state, we get 'too hung up on "historical errors" in a film', then we are missing the point of how Hollywood filmmaking operated in the Golden Age.[55] They are absolutely correct. Instead of fixating on factual errors, therefore, this book questions *why* Hollywood choose to represent the ancient past in certain ways and *how* Hollywood went about creating an on-screen image of antiquity. We must accept at the offset that producers, directors, designers and screenwriters (even some actors) often *knew* the historical facts, but they *chose* to make only flimsy nods towards historical reality and sometimes bypassed authenticity altogether.

A key fact sits at the core of this book: Hollywood always was, and has remained, a money-making business.[56] Filmmaking is an industrialised art form and its sole purpose was (and is) to generate cash – through film distribution, marketing and merchandising.[57] Getting bogged down by a film's historical errors will get us nowhere; let us explore instead *why* Hollywood chose to bring antiquity to life in the form it opted to take.

An epic film has a life beyond the screen and therefore this book will also explore the official rhetoric, marketing strategies, and publicity stunts Hollywood employed to sell its product – the ancient world – to its main target audience – the cinema-going public. As a result, this book will be more of a history of Hollywood filmmaking's impact on the popular culture of the twentieth century than it will be a study of the ancient world per se – although antiquity remains the fixed and the sole point of reference always. This book is about both the history of production and the production of history (Figure OC.11).

Throughout the book (as you have already experienced) you will be introduced to key primary sources which were produced during the Golden Age of Hollywood; these are our main study materials and they will provide us with the bone fide 'voice' of Hollywood filmmaking (see Text Box OC.5). Film historians must always contend with the sad fact that the film industry has long had a tendency to neglect – through accident, carelessness or intention – its own past. This means that there are often significant gaps in the record of the history of Hollywood filmmaking, some of which can never be filled: many early films are entirely lost, including the 1917 version of *Cleopatra*, existing only as titles in a back-catalogue or through numerous stills.[58] Much of the 1963 version of *Cleopatra* ended up on the cutting-room floor and is now feared lost. Lack of credits and the studio system practice of only naming on-screen the heads of departments means that the names of countless artists are lost to us. If Cecil B. DeMille and his films seem to loom large in this book, it is mainly as the result of DeMille's own archival presence.

Figure OC.11
Teamwork: the cast and crew of *Ben-Hur* (1959) assemble on the race-track set for a studio publicity photograph.

Text Box OC.5 Reading Beyond the Movies – Primary Sources

Film Scripts (Screenplays): Except for a few hundred classic films published in book form, it can be difficult to find accurate film scripts and most remain either unpublished as expensive collectors' items or unauthorised drafts. Moreover, some scripts of the Golden Age period were not finalised or published as coherent texts; sometimes acting or directing happened on a more ad hoc basis. Scripts which are available for consultation, however, offer rich insights into the original vision of a film. Film scholars can compare the writer's vision with the producer's and director's interpretations. The structure of scripts, character development, plot points and scenes can all be analysed. When there are multiple versions of a script created over time, they can be studied to see how derivative scripts are developed.

Pressbooks (Campaign Books): folio-sized glossy magazines (released as part of a press kit) sent to exhibitors (cinema owners or managers) which contain information about a new film. Pressbooks and related press materials date back to the 1910s when Hollywood studios released certain information about a film so that cinemas and exhibitors might disseminate details to the press. The major studios routinely designed and distributed carefully constructed advertising to help in the overall promotion of a film: most included background information about the film, the actors, the crew and other titbits about the film's creation as well as a breakdown of the advertising materials and merchandising tie-in products that are available to the cinemas. Exhibitors could order publicity materials from the pressbooks – lobby cards, posters and press releases were all included. Pressbooks are a superb source for analysing the official Hollywood rhetoric which accompanied a film's release.

Film (Souvenir) Brochures: distributed or sold to movie theatre audiences, colour film brochures were popular souvenirs of a visit to the cinema to see a favourite film. Lavishly illustrated, these glossy publications detailed stories of the making of the film, of the lives of the actors and images of sets and costumes. Like the pressbooks, the film brochures provide important information on Hollywood's official marketing of the movie.

Movie Stills (Figure OC.12): every Hollywood studio had a unit of stills photographers; they were required to capture in still photography many of the key moments of a movie as it was being made, the purpose of which was ultimately to use the images for publicity in newspapers, movie theatres and magazines. Rarely were movie stills copied from the celluloid negative; more commonly, at the end of a 'take', actors posed for the stills photographer who thereby artificially recaptured the on-screen moment. Large-scale outdoor shots were captured as they happened. (For a discussion of the stills photography process and purpose see Finler (2012).)

Publicity Shots (Figure OC.13): carefully posed pre-production shots and portraits of the movie stars in and out of costume were required for publicity. All the major studios hired professional, often leading, photographers to capture and sometimes 'create' stars' likenesses. Certain Hollywood photographers, like Clarence Sinclair Bull, were not only artists of the highest calibre, but became celebrities in their own right. (On

Figure OC.12
Buddy Baer as Ursus wrestling a bull. *Quo Vadis* (1951). Movie still. Glossy stills of key dramatic moments were sent out by the studios to newspapers and magazines in order to promote the movies shortly before they appeared in the cinemas. The stills were often accompanied by official tags. In this instance (typed on the reverse of the photograph) is the following: 'MAN VS. BEAST . . . Buddy Baer is fighting a wild bull in this scene from Metro-Goldwyn-Mayer's *Quo Vadis*.'

CLAUDETTE COLBERT
in Paramount Pictures

P1090-49E

Figure OC.13
A beautifully composed publicity portrait of Claudette Colbert, costumed for her role as
Cleopatra (1934). As John Kobal has put it, these portraits 'had nothing to do with
making movies, but everything to do with the selling of the dream that movies meant.'
This portrait, probably by Paramount's Eugene Robert Richee, has all the hallmarks of
great studio photography.

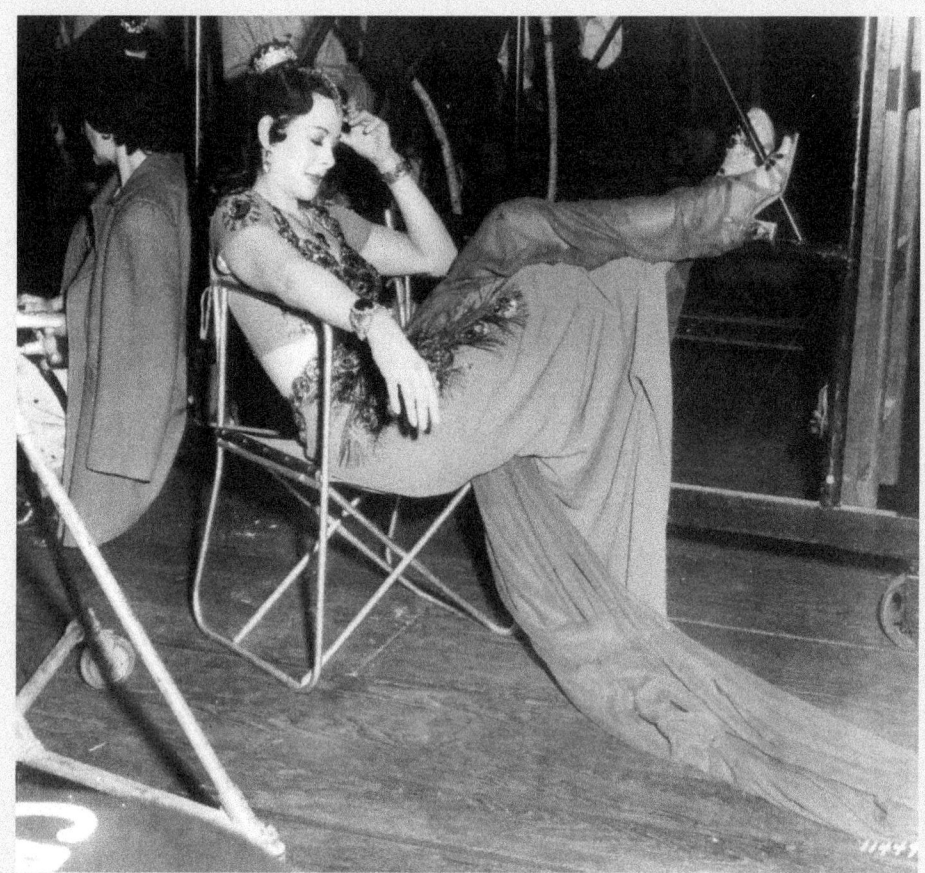

Figure OC.14
This candid shot of actress Hedy Lamarr shows her relaxing off-set during the filming of
DeMille's *Samson and Delilah*. She is in full hair and makeup, but wears only part of
her famous peacock dress (see Colour Plate 1).

Hollywood's publicity photography see Trent (1982); Fahey and Rich (1988); Pepper and
Kobal (1989); Dance (2008).)

Candid Shots (Figure OC.14): photographs of actors and crew in informal, 'off-duty',
moments. These images were regularly provided to the press and fan magazines, together
with publicity stills, to publicise the release of each new picture. Although these behind-
the-scenes photographs give the impression of spontaneity, showing actors, directors and
film crew in candid moments, they were often, in fact, carefully staged for the publicity
camera (see further Finler 2012: 119–79).

Wardrobe Reference Shots (Figure OC.15): a series of black-and-white photographs made
by the stills unit for the express purpose of providing costume, hair and makeup references for the Wardrobe (and related) department. These were often taken for continuity

Figure OC.15
Continuity reference photograph created for the Hair Dressing department during the
filming of *Cleopatra* (1963). These working reference shots have great value for the film
historian as they sometimes (as here) record costumes which were never used in the
final edit of a movie.

Figure OC.16
A giant billboard above New York's Rivoli Theatre in Times Square advertises the
imminent world premier of *Cleopatra*, which opened there on 13 June 1963. Designed
by Howard Terpning to capture the public mania for Elizabeth Taylor's love affair with
Richard Burton.

references, but they provide excellent evidence for the development of costume ideas
during a film's production and are sometimes the only evidence we have for costumes
which were dropped or changed during the filming process.

Designs: set and costume designs mainly exist in specialist collections, although they are
sometimes published in books and were even printed in contemporary film brochures.
Without doubt, these are key sources and should be studied wherever possible.

Posters and Lobby Cards (Figure OC.16): created for display in cinema lobbies, facades
and other prominent public locations, large posters and the smaller lobby cards. The main
studios lavished a fortune on publicity campaigns – from the modest 'one sheets' posted
on neighbourhood walls, to the gigantic 'forty-eight sheets' which covered the entire sides
of New York skyscrapers. The right image could seduce millions into the cinemas, and so
the studios employed some of the finest graphic artists of the age to design their posters.
Together with the tag-lines which accompany the pictures, posters are a rich source for
'reading' the 'meaning' of a film, as well as Hollywood's intended message. (For a discussion see Rebello and Allen (1988); for film exhibition see Hark (2002).)

Trailers: ever since the first known example in 1913, the movie trailer has been an
essential (sometime favourite) element of movie-going. Consisting of a series

**Salome*...inspired by Rita Hayworth
...a figure-flattering SeaMolds®**

Salome...sarong-skirted, with classical leaf-garland stenciled in
gold...is the fabulous SeaMolds Swimsuit by Flexees—
inspired by Rita Hayworth, fascinating as the famous court
beauty. You'll want two or three SeaMolds...to
swim, lounge, sun in the most exciting swimsuits
you'll see in '53. Salome SeaMolds: **$18.95**
       Other SeaMolds from **$12.95**

*Rita Hayworth, Stewart Granger, starring
in Salome, a Columbia Technicolor Picture.
Beckworth Corporation Production.*

flexees.

At better stores. For stores near you write Flexees, Inc., Dept. NY, 417 Fifth Avenue, New York 16

Figure OC.17
An advertisement from *The New Yorker*, dated 16 May 1953, used the star-power of
Rita Hayworth to sell the 'Salome' swimsuit. Hayworth wears nothing of this type of
outfit in the movie *Salome*, but this does not stop the ad campaigners, Flexees, claiming
that the bathing suit was 'inspired by Rita Hayworth, fascinating as the famous court
beauty'.

selected shots from the film being advertised (in less than two minutes, ten seconds), the trailer was created to attract an audience to the film, and excerpted moments from the most exciting or otherwise noteworthy sections of the film but without spoiling any storylines. They often provide an official narration and suggest the way we should 'read' the film (see especially Kernan 2005).

Advertisements (Figure OC.17): tie-ins were often promoted in magazines and news-papers, especially cosmetics and fashion items. Some movies were used to advertise products not directly related to the film. These advertisements alert us to the fact that Hollywood was a money-making industry which marketed its product in conjunction with other industries and manufacturers (see Sennett 1998; Massey 2000).

Fan Magazines: a great source of original Hollywood rhetoric and self-promotion, maga-zines like *Motion Picture Story* and *Photoplay* also dealt with gossip and innuendo sur-rounding the stars and provided advice on lifestyle and taste. Fan magazines offer a vivid insight into mass-marketed popular culture (see especially Basinger 1993; Stacey 1993; Barbas 2001; Slide 2010).

Reviews and cartoons (Figure OC.18): in the period 1915–65, most newspaper film critics and journalists tried to write for the masses. Many of the film reviews which were published in national or local newspapers were written by professional critics and other people in the entertainment industry or in public life, as well as by other filmmakers (this contrasts markedly with the wide dissemination of amateur film reviews to be found on the Internet). The opinions and observations of the critics are often valuable and provide a refreshing antidote to Hollywood's official 'voice' (see Keylin and Bent 1979; Perry 1989; Roberts 2010).

Figure OC.18
This affectionate cartoon pastiche of *The Ten Commandments* (1956) was found in the movie's pressbook and was produced for widescale use in newspapers.

As you read through the book use the text boxes to focus on important details and pay attention to all of the figures which are liberally placed throughout the text. Chapter 1 explores the way in which Hollywood publicised epic movies. It examines the way in which marketing experts created the rhetoric of selling the past to movie going America through pressbooks, newspaper and magazine copy, posters and other forms of artwork, as well as cinema trailers. Two selling factors dominated the process: the marketability of statistics and the marketability of research. The one was intended to overwhelm the audience by exposing the expense which went into bringing the past alive and the other was focused on justifying the cost in pursuit of historical authenticity. Both, as it transpires, were bogus claims.

In Chapter 2 the focus is on set design and the physical construction of the space of antiquity either created in the studio soundstages or on location. This chapter explores the work of Hollywood's great art directors and it attempts to 'read' sets as artificial forms of embellishment pretending to be reality. Dependent, in many respects, on nineteenth-century art, the Hollywood visualisation of the ancient world was also filtered through contemporary architectural aesthetic and fashions in interior design. Contemporary modes are also found in the costume designs created for epic movies, the focus of Chapter 3. This chapter explores the processes through which costumes were brought into realisation, from design inception to on-camera effect. While bound to the standard marketing ploy of historical authenticity, costumes were expressions of contemporary fashion and the film studios always had an eye on mass-marketing versions of epic costumes, hairstyles and make-up to the public. The chapter explores too the Hollywood ideal of masculinity and the male body expressed through epic costume design.

Finally, the focus of Chapter 4 is on movie stars and the roles they played in epic films. As the central component of the on-screen image of the past, the contribution that actors made to the creation, selling and appreciation of the epic genre cannot be overstated. The chapter questions the effect that the appearance of well-known movie stars had on the notion of on-screen history and turns its attention too towards the marketing of actors as historical figures. This often led to confusion, upset and the breakdown of the production process of putting antiquity on film. Movie stars are the most conspicuous rupture in the process of putting history onto film.

Admittedly, I have been selective in the materials I have decided to highlight in this study. From such a rich corpus of sources, I have opted to look only at the epic movies which seem to me to be the most important, the most representative or, sometimes, the least illustrative of the genre. Sometimes I have chosen films because of particular traits in design features or marketing devices. If some directors – and I'm thinking chiefly of Cecil B. DeMille here – appear more than others, then often it is because I think they are worth the attention. Some films (like the 1956 *The Ten Commandments*, both the 1934 and the 1963 *Cleopatra* movies, *Quo Vadis* and *Samson and Delilah*) appear here frequently – simply because I love them and I have things to say about them. But that is not to deny the value of other classics of the genre – *The 300 Spartans*, *Julius Caesar*, *The Last Days of Pompeii*, *Helen of Troy*, *The Story of Ruth* and many more – that do not get the coverage they deserve in these pages; had I more space, more time and more energy I would have included them all. My hope is, though, that this book will act as a springboard for future studies (perhaps my own included) and that individual epics (or groups of films) of the Hollywood studio era (and of more recent times) might be given more fruitful study, especially in terms of the production themes which I aim to highlight here.

It goes without saying that the key 'texts' in any study of Hollywood are the movies themselves. By viewing as many as one can one soon builds up a portfolio of movie-watching experiences and with that comes the realisation that the more epics one sees, the easier it becomes to identify the overarching trends of the epic genre. As Quentin Crisp, a veteran film-goer of seventy years, once insisted:

> The [best] way to go to the cinema is incessantly. The more often we visit the cinema, the more exciting the experience becomes, not the more boring, as one might expect. Films teach us how to see them; they are written in a language we must learn . . . We must go to the movies so often that, while remaining distant, the stars become calculable to us, allowing us to recognise and dote upon their gestures, the tones of their voices, their every idiosyncrasy. After a while, even the unseen presence of our favourite directors will become traceable.[59]

I would add to this by saying that over time the on-screen presence of the work of production designers, cinematographers, costume designers and even make-up artists becomes knowable. The more we watch, the more we recognise.

Almost every film referred to in this study is available on DVD or Blu-ray or to download digitally. As Martin Winkler has noted, there has never been a better time to study the epic genre, since contemporary technology aids our process of study; we can now 'read' a movie on DVD or through a download as readily as we might study from a book:

> We can view a film again and again at any time we wish, jump from one scene to any other within seconds, select a scene for particular scrutiny at slow motion, or even look at individual frames. In other words, we are now in the position to read a filmic work in a way similar to those in which we read a literary one. The new technology even enables us to find a particular moment in a film faster than we could find a certain passage or line in a work of literature by turning back the pages of a book, and so the term 'chapters' for a film's individual sequences or scenes in [DVDs] seems entirely appropriate.[60]

However, watching epic movies on our television or computer screens, or by downloading them onto our iPads and mobile phones, sets us far apart from the way in which the films were originally screened, and it is important for us to realise this dramatic shift in the viewing experience. In Hollywood's Golden Age films were only seen in cinemas; they were collective communal experiences for an audience at large who, of course, shared common experiences of the politics and socio-cultural events of the day. They read the same newspaper reviews of the films they watched together, the same fan magazines, and were subject to a common form of Hollywood rhetoric.

Nonetheless, we must be aware that there will never be any holistic 'reading' of a film and that no two members of an audience can ever have the same viewing experience. An individual's reading of a film can be tempered by numerous external and internal forces, ranging from the type of cinema in which the film is viewed (a luxury New York movie palace or a local drive-in) to an individual's own knowledge of (in the case of watching epics) ancient history or the Bible.

To get a little closer to the viewing conditions of the original screenings of these movies, where possible have the films projected (through a digital projector, no doubt) or take any opportunity to see them commercially projected in (usually) art-house cinemas. Although you might never be able to fully appreciate the vastness of a 1950s CinemaScope projection, you will nonetheless undeniably benefit from seeing the films magnified onto a screen and, viewing them as part of a group, you will note how an 'audience dynamic' informs your experience of watching the movies.

As you watch the films remember that you are viewing carefully constructed finished products of a multi-million-dollar industrialised art form. Nothing appears on screen that has not been meticulously thought through (except for a few continuity errors, or some anachronisms which creep into frame during the shoot). But certainly, *every* camera shot and each edit has been constructed to lead you towards reading the film in a certain way; every special effect, setting, prop and costume has been placed there for a purpose. Every close-up, gesture, shadow and movement has been choreographed for a purpose. Hollywood movies are finely crafted to persuade us to suspend our disbelief and enter into the on-screen reality. As casual viewers we are happy to accept, unquestioningly, what is projected in front of us, but as critical viewers we must engage with these films differently and we must never forget that we are observing an artificial product created by artistic experts.

As you watch the movies, do what Billy Wilder did so successfully when he crafted the last scene of *Sunset Boulevard*, his mini-epic-within-*film-noir* masterpiece, and think carefully about how the camera shots and angles effect our perception of a scene, how the editing impacts on the story, and how lighting, music and sound effects influence our viewing experience of the epic. Why is a set designed in a particular way? Why does scale matter? How is colour used in a scene? Think about the impact which costumes, hairstyles and makeup have on the way we engage with the films' characters and the movie stars who play them. Think about the acting styles too, as well as the movie stars who play the main roles – how do they integrate with the overall 'feel' and 'look' of the film?[61] What makes an epic film 'epic'? Keep all these of questions in mind as you consider how and why Hollywood interacted with antiquity. Think about *why* the films depict antiquity so and ask – 'What designs *did* Hollywood have on the past?'

Notes

1. Cited in Rosen (2001: 193) who examines the Tarsus barge sequence in detail, drawing attention to its 'virtuosity of spectacle comparable to that of the [1930s] musical'.
2. It should be noted that when the epic succeeds, the spectacle is organically connected to a human drama and the films earn their flamboyant set pieces (think of the crossing of the Red Sea in *The Ten Commandments* and the great chariot race of *Ben-Hur*) but the epic fails when it is made solely for its sensational elements.
3. Hirsch (1991: 275).
4. Blanshard and Shahabudin (2011: 44).
5. A good and detailed overview of the creation and afterlife of *Sunset Boulevard* is provided by Staggs (2002).
6. MGM boss Louis B. Mayer was furious at the film's exposé of Hollywood, and he thundered at Wilder, 'You have disgraced the industry that made and fed you. You should be tarred and feathered and run out of Hollywood!' See Block and Wilson (2010: 343).
7. For a concise but informative discussion of the *film noir* genre, see Keenan (2011). For a good discussion of the wider issues of Hollywood genre see Maltby (2003: 74–110); Casper (2007). Basinger (1986: 264) describes *genre* as a 'recipe', adding that:

   > *Genre* is the method of telling the story. In the shifting patterns of storytelling, the costumes and setting of a genre film might be called its objective parts, and its morality, its humanistic issues, might be called its subjective part. Each genre has an objective/subjective makeup. The subjective can change its meanings, be varied, and thus evolve. It responds to interpretation. The objective remains the same and is quickly recognised . . . Simply stated, we know ideology shifts over a period of time, but the 'genre' remains the same. New ideas are taught through familiar films.

8. Of the numerous biographies and studies of Billy Wilder's work, the most enlightening and engaging include Sikov (2000) and Chandler (2004). Simsolo (2011) provides a concise and well-illustrated introduction to Wilder's work.
9. Basinger (1999: 234). After one of the screenings Paramount held for industry insiders, the actress Barbara Stanwyck got down on her knees and literally kissed the hem of Swanson's gown, a gesture of accolade that briefly reinstated the old Hollywood order. Mary Pickford was at that screening too, but she left the performance early, too overwhelmed, it appears, to stay any longer.

10. The complete films of DeMille are chronicled by Ringgold and Bodeen (1969) with references to contemporary reviews.

11. Meyers (1999: xi). In *Sunset Boulevard*, Norma is also greeted by the real-life actor, Henry Wilcoxon, who was starring at the time as the Philistine prince Ahtur in DeMille's *Samson and Delilah*. As a DeMille stalwart (and later co-producer of DeMille's films) Wilcoxon had appeared in *Cleopatra* (1934) as Marc Antony and would later play Pentaur in the 1956 version of *The Ten Commandments*. For a very lively and amusing account of his life and work see Wilcoxon (1991).

12. Swanson (1981: 423). For Edith Head's inspirational costume work on *Sunset Boulevard* see Head and Castro (1983: 88–91); Staggs (2002: 126–33); Chierichetti (2003: 103–8); Jorgensen (2010: 157–63). The resonances between *Sunset Boulevard* and *Samson and Delilah* go deeper, as Wilcoxon (1991: 178) describes: 'look carefully at *Sunset Boulevard* and you'll see pieces of *Samson and Delilah* scattered about. At the New Year's Eve party at Webb's apartment, a statue of Dagon sits – looking very much like a Buddha gone wrong next to the telephone.'

13. For a definition and analysis of the term *mise-en-scène* see Chapter 2.

14. Cooke (2008: 101–2) analyses the *Sunset Boulevard* score.

15. Eldridge (2006: 12–13).

16. For detailed, solid, and informative overviews of the chronological development of the epic see Elley (1984); Solomon (2001); Richards (2008).

17. On *Judith of Bethulia* and the vogue for Bible stories in silent cinema see, importantly, Shepherd (2013: 161–9).

18. As we will explore, these early epics exploited the nineteenth-century vogue for theatrical spectacle and drew heavily on the established norms of gesture and iconography familiar to audiences of theatrical melodrama, giving silent films a timeless quality not attained by sound films. DeMille's *King of Kings* (1927), for instance, draws on the symbolic force of heroic gestures to give his Christ a suitably mystic aura unrealised in any Christ-film of the sound era. See Flanders (2006: 292–342).

19. See Drew (2001).

20. Cited in Paul (2013: 4). Hall and Neale (2010) date the use of 'epic' as a general descriptive term for film to a *Motion Picture Herald* article of 15 July 1911. On the ancient world in silent cinema see, importantly, Wyke and Michelakis (2013).

21. For *Cabiria* see Solomon (2001: 47–9).

22. Schickel (1996: 310).

23. Drew (2001).

24. See Llewellyn-Jones (2002a: 19–21).

25. See Birchard (2004: 363–4); Orrison (1999).

26. Golden (1996).

27. Forshey (1992).

28. See Llewellyn-Jones (2002a: 19–20).

29. Babington and Evans (1993: 91–139); Kinnard and Davis (1992).

30. Film stars and their epic roles are discussed in detail in Chapter 4.

31. Of course, the new millennium saw the triumphant return of the epic genre to the big screen with the release of Ridley Scott's *Gladiator* (2000). This mega-budgeted Roman spectacle was no doubt a gamble, but it paid off handsomely for everyone involved. In addition to being a tremendous winner at the box office, *Gladiator* also won the Academy Award for Best Picture – see Winkler (2004). The film established a trend for the return of the epic in cinemas: in (2004) Wolfgang Petersen's *Troy* opened to popular, if not

critical, success – see Winkler (2007a). In the same year Oliver Stone's biopic *Alexander* attracted less critical and popular acclaim than had been supposed – see Lane Fox (2004); Nisbet (2007); Greenland and Cartledge (2009). Forays into the field continued with Zack Snyder's *300* and a new spate of Greek myth movies; at the time of writing the omens for the future of (fantasy) epic looks good. For discussions of the contemporary epic in world cultures see Burgoyne (2010).

32. Discussions of the relationship between epic film and epic literature can be found in Elley (1984) and Santas (2008). See also, very importantly, Paul (2013).
33. DeMille (1960: 366).
34. Tanitch (2000: 50).
35. Rosenstone (1995: 46).
36. Rosenstone (1995: 29).
37. Cooper (1991: 19).
38. Ambrose (1996: 239).
39. For further debates about cinema's relationship with history see Chopra-Gant (2008).
40. McDonald Fraser (1988: 19).
41. Oliver Stone, cited in Carnes (1996: 306).
42. Fellini cited in Solomon (2001: 23). A good starting point to investigate the debate about cinema's relationships with history is Hughes-Warrington (2007).
43. Martin and Porter (1987: 674).
44. Sontag (1966: 279).
45. Sontag (1966: 279).
46. Shearer (2010: 300).
47. Vidal (1992: 84). Wyler is cited in Elley (1984: 87). As a young boy, the director Martin Scorsese had an intense cinematic experience watching an epic movie:

> I'd always wanted to make a film of the life of Christ, ever since I first saw Him portrayed on the screen in *The Robe* when I was eleven years old. I was an altar boy, and I was taken by our diocesan priest on a little field trip up to the Roxy. He hated the film for its absurdity, but I'll never forget the magic of walking down the lobby and getting a glimpse of that gigantic Cinemascope screen for the first time. And when I heard the music in stereophonic sound, it became confused in my mind with the Gregorian Chant for the Mass for the Dead, at which I used to serve every Saturday morning at 10:30. (Scorsese 1989: 117)

When Ridley Scott regenerated the epic with *Gladiator* in 2000 he acknowledged its success being dependent on the winning format created by the big-budget Roman epics of the 1950s – see Landau (2000). Likewise, Oliver Stone explained to the production team of *Alexander* (2004) that he had been deeply influenced by films such as *Ben-Hur* and *Intolerance* and that his *Alexander* was to be part of the long epic film legacy – see Lane Fox (2004: 124).

48. Joshel et al. (2001: 1).
49. Toplin (2002: 198, 203). See further discussion of the 'Americanisation' of history in McDonald (2011). The tyranny of the Hollywood studio system may have discouraged any radical approach to epic subject matter, yet it is important not to classify all epic films together; there have been many

honourable, popularly conceived Hollywood epics which stand head and shoulders over the commonly perceived detritus of many epic movies: *Intolerance*, *Ben-Hur* and *Spartacus* have attained a dignity and magnitude worthy of the literary epic and should not be dismissed merely because it inhabits the same genre-space as, say, the weak *Esther and the King* or *The Prodigal*.

50. The literature for this is full, but important. See especially Forshey (1992); Wyke (1997); Joshel et al. (2001); Cyrino (2004 and 2005); Grace (2009); Leib (2011). More generally on politics in Golden Age Hollywood movies see Maltby (2003: 268–308).
51. See Nadel (1993) and Wright (2003: 89–127).
52. Discussed in detail by Montserrat (2000).
53. Wyler, who was nonetheless inspired by DeMille's movies, did not regard the epic genre as conservatively as DeMille had done; he liked to quip that it took someone Jewish to finally make a good film about Christ.
54. Cyrino (2005: 59–120); Winkler (2007b).
55. Blanshard and Shahabudin (2011: 11).
56. For a focused discussion see Hozic (2001) as well as Sennett (1998).
57. See discussions in Hark (2002).
58. The American Film Institute lists the 1917 *Cleopatra* among its top ten most important missing films. For a discussion see Thompson (1996: 68–78). We do have some footage (albeit seconds) from the film. See, for example, http://www.youtube.com/watch?v=OWn7L2pL5dI (accessed 25 March 2017).
59. Crisp (1984: 8).
60. Winkler (2001: 19).
61. Kydd (2011) considers all of these points and more in a lively introduction to film studies.

CHAPTER 1

SEE! SEE! SEE! HOLLYWOOD SELLS THE PAST

As a spectacle, it is splendid. As a piece of . . . history, it is a gigantic joke.
Daily Herald review of *Solomon and Sheba* (1959)

Hollywood epics regarded 'History' as a spectacle. History Hollywood-style was a visual pleasure made up of a mix of obsession with period details and the ostentatious love of the grandiose. A sequence in DeMille's *The Sign of the Cross* exemplifies this point: the amphitheatre scene which occurs in the final portion of the movie features the kind of visual grandeur that was central to the epic genre, although the sequence begins outside the arena itself as the audience is shown a poster advertising that day's circus spectacle. The poster is first shown in Latin but the ancient language dissolves into English (a common filmic trope of the 1930s) although a somewhat haphazard use of the Latin 'V's and English 'U's helps maintain the Roman flavour of the 'original' poster:

> On the Last Day of May, NERO CLAVDIVS CAESAR will fvrnish 30 pair of gladiators [. . .] against 30 pair of gladiators [. . .] and 30 barbarian women from the North to fight 30 pygmies from Africa. There will be wild beasts and a hvnt with other great events and 100 CHRISTIANS taken in treason to be EXECVTED.

The on-screen text is accompanied by off-screen voices of Roman citizens commenting on the promised entertainments. 'It doesn't say how [the Christians] are to be killed, just "execution"', whinges one onlooker. 'You leave that to Nero', his colleague enthuses, 'it's bound to be in some interesting way!' This short dialogue plays on two levels, allowing us, the cinema audience, to wonder too what Nero has in store for the Christians while simultaneously prompting us to speculate on what the master showman Cecil B. DeMille has up his sleeve for our entertainment.

DeMille does not disappoint. A ten-minute-long sequence follows in which the excesses of the Roman arena are exposed. Rapid editing cuts between shots of the Roman spectators enjoying the grotesque horrors and the spectacle of death within the arena itself where a pair of elephants crush a man's head, a tiger mauls a young woman, crocodiles eat a girl trussed between two stakes, and another maiden is mauled (and perhaps violated) by a gorilla. The cinema audience is given both the panoply of the spectacle of ancient violence and the spectacle of watching ancient Romans behave badly and, as Tom Brown has noted, 'DeMille is one of the most blatantly spectacular filmmakers of classical Hollywood not only through the kinds of cinematic display he offered, but in the clear way in which he addresses the act of looking itself.'[1] But there is a further synergy between DeMille's 'Roman' viewers and his 'Hollywood' viewers in the way in which the arena spectacle is marketed. The Latin poster seen on-screen is in effect merely a variation of the studio marketing created for the cinema release of *The Sign of the Cross*. Pressbook advertising promised the movie-going audience a 'great spectacle: 50 Grecian dancing beauties . . . 40 gladiators in complete armour . . . 40 women more than six feet in height . . . alligators, gorillas, tigers . . . the sacrifice of 100 Christians . . . a faithful duplication of the Roman Circus'. For DeMille historical truth ('a faithful duplication of the Roman Circus') was unproblematically obtainable through a reconstruction of the artifacts – the look – of the past combined with hyperbolic spectacle. The past had to be seen to be believed and in Hollywood's terms this is what made antiquity marketable.

When we decide to go to the cinema to see a movie we might think that we are making a rational self-conscious decision. Perhaps to some extent that is true. But our choice of what we go to see is of course conditioned by what is playing at the cinema at the time and by much more. For weeks, perhaps months or years, we have been receiving information about the movie that is now playing in the local cinema (or, more likely today, the multiplex). When we went to the movies some months back, we saw a trailer advertising this current flick; then we read about its creation in movie magazines, newspapers and on the Internet. Perhaps we were transfixed enough to follow its development from conception to casting to filming to the moment of its release. (Consider the huge impact that Peter Jackson's *Lord of the Rings* and *Hobbit* trilogies have had on the public consciousness in terms of pre-release publicity; the *Harry Potter* franchise had a similar effect.)[2]

Then the artwork came out: posters and magazine-spreads – keeping us enticed, luring us in to buy a cinema ticket and be part of this cultural phenomenon. This was followed by television and radio slots publicising the film, alongside a myriad of official and unofficial website appearances. And at the time of the film's premiere, the movie tie-ins hit the shops: books, action figures, board games, clothing, t-shirts, lunch boxes . . . anything goes. Everything possible has been done by the production company to make sure that we buy the ticket and see *that film*. Free choice has very little to do with it; mass-marketing on an industrial scale predetermines how we will spend our leisure time and our money.

And it was ever so. Even without the power of the Internet (or the television, for that matter), the cinema-going public of Hollywood's Golden Age was under the same constraints, pressures, spells, lures and enticements as we are today. In her insightful and often humorously caustic 1939 study of the Hollywood film industry, the British sociologist-cum-movie fan, Margaret Thorpe, focused on the sociological effect American cinema had upon its public. She noted that:

> When any of the eighty-five million moviegoers walks down Main Street of an evening saying, 'Shall we go to the Majestic or the Bijou?' he imagines that he is making up his mind about his evening's entertainment. As a matter of fact, the nightly decision is very far from being a matter of free will. The choice was predestined months ago by forces . . . he cannot see.[3]

Tongue firmly in cheek, she goes on to describe how the film studios carefully plan their publicity campaigns (or 'exhibitions' as they were usually called) over an extended series of months with a military-like precision:

> National advertising campaigns have their routine procedure, and their special features if the picture is big enough. The companies [i.e. studios] design billboard, newspaper, and magazine advertising, make pressbooks of suggestions to theatre men, and plan material for lobby displays. Some of the posters, 'stills', 'blowups' and 'cutouts' for local use must be rented by the theatre but the [studio] makes them. Their quality and quantity vary with the importance of the picture. Of a feature film dear to his heart, a producer will announce his intention to run full colour pages in half a dozen magazines with national circulation, or promise to double his usual advertising, or agree to spend at least $100,000 . . . All this is dreamed and executed while the picture is in production. A feature campaign may get underway even before the cameras turn.[4]

What Thorpe is stressing here are facts that we have already recognised: that Hollywood has always been a money-making industry and

Text Box 1.1   Top Grossing Epic Films 1949–66

1949

Samson and Delilah	(Paramount)	**$11,500,000**

1951

Quo Vadis	(MGM)	**$11,902,000**
David and Bathsheba	(Twentieth Century Fox)	**$4,720,000**

1953

The Robe	(Twentieth Century Fox)	**$17,500,000**
Salome	(Columbia)	**$4,864,000**
Julius Caesar	(MGM)	**$4,741,000**

1956

The Ten Commandments	(Paramount)	**$43,000,000**

1959

Ben-Hur	(MGM)	**$37,000,000**

1960

Spartacus	(Universal)	**$14,000,000**

1961

King of Kings	(MGM)	**$25,000,000**

1963

Cleopatra	(Twentieth Century Fox)	**$57,777,778**

1966

The Bible: In the Beginning . . .	(Twentieth Century Fox)	**$34,900,023**

that mass publicity generates public interest. The public therefore buys cinema tickets to see a film and the revenue goes back into the industry. This is why Hollywood lavished so much attention on publicising its films with such flair and verve, and it is fair to say that between 1916 and 1966 epic movies were marketed with more ingenuity and more hoopla than any other movie genre. Because epic movies cost more money to make than other type of film it was imperative that they had to sell well to the public – not just to draw even financially, but to make a significant profit for the studios. Big films demanded big promotion.

From 1949 until 1966 epic films regularly appeared in the charts for successful box office receipts and during that period epics actually topped the box-office charts seven times (see Text Box 1.1). The Hollywood studios realised that by ploughing money into their biblical and historical pictures – and by advertising the fact that they had spent enormous sums on these projects – the financial payback could be very profitable. As Michael Wood has noted:

> The amount of money spent on [an epic] was part of what helped to sell the film – and the principle, presumably, that anything that

had cost that much had to be good, and also if it cost that much, we are invited to think, just imagine how much it will make. A projection of fabulous success for the movie becomes part of the movie's story before it even reaches the cinema. To be sure, this was always a Hollywood principle, but the epics consecrated it and interiorised it, so to speak, as if it were the only principle the industry had left . . . Only epics . . . insist on thinking so much about money while we are in the cinema. Every gesture, every set piece bespeaks fantastic excess. There is more of everything . . . we sit and brood about . . . the sheer extravagance of [it all].[5]

Part of the money-spinning appeal of the epic lay in its propensity to be used by the studios for technological innovation. Epic movies were frequently used as blueprints for developments in technical expertise and throughout the period covered by the book, there were several revolutionary technological advances first tried out in epic cinema: changes in film stock, colour processing, sound recording systems, special effects and projection – including CinemaScope and Technicolor (as we will go on to explore) – helped put the epic at the cutting edge of Hollywood filmmaking. As Blanshard and Shahabudin have noted, 'each technique promised a bigger and better experience, and it is understandable that filmmakers employed them in depicting the biggest, richest empire(s) the world has ever known.'[6]

Unfortunately critics usually condemned epic films as louche, hackneyed, money-making clichés, devoid of artistic merit (for instance, *New York Times* film-reviewer Paul Rotha dismissed DeMille's *Samson and Delilah* as 'manna for illiterates'),[7] yet at the height of their popularity in the 1950s, the public taste for epics seemed to know no limits. One man, recalling seeing *The Robe*, the first movie to be shot and shown in widescreen format, recounts the thrill of experiencing the scale associated with epics:

At last the lights went down and the curtains opened to what appeared to be an ordinary size screen and then the familiar Twentieth Century Fox logo and music came on. My friend . . . and I looked at each other – dead disappointed . . . Then the screen went black and the curtains opened until there in front of us was a curved screen . . . three times wider than normal . . . The hairs on the back of our necks tingled [and] there was a collective 'Ooh!' from the audience.[8]

For others though, epic movies were viewed with awe and considerable reverence. After watching *The Ten Commandments* in 1956, one audience member recalled:

The whole audience seemed to emerge from that [film] in hushed reverence. This was of course in the days when the [church] was not to be mocked, even if you didn't go yourself![9]

So great a sense of respect could epics command that in 1959 cinema managers were instructed by MGM that during screenings of *Ben-Hur*, no customers should be admitted to the auditorium and seated during the seven-minute long Nativity scene.[10]

The studios responded to audience enthusiasm by turning out more and more of the money-making epics, each one a more lavish spectacle than its predecessor, but every film remained true to the tried and tested formula which spelled 'epic'. The Old Testament's Golden Calf proved to be Hollywood's Cash Cow.

The purpose of this chapter, then, is to explore how, during the period 1916–66, Hollywood marketed epics. What ploys did Hollywood use to entice audiences into the movie theatres to watch an epic film? What experience of 'antiquity' did audiences have even before the film had begun? Moreover, this chapter will explore and expose the tension created between Hollywood's marketing ploys, which promised the audience an authentic experience of seeing, hearing and participating in the past, while simultaneously making the antique world palatable, marketable, 'modern' and thereby profitable.

Going to the Cinema

In an informative and sometimes surprising study of cinema audiences in 1930s America, Richard Butsch observed that in all the essential reasons for going to the cinema, the movie-goers of the early twentieth century differed little from those who go to today's multiplexes:

> During the 1930s . . . movie going settled into a form familiar to us today. The movie [itself, as well as] comfort and convenience . . . were the attractions. The audience was cross-class, more anonymous, less a community of friends and neighbours. Behaviour was less distin-guished by class. The same comments made in the 1930s about movie audiences can often be found in comments today. Talking and other noises became annoyances to adults in the audience. Working-class movie-going seems to have been transformed from a community experience into private consumption.[11]

The experience of going to the movies changed dramatically through-out our period of study, as much, in fact, as the architecture of movie theatres themselves changed too. Of course, the location of cinemas determined their size and decor, so that the movie-going experiences of individuals living in rural Iowa or Kansas was markedly different from those of urbanite audiences in the big cities like New York, Chicago or San Francisco, even though the demographic of class and cost might have been similar. Cinema-goers in rural America (and even rural Britain) sometimes made do with travelling picture shows set up in village halls or other types of community centres (like church or chapel vestries), or, if lucky, they enjoyed the comforts of vaudeville (music

Text Box 1.2   Picture Palaces of the Golden Age

Opened in 1925, the Capitol Theatre, Chicago was designed by John Eberson (who created several other Chicago cinemas including the Paradise and the Avalon). The Capitol's auditorium was decorated in an atmospheric style, and was modelled on an ancient Roman villa complete with statuary, vines and miniature temples. The Capitol's lobby and foyer areas also contained plaster copies of Greco-Roman reliefs, more statuary and mosaic tiled floors. Like the auditorium, the lobby had a *trompe l'oeil* blue starlit sky. Here is a short description of the Capitol Theatre in the year it opened (see Eberson 1925):

> The proscenium arch of the Capitol was conceived as a triumphal arch, supported on columns and roofed with a Roman tile roof surrounded by a stone balustrade . . . The entire stage . . . has a false proscenium resembling a Classic temple . . . Modified caryatids, sculptured human female figures, are used as column supports . . . The auditorium of the Capitol might be described as representing an Italian garden under a Mediterranean sky, featuring a moonlight night. On the left side of the auditorium is an Italian palace façade. The right side of the auditorium represents a terraced roof garden with a small temple building. Surmounting the whole is a representation of a deep blue sky with moving clouds and twinkling stars, creating a completely out-of-doors setting.

hall) theatres which divided their nightly programme between live acts and film screenings; increasingly throughout our period of study, more towns and even villages began to have purpose-built picture houses with comfortable seating, a permanent screen and a varied cinematic programme.[12] But city-dwellers might experience something very different: in the 1920s, cinemas in the major cities became veritable cathedrals of entertainment, with splendid edifices, lavish foyers and luxurious auditoriums. Appropriately they became known as picture palaces or dream palaces and they offered a rich panoply of entertainment (see Text Box 1.2; for the experience of watching epic movies within these cinemas see Text Box 1.3).

Harold Rambusch, a renowned theatre decorator, explained in an article of 1930 that:

> The vast majority of those attending our theatres are of very limited means. Their homes are not luxurious and the theatre affords them an opportunity to imagine themselves as wealthy people in luxurious surroundings. They may come here as often as they please by paying a small fee within their means and feel themselves to be the

Text Box 1.3   The Main Feature: Watching Epic Movies in the Golden Age

Going to the cinema was an important social experience; it was also meant to be a memorable one. Entry to cinemas was kept at an affordable price, even with inflation, so that prospective audiences would visit often; audiences attending first-runs and evening shows paid the premium price (matinees were cheaper):

Year	Average admission price
1935	25 cents
1939	27 cents
1940	29 cents
1945	40 cents
1950	45 cents
1960	80 cents

Cinema-going could be a lengthy affair and customers expected to be thoroughly entertained for their money. In the silent era, movies were often interspersed with vaudeville acts or live music but from around 1930 – until the late 1960s – the main feature film was always accompanied by newsreels, cartoons, serial episodes and a range of other short movies. During the Depression of the late 1930s a widespread use of another exhibition strategy appeared: the double feature, which paired selected shorts with two feature films, sometimes each of less than an hour in length. This popular programming strategy went hand in hand with the increased production of low-budget, sixty-minute, series-films (frequently Westerns) and other B-movies, which were designed to fit the requirements of the double feature. About three hundred different films were needed annually by a cinema that offered three changes of double-feature programmes each week. The double feature also allowed for a regularly scheduled intermission, which boosted concession sales (popcorn, sweets, drinks, ice cream and cigarettes).

The double feature with intermission breaks also became the standard programme at drive-in theatres during the 1950s, while some form of the balanced programme (combining shorts with a feature film) survived well into the 1960s. Overall, from 1950 onwards there was increased attention given to coming attraction trailers as part of the show and less emphasis on short films and cartoons.

The epic movies of the late 1950s and early 1960s (*The Ten Commandments*, *Ben-Hur*, *Spartacus*, *Cleopatra*, *The Fall of the Roman Empire* and *The Greatest Story Ever Told*) tended to be long, often running towards four hours, and it became customary to include a ten- or fifteen-minute interval at the midway point (this also helped to boost concession sales). In fact, directors of epics began to edit their movies with this in mind, commissioning intermission music from the score's composer and having an intermission caption, produced in the visual style of the film, projected onto the screen. There were no short movies accompanying epic films, and rarely were trailers for forthcoming movies even shown.

A large-scale epic film would open in big cities in an engagement much like a theatrical play or musical, often with components such as an overture, the first act, the intermission, the entr'acte, the second act and the exit music (the overture should not be confused with the main title music). The overture, recorded on film (and years later on tape) was always played *before* the beginning of the film, while the lights were still up and the curtains were still closed. (Until the 1980s most cinemas had curtains which covered the screen; they would open when the show actually began.) As the lights dimmed, the overture ended, the curtains opened and the film began with its main title music and opening credits. Likewise, the exit music should not be confused with the end title music. The exit music, also recorded without a picture but on film, was always played *after* the end of the film while the lights were up and the curtains were closed. As the lights came on, the end title music finished, the curtains closed and the exit music began.

A good example of this style of presentation is *Ben-Hur* (1959). Running almost four hours in length, the film was divided into all the above components, so that the film audience could experience the movie as if they were seeing a stage-play in a Broadway or West End theatre. It brought an element of gentility and sophistication to the movie-going experience.

Epic films of the late 1950s and early 1960s were always shown on a one- or two-performance a day basis; reserved seating was compulsory (one could not simply buy a ticket at the box office and go in to watch the film), and admission prices were always higher than those of regular screenings. The two-performance-a-day screenings were usually limited to Wednesdays (because most shops and banks closed for business at midday on Wednesdays), Saturdays and Sundays. During the rest of the week the films would be shown only once a day. Film brochures or souvenir programmes were often available at screenings of epic films, much as glossy programmes are made available when one goes to see a stage play or musical; these programmes contained photos from the film, photos and biographies of its cast and principal crew, and information on how the film was made (in a way, the glossy brochures were the forerunners of today's DVD commentaries and extras). (For excellent accounts of going to the movies in our period of study see Breakwell and Hammond (1990: 99–104) and Paul (2016).)

lords of all they survey. In our big modern movie palaces there are collected the most gorgeous rugs, furniture and fixtures that money can produce. No . . . emperors have wandered through more luxurious surroundings.[13]

A change in architectural style occurred in the 1930s when movie houses adopted the sleek lines of art deco as a form of decoration. A brochure published to advertise the 1930 opening of the San Francisco Fox Theatre touted its glamorous art deco sophistication:

> You enter the wide swinging doors of the great Castle of Splendour and behold: the silent magic of life's mirror, the Screen, in creations of its finest magicians . . . a myriad of multi-coloured lights . . . architectural beauties . . . soft miles of carpeted wonder in lounge and foyer . . . the vast magnificence of the palace of a king.[14]

Throughout the 1940s and 1950s cinemas promoted the latest trends in architectural and interior design.[15] In many cases, it was in the local movie theatres that many Americans (and British too) had their first encounters with modern architecture.[16]

Whatever the architectural design of the cinema, audiences of the Golden Age of Hollywood could experience unparalleled glamour, style and elegance when they entered through the doors of a major picture house. Movie going was meant to be a memorable, impressive and sophisticated experience: 'We sell tickets to *theatres*, not movies', boasted proprietor Marcus Lowe, while George Rapp regarded his theatres as social spaces where 'the wealthy rub shoulders with the poor'.[17]

For audiences of epic films, the experience of being inside a movie theatre could have an astonishing resonance with the images they would then experience on-screen. Take, for example, the extraordinary experience of the public who went to the Egyptian Theatre to view the first run of Cecil B. DeMille's silent masterpiece *The Ten Commandments* in 1924. Arabian and Far Eastern luxury offered an especially tantalising platform for early Hollywood, with its opulent Babylonian sets and lavish biblical epics, and the flirtation continued in the architecture of the cinema buildings themselves. It is not mere coincidence that Sid Grauman's Egyptian Theatre opened in 1922, the year that Howard Carter made his famous discovery in the Valley of the Kings and the King Tut craze swept through America.

The Egyptian Theatre was the original setting for 'Hollywood-style' premieres, and presented itself as an 'artistic monument to Egypt's glory' so that *Motion Picture News* was able to confirm that the entrance to the cinema was based on 'the gateways of Egyptian palaces during the days of Cleopatra'. The walls of the cinema were covered in faux-hieroglyphs and sphinxes, its foyers were planted with oasis foliage and the usherettes who showed clients to their seats and sold them cigarettes and popcorn were uniformed in belly-dance-style harem pants and gauzy yashmak veils.[18] Fittingly, when DeMille's film opened there, the *Los Angeles Examiner* enthused that: 'A premiere of a motion picture of note rivals the opening of the Metropolitan grand opera if the brilliant assemblage and wealth of fine costumes are considered.' Here was the perfect match of on-screen programme and cinema-going experience, as on-screen splendour spilled out into the theatre's auditorium and lobby. The audience didn't just watch *The Ten Commandments*, they experienced it; as Mae West (an unlikely fan of DeMille perhaps) later recalled, 'it was all glitter . . . All wonderful and full of a foolish magic which is the essence of motion picture making.'[19]

Film premieres were important aspects of any film's publicity campaign, for an impressive premiere was widely advertised and reported in newsreels, newspapers and magazines. Some epic movies attracted staggering amounts of public attraction in the months leading up to their premieres. DeMille's 1927 religious epic, *The King of Kings*, Hollywood's most lavish account of the life of Christ, was energetically marketed throughout America, with Paramount specifically targeting church groups of various denominations and sects throughout the country. (Remarkably, in 2004 Mel Gibson successfully promoted his movie, *The Passion of the Christ*, in much the same manner.) The public payoff was enormous: after a year of intense promotion, *The King of Kings* premiered at the newly opened Grauman's Chinese Theatre on Hollywood Boulevard. Beneath the playbill's huge panorama of Christ on the cross towering over Roman soldiers and mass congregations of the faithful, a new form of worshipper, the film-fans, flocked to see the movie and glimpse its stars and its famous larger-than-life director. 'Hundreds of Police Battle to Keep Crowds in Check', announced the next day's headlines in the *Los Angeles Times*, as a crowd of some 30,000 fans jammed the Boulevard, stalled traffic and forced VIP guests to abandon their limousines and walk to the theatre. Sid Grauman, real-estate tycoon, cinema proprietor and the 'father of the gala premiere', was delighted with the event: '30,000 persons fought to gain admittance to the opening of the showplace of the world . . . Never before has any box office turned away so many people,' he gloated. This was nothing short of *King of Kings* frenzy.[20]

Similar scenes accompanied the New York premiere of DeMille's *Samson and Delilah* during the Christmas holidays of 1949:

> Heralded by such a rolling and thundering of press agents' drums as might have announced the ground-breaking for Babel's stupendous tower, Cecil B. DeMille's *Samson and Delilah* was solemnly brought forth last night at both the Paramount and the Rivoli Theatres, in keeping with its elegance and size. And the first thing to be said about it, before the echoes have even died, is that, if ever there was a movie for DeMillions, here it is . . . Long lines of people formed three abreast last night in front of the . . . theatres, and directed by strong details of policemen made their way into both theatres for the première . . . The crowd, estimated at 3,500 by the police, began gathering at 7pm on Forty-third Street, between Broadway and Eighth Avenue, for admission to the Paramount. The lines stretched on both sidewalks for almost the entire block. The theatre opened its doors at 7:45pm, and the crowd filed through in an orderly manner. Some fifty policemen

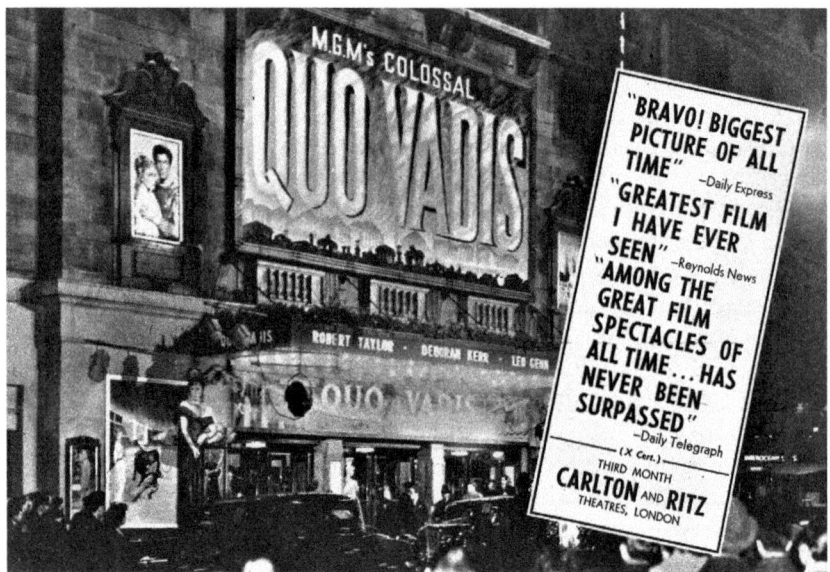

Figure 1.1
Newspaper advertisement showing the marquee display erected for *Quo Vadis* (1951) at the Carlton Cinema, London.

were on duty on West Forty-third Street, and a like number handled a crowd of 2,000 at the Rivoli Theatre.[21]

Like all epics, *Quo Vadis* also premiered with equal amounts of enthusiastic trumpeting (see Figure 1.1 and Figure 1.2), but, infamously, it was Mankiewicz's *Cleopatra* which attracted the most widespread, frenzied, public hysteria by the time it opened at the New York Rivoli on 13 June 1963. From the moment Elizabeth Taylor was signed up to play the Siren of the Nile (with a then unprecedented one million dollar contract; it is estimated that she eventually made nine million dollars from *Cleopatra*), the public was seized by an unquenchable thirst for all things Liz (or all things Cleo – it's hard to say which). The mania only escalated as her affair with Richard Burton hit the news headlines and an amalgamated 'Liz and Dick' blurred into the on-screen lovers Antony and Cleo (see Chapter 4 for a fuller discussion of the Taylor-Burton phenomenon). In the early 1960s Cleo-mania completely gripped the world.

In spite of *Cleopatra*'s colossal $44 million dollar budget, the movie nevertheless recuperated its projected losses (a fact often overlooked by the film's detractors) as Twentieth Century Fox went into overdrive with its slick publicity machine. Business at the Rivoli alone was brisk and the movie quickly sold out for four months (all in all, the studio collected $20 million dollars in pre-release grosses) and by 1966, when Twentieth Century Fox sold the television rights to ABC for five million dollars, *Cleopatra* had broken even.[22]

Figure 1.2
Advertisement for *Quo Vadis* (1951) intended for mass publication in newspapers.

Promotional Activities and Merchandising

As a new epic film went into production, a slick publicity campaign was developed by the studios in Hollywood and was subsequently managed in New York, the advertising capital of the USA during our period (as those familiar with the hit TV series *Mad Men* will recognise).[23] The promotion of material for distribution to exhibitors (as cinema managers were known in the trade) ran alongside the promotion of the movie stars to the fan magazines and newspapers, and the studios carefully controlled every aspect of the process; they submitted all promotional material to the Advertising Advisory Council (AAC), an important and influential branch of the Production Code Administration. Here all advertising materials, including posters, pressbooks, sketches and designs, publicity stories, TV and radio ads, and ideas for gimmicks were assessed for suitability and moral integrity (because of the Production Code, all references to profanities, nudity and other types of vulgarity were rigorously censored).

Serious money was invested into a new movie's publicity campaign which usually started before the film had even gone into production. For instance, United Artists vice-president Max Youngstein authorised a $3 million dollar budget to promote the release of *Solomon and Sheba* (the film itself cost $6 million dollars to make). Launched in June 1959, six months before the film's premiere, a special publicity unit was created under the leadership of Roger Lewis who declared that: 'We intend to carry our programme through to the world's exhibitors and moviegoers with an impact and awareness that has never been achieved.' Special emphasis was laid on cooperative advertising with a heavy emphasis on TV, newspaper and magazine slots ('blue-chip promotions' – or 'teasers' – as they were called). *Solomon and Sheba* benefited, for instance, from marketing deals with, among others, Sabena Airlines, the Galliano Wine Company, Blue Fox Perfume, Lustre-Crème and Fleetway Pajamas. Variety in marketing partners was vital because, as Roger Lewis liked to remind his staff, 'Teasers arrest attention; ads capture sweep, boldness, intimacy.'[24]

An epic's promotional campaign was aimed at different segments of the potential audience, although it was recognised by the studios that certain types of marketing worked better with some segments of the population than with others. No single audience was exposed to all the publicity material created for any one film and some studios developed systems for identifying specific public markets. A good example of the kind of hyperbolic approach taken by the studios in publicising movies to different strands of an audience was the so-called 'three-way exploitation' strategy recommended by Paramount for the general release of *The Sign of the Cross*. The pressbook of 1932, shows how the studio divided the potential ticket-buying public into three distinct areas, 'the masses', 'church-goers' and 'schools', and exhibitors were instructed to target these groups with very different types of advertising and not to 'mix your issues' (see Text Box 1.4; interestingly, the pressbook for the film's 1944 (post Production Code) reissue repeats the same wording almost exactly, omitting mention of sex but briefly citing 'depravity').

Solomon and Sheba benefited from much the same approach, and while the obvious charms of Gina Lollobrigida as the Sheban Queen were marketed in fashion ads, lifestyle campaigns and gentlemen's magazines, the spiritual and educative potential of the movie were not overlooked: 'It is a time-tested industry axiom that religious spectacles are big box office', reassured the pressbook, adding that 'the inspiration of religion' would guarantee an audience for the film, making *Solomon and Sheba* 'one of the surest shots in the annals of the industry'. In terms of scholastic profitability, Hardy R. Finch, a noted author and tutor, was hired by the studio to serve as a special educational consultant and to prepare materials, study guides and campaigns for more than 10,000 grade schools, high schools and colleges throughout America in which the history, art, religion, literature and geography relevant to *Solomon and Sheba* were emphasised. Global publicity plans included an education pack aimed at the universities and colleges of Europe – although there is no evidence of this ever happening.

The Egyptian was marketed with a similarly ruthless ad campaign which not only boasted of a nationwide newspaper coverage 'from coast to coast' (as the pressbook put it), but also an aggressive 'round the clock TV campaign [that] reaches into 25 million homes!' As the pressbook stated, 'More than the modern version of the door-to-door salesman,

---

Text Box 1.4   *The Sign of the Cross*: 'Three-Way' Exploitation

The Masses . . . who are not enthusiastically interested in religious themes or educational value. Sell them SPECTACLE – the glitter, the excitement, the thrills which characterized Rome at the height of her power and depth of depravity. Here is stock drama and sex suggestion they understand and will buy. These elements should dominate your newspaper publicity, your ads, lobby and general exploitation.

Church-Goers! Here the appeal is tremendous. Reach this class thru the clergy, thru sermons, thru direct mail. This phase of your campaign is quiet. It is out of the newspapers and away from the mass public.

Schools . . . The educational appeal of *The Sign of the Cross* is powerful. The Los Angeles Board of Education has already ASKED for a complete set of production stills on *The Sign of the Cross*. DeMille's great spectacles are always historically accurate. Contact the schools in the same direct, out-of-the-newspapers fashion as you do the churches.

DON'T MIX YOUR APPROACHES! REMEMBER: DRAMA AND THUNDER AND SEX FOR THE GENERAL PUBLIC . . . RELIGIOUS APPEAL FOR THE CHURCHES . . . EDUCATIONAL INTEREST FOR THE SCHOOLS! HAMMER EACH APPROACH FOR ALL THEY'RE WORTH! THEY'RE WORTH PLENTY!

Pressbook, 1932

---

television gets past the doorstep into the family circle. It helps the family – every member of it – decide what it wants. You'll know they want *The Egyptian* when you play [this advert].' Lucrative deals made with television production companies meant that the American public was slowly barraged with advertisements for *The Egyptian*. The movie was even promoted during the *Ed Sullivan Show*, America's top-rated family entertainment programme. Behind the big publicity push was the need to grab the attention of the diverse mass of the American public.

Surviving documentation from the pre-production period of Mankiewicz's *Cleopatra* similarly shows how keenly Twentieth Century Fox marketed the film to a diverse mass audience. Writing to the director in April 1961, the producer, Spyros Skouras, expressed his concern for 'impressing a greater impact on the public', and to that end he ordered Mankiewicz to supply him with

[S]ome authentic footage – as it will appear in the picture – say, about 1250 feet. My plan is to have demonstrations in 175 cities throughout the world . . . Invitations to these screenings would be extended to exhibitors, historians, clergymen, critics and newsmen, of course, in fact people in practically all walks of life. We will set up two or three of these demonstrations in every city, based upon the response to our invitations. I assure you that if this can be done, even the presently phenomenal audience penetration will be augmented to greater heights than ever before achieved for any medium in the history of the entertainment world.[25]

In 1965 *The Greatest Story Ever Told*, one of the last postwar biblical epics, was put on general release through United Artists (the studio also provided production finance at $21 million dollars). Directed by George Stevens for his own company and filmed in Ultra Panavision 70, *The Greatest Story Ever Told* was also, at that time, the most expensive movie ever filmed in America and the second most expensive film made worldwide (its cost was only outdone by the profligacy of Twentieth Century Fox's *Cleopatra*). Inspired by Fulton Oursler's book of the same title, Stevens insisted that *The Greatest Story Ever Told* would be unlike any other biblical epic and while in the astonishing cinematography and controversial casting of the film he was true to his word, the marketing and selling of the film was curiously conventional and employed publicity strategies adopted for the selling of almost all epic movies since the 1920s.[26] As the film was nearing completion of production, the head of publicity, Maxwell Hamilton, issued a memo entitled *Post-Production and Pre-Release Promotional Activities* in which he set out the main areas in which promotions could best be put into operation (Text Box 1.5 quotes a memo issued by Hamilton, dated 13 June 1963).[27] It clearly demonstrates the kind of creative thinking that was needed to sell an epic and the numerous conventional strategies which had to be employed by the studios.

Fortunately throughout Hollywood's Golden Age, the appetite displayed by exhibitors and public alike for ever more publicity material was insatiable. The studios obligingly responded. As Tino Balio summarises:

> Nothing was too private if it interested the public, nothing too trite if it got copy, and nothing was too exaggerated if it sold a ticket . . . Material freely found its way into any newspaper, magazine, or radio station in the country. Good, bad, or ridiculous, someone would be willing to read it, enter it, or buy it . . . Previews of coming attractions whetted the appetites of loyal fans. Magazine articles, Sunday features, and news items . . . and, of course, movie ads in the local newspapers stoked the interest of casual moviegoers.[28]

For their part, the exhibitors were responsible for disseminating to the movie-going public the publicity materials showered on them by the studios' advertising offices and for making sure that the consequent box-office receipts were lucrative. After he had booked a picture, an exhibitor received the official pressbook, a folio-sized glossy trade magazine crammed with pre-written publicity stories for use in local newspapers or radio and television slots, movie stills, lobby cards and posters – all of

Text Box 1.5   Selling *The Greatest Story Ever Told*

Post-Production and Pre-Release Promotional Activities

Memo from Maxwell Hamilton, June 13 1963

Publications, including a souvenir programme brochure; a book on the making of the film; a reprint of the original [Foulton] Oursler novel; school study guides and children's books; a compilation of scholarly research materials; a biography of [the director, George] Stevens; and the screenplay of the film.

A travelling exhibition of props, costumes and photographs from the film, arranged by the Smithsonian Institute, to tour museums in key cities; 51 other exhibits produced for use in department stores, churches, Sunday schools and other schools; and a stand at the New York World's Fair.

Audio-visual aids, such as film strips, slide presentations and models.

A thirty-minute colour documentary on the making of the film, for showing on network television at Easter 1964, and subsequent distribution to clubs, schools and churches, and as an extended theatrical trailer.

TV and radio promotions, including news programme reports, taped interviews and appearances by stars of the film.

Pressbooks for exhibitors, containing suggestions for local promotions and advertising.

Previews, especially for religious leaders, educators, leading industrialists, government officials, psychologists, youth leaders, boy and girl scout officials, and others concerned with juvenile problems.

Gifts for the press and religious leaders, including 'tasteful mementoes' of the film.

Testimonial dinners and awards honouring [George] Stevens.

Commercial tie-ins.

which were obtainable for order on the payment of a fee (see Figures 1.3, 1.4, 1.5 and 1.6). The pressbooks, always overblown, often overzealous and full of exaggerated hyperbole, are nevertheless unique sources for the study of epic films as they highlight the official rhetoric and marketing strategies employed by the studios to sell their products and they also inform us how the movie-going public first encountered newly produced Hollywood epics and, by extension, experienced the ancient world. Take these diverse examples of headlines drawn from the *Quo Vadis* pressbook, each of which was accompanied by some snappy 'copy' (a few columns of text) ready to insert into local newspapers or magazines:

Figure 1.3
Poster advertisement for *Solomon and Sheba* (1959). The film was marketed with an aggressive publicity campaign incorporating colourful, eye-catching artworks, such as this poster by Frank McCarthy. Pressbook.

BREATH-TAKING COLOR, SPECTACLE AND PAEGANTRY IN MGM'S EPIC 'QUO VADIS'

DEBORAH KERR RECALLS 'QUO VADIS' AS FASCINATING ACTING EXPERIENCE

14-KARAT GOLD DRESS!

WIRE FENCES PROTECT CAMERAMEN FROM LIONS

INSPIRATIONAL MOMENTS IN RELIGIOUS HISTORY HIGHLIGHTED IN 'QUO VADIS'

Similar eye-catching headlines were produced for *The Silver Chalice*, the otherwise disappointingly dismal epic made infamous for awk-

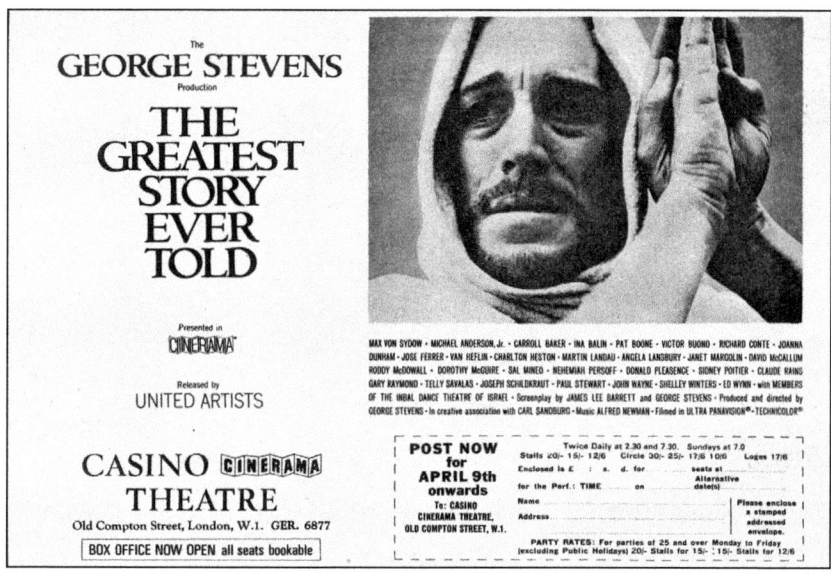

Figure 1.4
British newspaper advertisement and booking-slip for *The Greatest Story Ever Told* (1965).

wardly propelling an uncomfortable young Paul Newman into the limelight:

LARGEST SETS EVER BUILT FOR PICTURE

'SILVER CHALICE' COSTLIEST SCREEN PROP EVER DESIGNED

DEARTH OF DROMEDARIES HALTS CAMEL CARAVAN

LUCK PLUS TALENT KEYS FAME OF NEW STAR PAUL NEWMAN

Time and time again, the pressbooks rehearse the unchanging rhetoric of the epics' visual splendour, popular appeal and moral integrity. Repetitive as they undeniably are in the techniques which they employ and the imagery which they produce, pressbooks were the bona fide 'voice' of Hollywood and therein lies their unquestionable importance as sources.

The exhibitors were encouraged to attract different sections of a potential audience by creating a series of stunts and marketing gimmicks. To help with this, the pressbooks offered advice on effective marketing ploys (see Text Box 1.6 and Figures 1.7, 1.8 and 1.9). Many epics were promoted with competitions and visual gimmicks reminiscent of popular fairground attractions (strongman contests, camel rides, and exotic dancers), although some epics with loftier aspirations took a different marketing approach: the pressbooks for *Spartacus*, *The Fall of the Roman Empire*, *The Greatest Story Ever Told* and *King of Kings*, for

Figure 1.5
Pressbook advertisement for the purchase of freestanding cut-outs for lobby display.

instance, placed their emphasis more on scholarly and cultural tie-ins like books, music and travel.

Beauty contests were specialities of the particularly ambitious exhibitor and many epic films were promoted with the aid of a community pageant (see Figure 1.10). Unsurprisingly, this was part of the marketing ploy of Mankiewicz's *Cleopatra* where the pressbook recommended that the 'competition should be run on the lines of 'The Search for a Modern Cleopatra'. The release of Columbia Pictures' *Salome* was also heralded with a beauty contest with the same quest: 'Girls! Girls! Enter the Rita Hayworth *Salome* Beauty Contest! A photo of you in a bathing suit may

Figure 1.6
Robert Taylor and Deborah Kerr in a photograph commissioned by MGM as a publicity
gimmick for *Quo Vadis* (1951). Taylor plays up his all-American-boy image by reading the
Los Angeles Examiner, while Kerr plays the English rose and examines *The Times*. Great
friends off set, Kerr and Taylor were happy to oblige studio demands by posing for such
knowingly inane publicity shots. Such images were included in pressbooks and were made
widely available for use in the press.

bring you fame and fortune! We are searching for a nation-wide, modern-
day Salome!' (*Salome* pressbook, 1953). But the biggest beauty contest
tie-in was spun around the release of *Esther and the King* in 1960: 'Who is
America's Queen Esther?' asked the pressbook. 'Unique Contest Seeks
Fairest in Land', it went on to enthuse. Local exhibitors were encouraged to take part in a nationwide search for America's newest beauty
and, drawing inspiration from the Old Testament story wherein the
humble stay-at-home Esther (played on-screen by Joan Collins) became
queen of the Persian empire as a result of an ancient, genuinely biblical
'Miss Persia' beauty competition. The pressbook stressed that the lucky
winner (who would be judged on both beauty *and* personality) would
get the experience of a lifetime: an all-expenses air trip to Hollywood, a
week's stay at the Sheraton Hotel, an appearance on Movietone News,
and a screen-test at the Casting Department of Twentieth Century Fox
(see Figure 1.11).[29]

A PROVEN BEST SELLER !

The best selling book of all time in this country sold 1¼ million copies. The BEN-HUR souvenir book has to date sold 1 million! It has 36 pages (18 in full colour).

Sale price to your patrons is 2/6—an absolute bargain in that they cost you only 1/10½d. per copy, ON SALE OR RETURN! Therefore, you can't lose! Past experience has told us:—

1. That these books sell at the rate of ONE to every FIVE patrons.

2. That they also sell extremely well PRIOR to playdate and thus stimulate interest in the film.

3. That for a small commission your staff will make them a best seller for you!

For supplies please contact Publicity Dept., Metro House, stating:—

Playdate

Date books required

How many books you want for your ENTIRE run!

Unsold copies should like-wise be returned to M-G-M's Publicity Dept.

 ★ ★

This is the specially prepared double crown poster piece advertising the souvenir book.

This is available from N.S.S. at the price of 2/- each.

ON SALE HERE

THE LAVISHLY ILLUSTRATED 36-PAGE SOUVENIR BOOK OF THE FILM

PRICE 2/6ᵈ

Figure 1.7
How to sell the *Ben-Hur* souvenir book. Pressbook advertisement (1959).

Figure 1.8
How to sell *Solomon and Sheba*. The pressbook advised exhibitioners to stage this scene in the cinema lobby using white-powdered water and a willing female employee. The bath scene was a definitive cliché for female stars in epic movies. Lobby card (1959).

COSTUMES FOR YOUR OPENING NIGHT

Make a good impact on your opening night of "Cleopatra" by having your staff dressed in appropriate costumes. This is also good for publicity in your local press if you can have a costumed girl photographed with local civic dignitaries.

20th Century-Fox have laid on a service with Messrs. M. Berman Limited, the famed Theatrical Costumiers which will guarantee you excellent, authentic costumes. Shown here is the outfit for a Roman Soldier.

The costumes are supplied with shoes, head-dresses, arms, shields, etc., and the following are available:—

MEN	**WOMEN**
Roman Soldiers	Roman Slave Girls
Senators	Egyptian Girls
Roman Cavalry Soldiers	

The men's costumes are available on hire at £4 4s per week and the women's costumes on hire at £5 5s per week. When ordering you should state (for men) height, shoe, hat, chest and waist measurements. (For women) height, bust, waist, hips and shoe measurements.

Please note that you should select men of fairly large size, if possible between 5 ft. 8 in. and 6 ft. and the girls should be of average height and build. Do not use anybody over 6 ft. or anybody too small.

The "Roman Soldier" costume available from Messrs. Berman, Ltd.

Figure 1.9
How to advertise the opening night of *Cleopatra*: hire costumes for cinema staff. Pressbook (1963).

Besides the advertising materials and gimmicks which were offered and promoted by the studios, the pressbooks also allowed exhibitors to buy into a range of goods which could be put on sale at the cinema or in local department stores or other retail outlets and, therefore, exhibitors were encouraged to work closely with local store managers and shop keepers for mutual benefit (see Figure 1.12). Financial concerns impinged not only on the production, but on the way that the film was sold too and while a director may have intended to promote a particular message in his film, sometimes advertising executives were keen to play up something different altogether. To a large extent, product 'tie-ins' (a bona fide Golden Age marketing term, used alongside the phrase 'tie-up') often undercut the lofty aspirations of the epic. Take, for instance,

Text Box 1.6   Small-Town Exploitation: Publicity Gimmicks

The following examples of marketing stunts are all *genuine* suggestions to be found in the pressbooks of the period; exhibitors were encouraged to publicise epic films in some weird and wonderful ways . . .

Samson and Delilah pressbook, 1949

Strength Tester: An idea that is bound to attract attention is a strength-testing machine placed in your lobby. Always a favourite in amusement parks and penny arcades as well as carnivals, this machine is perfect for your 'Samson' playdate. Called 'The Samson Strength Tester', it could be used effectively to create added excitement for your playdate.

Quo Vadis pressbook, 1951

Latin Sayings Contest: 'Quo Vadis', which means 'whither thou goest', is one of the many Latin expressions which have become part of the English language. Interest high schools and local newspapers in a contest in which the reader translates Latin expressions. The first correct answers will win complementary passes or promotional prizes.

David and Bathsheba pressbook, 1951

Man and Boy: Simulate David and Goliath on the streets of your town with this walking stunt. Employ the tallest man in town and a small boy to parade the streets on the opening day of your *David and Bathsheba* playdate, calling attention to the historic situation featured in the film.

Slingshot Contest: Organise slingshot teams in the grade schools and boy scout troops. Prepare an archery bull's-eye under local boys club supervision, where competing teams can vie for top prizes (promoted via lobby cards from local sports outfitters). All contestants get passes for playdate. Contest judges to be playground director, boy scout troop leader and similar organisational leaders.

Salome pressbook, 1953

Salome and Her Dance: America's foremost dancemaster, Arthur Murray, has created a 'Doing the Salome' dance routine, inspired by . . . 'Salome' in which Rita Hayworth performs the sensuous Dance of the Seven Veils. More than 200 Arthur Murray dance studios around the country have been advised of this tie-in and urged to work with local promotions . . . Salome and her Dance of the Seven Veils have both been synonymous in the mind of man for 2000 years. Capitalise on this fact by working as many as possible of the stunts suggested here . . . whatever called for, get an Oriental feeling into the act, relating it closer to the picture.

Dancing in Streets: Send an Oriental dancer around town dancing on a float to sell everyone on the big show at your theatre. Gay and easy decorations can be made from poster cutouts and a record player can supply the hot music. Dancer is a cinch to wow lunch-time crowds!

Dancing Girls: Send dancing girls out on the streets with signs announcing 'Salome Dances the Dance of the Seven Veils Tonight at the State Theatre.'

Dance with 'Salome': Give a lucky serviceman a date with a 'local Salome', a dancer from one of the night clubs or theatres. Send them on a round of all the dance spots in town. With the press agents for the night clubs and hotels joining in, you should get reams of space for this serviceman's 'King for a Night' stunt.

The Silver Chalice pressbook, 1954

Unusual Street Bally! If your city has a zoo, or you are otherwise able to enlist a live camel, *this* is *your* stunt! Decked out in Oriental trappings and satin banners, it's a real attention grabber – and certainly good for a news photo. If camel is not feasible, a couple of white horses mounted by veiled gals and led by burnoose handlers will do the trick!

Solomon and Sheba pressbook, 1959

Sheba's Toys Caravan: Offer commanding officer of nearest US Marine Reserve unit the services of a local 'Queen of Sheba' caravan to help him collect 'Toys for Tots'. As the Marines carry on such a campaign every year favourable press coverage is practically guaranteed. Special items for this stunt include: 1. Pictures of local 'Queen of Sheba' with Marine Corps leaders as honour guard; 2. Have a 'Queen of Sheba' on duty at central collection point; 3. 'Queen of Sheba' hands out toys from the land of Sheba.

Cleopatra pressbook, 1963

Ballroom Contests – Fancy Dress Night: Many ballroom managers are only too willing to 'jump on the bandwagon' to tie up with an important picture, and we feel that in 'Cleopatra' you have an ideal film on which to suggest a co-operative campaign . . . Arrange a 'Cleopatra Night' fancy dress ball on the busiest night of the week before 'Cleopatra' opens in which all the dancers are invited to attend in costumes of the period – the girls as Cleopatra or Roman or Egyptian slave girls, and the men as Roman soldiers, senators, etc. Make sure that there is plenty of publicity for the film in the ballroom, and offer prizes for the best costumes.

Travel Agents Tie-Up: Contact your local travel agents for window displays featuring posters emphasising the beauty of Rome and other parts of Italy together with stills and publicity for the film. You could use the line 'Cleopatra conquered Rome – Rome will conquer you.'

'Cleopatra' Menus: Contact your local good-class restaurant to put together special 'Cleopatra' dishes on the menu for a week before your playdate, together with credits for the picture. As a suggestion, you could use 'Sole Cleopatra', 'Crepes Suzettes Elizabeth Taylor', 'Entrecote Mark Antony', etc.

Figure 1.10
On 17 December 1949, two lucky girls pose for a photograph alongside a blow-up image of Hedy Lamarr to promote the New York premiere of *Samson and Delilah*. They are Louise Hartung of Far Rockaway, NY, and Merle McHugh of New York City; both girls were chosen from a group of six Hedy Lamarr 'doubles' and were invited to act as glamorous hostesses for the evening. The New York Bureau's press office noted that 'the girls wear costumes from the picture', although in reality the costumes are rather poor imitations of the on-screen designs and were probably made cheaply in New York.

Figure 1.11
Still from *Esther and the King* (1960). King Ahasuerus of Persia (Richard Egan), in the
company of chief eunuch Hegai (Robert Buchanan), observes a bevy of beauties within his
harem. This scene was the inspiration behind a campaign to find America's modern Esther.
The pressbook promoted an idea very much in keeping with the burgeoning 1960s
American civil rights ideology: 'Just as the first Queen Esther Contest was international, the
1960 version will be open to beauties of all faiths, races and nationalities.'

Figure 1.12
Ben-Hur toys and games were widely available from toy stores all over America and Britain.
Here Charlton Heston and Stephen Boyd anticipate playing the chariot race board game.
Publicity shot (1959).

the promotion of Coca-Cola in a 1932 advertisement for *The Sign of the Cross* (see Figure 1.13) or the male underwear sold as a tie-in to promote *Quo Vadis* in 1951 (see Figure 1.14), and the 1959 Maidenform brassiere advertisement (see Figure 1.15) which so clearly takes its playful visual reference from *Ben-Hur*.[30] Here we see two types of advertising at work: the official tie-in (Coca-Cola and the *Quo Vadis* shorts) and the opportunistic marketing ploy of a leading ladies' hosiery company exploiting the popularity of a major new Hollywood film (the *Ben-Hur* bra). All kinds of goods were promoted as official or unofficial merchandising tie-ins: children's toys and board games, male and female fashion items, home furnishings, food and drink, music and leisure activities. To retailers, epic films were highly marketable.

Posters: Advertising Antiquity

The major studios dominated cinema bookings and on the release of a new film, particularly any costly epic, the studios made sure that their latest picture flooded the market.[31] Never entirely confident of their publicity strategies and stunts, the Hollywood studios needed to ensure that the cinemas were well attended and the films were financially (if not necessarily critically) successful and they therefore spent considerable time, attention and costs in designing, producing and displaying advertising posters and in creating and showing movie-trailers, for, as Adolph Zukor propounded, 'what is good art is good advertising . . . the most satisfying design will sell the product the best . . . What's good *sells*.'[32] Important marketing tools, movie posters (and other types of publicity art) and movie trailers are significant sources for understanding how the epic genre was conceived of in the Golden Age because they provide a vivid and abbreviated vision of what Hollywood's epic movies were all about. Posters and lobby cards highlighted the visual parameters of the film being advertised and spotlighted its main themes through catchy tag-lines and captions, while trailers provided a précis of a movie into a series of visual highlights and demonstrative narration and musical scoring. Let's explore these powerful marketing devices further.

As we have noted, movie campaigns could be as elaborate as an exhibitor's publicity budget allowed, but the one thing which was guaranteed to bypass all of the marketing gizmos of the industry was the poster. The job of the poster was to sell or magnify the movie's essential qualities – its essence – at a single glance and therefore the epic poster had to be as sensational as the product it was selling. Film posters had to resonate with potential ticket buyers where it most mattered: at the point of sale, the movie theatre's box office itself. No other motivation was needed. Charles Schlaifer, one-time advertising vice-president for Twentieth Century Fox, was willing to concede: 'My main concern with a poster was, "Would people *look*, rush to the box-office and buy a ticket?" If that didn't happen often enough, I'd be out of a job.'[33]

Between scenes of Paramount's super picture of Rome, THE SIGN OF THE CROSS — Fredric March as Marcus Superbus, Claudette Colbert as Empress Poppaea and Director Cecil B. DeMille.

PHOTOGRAPHED IN NATURAL COLORS BY NICKOLAS MURAY

The pause that refreshes
"stops the show"

Director DeMille plays host to Marcus Superbus (Fredric March) and Empress Poppaea (Claudette Colbert) with a pause for ice-cold Coca-Cola. Underneath the grandeur that was Rome, they're hard-working actors. Getting hot, tired and thirsty—just as you and I . . . *The pause that refreshes* means to bounce back to normal. Paramount's Hollywood studio provides for it with a fountain in the restaurant and bottled Coca-Cola on the sets. In the part you play in this workaday world, it's ready around the corner from anywhere—and so easy to keep a few bottles in your refrigerator at home.

Figure 1.13
Everything stops for . . . Coca-Cola, even the decline of Rome. Cecil B. DeMille enjoys a refreshing Coke with Frederic March and Claudette Colbert between takes on *The Sign of The Cross*. Magazine advertisement (1932).

Figure 1.14
Magazine advertisement for Munsingwear rayon boxer shorts. The wearer is invited to 'make like Nero' while his adoring 1950s wife, empress-like, watches on. *Quo Vadis* tie-in (1951).

Leading popular artists and graphic designers – men like Jack Davis, Tom Jung and Bob McCall – were hired to create poster images. One influential designer especially noted for his work on epic movie imagery was Frank McCarthy, who began his career in the 1940s as a commercial illustrator and whose vivid works were used to enliven the covers of paperback novels and magazine covers. In the 1950s he went on to create elegant, colourful and dramatic images to promote epics such as

I dreamed I drove them wild
in my *maidenform bra*

COUNTERPOINT*...new Maidenform bra made with super-strong Spandex—new, non-rubber elastic that weighs almost nothing at all yet lasts (and controls you) far longer than ordinary elastic. Exclusive "butterfly insert" adjusts size and fit of each cup as it uplifts and separates! Cotton or Spandex back. White. From 2.00.

Figure 1.15
Maidenform bra magazine advertisement (1959).

The Ten Commandments and *Solomon and Sheba*. McCarthy was an accomplished draftsman and a sensitive artist with a flair for composition and expressive portraiture and his painted portraits of actors in character are masterful representations of the pulling-power of movie stars. Today his works are generally classified as modern masterpieces of poster art (Colour Plate 2).

From the mid-1920s posters became standardised in terms of size and, subsequently, cost. These ranged from 'advance' or 'teaser' one-sheets (27 × 41 inches) that heralded the arrival of a new movie weeks

Figure 1.16
Unknown workmen exchange words about the charms of Gina Lollobrogida as the Queen
of Sheba. Painted on canvas, large-scale poster art such as this was often hung in cinema
foyers to celebrate the release of a new movie. This portrait of the actress is the work of the
master poster artist Frank McCarthy.

or months ahead of its screening (these cost exhibitioners on average
15 cents per sheet in the 1930s) to the six-sheet (81 × 81 inches) created
in vivid colours and intended to catch the eye from a distance with
its striking design. The largest standard size poster was the 24-sheet
billboard (9 × 24 feet), intended to be traffic-stoppers (see Figure 1.16),
although in the 1950s (and into the 1960s) even 48-sheet billboards were
produced, a fitting tribute to the growing scale of the epics themselves
(see earlier, Figure OC.16).[34] As Stephen Rebello and Richard Allen
note, these gigantic images 'overpowered the viewer through sheer
dimension, hue, and composition. Perhaps due to the horizontal nature
of the format, they often showed their stars in states of voluptuous
dishabille.'[35]

What constitutes a successful epic movie poster? Several features
need to be acknowledged in answering that question, for while there
were developments in artistic trends in poster design and nuances
in trends can clearly be traced decade through decade, in general
throughout our period posters designed to sell epic films employ
regular features. Title dominance is, of course, the aspect most looked

Figure 1.17
Title dominance: *Cleopatra* (1934). Pressbook.

for in poster designs (see Figure 1.17) and epic movies capitalise on
that idea most successfully because of the vastness of scale looked
for in the genre as a whole (see Figure 1.18). The striking design of
the poster of the 1959 production of *Ben-Hur*, for instance, sees the
film title carved from the mammoth rock face of the chariot arena set
which plays a central scene in the movie. Architectural elements such
as colossal statues emphasise the setting, while the diminutive horses
and chariots and the cheering crowds of spectators highlight the scale
of the spectacle (see Figure 1.19). The same elements appear in the
poster for Bronston's production of *Kings of Kings*, although here the
rock-face design is deep enough to have the key marketing tag-line
carved into it: THE POWER, THE PASSION, THE GREATNESS, THE
GLORY (see Figure 1.20).[36]

A word must be said here about film titles. An evocative tile is the
most effective sole element in a marketing strategy, given that the film's
name is relentlessly pushed into the marketplace on giant billboards,
print ads and many other forms of dissemination. There is little room
for manoeuvre of course for films based on books or plays (and both
Quo Vadis and *Ben-Hur* benefited from the popularity and 'title-appeal'

Figure 1.18

Dominance of spectacle: *Demetrius and the Gladiators* (1954). The poster design, rich in painted images and screen shots, foregrounds the most marketable aspect of the title alongside its most sellable technical feature: CinemaScope. Pressbook.

Figure 1.19

Monumentality 1: the poster for *Ben-Hur* (1959). The intimidating Gladiator statues are seen in many shots during the chariot race sequence. The poster draws heavily on the production designs of Henry Henigson, William A. Horning and Edward Carfagno.

Figure 1.20
Monumentality 2: poster design for *King of Kings* (1961).

enjoyed by their pre-celluloid ancestors), but for the majority of films, the choice is open-ended. Hollywood has recently enjoyed an affinity with punchy one-word titles (*Avatar*, *Up*, *Gladiator*) but few films in the Golden Age took this approach (consider *How Green Was My Valley*, *All Quiet on the Western Front*, *Meet Me in St Louis*). The exception of course were epic titles. Movie titles capitalised on the celebrity of ancient names: *Spartacus*, *Cleopatra*, *Hannibal*, *Barabbas*, or on the coupling of names such as *Samson and Delilah*, *Solomon and Sheba* or

David and Bathsheba. As a marketing ploy, these famous names were then intimately tied into movie-star personas in a handy 'double sell': Hedy Lamarr and Victor Mature, Yul Brynner and Gina Lollobigida, Gregory Peck and Susan Hayward. Epic marketers felt that titles should describe the genre of the films so that fans could identify a movie's potential appeal. Communicating too much of the arc of a story might be a negative though and so epics tended towards short titles which hinted at monumentality: *King of Kings*, *The Silver Chalice*, *The Sign of the Cross* or *The Robe*. The badly named *Demetrius and the Gladiators* has the ring of a B-movie title, lacking as it does nobility and magnitude; it is a 'romp-title', but perfectly fitting for a film which was, after all, a popular spin-off of *The Robe*, altogether a more worthy epic.

In both the *Ben-Hur* and *King of Kings* posters, architectural elements drawn from the production design of the movies themselves are cleverly incorporated into the massiveness of the rock faces (the circus arena and the steps of the temple of Jerusalem). Some epic posters fixate on these architectural splendours as the main selling point: a photograph of the vast set of the Roman Forum, for instance, dominates the poster for *The Fall of the Roman Empire*, articulating the notion that, in spite of the A-list movie stars who are referenced in portrait headshots surrounding the main image. It is the setting itself which is the focus of attention. The set has the pulling-power (see Figure 1.21).

Of course, star images were in themselves very important marketable components and poster designers capitalised on the obvious selling-power actors brought to film advertising. This cannot be underestimated. When a top-billed actress such as Claudette Colbert was matched with a historical legend such as Cleopatra, the resulting poster design gave focus to that perfect heavenly alignment, a marketing manager's dream, with the film's co-stars (William Warren and Henry Wilcoxon) operating as mere satellites in the background (see Figure 1.22). On other occasions, movie stars vied with one another for space on the canvas as producers pushed to promote the galaxy of talent scheduled to appear in the latest release (see Figure 1.23).

The use of actor-images in poster marketing was not without its controversies, however. Famously, the first version of Howard Terpning's poster art for *Cleopatra* (1963) was created without Rex Harrison who, as one of the top billed stars, was angry to find himself left out of the artwork. The original *Cleopatra* poster only depicted Richard Burton and Elizabeth Taylor in a seductive and romantic pose which the studio, quite happy to parlay the publicity surrounding their courtship, used to its advantage in the film's publicity. Harrison was not content to be overlooked in this manner and sued and won a lawsuit against Twentieth Century. His portrait was thereafter inserted into the poster (see Figures 1.24 and 1.25).

Poster art frequently used painted montages of scenes from the film to suggest the action or romance which audiences would enjoy in a screening (see Figure 1.18 earlier and Figure 1.26), although just as frequent

SAMUEL BRONSTON PRESENTS

SOPHIA LOREN
STEPHEN BOYD · ALEC GUINNESS
JAMES MASON · CHRISTOPHER PLUMMER

THE FALL OF THE ROMAN EMPIRE

(U)

CO-STARRING
JOHN IRELAND · MEL FERRER · OMAR SHARIF
AND
ANTHONY QUAYLE Directed by ANTHONY MANN

Original Screenplay by BEN BARZMAN · BASILIO FRANCHINA · PHILIP YORDAN · Music by DIMITRI TIOMKIN
Production Designers, COLASANTI and MOORE · Executive Associate Producer, MICHAEL WASZYNSKI · Produced by SAMUEL BRONSTON
Photographed in ULTRA-PANAVISION®   Colour by TECHNICOLOR®

DISTRIBUTION

ROYAL WORLD PREMIERE TUESDAY 24th MARCH AT 7.30 pm
in the presence of His Royal Highness
THE DUKE of EDINBURGH and ADMIRAL OF THE FLEET EARL MOUNTBATTEN OF BURMA
ASTORIA THEATRE CHARING CROSS RD. W.C.2
BOOK NOW FOR MARCH 25 ONWARDS AT THEATRE AND USUAL AGENCIES   TEL: GERrard 5385
Separate performances daily at 2.30 pm & 7.30 pm Sundays 6.30 pm

Figure 1.21
The selling-power of the set. To a large extent eschewing the marketability of some of
Hollywood's finest actors, this version of *The Fall of the Roman Empire* poster fixates
instead on architectural supremacy (1964).

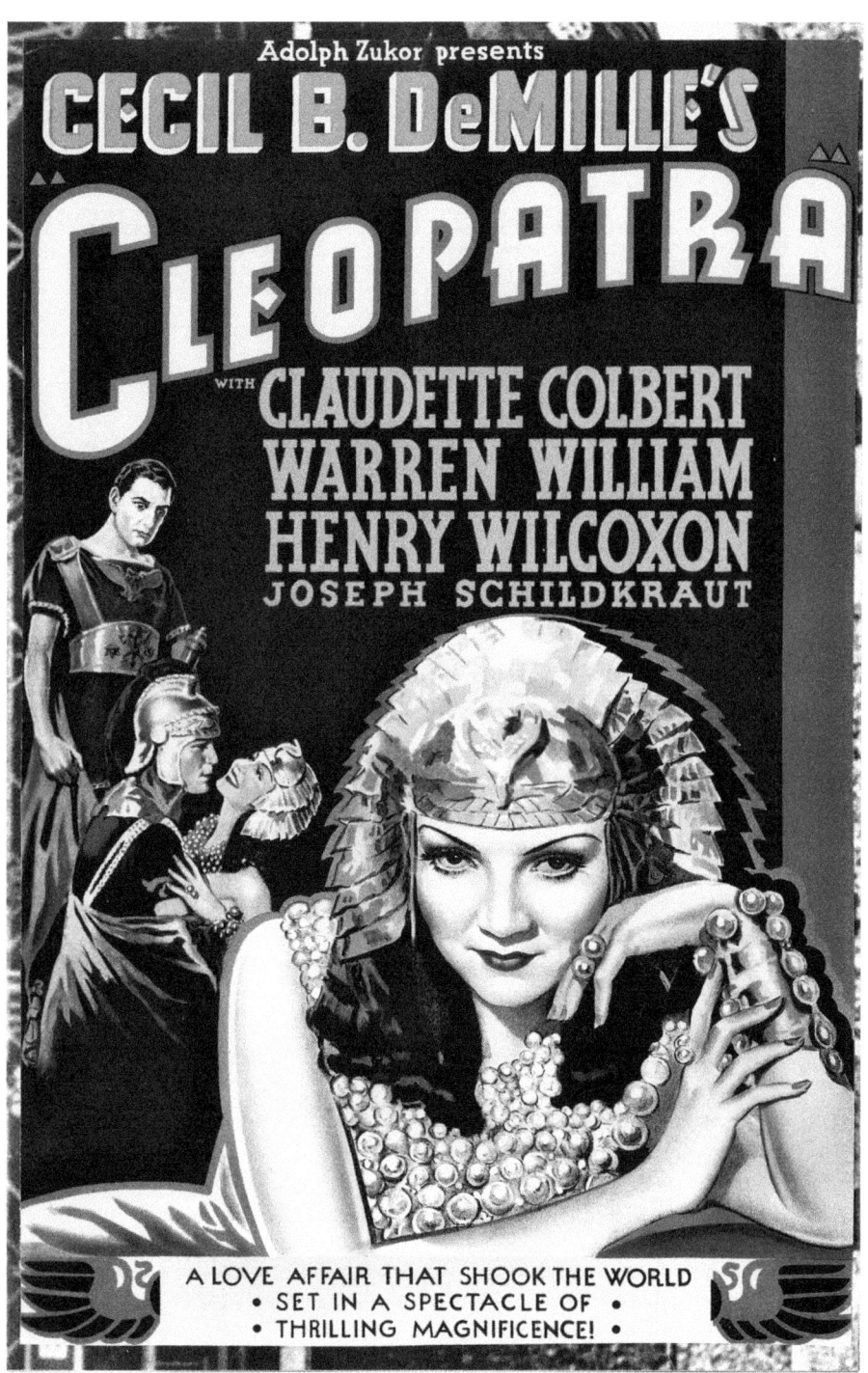

Figure 1.22
The selling power of the star: Claudette Colbert and Cleopatra in perfect Art Deco
alignment (1934).

Figure 1.23
Movie stars vie for space in this version of a poster produced for *The Fall of the Roman Empire*.

were the posters which used the technique of marrying painted images together with photographic stills from the films (see Figure 1.27). Less successful though was the comparatively bland poster created for *The Bible: In the Beginning . . .* with its thumbnail photographs scattered sparsely across the sheet (see Figure 1.28). Its boastful tag – 'THE MOST BREATHTAKING SPECTACLE – was undermined by the austerity of the images themselves. In itself this poster is symptomatic of the death-

Figure 1.24
Following a successful lawsuit, Rex Harrison's portrait was integrated into the *Cleopatra* poster design, although somewhat awkwardly.

throes of the epic movie which occurred in the mid-1960s, and the rheto-ric of the poster is an uncomfortable last gasp of Golden Age glamour set in a design scheme of stark, modernist, 1960s simplicity.

While technological advances in cinematography might be incorpo-rated into poster art (see Figure 1.29), by and large epic movie advertis-ing tended to be, like the films themselves, solidly conservative. Movie star headshots, action montages, photography-based screen shots and architectural spectacle were the standardised apparatuses of the suc-cessful epic poster, with references to antiquity only coming inciden-tally in the costume and hairstyles worn by the actors, or the pillars, chariots and temples of the set details. Attempts at a more avant-garde representation of the antique past rarely met with approval. The press-book for *Samson and Delilah* incorporated a whole page dedicated to 'famous' artists' paintings based on [the story]', where Rembrandts and Rockwells rubbed shoulders with new takes on the old story, such as those created by Ben Stahl, Peter Helck and Al Parker. The striking painting by John Atherton (see Figure 1.30), based upon the unforgiving human representations found in Neo-Assyrian art, might have made

Figure 1.25
A second poster design commissioned for *Cleopatra* gave equal weight to the two male leads, although all eyes focus on Elizabeth Taylor.

Figure 1.26
Painted montage poster for 1963's *Cleopatra*.

Figure 1.27
Overblown and over-fussy, the DeMillian extravaganza of *Samson and Delilah* is marketed with painted and photographic images and a plethora of text.

for an exciting starting point for the film's production design, but sadly Atherton's naively beautiful vision of the ill-fated Israelite hero and his Philistine lover did not suit DeMille's taste for a more overtly glitzy antiquity.

Figure 1.28
Spartan in its austerity, the poster for *The Bible: In the Beginning . . .* (1966) looks uncomfortable with its old-fashioned marketing tags.

Film poster images share space, of course, with text. In fact there is often a mass of text on the epic film posters, given that producers had a particular penchant for providing potential audiences with production-related facts. The names of movie stars and directors are therefore encountered alongside those of screenwriters, composers and the producers themselves, in conjunction with the latest industrial and

Figure 1.29
This poster advertisement for *The Egyptian* (1954) uses the standard visual formula of movie star portraits and a painted scene montage to sell the film, although the technological wonder of CinemaScope is given the most emphasis, with the curving three-dimensions of the new screen ratio being marketed as the most exciting feature of the movie. Pressbook.

Figure 1.30
According to the *Samson and Delilah* pressbook, DeMille commissioned art works to be used as newspaper reproductions, for lobby displays and as exhibits in libraries, museums and art schools. This painting, *Samson and Delilah*, by John Atherton, was created for Paramount as a taster for the design concept of DeMille's movie.

technical features on offer such as WideScreen, Technicolor, Camera 65 or 70 mm Super Technirama. Production companies too are listed alongside distributors.

Most space though was reserved for the all-important tag-lines (or slogans), the catchy and enticing short phrases used by marketers and film studios to advertise and sell a movie (and create 'buzz'). In Golden Age Hollywood tag-lines often summed up the plot and set the tone or

themes of a film. Movies could have multiple tag-lines and the composing and creation of copy for posters and trailers was generally regarded
as the first important step in marketing a movie and setting a strategic
direction for the product. These soundbite epigrams were placed on
film posters above or below the film's title, and on the merchandise
sold alongside a film's release.[37] Unsurprisingly, epic movies tended to
utilise tag-lines (see Figure 1.31) which emphasised the scale, surge and
splendour of the production, alongside obligatory notions of history,
faith and, of course, sex:

> 'An Epic Film that Sweeps Across the Horizon of Ancient Times!'
> (*Sodom and Gomorrah*)

> 'The Mightiest Story of Tyranny and Temptation Ever Written – Ever
> Lived – Ever Produced!' (*The Silver Chalice*)

> 'The Screen's Greatest Drama of Heroic Faith and Inspiring Spectacle'
> (*The Sign of the Cross*)

> 'Flaming Story of History's Most Fabulous Era!' (*Androcles and the
> Lion*)

> 'The Glory that was Egypt! The Grandeur that was Rome!' (*Cleopatra*,
> 1934)

> 'It Rings with the Power of Human Valour! It Blazes with the Surge of
> Human Passions!' (*Spartacus*)

> 'Egypt in all its Glory and Transgression . . . 1500 Years Before the
> Birth of Christ!' (*The Egyptian*)

> 'Gigantic Spectacle Drama!' (*The Last Days of Pompeii*)

> 'The Barbaric Love that Left the Great Pyramid as Its Landmark!' (*The
> Land of the Pharaohs*)

Some tag-lines concentrated on the often-voiced epic obsession with
budget, such as *The Prodigal*'s boast: 'Two Years in the Making! A
Fortune to Produce!' With characteristic smugness, Cecil B. DeMille's
main slogans for the Technicolor remake of *The Ten Commandments*
were simply 'The Supreme Motion Picture of All Time!', 'The Greatest
Event in Motion Picture History', 'The Most Significant Human Drama
Ever Lived!' and 'The Mightiest Human Drama Ever!' It took a brave
producer to commission a poster without a tag-line, but with the right
combination of star-power and off-screen scandal it could be done: the
original marketing of Mankiewicz's *Cleopatra* was undertaken without
any slogan and it was only after the Burton-Taylor affair became global

Figure 1.31
Explosive montages are used for a poster advertisement for *David and Bathsheba*. The elegant restraint and clarity of the design is compromised by the over-wordy and grandiose tag-lines enjoyed by the studios.

news that a tag-line was added: 'The Motion Picture the World Has Been Waiting For!'

Trailers: The Art of Persuasion

Movie trailers are 'free samples' of a film, packaged to convince an audience to come back for more when the film opens in the cinemas.[38] Like any other form of advertising, epic film trailers were as much a reflection of the dominant marketing trends of the period as they were of the films they were selling. A trailer was made by marketing experts from pieces of the film and was (and still is) meant to encapsulate what the film was all about. In the Golden Age, a movie's director had little or no say in the creation of the trailer.[39] The history of the movie trailer shows that film previews have almost always been in the process of evolving, and they have almost always been directly influenced by the pop-cultural landscapes that created them.

Coming attractions have been part of the movie-going experience for over a century now. In the early days of cinema, movie houses ran trailers after a film's conclusion rather than before a film began – they were called 'trailers' because they trailed the feature film. In the blockbuster-rich 1950s, film trailers were built around how one might sell a moving picture to a stage-going audience or to someone listening on the radio. It was the era of the 'hypersell'. After all, in this period there were so many films in circulation and so many people going to the movies that marketing executives consistently went over the top with hyperbolic copy such as: 'This is the greatest movie of all time!'

Epic films, by their scale, cost and, most significantly, length, demanded equally lengthy trailers. Viewing an epic trailer such as that produced for the release of *Quo Vadis* in 1951 reveals that the time taken between cuts, the sonorous voice-over and the overall pacing make for a very formulaic experience (see Text Box 1.7). By today's standards, the *Quo Vadis* trailer drags: it runs just over five minutes in length and the tone is weighty and reverential, with much emphasis given to title cards and actors' names – an image that evokes the legitimate stage more than the silver screen. The *Quo Vadis* trailer works in the service of the rhetoric of stardom. It promotes an ensemble cast and has an overdetermined focus on stardom, promoting both its stars and the 'historical' characters they play. The trailer also nods towards the 'behind-the-scenes' promotional world of Hollywood in ways that illuminate the magnitude of the production, with emphasis on 120 speaking parts and 'thousands and thousands of players in one scene'.

Trailer rhetoric was subsequently used in other types of marketing strategy and the synergy between trailer dialogue and advertising was kept deliberately tight. The giant *New York Times* advertisements for *Quo Vadis* proclaimed: 'Your Eyes Have Never Beheld Such Sights! The world's most wicked empire in all its pagan grandeur! Here at last is . . . the most colossal movie you are ever likely to see for the rest

Text Box 1.7   *Quo Vadis* Trailer

Trumpets blast a fanfare.

[Screen card reading:] 'To our patrons –'

[Cut to screen card reading:] 'We of this theatre take great pride in announcing completion of arrangements that will bring to our screen the attraction
which has been universally acclaimed –'

[Cut to new screen card reading:] '"The Greatest Motion Picture Of Our
Time". The Management'.

Trumpets blast a second fanfare.

Title Card: METRO-GOLDWYN-MAYOR OFFERS A TRIBUTE TO THE
FINEST IDEALS OF THE HUMAN SPIRIT:

Title Card in gold lettering: QUO VADIS

Triumphant music underscore.

Narrator's Voice [over scenes of marching legionaries on the Appian Way]:
'After more than 12 years of conception, of planning and actual production, *Quo Vadis* has been completed and a dream has been fulfilled. *Quo
Vadis* was filmed in Rome, amid the actual sites of its historic locale.
Through the vivid reality of colour by Technicolor, Imperial Rome is
recreated – glorious and corrupt, awesome and hallowed. [Cut to close
up of Robert Taylor in a chariot] Here you will meet with Marcus Vinicius.
Robert Taylor, through a performance of masterful artistry, will lose his
own identity and will have become Marcus Vinicius – brave warrior,
generous and yet capable of great cruelty and unbridled self-will [Shot of
Vinicius driving his chariot through a market stall, overturning the goods].

[Edit. Cut to Vinicius entering a house. Interior. Two shot of Robert Taylor
and Deborah Kerr] And here, with Marcus Vinicius, you meet Lygia,
a Christian slave-girl who in time will dominate his life. [Close up of
Deborah Kerr]. Deborah Kerr is Lygia.

[Edit. Cut to close up of Leo Genn] A pagan to his fingertips, is the suave and
ironical Petronius. The eminent actor Leo Genn recreates Nero's arbiter
of elegance.

[Edit. Long shot of Peter Ustinov] And here is history's most evil genius:
Nero!

Nero (calling out in distress): Tigellinus!! Tigellinus! Where is my guard?
Tigellinus!

[Close up on Peter Ustinov]

Narrator: Under the forehead of a demi-god and the face of a beast, he
was a drunkard and a sensate, full of changing desires, swollen with fat
and crime. So has history described him and so he is recreated by Peter
Ustinov in a magnificent performance. [Edit. Close up of Patricia Laffan,
with a leashed cheetah] The Empress Poppaea, calculating wife whose
hand shaped the fate of Nero's world.

[Edit. Cut to close up of Buddy Baer] The giant Christian slave Ursus, a man
of tremendous strength and the gentleness of a child. [Edit. Close up of

Finlay Currie amidst crowds of Christians] Here the fisherman Simon called Peter.

Narrator: In all there are one hundred and ten speaking parts in *Quo Vadis*. [Edit: crowd scenes] An unprecedented cast of thirty thousand men, women and children. You will see thousands upon thousands of players appearing in a single scene. No achievement in entertainment history has equalled the panoramic spectacle, the power, the compelling human drama of *Quo Vadis*. It is an experience which cannot be compared with anything you have ever known before. [Edit. Scenes of Christians thrown to lions. Edit. Interior: Nero's banquet]. You witness the infamous revelry of a night in Nero's court. [Edit. Scene: Christian gathering] You stand with the Christians in the catacombs. [Edit. Shot of Buddy Baer fighting a soldier] See the battle of the giants! [Edit. Robert Taylor and Deborah Kerr kiss]. And know the love of Marcus Vinicius and Lygia. [Edit. Long shot: the circus arena] The spectacle of Nero's circus! [Edit. Clip. Buddy Baer fights a bull] The terror of the arena as Ursus stands alone against death! [Edit. Longshot: fire of Rome with Peter Ustinov, lyre in hand] And here a happening which will be remembered as long as history: the burning of Rome! [Edit. Extended shots of fire, collapsing buildings, people screaming].

Trumpet fanfare. [Edit: longshot: Roman triumph parade].

Narrator: Standing here in the shadows of antiquity's pagan gods, you will join with Rome's cheering multitudes as they honour their victorious warriors and you'll know why Quo Vadis has been called 'The most genuinely colossal movie you are likely to see for the rest of your lives.'

Music: chorus sing theme – *Quo Vadis Domine*.

Screen Card in gold: QUO VADIS

Screen Card in gold: BASED ON HENRYK SIENKIEWICZ' NOVEL OF FAITH AND ROMANCE

Screen Card in gold: METRO-GOLDWYN-MAYOR'S FINEST MOTION PICTURE

Screen Card in gold: IN COLOUR BY TECHNICOLOR

[Music reaches a climax; fade to black]

of your lives!' In keeping with all the ballyhoo and employing stills from the movie, newspapers and magazines ran with headlines lifted from the trailers: 'The triumphal return of Roman legions with their shackled captives, to the acclaim of thousands and thousands!', 'The half-crazed emperor and his wicked empress entertain hundreds at their palace with an all-night feast and revel!' and 'The mighty Ursus wrestles in the arena with a maddened bull, to save Lygia tied to a stake!'

A special teaser-trailer commissioned to promote *David and Bathsheba* (titled *Once in 3000 Years*) took a very different approach. It shows

Gregory Peck, having been called to the Twentieth Century Fox studio, in conversation with director Henry King:

> KING: Greg, I've got some news for you. You will play King David. How does that strike you?
>
> PECK (laughs): How does it strike me? Why, I've been fascinated by David's story in the Bible ever since I could read.
>
> KING: Well, the role is yours, Greg. The greatest of your career . . . The drama of a man who had everything and lost his God, a King who fell in love with another man's wife. One of the most passionate love affairs of all time. But above all a wonderful story of faith.

Gregory Peck leaves King's office and tours the various studio departments which are a hive of activity as they prepare for filming. A series of scenes from the film dissolve one into another as Peck provides the voice-over:

> PECK'S VOICE: With this as the beginning, an impressive succession of scenes came before the Technicolor cameras.
>
> Thousands of soldiers besieging the walls of Rabbah, countless shields, spears, swords and armour were painstakingly recreated for these scenes.
>
> Herds of camel and oxen in the colourful caravan bringing the Holy Ark to Jerusalem . . .
>
> David's Forbidden love with the woman Bathsheba, played by Susan Hayward . . .
>
> The giant Goliath and young David in mortal combat... as Philistine hordes watch in awe . . .
>
> The mob stoning the adulteress outside the gates of Jerusalem – the biblical penalty for such a sin . . .
>
> The psalm-singing shepherd boy who became David the King!
>
> 'Thou annointest my head with oil; my cup runneth over. Surely goodness and mercy shall follow me all the days of my life: and I will dwell in the house of the Lord forever.'
>
> [TITLES IN PARCHMENT]
>
> *DAVID AND BATHSHEBA*

Cinematic trailer spectatorship is, of course, a very heightened spectatorial mode, 'an arena where spectators tend to evince greater awareness of themselves as a collectivity'.[40] Recent film scholarship has called to attention the relationship between film spectatorship and shopping, specifically the 'shop' window analogy. Audiences shop for films and, as Tom Gunning has noted, a 'cinema of attractions', an appellation which suits the epic film admirably, is

> less . . . a way of telling stories . . . than a way of presenting a series of views to an audience, fascinating because of their illusory power

... and exoticism ... a cinema that displays its visibility, willing to rupture a self-enclosed fictional world for a chance to solicit the attention of the spectator.'[41]

With their constant references to the process of filmmaking and the magnitude of labour involved in bringing the past to life, epic film trailers use text and image in ways that attract the spectator's attention in a contradictory way by saying both 'here is the actual historical past' and 'here is the effort we put into making it look real.' Epic trailer spectatorship, like all forms of epic marketing, highlights the presence of this doubleness.

Statistics Sell

Statistics were trumpeted in Hollywood marketing as a certain way of grabbing an audience's attention. As early as 1916 Griffith's *Intolerance* was marketed with tags like 'Thrills! Mystery! Romance! Adventure!' and with the visual promise of '125,000 PEOPLE, 7,500 HORSES, 1,200 CHARIOTS, 3,000 SCENES!' In 1921, Edwards' production of *The Queen of Sheba* (see Figure 1.32) was being sold as 'The Love Romance of the Most Beautiful Woman the World Has Ever Known! Visualized with a Background of Unbelievable Gorgeousness! 10,000 ACTORS! 671 SCENES! 500 CAMELS! 500 HORSES!'[42] The souvenir brochure for the 1923 version of *The Ten Commandments* proudly listed the statistics behind the 'magnitude of this colossal production':

> **Material actually used** – 15 tons modelling clay; 300 tons of plaster, 550,000 feet timber; 57 miles cable wire. **Weight of sphinxes** – nearly four tons each. **Equipment of Camp DeMille** – water pumping 36,000 gallons daily; electricity daily consumption 1000 kilowatts; 2 dining halls; 1000 sittings each ... fleet of motor cars 47; 850 mechanics; 125 cooks ... **Animals** – 900 horses; 200 small mules; 50 camels; 1,000 cattle; 500 sheep and goats; 300 head of poultry; 50 dogs ... **Camp Synagogue** – presided over by Rabbi Aaron Markadov, assisted by an interpreter; **Camp School** – 7 teachers and 60 registered children under the age of 14; **Camp Orchestra** – Miss Ruth Dickey conductor and ten musicians. **Costume and harness** – 16 miles of cloth for over 3,000 costumes; 3 tons leather for 250 sets chariot harness; 2 tons talcum for actors' faces; 500 gallons of glycerine to grease their bodies.

The pressbook reiterated the essentials, with a few extra figures thrown in for good measure:

> Height of the set – 120 feet
> Width of the set – 720 feet
> Statuary in the set – 1,000,000 pounds
> Number of construction workers employed – 1,500

Figure 1.32
The Queen of Sheba (1921) was marketed on its 'Unbelievable Gorgeousness' –
represented by Solomon's harem of concubines and the alluring charms of Betsy Blithe.
Poster advertisement.

Lumber in the set – 500,000 feet
Amount of nails – 25,000 pounds
Amount of reinforcing cables – 75 miles
Number of actors on the site – 3,500
Number of cooks – 125
Number of sandwiches per day – 7,500
Number of oranges per day – 2,500
Number of apples per day – 2,500
Number of chariots built for the film – 300
Number of animals on the site – 5,000
Number of pounds of hay per day – 20,000
Number of pounds of manure per day – Plenty

Remarkably, the *Ben-Hur* souvenir brochure was reiterating the same
tried and tested marketing devices in 1959, demonstrating once more
the deep conservatism of the epic genre.[43] The brochure's 'Random
Revelations' note, for instance, that 'Many women in Italy gave their
hair for *Ben-Hur*. More than four hundred pounds were assembled at

Cinecittà Studios.' There were two blacksmiths, it transpires, hired to care for the seventy-eight horses used in the chariot race while two doctors and two nurses maintained a twenty-bed infirmary at the edge of the arena. The whole population of the mountain village of Arcinazo voluntarily uprooted and relocated one hundred miles in order to play the residents of Nazareth while Rome's newspapers told men with beards to present themselves at the studio: 'In anticipation of such a call Romans had started growing beards months before; more than five thousand showed up the day after the newspaper advertisement had appeared.' Obligatory number crunching was also included. The set for the chariot race sequence, 'modelled after the ancient circus in Jerusalem', kept more than a thousand workmen occupied 'for a year carving its graceful oval face from a rock quarry which covered eighteen acres of studio property'. The arena statistics are noted as:

Close to 1,000,000 feet of lumber
1,000,000 pounds of plaster
250 miles of metal tubing
40,000 tons of white sand imported from nearby Mediterranean beaches.

MGM ploughed $15 million into the story of Judah Ben-Hur; committing such a large budget was always a gamble (although with *Ben-Hur*'s pedigree on stage and screen in the early 1900s some guarantee of popularity was ensured). But given that the 1959 movie was such a colossal undertaking – a 220-minute film involving three production units – part of the marketing potential was to exploit the budget as an audience enticement. Lists of lumber, plaster and metal tubing, or of wigs and beards for that matter, demonstrated that every dollar and cent had been spent on creating this extraordinary feature film and that, therefore, *Ben-Hur* (and every other epic film, given that statistics-based marketing ploys remained consistent throughout our period of study) was something worth seeing.

Voyeurs of History?

Both epic movie posters and trailers exploited the notion of sight. Audiences were customarily invited to witness the lavishness and breath-taking spectacles of antiquity. Given its focus on the infamous Dance of the Seven Veils, *Salome* provides an appropriate example of this visual fixation. With auburn-haired love-goddess Rita Hayworth in the eponymous role, shedding the gossamer scarves as she moved, the film promised 'Pomp, Pageantry, Spectacle Unsurpassed! The Glory and Excitement of Rome . . . in all its Greatness and Badness!' and ensured audiences, with a thinly veiled double-entendre that 'Your Eyes Will See the Glory!'

The extravagances and excesses of Hollywood's formation of the past were emphasised time and again in the studio publicity through the concept of the gaze: 'The All Time Spectacle' (as *Solomon and Sheba* was marketed) of the ancient world. In fact the trailer for *Solomon and Sheba* promises the audience, 'A Thousand Marvels!' and invites them to 'Behold! The Mightiest Spectacle the Screen Has Ever Encompassed: The Days of Battle, the Nights of Desire that Shook the World', and continues (using a gyrating Gina Lollobrigida as further visual entice-ment), 'Behold! The Many Sins! The Pagan Revels! The Wine-Bathed Orgy Before a Graven Image!' Consequently the audience does indeed 'Behold!' the inevitable outcome of all this debauchery: 'The Wrath-Filled Lightning Bolt Over the Earth!' A cut to clashing chariots follows: 'Behold! The Desert-Quaking Charge of the Pharaoh's Chariots! The Miracle of Blinding Light!' and, in a clip that too readily gives away the film's most thrilling moment, the audience must prepare themselves to 'Behold! The Terrifying Death-Plunge of the Egyptian Host!' 'Behold!' comes the final reassurance, 'Above All! The Love Story of the Ages! Yul Brynner and Gina Lollobrigida: Solomon and Sheba'.

As might be expected, DeMille marketed his version of *Cleopatra* with particular visual panache which emphasised the – somewhat salacious – visual spectacle of the production:

A LOVE AFFAIR THAT SHOOK THE WORLD . . . AND TOPPLED
   TWO EMPIRES!
CLEOPATRA
Cecil B. DeMille's tremendous pageant of unrivalled splendour!
WONDERS THAT DAZZLE THE HUMAN IMAGINATION!
CLEOPATRA'S PARADISE, a Love Boat 500 feet long, where Antony
   is wafted to unknown delights by the sloe-eyed Temptress of Egypt!
GALAXIES OF ROMAN BEAUTIES bathing in rose-scented palace
   pools, laughing over the latest scandal with Roman court dandies!
GIANT WAR GALLIES hurling fire balls, armies of men in holocaust
   of battle, all for a woman's love!
BALLET OF THE SINUOUS 'LEOPARDS', the Dance on the back of
   the Sacred Bull, performed by the 100 Sea Maidens!
ROME'S CONQUERING HORDES shocked into silence by what they
   see in the crimson-columned throne room at Alexandria!
THE RITES TO ISIS, Goddess of Love, into whose worship Antony is
   initiated by the singing handmaidens!
CLEOPATRA BORNE IN CAESAR'S TRIUMPH, dazzling the Roman
   multitudes, decked in priceless gold and jewels, as the Great White
   Queen of Egypt!
THE LAST EXQUISITE LOVE TRYST of Antony and Cleopatra, the
   weeping slave sent for the fatal stinging asp! 'I am dying, Egypt,
   dying, but the world is well lost for love!'
A PARAMOUNT PICTURE

With such prominence placed on the compelling need to 'look', the studio marketing experts hoped that, like Lot's wife, audiences would find it impossible to turn away from the on-screen spectacle. Audiences were charmed into their cinema seats through the pure hedonism of the visualisation of antiquity.

Joan Staiger has noted that the successful marketing campaign achieved best results through a combined focus on 'realism, authenticity and spectacle'.[44] To call attention to the spectacle in a film, tag-lines specifically capitalised on this quality: SEE! SEE! SEE! (Colour Plate 3). A poster for Rosen's *Alexander the Great* goes as far as to list the film's 'Spectacles' in orderly columns which include 'The Mass Marriage of Thousands of Persian Women', 'The Charge of the Knife-Studded Chariots', 'The Cutting of the Gordian Knot' and 'The Massive Stone Gods of Babylon' (see Figure 1.33).

The audiences of epic movies were encouraged to believe that by choosing to see one of these grandiose films they were conceivably among the 'cast of thousands' in the battle scenes or glamorous pageants. Ancient history on film therefore needed to be spectacular for that belief to be sustained and any depiction of private or intimate moments in history would risk disrupting this by reminding audiences that they were 'voyeurs' *of* history and not participants *in* history. We should remember that the worthiness and historical 'veracity' of the epic film was often augmented by voice-overs in lumbering prologues and opening titles which showed ancient documents being unfurled as 'history' was narrated on-screen. *Samson and Delilah*, for instance, begins with an ancient parchment being opened to reveal the film's title written in large archaic-style lettering. 'History', it seems, is written in pretentious calligraphy, in gilt and with a capital H, with the words 'In the Year of Our Lord', followed by a concise summary of 'the story so far'. Maps often accompanied the prologues, promising the viewer epic scope, empire building and adventure.

One particularly effective technique employed for the opening credits of *Cleopatra* (1963) was the notion of using faded ancient painted frescos – which slowly regain colour and come to 'life' – to make the connection between the past and the present. The audience is asked to believe that what is witnessed on the screen is the ancient world of Cleopatra brought to life and the proof of this are the frescoes themselves. A series of paintings are used during the opening credits, depicting settings and scenes later witnessed in the movie, until an old battle scene begins to merge with footage of soldiers moving and funeral pyres burning. A voice-over places us in the historical timeframe: '. . . and so it fell out that at Pharsalia, in Greece, Caesar put his legions against those of the Great Pompey and did destroy them. Thus, by the folly of war amongst themselves, came the Romans to count Roman dead.' The movie closes in the reverse manner as the film footage of Taylor-Cleopatra lying in state following her suicide dissolves back into increasingly grainy, fragmented wall paintings, with the voice-over taking line's drawn from Plutarch's *Life of Antony*: 'And the Roman asked. "Was this well done of your lady?" And the woman replied, "Extremely well as befitting of

Figure 1.33

A painted montage and a list of spectacles helps to sell Rosen's *Alexander the Great* (1956). Poster art.

so many noble rulers."' The picture fades to black and the circle from present-to-past-to-present is cleverly completed.

DeMille Sells the Past: The Marketability of Research

When Cecil B. DeMille's remake of *The Ten Commandments* had completed filming and was ready for cinema try-outs, a trailer was shot to help promote the picture's marketability. That trailer ranks among the most bizarre Hollywood marketing ploys ever seen, not because of any grotesque multi-million dollar budget or of any on-screen excesses, but by its sheer pomposity. Running at over ten minutes in length, the lumbering trailer takes place in DeMille's oak-panelled office, where the master himself gives us a wordy lesson in theology, geography, ancient history, biblical Hebrew and art history. The audience is talked at and, in the style of any good lecture, is shown some visual aids: sketches by Doré, sculptures by Michelangelo and paintings by Van Dyke. Interspersed among these authentic artworks, which happen to be scattered about DeMille's office, are production sketches and props – the rush-basket which carried the infant Moses (Frasier Heston),[45] and the tablets of stone carved from 'the red granite of the Holy Mountain, Sinai, itself', DeMille assures us. 'This Canaanite lettering of the Bronze Age', he goes on to say, pointing to the inscribed letters on the pink stones as though they were genuine museum artefacts, 'is a forerunner of the Hebrew alphabet, the Greek alphabet, and our own alphabet today.' Maps are unfurled and scrutinised, huge, dusty tomes are opened and pored over, screen-props are waved in front of the camera in the most hubristic, verbose and hyperbolic demonstration of directorial vision in screen history. Why? The answer is simple: because for DeMille selling the idea of historical credibility was everything. Thus the lavishly illustrated colour brochure created for the premiere of *The Ten Commandments* proudly announced that:

> THE TEN COMMANDMENTS IS AS AUTHENTIC AS RESEARCH, DEDICATION AND HUMAN LABOUR COULD MAKE IT

and boasted that DeMille 'set a standard for absolute authenticity in every detail'.

Of course, in the Bible, the story of Moses stops at the moment he is discovered in the bulrushes by Pharaoh's daughter and picks up some thirty years later when Moses is a prince of the royal house. In order to fill in that gap, and make the picture both marketable and credible, DeMille needed to fill in the thirty-year gap and he did so by drawing on traditions of Moses' life found in the Jewish Midrash, rabbinic commentaries, the Koran and the classical works of Philo, Josephus and Eusebius (as well as a 1949 novel by Dorothy Clarke Wilson called *Prince of Egypt*, which appealed to him greatly).

Using this background knowledge as justification ammunition, *The*

Ten Commandments opens not with the usual epic spectacle of slaves or chariots or even pyramids, but with an awkward Prologue which places the figure of DeMille himself in front of a huge projection screen, masked by silver brocade drapes. A close-up of DeMille follows, and he speaks:

> Ladies and Gentlemen, young and old! This may seem like an unusual procedure . . . speaking to you before the picture begins, but we have an unusual subject: the story of the birth of Freedom, the story of Moses. As many of you know, the Holy Bible omits some 30 years of Moses' life . . . from the time he was a three-month-old baby and was found in the bulrushes by . . . Bithiah, the daughter of Pharaoh and adopted into the court of Egypt . . . until he learned that he was Hebrew and killed the Egyptian.
>
> To fill those missing years we turned to ancient historians such as Philo and Josephus. Philo wrote at the time that Jesus of Nazareth walked the earth, and Josephus wrote some fifty years later and watched the destruction of Jerusalem by the Romans. These historians had access to documents long since destroyed . . . or perhaps lost, like the Dead Sea Scrolls.
>
> The theme of this picture is whether men are to be ruled by God's law, or whether they are to be ruled by the whim of a dictator like Ramses. Are men the property of the state . . . or are they free souls under God? This same battle continues throughout the world today.
>
> Our desire was not to create a story, but to be worthy of the divinely inspired story created 3,000 years ago: the Five Books of Moses. The story takes three hours and thirty-nine minutes to unfold. There will be an intermission. Thank you for your attention.

The opening titles for *The Ten Commandments* then run and after the cast and crew are listed, special prominence is once again given to DeMille's source materials:

> This work was compiled from many sources and contains material from the books:
> *Prince of Egypt* by Dorothy Clarke Wilson
> *Pillar of Fire* by Rev. J. H. Ingraham
> *On Eagle's Wings* by Rev. A. E. Southern
> Those who see this motion picture – produced and directed by Cecil B. DeMille – will make a pilgrimage over the very ground that Moses trod more than 3,000 years ago –
> In accordance with the ancient texts of:
> Philo
> Josephus
> Eusebius
> The Midrash
> and
> THE HOLY SCRIPTURES[46]

'I have sometimes likened the producer to the restorer of a broken mosaic,' DeMille once wrote. 'Some parts of the mosaic can be supplied by the historians. The missing parts . . . the producer must supply; but the integrity of the whole work demands that what the producer supplies must fit in with what history knows.' He elaborates his point by referring to the so-called 'Alexander mosaic', a fragmentary floor covering found in an aristocratic Pompeiian house which shows Alexander the Great on horseback fighting Darius, the Great King of Persia:

> The duty of an historian is to give an accurate report of known and proven facts. The duty of an historical dramatist, however, is to fill in the crevasse between them. The absence of legs from both Alexander and his horse Bucephalus in the damaged Pompeiian mosaic of the Battle of Issus is no proof that legless men or horses existed. It is for the dramatist to fill in all the missing pieces of the mosaic of history.[47]

In order to fill in these missing pieces of history, Hollywood publicity departments were keen on stressing the laborious academic research that went into the recreation of ancient locations and costumes, and on claiming that what was being witnessed on the screen was as authentic a recreation of ancient life as could be hoped for. But DeMille was particularly obsessed with the idea of historical research and with the kudos to be obtained from persuading his audience that it was witnessing on-screen accurate recreations of the past. However, as will be seen throughout this study, his obsession with the *idea* of historical precision and his desire to realise lavish movies with mass appeal were contradictory: what DeMille claimed to do and what he actually did were two different matters. For DeMille the selling of the past (*his* version of the past, that is) as accurate has great marketing potential. A teaser-trailer for his medieval-era epic *The Crusades*, for instance, demonstrates this fact. It shows DeMille sitting on top of a studio boom directing the action on the studio floor from on high. He calls 'Cut!' and swoops down, *deus ex machina*-like, and focuses on the costume of a young female extra: 'What's that girl doing over there with a 1935 headdress!?', he bursts out. 'You know, this isn't a fantasy, it's history! She looks as though she just walked out of a beauty salon!' With this kind of on-screen bombast, DeMille helped create his own myth as a devotee to, and high priest of, fact.

Even in his formative period of filmmaking (pre-1923), studio publicity already emphasised DeMille's army of research assistants and the years of background work which ensured a historically correct recreation of antiquity. DeMille claims to have developed his proclivity for historical research early on, when he routinely sent his secretary into public libraries to collect books on costume, architecture, armaments or whatever subject occupied his mind at the time.[48] Certainly, by the late 1920s DeMille's offices contained one of the biggest research libraries in Hollywood, and DeMille began to see himself as something of an

Figure 1.34
DeMille (with a studio employee) is shown in his office during the making of *The Ten Commandments* (1956). With piles of research files stacked up behind him and with sketches, artworks and photographs pinned to the walls, this was an image which DeMille carefully engineered; he utilised this scholarly persona in his long-winded film-trailer. Studio publicity photograph.

academic, an expert in biblical history and Judeo-Christian theology (see Figure 1.34).[49] When asked if DeMille was really concerned with research and accuracy or if it was just part of his self-promotion, his scriptwriter, Charles Bennett, responded, 'Oh yes, he had a research department working with him all the time. Everything had to be accurate, even to the kinds of plants that would be in a particular area. He was very thorough in that way ... and very good.'[50] Interestingly, in their interaction with DeMille's movies, critics and reviewers often echoed the laborious research details that underpinned a film's production (see Text Box 1.8).

DeMille was to regard himself as the instigator of the concept of the 'research department' and regarded the creation of the post of 'research consultant' one of his most valuable contributions to movie-making. In DeMillian philosophy, the research consultant was a lynch-pin in his production crew. As he noted, '[the research consultant] with scholarly objectivity ... must often be a 'No'-man to the wider fancies of producer, director or writers ... His most important function is to see that what goes into a picture is authentic for the time and place of the movie.'[51]

Text Box 1.8   Reviewing DeMille's Authenticity

Figure 1.35
William Warren and Claudette Colbert as Caesar and Cleopatra: *Cleopatra* (1934).
Film still.

During the hour and a half that audiences will spend in the theatre watching the unreeling of the film [*Cleopatra*], they will be, in fact, seeing the results of several thousand persons over a period of more than a year. The work of actual photography took only two months. Those two months, the Studio reports, were merely the climax of a year's toil.

To explain that statement, the producers cited an illustration: in a room of Cleopatra's palace at Alexandria, Julius Caesar is portrayed seated in an Egyptian chair, toying with models of instruments of war and dictating terms to Egyptian officials.

The scene appears simple enough, but to bring it to life the following details had to be settled: What sort of room was it and how was it furnished? How did Caesar and Cleopatra dress? What were the details of the soldiers' uniforms? Who were the dignitaries Caesar was addressing and what were the terms he was making? How was Caesar's hair cut? These were a few of the questions.

Eight months were spent answering them. Jeanie Macpherson, one of DeMille's scenarists, was in charge of a research staff of twelve. Some of the world's largest libraries and museums were called on for help; almost every known book on the chief figures in the story was obtained and read.

The research staff split into subdivisions. One handled incident and action; another took up architecture, interior decorating; a third specialised on props, ranging from Cleopatra's hairpins to water clocks. Sketches were made of costumes, chariots, chairs, buildings, beds and boats. Artisans were set to work reproducing them in metal, cloth, plaster or wood. Skilled workmen in the Studio foundry turned out swords, helmets, spears, armour and chariot fittings. Carpenters began building the sets.

This went on for months. Meanwhile, the casting director, Billy Gordon, had to select Romans and Egyptians from among Hollywood's thousands of extras. They needed as many as 700 for a single scene. Finally the cameras began grinding and continued for two months. It took longer to edit and cut the film, score the music to certain parts of it and add sound to others.

'C. B. DeMille's "Cleopatra"', *New York Times*, 12 August 1934

In 1945 a Swiss-born historian named Henry Noerdlinger joined DeMille's Research Department and quickly established himself as a very able and patient co-worker. Earning the complete trust of DeMille,[52] he undertook the research for, firstly, *The Unconquered* (1947) and then *Samson and Delilah* (see below). For *The Ten Commandments*, he commissioned Noerdlinger to oversee the publication of his research notes compiled from the works of eminent Egyptologists, theologians and historians (the cost of the research, it has been suggested, took up 2 per cent of the film's entire budget).[53] DeMille then arranged to have the work published under the title *Moses and Egypt: The Documentation to the Motion Picture of 'The Ten Commandments'* and distributed by the

University of Southern California. DeMille himself, in a wordy introduction to the volume, noted the lengths to which Noerdlinger had
gone in order to compile the book (a tally of publications was used
as evidence for the quality of the research) and gave reasons for its
composition:

> In our research ... we have consulted some 1,900 books and peri-
> odicals, collected nearly 3,000 photographs, and used the facilities
> of 30 libraries and museums in North America, Europe and Africa
> ... Students will find here a distillation of materials for which other-
> wise they would have to search in many places, but which are here
> arranged and collated for ready reference ... I consider it money well
> spent to bring to the screen the results of the work of so many patient
> and selfless scholars whose labours ... have helped make [antiquity]
> live again. Research does not sell tickets at the box office, I may be
> told. But research does help bring out the majesty of [the past].[54]

Scott Eyman's study of DeMille's creation of *The Ten Commandments*
has noted that 'the book would be criticised as an example of "pseudo-
history" because Noerdlinger gathered every possible source, canonical
or not, without attempt to authenticate one over the other or to reconcile
contradictions.'[55] In fact in March 1957 the Biblical and Archaeological
Research Fund listed several errors they found in the picture.[56] DeMille
hit back with a four-page, single-spaced, point-by-point refutation
printed in the San Francisco newspapers, with Noerdlinger himself
arguing that *Moses and Egypt* was not supposed 'to give full justice to
any given subject, but rather to point out what we did in the picture
and with what justification.'[57] He hinted at the notion that a filmmaker
needs to narrate the story with imagination and that events might be
'telescoped' for dramatic effect.

The telescoping of events was not the problem though when it had
come to finding a rationale for locating DeMille's version of the story
of Samson and Delilah in a specific historical period. DeMille and
Noerdlinger found this problematic. Deciding on the chronological
period in which to place the film was difficult and the director was
forced to ask himself just when 'one of the greatest love stories in history
or literature' was set.[58] As it stands in the sixth chapter of the Book
of Judges, the account of Samson's sexual involvement with Delilah
is astonishingly brief. This was not a problem for DeMille who once
declared that he could make a film out of any two pages of the Bible
('with the exception of the Book of Numbers'), but with so little to go on
in the Samson and Delilah story, he opted to pad out the plot with scenes
taken from a little-known novel, *Judge and Fool*, by Vladimir Jabotinsky.
The novel, like the biblical book, is set in and around Canaanite and
Philistine cities of the Levant in the Middle Bronze Age. But what did
this period, this locale and these names mean to the average cinema-
goer? Very little, it was supposed. Moreover, did the audience have a

preconceived vision of ancient Hebrew and Philistine life? The answer, it was decided, was no.

DeMille had no idea about the period either. He sent Noerdlinger on a quest and, with some credibility (drawn from the latest scholarly research), Noerdlinger came up with a solution: the Philistines, he said, were an advanced Mediterranean race who swept into the Levant and Egypt during a great migratory period of the Late Bronze Age. They shared a cultural heritage with a very sophisticated island race, the Minoans; therefore, the 'look' of the film, of the Philistine scenes at least, should be Minoan.[59] DeMille read Noerdlinger's notes thoroughly and gave the go-ahead for the publicity department's blurb:

> The civilization represented in this particular biblical picture is known as the Minoan Civilization, about which not a great deal has been known until relatively recent times . . . Mr DeMille [has] exceeded his own demanding nature by spending fourteen years in researching the manners, customs, flora, fauna, dress, habits and other indices of Minoan culture.[60]

The Minoans therefore became a convenient handle for Hollywood's recreation of Philistine society, regardless of any sure and secure histori-cal evidence for such a close identification between the two civilisations. Yet the DeMillian publicity machine assured cinema audiences that they were witnessing painstaking recreations of the original look of the ancient Philistine-Minoan world (whatever that was), skilfully brought to life by an army of experts. The boast lead Richard Condon, DeMille's press agent, to note, 'We've got more on Minoan culture than Arnold Toynbee.'[61]

But of course, by their nature, epic films do not show an honest view of ancient life. Ever since D. W. Griffiths' *Intolerance*, movie-makers had strived to get specific historical points right, but on certain issues, epic treatments could be very lax and were often way off the mark of any historical authenticity, not only in the details of narrative, script, sets and costumes, but in the whole generic ambience of a film.[62] But then we must recall that historical authenticity was not necessarily looked for. As we will see, the contemporary marketability of the past often trumped any desire to recreate accuracy, and even DeMille readily suc-cumbed to the idea of 'profit over period'. Moreover, it is important to remember that the shared reception of epic films by any audience was not (and never can be) wholescale; received notions of what was historically right or wrong varied between audience members, and so Hollywood continued to advance the illusion that what was depicted on screen was a realistic depiction of the past according to the expectations of the cinema-going public.[63]

The much-ballyhooed DeMillian penchant for research (bogus or otherwise) left its mark on Hollywood (see Text Box 1.9). When Howard Hawks, no great admirer of the Cecil B. DeMille school of filmmaking,

Text Box 1.9   Alexander's Researcher

Except by inference (notably on the part of respectful subordinates) a producer is only seldom a qualified expert on the more arcane aspects of his own films. And why should he be? As one noted Hollywood producer of costume movies has said, 'I don't even know what a pewter mug is made of, much less the particular kind of mug used by Osric the Ornery back in the eleventh century. So I hire experts to tell me, authorities who have devoted an entire lifetime to the subject of pewter mugs.'

On the other hand, there are such producers as Robert Rossen, representing a type as rare in Hollywood as a third hand. Rossen . . . is a scholar and doesn't care who knows it. Before making a film on any subject, he goes to extreme lengths to imbibe it and ingest it, to learn it, to learn it inside-out, upside down, and even outside out and right side up.

Epic Task

Students of movie advertisements are undoubtedly familiar with the breathless proclamation that a picture has been 'three years in the making!' Translated into fact, this could mean that (a) the producer has spent three years trying to raise money, or (b) four weeks making the picture. Well, Robert Rossen had his new film, *Alexander the Great*, in preparation for three years because it took him that long to acquaint himself with the great man (Alexander the Great) and his times (356–232 B.C.); and approximately eight months before the cameras because he had conceived of the film in epic proportions and nobody – no matter how fast or how economy-minded – can make an epic in less than eight months.

Rossen began his research on *Alexander the Great* in the neo-Hellenic atmosphere of the Connecticut countryside, a significant remove from the cockpits of Hollywood. Here, in a study built over a garage, he set about separating the chaff of myth from the breadstuff of fact, hampered no end by the mists of twenty-three hundred years of elapsed time and the – indeed – mythic accomplishments of the man who was King of Macedonia and Captain General of Greece at twenty, conqueror of the known world at twenty-six and dead at thirty-three. He read everything that could be found on Alexander, and haunted the great libraries, museums and foundations of New York and New England.

Next, he sifted, selected and recorded all he had learned about Alexander, and tried to fix the man's character by a sort of psychiatric technique. How much was Alexander's ambition driven by his intense rivalry with his father? What were the influences of his tutor, Aristotle, of his father's ambitions, of Demosthenes? etc., etc.

One thing became immediately clear. The brief span of Alexander's life was crowded with a surfeit of dramatic incidents in all of which he was the central figure. The great problem for Rossen, once he had evolved a pattern from the mountainous accumulation of his research and notes, was that of selection. He was possessed of an embarrassment of riches.

Career Highlights

Regretfully, but of necessity, since he was concerned with making *Alexander the Great* a mere epic rather than a marathon film, he eliminated a lot of wonderful stuff, retaining some forty-five chronological highlights as the basis of the story, including the battles of Cheronea, Grancius and Gaugamela; the siege of Miletus; Philip's macabre dance over the corpses after Cheronea; the crossing of the Hellespont; Alexander's first glimpse of the fabulous wealth and splendour of the Persian court; the burning of the palace of Persepolis; the mass wedding ceremony of 10,000 Macedonian men to Persian women; and, of course, Alexander's death at Babylon.

With the draft of a screenplay in hand, and accompanied by his family and two enormous tin trunks crammed with indexed research material and a sizeable bibliography for detailed reference, Rossen departed in further pursuit of knowledge. Rome for sidelights, Greece for a study of the famous Alexandrian landmarks. Spain to select location sites that would match the original. London for access to the renowned museums, libraries, archives and antique book shops, with special emphasis on the British Museum and the Royal Hellenic Society.

Meanwhile the script was being rewritten, reshaped, polished to a high gloss. And, one fine day, satisfied that he had done his very best, Rossen went off to Spain to transmute three years of study into a movie.

Alexander the Great was three years in the preparation, eight months in the making. On the level!

New York Times, 11 December 1955

was coerced into directing *The Land of the Pharaohs* he too found comfort and publicity opportunities in promoting his research department. 'I don't know how a pharaoh talks,' Hawks admitted – and for Hawks this was a big issue; his films were always based on dialogue, gesture and intimate exchanges between characters. To make any serious headway with the script (written in part by William Faulkner), the story of which centred around the construction of the Great Pyramid, Hawks and his writers had to be clear on how they were going to show the pyramid being built. He consulted Jean Philippe Lauer, allegedly one of the world's most prominent Egyptologists, who laid out the most accepted theories about the construction of the pyramid and, for the crucial matter of the ending of the film in which the dead pharaoh's burial chamber is forever sealed with the entourage of his servants and his treacherous wife, the way in which tombs were sealed. Hawks found courage in his conversations with the scholar to press ahead with the picture and thereafter appointed Noel Howard as Head of Research on the project. When the special effects man announced that he was beginning work on the construction of thirty chariots for the pharaoh and his officers, it was Howard who had to inform the production team that the wheel did not exist in Old Kingdom Egypt, and neither did the chariot. For that matter, Howard added, at that date Egypt did not know either horses or camels. The film's animal-wrangler was crestfallen. Hawks was compelled to take Howard aside, saying to him, 'I'll make a deal with you . . . I'll give up the horses, but for God's sake, Noel, let me have the camels.'[64]

Concluding Thought

In Hollywood's version of the ancient world we see the contemporary world as we imagine it must have been in antiquity. Hollywood's ancient world must seem ancient but be modern. In creating this illusion, the world of the American epic movie becomes a model for modern American attitudes. The Hollywood marketing processes which sold twentieth-century America its concept of antiquity embraced this idea with verve and vigour. Ancient history was shaped to fit the needs of the time – this explains why, for instance, the 1959 version of *Ben-Hur* focuses on the unity of Jews and Arabs while the 1925 version omits this altogether. In 1925 the state of Israel did not exist and no politics could be linked to the portrayal of a Jewish hero.

To conclude this chapter, let us note one more piece of epic marketing (see Figure 1.36): it is a display advertisement for *The Egyptian* printed in the *New York Times* on 22 August 1954. The advert, while foregrounding the design concept in elegant pictorial form (highlighting that the film is in CinemaScope and stereophonic sound), is nonetheless text-heavy and promotes the rhetoric of research as the major marketing tool:

> What was life like 33 centuries ago in the 18th Dynasty when pagan Egypt flowered as the centre of civilisation? Why did Sinuhe, the learned Egyptian physician, who tells the story, believe that he would live eternally in mankind? Why was Akhnaton, Mighty Pharaoh, King of Upper and Lower Egypt, the first wise man in history to leave his throne because of monotheistic beliefs? What did the Queen of Cities – Thebes of the Hundred Gates – look like? These and hundreds of other baffling questions had to be answered before a camera turned on this truly trail-blazing film about a civilisation . . . 1500 years before the birth of Christ. After three years of painstaking research in Egyptology, Producer Darryl F. Zanuck . . . now comes a motion picture of exquisite beauty, compelling force, and overwhelming spectacle – 'The Egyptian'.

For cinema-goers the ancient world was one great sweep of time and epic movies often gave shape to history by combining events, adding fictitious episodes, overwriting the past and, as we will go on to see,

Figure 1.36
Selling research: large double-page spread advertising *The Egyptian* (1954). Pressbook.

emphasising the material authenticity of sets, costumes and props. Precise facts were of little interest; what was of vital importance though was the *illusion* of facts.

Notes

1. Brown (2016: 201).
2. See Matthijs and Pomerance (2006).
3. Thorpe (1939: 28).
4. Thorpe (1939: 29).
5. Wood (1975: 169).
6. Blanshard and Shahabudin (2011: 11).
7. Reviews of the period usually offer caustic (if amusing) takes on the epics which are not necessarily typical of public taste. Take, for example, Dilys Powell's very sharp but comic anti-epic list, 'Scripture Prizes 1932–61', published in the *Sunday Times* in 1961:

    Most Vulgar: THE SIGN OF THE CROSS
    Most Nauseating: QUO VADIS
    Most Exhausting: THE TEN COMMANDMENTS
    Most Nondescript: THE ROBE
    Most Luxurious Blood-Baths: SAMSON AND DELILAH
    Most Idiotic Dialogue: THE BIG FISHERMAN
    Most Genteel Orgy: SOLOMON AND SHEBA
    Special Chariot Race Award: BEN-HUR

    Richards (2008: 54) suggests that there existed among professional critics 'a middle-class puritan distaste for excess'.
8. Martin (2000: 106).
9. Martin (2000: 107).
10. Solomon (2016: 771).
11. Butsch (2001: 119).
12. On the diversity of cinema buildings and cinema-going experiences see Hark (2002) and Wallen (2002).
13. Rambusch (1930: 2). See also Kinerk (1998).
14. Fischer (2003: 187).
15. See further Naylor (1988); Grey (2011).
16. Thorpe (1939: 36–7).
17. Fischer (2003: 187).
18. For an overview of Egyptian-inspired cinema architecture, see Curl (2005: 380–9). More generally on modern Egyptomania see Huckvale (2012).
19. Karnes (1986: 560).
20. Almost a year after its Los Angeles release, the *New York Times*, 22 January 1928, reported on the London opening of *The King of Kings*:

    [I t is] worth recording the reception that London has given to *The King of Kings* . . . It was shown first at the Royal Opera House, Covent Garden . . . The exhibition of this picture has provoked heated and widespread controversy . . . [and] the interest taken in the film is proved by the fact that *The London Times* devoted its principal editorial article to a discussion of it on the morning after its exhibition and that correspondence on the subject still continues.

21. *New York Times*, 22 December 1949: 'LAVISH DEMILLE FILM ARRIVES; *Samson and Delilah* Has Its Premiere at Two Theatres, Rivoli and Paramount.' Other premieres were less circumspect: when *Salome* opened at New York's Rivoli Theatre, crowds were so dense and so desperate to see its star, Rita Hayworth, that they came close to rioting. As the *New York Times* (25 March 1953) reported: 'It was a miracle . . . that no one – especially Miss Hayworth – was hurt in the crush . . . Honoured guests were pushed into the lobby of the theatre and held there before police were able to check the excited crowd.'
22. Kamp (2000: 273).
23. On New York advertising in the 1950s and 1960s see Vargas-Cooper (2010).
24. *Independent Film Journal*, 44 (10), 31 October 1959. Special edition on *Solomon and Sheba*.
25. Cited in Chrissochoidis (2013: 81).
26. For an overview of the film see Solomon (2001: 187–9) and Richards (2008: 130–2).
27. As cited in Hall (2002: 177).
28. Balio (1993: 168).
29. For her part, Joan Collins was less than impressed by *Esther and the King*: 'It was full of pseudo-Biblical, banal, Hollywood dialogue . . . It really was crap,' she recalled candidly in her autobiography. See Collins (1979: 189).
30. On the Maidenform bra advertising campaigns of the 1960s see Vargas-Cooper (2010: 49).
31. See Holston (2013).
32. Quoted in Rebello and Allen (1988: 13).
33. Quoted in Rebello and Allen (1988: 47).
34. For a full discussion of poster sizes and terminology see Rebello and Allen (1988: 37–45) and Bassoff (2000: 19–21).
35. Rebello and Allen (1988: 44).
36. *El Cid* of 1961 (dir. Mann) was marketed in the same way, with huge stone lettering spelling out the protagonist's name. See Bassoff (2000: 98–9).
37. According to www.taglineguru.com a poll of the Top 100 American Movie Taglines placed *Alien* (1979) at the pinnacle of their list: *In space, no one can hear you scream*. The website based its results upon four criteria: suitability, creativity, originality and memorability.
38. See comments and discussion by Marich (2005: 28–33).
39. See especially Kernan (2004) for the history of the movie trailer in America, although little attention is paid to the epic trailer per se.
40. Kernan (2004: 5–6).
41. Gunning (1990: 57).
42. *Milwaukee Journal*, 27 November 1921.
43. On the marketing of the 1959 *Ben-Hur* see Solomon (2016: 766–74).
44. Staiger (1985: 99).
45. An incident blew up after the shooting of the baby in the basket sequence when DeMille and Henry Wilcoxon noticed, on viewing the rushes, that baby Moses' nappy pin could be seen. Too late to reshoot the sequence, the scene was released in VistaVision and 'safety pin' letters began to flood into Paramount from disgruntled fans. See Wilcoxon (1991: 313–15).
46. Following DeMille's precedent, other examples followed:

    Opening titles for *The Greatest Stories Ever Told*:
    Based on the Books of the Old and New Testaments, other ancient writings, the book 'The Greatest Story Ever Told' by Fulton Oursler and Writings by Henry Denker.

Opening titles for *Cleopatra* (1963):
Based upon histories by Plutarch, Suetonius, Appian, and other ancient
sources and 'The Life and Times of Cleopatra' by C. M. Franzero.
The British movie *Carry on Cleo* (dir. Thomas, 1964) parodied the trend:
'. . . from an original idea by William Shakespeare'.

47. In Noerdlinger (1956: iii).
48. DeMille (1960: 105).
49. A committed Christian, DeMille read the Bible on a daily basis and delighted
    in inviting cardinals, bishops and rabbis onto his sets in order to debate
    some theological point. Billy Graham once confessed to David Frost that
    DeMille was a great Bible student who once corrected his scriptural error
    regarding *The Ten Commandments*. See Frost (1997: 137). A good study of
    DeMille's Christian faith is provided by Forshey (1992).
50. Server (1987: 28).
51. DeMille (1960: 106). DeMille's usual methodology was to have an artist
    sketch and even paint scenes in advance of shooting; all the historical
    components of the scene had to be included within the sketch and the final
    shot.
52. DeMille wrote of him: 'Noerdlinger has been the most thorough and accu-
    rate research consultant I have ever had, making himself as much at home
    among the pyramids of the Pharaohs as in the tinsel and spun-candy world
    of the circus' (cited in DeMille 1960: 360). In the publicity brochure DeMille
    proudly notes that 'Mr Noerdlinger drew upon a lifetime of exploration into
    archaeology, history and writings on antiquity to provide a solid foundation
    of facts for the work of the screen writers, costume and set designers, etc.'
53. Forshey (1992: 136).
54. Noerdlinger (1956: 2–3). On *The Ten Commandments* see also Solomon (2001:
    142–58) and (Orrison 1999). In spite of (or because of) its spectacle, not all
    reviews of the film were favourable. *The Weekly Variety*, 10 October 1956,
    noted: 'Emphasis on physical dimension has rendered neither awesome
    nor profound the story of Moses. The eyes of the onlooker are filled with
    spectacle. Emotional tug is sometimes lacking.'
55. Eyman (2010: 440). After DeMille's death a story went around Hollywood:
    'When DeMille reached the pearly gates, Saint Peter shook his head sadly.
    "I'm sorry, Mr DeMille, but your name is not on the list." "Listen, buddy,"
    replied DeMille, "I made you and I can break you"' (cited in Brynner 1989:
    79).
56. Five months earlier *Awake*, the Jehovah's Witness publication, had also listed
    the film's errors. See Forshey (1992: 139).
57. Eyman (2010: 440). For Noerdlinger's discomfort about setting a precise date
    for the setting of *The Ten Commandments* see Birchard (2004: 352).
58. Cited in DeMille (1960: 364).
59. Evidence leaves little doubt that the Philistines came immediately, though
    probably not ultimately, from the Aegean. They were probably one of the
    Sea People who, in the second millennium BCE, uprooted by the collapse
    of the Mycenaean palace civilisation, migrated from the Aegean, via Crete
    and Cyprus, to the Near East. For an interpretation of Philistine culture see
    Coogan (1999: 201–5).
60. *Samson and Delilah* pressbook (1949).
61. Cited in Higham (1973: 289). Toynebee (1889–1975) was a British historian,
    known for his view of the past as a succession of civilisations rather than
    political entities. He published his twelve-volume *A Study of History*, a com-

parative study of twenty-six civilisations in world history, between 1934 and 1961.

62. See comments in Solomon (2001: 25–7).

63. Of course, it should be noted that DeMille was not alone in his commitment towards historical research; note Harris (1996: 42):

> The filmmakers [of *Spartacus* (1960)] showed some desire to know what actually happened, but they had no notion how to find it. [. . .] Meanwhile a research assistant could have gathered all the ancient textual evidence (from Appian, Plutarch, and others) in ten pages. A hundred pages would have given a wealth of historical background. Such a procedure seems unimaginable; yet a vast effort was devoted to creating physical details.

64. McCarthy (1997: 522). See also Combs (1997).

CHAPTER 2

ILLUSION MAKERS: PRODUCTION DESIGN

Like Rome, the sets were not built in a day . . .
   The art, the imagination, the faithfulness to detail . . . that was poured into the making of the movie reflects life as it was in a distant civilisation.
Cleopatra pressbook (1963)

L et's begin this chapter by looking at an image – Figure 2.1. It is a scene from *The Robe*, starring Richard Burton and Victor Mature, both of whom are in the shot. The setting is the hill of Golgotha, outside the walls of Jerusalem; a group of Roman soldiers gamble for the possession of a garment that had belonged to a prisoner, Jesus of Nazareth, now hanging on a cross at the rear of the scene. The sky is grey, the earth is barren; the atmosphere is solemn. Look again at the photograph and fix your eyes on the upper right-hand corner. Something odd is happening: the sky seems to have stopped and is replaced by heavy-duty lights which throw their beams down below. This is part of a studio lighting rig and the moody sky, the hills of Judaea and the walls of the Holy City, it becomes clear, are merely painted scenes on a canvas backdrop stretched taught from a high curtain-track.[1] This painted cyclorama, as it was known, provides the

Figure 2.1
The Hill of Golgotha, outside Jerusalem. A studio set using a vast painted backdrop. Note the lighting rig in the top right-hand corner. *The Robe* (1953). Production shot; never circulated.

illusion of space and depth: 'the cinematic backing . . . is viewed from only one vantage point, the eye of the camera. The backing viewed on a film . . . is a substitution for the real, intending to fool the eye of the audience.'[2] And what then of the earth mound at the front of the scene, the place of the crucifixion? That too, of course, is an illusion. For this is an artificial landscape skilfully created from plaster, wood, canvas and paint effects (see Colour Plate 4).

While all films start with the story, design decisions quickly follow. With the ostensible purpose of serving the narrative, design actually plays a far more crucial and central role in articulating not only the period of an epic film's setting, but acts too as embellishment in its own right, obliging the spectator to read design as an intrinsic necessity of the narrative. In epic films, gigantic sets are used to show the sweep of history and the processes and costs of the film industry (Colour Plate 5). Set designs were an integral aspect of selling movies and, as art director Henry Grace noted, 'Mediocre sets never hurt a good film but good sets often helped a mediocre film.'[3]

Film design, known in the industry as production design or art direction, establishes the overall visual feel and look of a film by creating
the settings, spaces and images which serve as the film's backdrop
and helps to develop narrative structure and support character identities and rationales. Filmmaking is a holistic, collaborative process,
involving hundreds of people, from directors, actors, screenwriters and
cinematographers, and the art directors themselves work alongside an
army of specialist artists and craftspeople to create the architectural
illusions of the film by taking a blank studio sound-stage and turning
that empty space into on-screen reality. In the case of epic movies, art
directors and their team of workers travelled back in time in order to
create a vision of the past which was integral to the story of the film (see
Text Box 2.1).

In Hollywood's Golden Age the art direction of epic movies was as
rigidly controlled as any other part of the studio system. The art department was a male-dominated section of the industry, often employing
a mixture of Americans and European artisans, which, like any other
factory, produced concept sketches, scale models, architectural render-
ings and full-scale sets on a hectic, often gruelling, six-days-a-week
schedule – all under the ever-watchful eyes of the budget-conscious
Studio heads.[4] Strong art directors like Cedric Gibbons, Hans Dreier and
John De Cuir brought together more artists and artisans on the same
projects than any other enterprise in the history of modern American art.
The big studio art departments experienced yearly changes in person-
nel, but most people remained for long periods of time in one studio.
Most art directors stayed with major studios for much of their careers,
helping develop, thereby, distinctive studio styles (Text Box 2.2).[5]

A 1944 *Life Magazine* article celebrated the skills of the art department
as the embodiment of the tension between creativity and manufacturing
which defined Hollywood movies:

> In the fifty years since the motion picture was invented, its technicians
> have turned out ever more convincing series of illusions. This ability
> to make its audiences believe they are looking at the real Sahara or
> a real battle has done much to place Hollywood in its preeminent
> position . . . As a consequence, no group of men is more respected in
> Hollywood than the illusion makers. They must understand lighting
> and electronics and know the crafts of carpentry and plumbing and
> painting. They must be engineers and artists, fully aware of the prob-
> lems of stress and colour and perspective. And finally, they must be
> able to organise quickly, and fairly cheaply, the myriad details which
> go into the manufacture of a German town, an Alaska tundra, or a
> fake submarine. For all these versatile abilities they are very highly
> paid.[6]

It was the ability of the production artists to transcend time and
space that Hollywood exploited with most enthusiasm. A Paramount

Text Box 2.1   Epic *Mise-en-Scène*

Originally a theatre term meaning 'staging' and referring to the spatial arrangement of performers and properties on a stage for a theatrical production, *mise-en-scène* was a term adopted by filmmakers to signify the same practice in the framing of shots. It denotes all of the elements which are included within a frame – set, props, costumes, lighting, actors and, indeed, action too. American filmmakers working within the Hollywood system used *mise-en-scène* to project their own sense of individuality. The *mise-en-scène* could therefore have the potential to determine the specificity of cinematography by allowing individual directors and other types of filmmakers, such as art directors, to develop a particular individual style.

A still from *The Sign of the Cross* (Figure 2.2), for instance, demonstrates DeMille's distinctive form of *mise-en-scène* – a dense packing of the frame, rich in detail; a static tableau-like artifice of such opulence that some might read the composition as 'high camp'. *The Sign of the Cross* is an extraordinary example of a spectacle produced on a budget. Filming began on 24 July 1932 and ended only eight weeks later; DeMille stayed within his $650,000 budget, and the film was ready for release on 30 November. DeMille achieved his customary 'look' of decadence by seducing viewers with images of

Figure 2.2
DeMillian *mise-en-scène* 1: *The Sign of the Cross* (1932). Publicity still shot on set.

sumptuousness (bowls of burning incense, garlanded archways, imposing statuary, burnished pillars, curtained banquet rooms, orgy-friendly couches) and a world that looked
vaster than the one recreated on Paramount's cramped sound-stages. But clutter worked
to the film's advantage. By filling the frame with all sorts of faux classic artefacts – kitsch,
perhaps – DeMille gave audiences a Neronian Rome that conformed to their image of an
age of surfeit without causing him to exceed his budget.

The work of the art director, Mitchell Leisen, served the particular aesthetics DeMille
identified as 'ancient' and demanded in his productions. Indeed, the glossy *Sign of the
Cross* film brochure boasted of how 'Interior settings, duplicates of Nero's famed Palace
of Gold, and of the houses of wealthy patricians, were built in the studios. These were
reproduced with lavish detail.' The same elements are at work in *Cleopatra* in 1934 (Figure
2.3); in this densely packed frame DeMille masterfully retains an undiminished sense of
panache. Space is at a maximum, but the frame does not feel overblown, and through his
skilful use of tableau he creates a far superior and stylish entry into Rome for his Egyptian
queen than Mankowitz managed in 1963.

The massive sets created for the 1925 *Ben-Hur* by Horace Jackson and Arnold Gillespie
and supervised by the talented Cedric Gibbons were certainly in keeping with the MGM
house-style and display a certain aesthetic often associated with a Gibbons design. His
Rome was created on an unbelievable scale and was full of extravagant detail. A breath-
taking chariot race staged in a vast sporting arena was a triumph of MGM design; the set
was adorned with colossal statuary built into the spina (the central area around which
the chariots race – see Figure 2.4) which became a major feature in the publicity for the
movie. When Edward Carfagno and William Hornung came to design the 1959 remake
they self-consciously emulated the 1925 design by echoing the spina sculptures (Figure
2.5) and other architectural elements of the earlier movie, in effect suppressing their own
artistic creativity in order to recreate the *mise-en-scène* of the Niblo film.

Joanna Paul (2013: 151) was perceptive in noting that, 'even whilst remaking an earlier
film, the newer version seeks to replace it, to show that the latest version is the definitive
one,' and indeed technological innovations between the 1925 and 1959 versions, not
least the invention of sound, colour and widescreen, demarcates the fact that in many
respects Wyler's *Ben-Hur* in many ways transcends Niblo's version; nonetheless in terms
of *mise-en-scène*, Hollywood's conservative self-referencing is blatantly apparent. Both
versions of the chariot race employ the same framing techniques and the same key action
points: long shots, crane shots, close-ups of the horses, clashing wheels, chariot smashes,
whipping of drivers, crows shots, lap-indicators and a myriad of shared screen images. As
Gore Vidal (1992: 84) has claimed, 'William Wyler studied not Roman history but other
Roman movies in preparation for *Ben-Hur*.'

Hollywood epics repeat tried and tested visual topoi with regularity. The *mise-en-scène*
of epic movies harken back to popular prototypes – earlier movies, oil paintings and lithographs – in order to provide audiences with not just spectacle, but a comfortable familiar-
ity. Lounging despots devouring grapes on quilted couches, gyrating dancing girls, golden
sphinxes, orgies, asses milk baths, the destruction of temples, gladiators hailing Caesar and
Caesar responding to the accolade by turning down his thumb are some of the many motifs
Hollywood falls back upon in its commitment to create the *mise-en-scène* of antiquity.

Figure 2.3
DeMillian *mise-en-scène* 2: *Cleopatra* (1934). Production still.

Figure 2.4
Ben-Hur (1925). Sets by Horace Jackson and Arnold Gillespie, supervised by Cedric Gibbons. Production still.

Figure 2.5
Ben-Hur (1959). Sets design by Edward Carfagno and William Hornung. Production still. Pressbook.

Text Box 2.2   Notable Epic Art Directors

Ken Adam	*Helen of Troy; Sodom and Gomorrah*
Roland Anderson	*Cleopatra* (1934)
Herman Blumenthal	*Cleopatra* (1963)
Hilyard Brown	*Cleopatra* (1963)
Ben Caré	*The King of Kings*
Edward Carfagno	*Quo Vadis; Ben-Hur* (1959)
Mario Chiari	*The Bible: In the Beginning . . .*
George W. Davis	*David and Bathsheba; The Robe; The Egyptian*
Richard Day	*Solomon and Sheba*
Hans Dreier	*Cleopatra* (1934); *Samson and Delilah*
Randall Duell	*The Prodigal*
John de Cuir	*Cleopatra* (1963); *The Big Fisherman*
Ferdinand Earle	*Ben-Hur* (1959)
Cedric Gibbons	*Ben-Hur* (1925); *Quo Vadis; Julius Caesar*
Buddy Gillespie	*Ben-Hur* (1925); *Ben-Hur* (1959)
Harold Grieve	*Ben-Hur* (1925)
Anton Grot	*The King of Kings; Noah's Ark*
William Horning	*Quo Vadis; Ben-Hur* (1959)
Paul Iribe	*The Ten Commandments* (1923); *The King of Kings*
Edward Jewell	*The King of Kings*
Mitchell Leisen	*The King of Kings; The Sign of the Cross*
Boris Leven	*The Silver Chalice*
Albert Nozaki	*The Ten Commandments* (1956)
Eric Orbom	*Spartacus*
Hal Pereira	*The Ten Commandments* (1956)
Walter Tyler	*Samson and Delilah; The Ten Commandments* (1956)
Lyle Wheeler	*The Robe; The Egyptian; Demetrius and the Gladiators; The Story of Ruth*

advertisement of 5 February 1921, for instance, boasted under the head-line 'East, West, Paramount's Best', that:

> Whatever objects are needed in a Paramount Picture to evoke the right dramatic atmosphere, those objects are sought and photographed, even if they are continents apart – the Sphinx of the Egyptian Desert, the queer architecture of ancient China, the landmarks of modern Europe, the great airships that ride the sky . . . East or West, all that's best!

The big movie studios took pride in their ephemeral architecture and used the sets as selling points; the souvenir brochure of *The Ten*

Figure 2.6
Plate from a family bible, c.1920 taken from *Israel in Egypt* by Sir Edward John Poynter. The popular painting depicts dozens of Israelite slaves pulling a sculpture of a lion and is set against a composite Egyptian background which includes (a-historically) temples, villas and pyramids. Poynter became interested in Oriental themes very early in his career and *Israel in Egypt* can be considered his first major success. The piece took him three years to complete, and in 1867 it was exhibited at the Royal Academy in London.

Commandments (1923), for instance, pronounced: 'Splendor in Staging! Brilliance of Setting! You experienced fans have actually come to take these for granted in every Paramount Picture where the story requires them.' 'This shows', notes Juan Ramírez in his careful study of the history of film architecture, that on occasion, 'movie architecture could attain nearly the same level of adulation as did the studios' notoriously mythologised stars.'[7]

Victorian art and Its Hollywood Legacy

Hollywood's penchant for the grandiose vision of antiquity was anticipated by the late nineteenth-century Royal Academy painters Edwin Long, Lawrence Alma-Tadema, Frederic Leighton, Edward Poynter and John William Godward, as well as the more flamboyantly sensual French artists Jean-Louis Gérôme, Eugène Delacroix and Gustave Moreau– all of whom spiced up ancient history, cleaned it of dirt and overlaid it with a Victorian love of fussy detail and, importantly, brought to their works a fascination for new archaeological finds which they enthusiastically embedded into their painted canvases (Figure 2.6).[8] The ancient world as conceived by these nineteenth-century artists was lavish – far grander than the antiquity of actuality – and early filmmakers such as D. W. Griffith and Cecil B. DeMille, familiar with these works, especially through the popular prints and lithographs published in newspapers and magazines and in illustrated bibles which were popular in the home, capitalised on the look of antiquity which the artists conjured in paint.

The legacy of these 'widescreen painters' on Hollywood epic film-making is vividly clear and, in effect, it is not too glib to state that Victorian artists created the successful stereotypes of how the ancient world would look for the next one hundred and twenty years. When it came to undertaking research for *Gladiator* (2000), for instance, Ridley Scott is noted as saying that, 'The best references on any period in history, of course, are its painters. So before we shot, I started to look at the Napoleonic painters and other artists.'[9]

One of the most sought-after picture books in American homes of the early twentieth century was *The Family Illustrated Bible* with engravings by the French artist Gustave Doré (from original drawings he had created in 1865) which was first produced in 1870s and was still selling widely in America in the 1940s. Doré was much admired for the way in which he used research – photographs of the Holy Land, archaeological collections in the Louvre – together with psychological realism in his portraits of the heroes of the Bible mixed with, unquestionably, a distinct flair for theatricality (Figure 2.7).[10] The art critic Arthur Miller once wrote that Doré's work had 'made an indelible impression' on Cecil B. DeMille, noting that, 'he will tell you that Doré is his favourite artist. Perhaps DeMille is the reincarnation of his idol, come back to a second and even greater earthly success.'[11] Charles Higham too notes the artist's hold on the young DeMille and that his favourite book as a child had been the 1891 edition of Doré's *Bible Gallery*, a collection of illustrated scripture stories including such classics as 'Ruth and Boaz', 'The Judgement of Solomon', 'The Sermon on the Mount' and 'The Prodigal Son'.[12] Doré's impact on the visual aesthetics of DeMille's version of antiquity is clear to see and it goes a considerable way towards accounting for DeMille's lifelong devotion to theatrical tableaux which were not just a product of his early silent-era films but even of his mature widescreen works (Figure 2.8).[13]

The legitimate stage also took its inspiration from the popular paintings of the nineteenth century and the vogue for ancient-world spectacles, and theatre designers of the Edwardian age were praised for their approximations of artists' works. A review of a popular stage-play, *Joseph and his Brethren* of 1913, for instance, raved that 'every scene was like a composition by an old master ... And by relying entirely on artistic painting, fine stage perspective and fine lighting, Gates and Morange (the scene-painters) produced [a] ... convincing illusion.'[14] The link between theatre set-designs and those adopted by early filmmakers are clear to see, so much so in fact that enthusiastic stage reviews might well be referring to cinematic portrayals. Take, for instance, this review of the design of the stage-drama *The Life and Principate of the Emperor Nero* (1906):

> The beauty and magnificence of the scenes was overpowering, the luxurious life of the Roman Emperors being brought before us in all its lavish splendour. The stately palace, finely painted by Mr Joseph

Figure 2.7
Print from *The Family Illustrated Bible* (1890s) by Gustave Doré showing Moses and the tablets of the law.

> Harker, which formed the background for the first and second acts . . .
> may be briefly mentioned as examples of what our scenic artists can
> do when given full scope . . . Archaeological accuracy . . . introduced
> in a scene of Roman revelry . . . beggared description . . . by the sump-
> tuous liberality of its arrangement.[15]

It is the artistry and 'archaeology' of the scene designs which draws the
attention, and in this respect there are clear reflections in the subsequent
reception of film sets.[16]

Figure 2.8
Realising a childhood dream: DeMille's vision of Moses (Charlton Heston) based on the artwork of Doré. *The Ten Commandments* (1956). Staged production shot.

In Griffith's epic masterpiece *Intolerance*, the pictorial traditions of academic history paintings are used to good effect, most prominently in the designs of the Babylonian story's scene of the 'Marriage Market' (Figure 2.9), a setting conscientiously created from the popular 1875 oil painting by Edwin Long (based on a passage from Herodotus' *Histories* 1.196), which was widely distributed in printed media into the 1930s (Figure 2.10).[17] Bernard Hanson's carefully considered examination of the visual sources for *Intolerance* revels that not only was Griffith faithful in reproducing the details of the painting, 'the slave block, the

Figure 2.9
The Babylonian Marriage Market as depicted in *Intolerance* (1916). Production still.

auctioneer's stance, the metal gate, the gestures, the costumes, and even
the expression on the faces of the waiting women', but he even took
his audience through the process of looking at the painting. Griffith,
through a complicated edit of sixty shots, 'lyrically and humorously
transformed [history] through the looking-glass of nineteenth-century
painting into the reality of the magic world of the movies.'[18]

There is nothing technically naive about the crafting of this film and
Griffith's use of the camera is astounding. He loves miniature detail, and
his camera dwells in close-up on actors' eyes, hands and detailed, well-
chosen props and costumes. Nothing, it appears, is left to chance; every
shot is meticulously thought through and expertly designed – although
we know surprisingly little about the production design process of the
film per se (we know that Frank Wortman and Walter L. Hall designed

Figure 2.10
The Babylonian Marriage Market by Sir Edwin Long (1875) was turned into a very popular
print and was readily available for inexpensive purchase.

the sets, although they are not credited in the film).[19] But Griffith's skill is
in utilising the full potential of the camera, and from the micro-detail of
the close-up, he expands his vision to flood the screen with armies (quite
literally) of movement. The scene of the bacchanal that is Belshazzar's
feast, set in the courtyard of the Babylonian temple of Ishtar (Figure
2.11), begins with a high-perched long-shot of the vast, multi-levelled
set, packed to overflowing with costumed extras. The camera sweeps
down to ground level to watch the gyrations of the scantily clad priestesses of the goddess, before ascending again in one smooth swoosh to
take us high up onto the balconies and rooftops of the temple. To get this
shot, Griffith placed his camera on an elevator platform on tracks, a sort
of pre-cursor to the crane. It is an extraordinary moment.

The design of the great courtyard, one of the most famous sets in film
history, incorporates many elements of ancient Near Eastern design,
although they are drawn from a variety of mismatched sources: the
staircases on the sides and the centre of the courtyard are duplicated
from the staircases of the palace of Darius the Great at Persepolis; lion
images, a common Babylonian motif, decorate the balustrades; eagle-
headed winged servants drawn from Assyrian reliefs appear on the
massive pillars and a tree of life and numerous rosettes and palmettes
compete for space on the archways at the rear of the set. A huge statue
of the goddess Ishtar nursing a child is placed between the columns of
the right-hand side of the courtyard complex. Huge elephant figures
surmount each column – a major historical discrepancy demanded by
Griffith who borrowed the inspiration from the set of the Italian film

Figure 2.11
Epic vastness: Belshazzar's feast in the courtyard of the temple of Ishtar. *Intolerance* (1916).
Production still.

Cabiria. This kind of generic 'ancient Near Eastern' architectural eclecti-
cism, together with the elephant-topped columns, may belie Griffith's
claims of 'authenticity', but for most audiences *Intolerance*, with its
technical brilliance, afforded the perfect 'living' representation of that
wicked, doomed city of Babylon familiar to them from their (static)
picture bibles. Marcus Becker is correct to emphasise that:

> It may be inferred that the appeal of early film recreations of ancient
> worlds depended not only on pictorial or dramatic elements which
> can be traced back to the practices of history painting or theatre but
> to perceptual modernity ... The discontinuity of camera glances with
> which the audience was confronted, and the rapidly shifting temporal
> accessibility of cinematic images, contributed to a radically new repre-
> sentation of ancient worlds at the beginning of the twentieth century.[20]

It is clear that the nineteenth century paintings of ancient life, coupled with
flamboyant stage designs, heralded the way for the filmic recreations of
the twentieth century. But in a conceit typical of Hollywood filmmakers,
many directors employed artists to recreate scenes from their movies on
painted canvas in a kind of postmodern homage to the origins of cinema.
Pressbooks frequently advertised set reproductions of painted artworks

which could be used to adorn cinema lobbies and we have noted already the dependency on the painted image in poster advertising.

DeMille, we have seen, frequently exploited the talents of artists for his publicity campaigns and worked closely with the painter Dan S. Groesbeck for many years in perfecting the colourful, pageantry-filled Doré-inspired visions for his films. A visitor to DeMille's office at Paramount Studios in the 1930s or 1940s would have found the walls covered with Groesbeck sketches. DeMille had discovered the artist's remarkable talent for 'visualising' a dramatic scene and setting it down in detailed sketches and drawings while working on his 1923 version of *The Ten Commandments* and from 1926 DeMille used Groesbeck's sketches of sets, costumes and characters for all of his biblical and historical films, including *King of Kings* and *Samson and Delilah*, in which Groesbeck's vision had been particularly influential. But Groesbeck's death in 1950 left DeMille looking for a new concept artist in order to undertake work on the remake of *The Ten Commandments*; on the recommendation of fine-art publicist Herman Stolpe in 1954 DeMille contracted Arnold Friberg as chief production artist for the movie.

Friberg was based in Salt Lake City and was working on an illustrated version of the Book of Mormon when Hollywood beckoned. On hearing the call, Friberg gladly dropped the Mormon art project for the time being, not least because, like DeMille, he had always been inspired by Gustave Doré and the works of Alma-Tadema, who had painted ancient Greek and Roman scenes with uncanny realism and a sense of authenticity. The kind of realism offered by these sources (and demanded by cinema work) was welcomed by Friberg who had always scorned modern art, saying in 1954:

> I have plenty of enemies . . . among artists who resent my earning a living. They think I should go off and starve while painting something 'significant'. I am doing what I want to do – painting pictures people want and understand. I have no burning ambition to create the kind of 'art' which the confused critics praise for its 'plastic significance', 'fluid lines', and 'inner awareness', or (heaven forbid) 'must be understood on three levels.'[21]

He completed fifteen major paintings for the film, and Paramount showcased them in an exhibit that toured the world (Colour Plate 6). The exhibit included Friberg's twelve portraits of the movie's stars and many sketches in pencil, watercolour and oils. The full-colour souvenir brochure produced for the release of the *Ten Commandments* was completely given over to reproductions of Friberg's paintings and sketches and in which the artist was praised for 'combining rare artistic skill with a profound respect for the most minute historical details' (see Text Box 2.3). In later life, Friberg emphasised that these were not paintings made from the motion picture, but rather, the movie took its artistic direction from the paintings.[22]

Text Box 2.3 *Paramount News:* **Arnold Friberg and** *The Ten Commandments*

For the first time in motion picture history, the entire pictorial content of a souvenir programme for a film will be a treasure of the finest colour reproductions of original paintings executed for the purpose by a great artist.

This was revealed today with the announcement that Arnold Friberg, the noted religious artist and illustrator of Salt Lake City, has been signed to provide the entire programme for Cecil B. DeMille's production of 'The Ten Commandments.'

Friberg will design the book itself and will execute more than a dozen major oil paintings for full-page and double-spread reproductions of such spiritually far-reaching events as the giving of the Ten Commandments to Moses on Mount Sinai; the first Passover; the halting of the Hosts of Pharaoh by the Pillar of Fire, and the Parting of the Red Sea. Similar reproductions will be made of others of his paintings of scenes in the film and of character studies.

This booklet of art treasures, an innovation created for 'The Ten Commandments', directly evolved from Friberg's work on the picture for well over a period of two years of pre-production and actual shooting.

Friberg, working directly with DeMille during this period, executed scores of oil paintings and sketches as advance visualisations of Biblical scenes, created studies of the major characters before casting began and additionally designed many of the costumes for Charlton Heston as Moses, Yul Brynner as Ramses II, Sir Cedric Hardwicke as Sethi the Just, Vincent Price as Pharaoh's master builder and others.

Friberg, commissioned by David O. McKay, president of the Church of Jesus Christ of Latter-Day Saints, to execute a series of paintings illustrating the Book of Mormon, was given a sabbatical to fulfil his work for the film and to execute the programme because of the importance as a world influence for good placed on the motion picture, 'The Ten Commandments', by church leaders. Though Friberg has far from completed his work on The Book of Mormon, his earlier paintings when reproduced as magazine inserts won for him two successive years the award from the Lithographers' National Association for the finest inserts of the year.

As a child in Phoenix, Arizona, Arnold Friberg demonstrated exceptional artistic talent before school age. He later attended the Chicago Academy of Fine Arts, and was highly successful in the related fields of commercial art – calendars, book design, illustration, etc. – in such centres as Chicago, San Francisco and New York.

However, inspired by Cecil B. DeMille's earlier production of 'The Ten Commandments', and later through other DeMille Biblical screen subjects,

Friberg's ambition for many years had been to devote himself entirely to painting Biblical subjects.

When he completes his present work for the forthcoming epic dramatisation of the life of Moses, he will resume work on his paintings for the Book of Mormon, and hopes when this work is finished, to devote the next ten years or more illustrating the entire Bible.

'The Ten Commandments' is regarded as the peak achievement of DeMille's long career. The Paramount film is in VistaVision and Technicolor.

Paramount News: a news items released to Paramount Picture employees, 1955.

Sets as Embellishment

We have seen that the visualisation of the 'real world' of the ancient past was a major marketing feature for the Hollywood studios and that advanced publicity often lauded art direction as the most expressive financial and narrative aspects of production. *Ben-Hur* was pre-sold on the thrill of the chariot race track and the spectacle of the vast stadium in which it was staged; *Samson and Delilah* was marketed to audiences who knew the temple of wicked Dagon would collapse at the movie's climax; *Land of the Pharoahs* promised audiences that, somewhere, there would be pyramids and tombs, while those watching *The Last Days of Pompeii* knew there would be a volcano and countless falling pillars.

Part of the marketability of the epic was the guarantee that the film would incorporate multiple sets and locales (see Text Box 2.4). In epic movies there are frequent changes of setting, more so than in some other film genres and significantly so than the one or two sets seen in stage-plays. An epic's art director had to be selective in deciding what sets to build, depending on how long and how much of it would be seen on screen and upon the action that was called for by the script. While epics liked to promote the image of the construction of mammoth-sized sets, in reality extremely small fragments of sets were often constructed, suggesting vast scale and limitless space. A studio-promoted image showing DeMille hard at work shooting a scene of *Cleopatra* neatly demonstrates this conceit (Figure 2.12): the setting of Cleopatra's Tiber-side villa occupies only a corner of the sound-studio, where a raised platform, a few strategically placed pillars, and swathes of draped satin are all the details needed to create the illusion of opulence and scale (Figure 2.13). Conversely, a huge setting might function for only a matter of minutes on screen. The vast golden throne room, with its enormous statue of the falcon-god Horus, makes only two fleeting cameo appearances in the Mankiewicz *Cleopatra*, but satisfied the audience expectation for lavishness and size which the marketing of the movie had long heralded (Figure 2.14).

Text Box 2.4   Setting the Scene

Scripts frequently contain descriptions and visualisations of the sets and the action which would be encountered during the filming process. Art directors were required to keep abreast of developments in the scriptwriting process and note and respond to the changes of locale, new settings or deleted scenes as the production developed. Drafts of scripts sometimes show how faithfully the art director responds to the screenwriter's vision, although others inform us of how changes to the script necessitated changes to the design.

The Sign of the Cross (1932)

Scene A-1

FULL SHOT – FIRE SET

The set consists of a stone ledge, or platform, jutting out from a blank wall. At the right, and down a few steps from the ledge, is another platform. At the extreme left the wall ends, just inside the frame line. Through that aperture may be seen a limited vista of burning Rome in the distance.

Over the scene plays the flickering light of a fire in the city below.

As the dissolve comes through, the roar of the flames subsides somewhat while the accompanying music on the lyre comes up into fuller volume.

Sound: (Music on lyre, heard over faint roar of flames)

On the upper ledge, seated on a great chair, or throne, is Nero, Sixth of the Caesars, Emperor of Rome. He holds a lyre on his knee and plays wildly on it as he looks past camera, out of scene, upon the burning city below.

On a lower platform [*sic*] at the right is a group of his courtiers, standing in awed silence.

Cleopatra (1934)

Sequence C-1

BOOM SHOT – ATRIUM CAESAR'S HOUSE – ROME

The angle is down from the BOOM, as the scene FADES IN, taking in a FULL VIEW of the atrium. This is a magnificent court, paved with mosaics, flanked by four Corinthian columns, upholding the roof around a wide light-well. Under the light-well is a fountain, with bronze Tritons and dancing nymphs shooting jets of water into a white marble basin, in which grow luxurious water plants. The doorways around the atrium are closed by rich, heavy curtains.

An afternoon party, of an informal character, is in progress. Some thirty or forty guests, men and women, of the Roman patrician class, are standing chatting in groups about the atrium. A small string orchestra of the period is playing in one corner.

Cleopatra (1934)

Scene C-24

BOOM SHOT – BATHS – (NIGHT)

THE BOOM TAKES IN A FAIRLY FULL SHOT of the baths, showing dimly through the steam and general activities.

Sound: (Splashing, etc.)

THE BOOM MAKES A QUICK SPECTACULAR SWING, PICKING UP different portions of the bath and GOING ON, IMMEDIATELY. There are fat men, their midriffs encased in Turkish towels, sitting on the steam bench. There are thin, effeminate youths, shrieking coyly as they dip into the cold tank, there are slaves rubbing and slapping fat bankers lying face downward on tables – a swift, panoramic view.

Quo Vadis (1951)

Scene 16 [early draft of a script, later substantially altered]

Antium – An enormous tent is erected on the beach.

The Emperor Nero sits, fanned by Nubians, in front of the model of a city.

Tigellinus is beside him, and the freedman Phaon with dividers and triangles explains the model, its street, its blocks, its bridges, its squares and forums.

It is the model of a new Rome.

And Nero looks as it through his emerald, drinking in the words of the Architect, who creates before his delighted eyes the new city, with new temples, new palaces, new circuses . . . NERONIS it is to be called.

There is a certain glint in Nero's eyes as he hears the names spoken for the first time . . . !

The new Rome on the old seven hills . . .

Phaon: A new city. To be raised – with your consent – from new foundations; and to be called Neropolis – with your permission. Here will be the Forum – vast and majestic and open to the sun- with a Temple of Jupiter facing the temple of that unworthy deity from [whom] the city wall derives its name. And here at the centre, a colossal statue of the same humble individual – unless of course my Lord prefers some other arrangement – unless of course my Lord prefers some other arrangement. Ten proud bridges, conveniently linking the various quarters – or perhaps my Lord would rather have an even dozen. The new Via Sacra, running from the Imperial Gardens straight across to a new Circus Maximus – worthy I think to be called The (Colosseum). But of course any of this can be changed about as the Arbiter may direct . . . And be good enough to notice – temples, palaces, treasuries, theatres, bridges, monuments . . .

Figure 2.12
Creating the illusion: studio publicity shot of DeMille directing a scene from *Cleopatra*
(1934).

In general, Hollywood's art directors presented a very conform-
ist vision of the ancient world. Epic art direction did not take risks.
Hollywood's coordinated conception of epic settings was clearly a
function of finance, because the studio heads believed that big budget
films could not risk challenging popular notions of ancient life with
revisionist (or even overly accurate) visual depictions of the ancient
world as foreign, or perilous, or savage, or even dirty. Movie-goers had
a preconceived idea of what Rome or Egypt was *supposed* to look like,
and any film that seriously challenged these traditional preconceptions
was not likely to gain popular acceptance or do well at the box office
(see below).[23]

Figure 2.13
On-screen illusion: the set in Figure 2.12 as it appears in *Cleopatra* (1934). Production still.

Figure 2.14
Joe Mankiewicz directs the scene of Cleopatra's coronation, 1962. Candid shot.

The 1954 film *The Silver Chalice*, set in late first century CE Syria and Judaea radically altered the standard epic design formula. Dealing more usually with gangster flicks and musicals, the producer, Victor Saville, had never created a religious epic, nor had he worked CinemaScope, but he was determined to try a new approach to filmmaking. Instead of having the standard elaborately realistic settings of the standard epic, he hired theatrical designers Boris Leven and Rolf Gerard to create dramatically stylised sets (Colour Plate 7), pronouncing that:

> It has long been my contention that colour has been used indiscriminately in the film industry. There have been tremendous splashes of colour in the backgrounds, often to the detriment of the principal characters in the scene and in the long-run, the film. In the CinemaScope and WarnerColor production of *The Silver Chalice* the action centres in three settings during an era of unprecedented sumptuousness of colour . . . In the first scenes our sets are austere and everything is in white marble . . . an all-white marble background of stylised constriction. In the second . . . we use gold background sets entirely. In the third . . . we use heavy red, gold, and black.[24]

Although the pressbook publicised that these were the 'largest sets ever built' – 'four acres on the back lot were the sites for setting representing the wicked city of the Near East, the Court of Petitioners on the Tiber, a bacchanalian banquet hall, the Pagan Pavilion and the Golden city' – the film's avant-garde employment of colour and lighting, together with the strange surreal and impressionistic sets designed by Boris Leven (coupled with a poor script) did nothing to help the film's box-office takings. Otis Guernsey of the *New York Herald Tribune* described the sets as looking 'like a little theatre production of *Quo Vadis*' (although a review in *Fortnight* called them 'remarkable').[25] *The Silver Chalice* was an unmitigated flop.[25] A more recent reviewer has noted that:

> Boris Leven's sets are distractingly weird. Huge interior rooms (what's holding up all those ceilings?) have featureless walls and oversized doors. Exterior sets are built full-scale but look like cardboard cut-outs, reminding us of Leven's purposely artificial designs in [1953's] *Invaders from Mars*. The matte paintings and backdrops are like something out of Dr. Seuss. The rooftops of Jerusalem could be from a UPA cartoon; Basil's view of a field of crucified Christians is a complete abstraction. Something is amiss with the entire design scheme – many scenes look like raw conceptual storyboards.[27]

In a similar vein, Paul Roen judged the film as:

> an exercise in wretched excess, particularly when the scene shifts to the court of the emperor . . . Turquoise-skinned kootch-dancers, clad in bright yellow, twirl around and wave their asses at the camera like

a bunch of chorus girls from Las Vegas . . . The emperor is tempted
with tray after tray of gold plated delicacies ('Aged grasshoppers,
fried in honey to a light, golden-brown').[28]

Foster Hirsch sees things differently, recognising *The Silver Chalice* as an
'experimental Hollywood epic' in which the 'sense of ancient architecture is fanciful yet informed, and the film is enhanced by its delicate use
of colour and strong contrasts between black and white.' He compares
Leven's designs favourably alongside the elegant designs created by
William Cameron Menzies for Douglas Fairbanks' production of *The
Thief of Bagdad* (dir. Walsh, 1924), and notes correctly that the 'film's
lyrical design avoids completely the weighty, baroque ornamentation
that is standard for epic subjects.'[29] This though was part of the film's
undoing.

Hollywood's view of the antique world was *based* on historical reality
and was marketed through the rhetoric of historical precision, but
tended, nevertheless, to be glamorised, gilded, gaudy and, ultimately,
contemporary. The immaculate palaces, temples, forecourts, arenas,
barges and marketplaces of the epic milieu, the burnished gold, the
marble, the silks and draperies, the fountains and manicured gardens
look inescapably like the opulent hotels, bars, cafes, shopping malls, of
twentieth-century California or New York. The epic's ancient settings
were always tinged with a contemporary design aesthetic and a heavy
infusion of the costly and the fantastical. Amazed at the visual magnificence of the 1956 *The Ten Commandments*, the movie mogul James
Thurbur exclaimed, 'Jeez, it makes you realise what God could have
done if He'd had the money!'[30]

The dazzling beauty of the epic sets, with their rigorous denial of dirt,
squalor and dreariness suggests a conspiratorial revision of historical
truth on the part of Hollywood (Colour Plate 8). The typical *mise-en-
scène* of the epic film was too elaborate and too systematic to pass off
as an accident, and so the studios' claims of aiming for authenticity
through design can only be seen as hollow lies, or as Maria Wyke puts
it, 'a masquerade'.[31] But ultimately these deceptions helped make the
epic genre the success it was. John Cary goes some way towards explain-
ing the dichotomy: 'If authenticity is brought into our conscious too
laboriously, the drama suffers.'[32] With remarkable foresight, in a 1929
interview the highly esteemed French architect and designer Robert
Mallet-Stevens noted that 'the spectator must find on the screen the
vision of the past to which he is accustomed', anything else would lead
to discomfort and rejection.[33]

Hollywood epics are often alike as peas in a pod. Consider those
made in the 1950s: all are in colour and most are widescreen; all contain
periodic crowd scenes to show off how the budget has been spent; lighting design is consistently bright and high-key to show off the sets. In
short, epics conscientiously mimic one another and in the process they
mould audience expectations and (literally) build our image of a period.

As Charles Tashiro has noted:

> Hollywood has trained us to think of Roman life as occurring in large villas, temples or palaces, thick with Corinthian columns, constructed largely of marble . . . No doubt some people did live in such circumstances, just as some people today inhabit the photographic spaces spread out in the pages of *Architectural Digest*. How typical such a life was, how relevant it is to an understanding of the period, and for that matter, how true it was even for that limited class of people who could enjoy it, is a matter of debate.[34]

If Hollywood publicity agents stated that the panorama of Rome, the arena of the Colosseum, the walls of Troy, the Hanging Gardens of Babylon or Cleopatra's barge were faithful recreations of the originals, then audiences were prepared to go along with them. Studio publicity stressed the academic research that went into the recreation of ancient settings and stressed that what was being witnessed on the screen was authentic. The pressbook for *Solomon and Sheba* highlights that:

> Construction of Solomon's temple posed many problems for the research staff, since many weeks had to be spent searching not only the Bible but also the works of other authorities on the period to establish the exact dimensions mentioned. Translation of Biblical cubits into . . . modern-day inches and feet . . . became a major project which had to be solved before the architectural designers could begin their work... [The final designs] were absolutely authentic and would bring the picture full approval from Biblical scholars and historical experts.

The *David and Bathsheba* pressbook made similar broadcasts:

> The majestic splendour that was Jerusalem during the reign of King David came to life again . . . The walls, towers and palaces that made the capitol city a thing of wonder in Biblical times was rebuilt . . . for David and Bathsheba . . . at a cost of $250,000 . . . Months of preparation kept the lights burning late at the studio while members of the research and art departments worked on the myriad of details which preceded the resurrection of an ancient civilisation . . . Made at the home of Twentieth Century Fox Studios, eight sound stages and large portions of the back lot were utilised. The corridors and main court of David's palace, for instance, boasted eight thirty-foot columns, six feet in diameter . . . Under the directorial hand of Henry King and Chester C. McCrown, a retired international authority on biblical history, archaeology and geography acting as adviser, the largest order of sets in recent film history was assembled. Among them were the walls and gates of Jerusalem, the walls of besieged Rabbah . . . the king's palace, the Tabernacle housing the Ark of the Covenant, and tent encampments of the warring hosts of Israel.

The fact that very few cinema-goers were equipped to judge the accuracy of a period reconstruction means that they accepted that the filmmakers had indeed done their homework and that they were watching well thought-through reconstructions. The further back in time the films were set, the more likely the audience was to accept the visualisation as true because they had no easy frame of reference to draw on. Audiences drew on stereotypes of past cultures to build their on-screen visualisations; they wanted Rome or Egypt to look a certain way and rejected attempts that challenged those expectations.

Cleopatra's Palace: Problems in Historic Set Design

An interesting case study focusing on the problems of locating a historical 'look' for a film can be had through an examination of the production design of Hollywood's three *Cleopatra* films (1917, 1934, 1963) because when it comes to representing the hybrid world that was Ptolemaic Alexandria, where Greek and Egyptian cultures melded and morphed, Hollywood clearly found itself in a dilemma. The art directors of the three films experienced difficulty in visualising a Hellenistic city that – according to historical data – merged traditional and well-known Egyptian architectural motifs with elements of, equally familiar, Greek architecture. What should Hollywood do with a crossbreed culture? Archaeological finds at Alexandria and investigations into the literary sources suggested that the vast palaces of the Ptolemaic monarchy were principally Greek in design and construction although they included notably impressive and often monumental pharaonic structures too. These Egyptian-style structures were either built by the Ptolemies themselves in imitation of ancient building styles or else they were genuine ancient buildings pilfered from their original locations by the Greek-speaking rulers.[35]

On a preliminary viewing, the opening ten minutes of Mankiewicz's *Cleopatra* seem to confirm the publicity announcement that:

> Untold effort has gone into the over-all design of the physical production of *Cleopatra*. The Forum set . . . covered twelve acres and included reconstructions of ten of the original buildings in the Roman Forum. Also built were numerous temples, triumphal arches and palaces. Even larger than the replica of the Forum was the Alexandria set . . . Before the Alexandrian Palace rose in magnificence, three architects and twenty-four designers had been called in to assist [art director] John de Cuir.[36]

The film opens on the bloody spectacle of the aftermath of the Battle of Pharsalus as the bodies of the dead are burned on funeral pyres and then cuts to the first of the movie's many 'spectacle' scenes, the wharf-market and royal palace at Alexandria (Figure 2.15). The establishing panorama shot along the coastline provides the audience with an unrivalled

Figure 2.15
The wharf market and royal palace at Alexandria. Set designed by John De Cuir. *Cleopatra*
(1963). Production shot.

recreation of the ancient city and includes such landmarks as the Pharos
lighthouse. De Cuir had only three months to build the ancient city on
the production's Cinecittà lot, although a previously thwarted attempt
to build the set on locations in England (Figure 2.16) had given him
plenty of time to perfect his designs and consult his research notes. As
De Cuir himself recalls:

> I was on Cleopatra for two years while it was a Walter Wanger pro-
> duction – with sets worth $250,000 already built on the [Pinewood] lot
> – when Elizabeth Taylor came into the project. The film was going to
> be made in London, then they moved to Italy. Robert Mamoulian was
> going to direct – I worked closely with him on the design – but then
> Joseph Mankewicz took over. With a new director, my Rome – Rouben
> Mamoulian's Rome – didn't look at all like the gold and marble Rome
> you see in the finished film. We wanted a realistic Rome, closer to that
> of *The Robe*, earthy in colour and texture.[37]

Regardless of the unwanted glitz and vulgarity of the sets reimagined
by De Cuir (more Caesars Palace, Las Vegas than truly Ptolemaic
Alexandria), the architectural elements nonetheless alert the viewer to

Figure 2.16
The first attempt: De Cuir's original Alexandria set built in the open air of Pinewood
Studios, London is engulfed in freezing mist, drizzle and wind, c.1961. Candid shot.

the fact that the story is set in a bona fide Hellenistic city. The palace
facade looks authentic enough to satisfy the purists; there is certainly
no hiding the fact that its inspiration is Greek for it is embellished with
Doric columns, sculpted pediments and painted metopes. But the set
design neatly incorporates some Egyptian elements too: human headed
sphinxes, a great scarab beetle, a seated statue of Isis, an Egyptian-style
kiosk and, of course, a giant sphinx guarding the entrance to the harbour
itself all help the viewer to locate the Egyptian spin on the otherwise
essentially Hellenic design. Interestingly, recent (underwater) archaeological investigation at Alexandria supports De Cuir's vision; the later
Ptolemies utilised large-scale Egyptian architecture on a more routine
basis than was once supposed. Alexandria, and especially the royal
quarter, would have been an eclectic mixture of Greek and Egyptian
building styles.[38]

However, upon stepping inside the palace, the cinema audience
enters another world; here the Hellenistic elements of the facade give

Figure 2.17
Cleo is rolled out in front of Caesar. The vast inelegant interiors of Cleopatra's Alexandrian
palace employ papyrus-effect wall decorations and a rather clumsy large-scale pharaonic
sculpture. Set design by John De Cuir. *Cleopatra* (1963). Production still.

way to a riot of Egyptianising motifs (although the occasional piece of
classical sculpture is allowed to creep in). Cleopatra's palace is vast; its
throne rooms, reception rooms, dining rooms and private chambers
glisten and gleam with mosaics and alabaster columns. Caesar's massive
guest-chamber, for example, has a highly polished marble floor and a
papyrus-effect wall-mural that depicts a variety of pharaonic religious
scenes more fitting for a New Kingdom tomb or temple than a palace
(Figure 2.17).

The tomb-like decoration of the palace is made even more obvious in
other sets, such as a corridor leading into the queen's apartments which
is decorated with raised golden bas-reliefs, winged pediments and
gilded guardian statues. It is interesting to note how frequently well-
known images of earlier Egyptian artworks are utilised within the set
design to create this image of timeless Egypt: one of Cleopatra's private
chambers, for example, is furnished with chairs and tables modelled
on those found in the tomb of queen Hetepheres of the Egyptian Old
Kingdom,[39] while her barge is hung with expensive 'Grecian' drapes but
also includes copies of the famous black-skinned guardian (or *ka*) statues
discovered in the tomb of Tutankhamun (Figure 2.18).[40]

Elizabeth Ford and Deborah Mitchell have made the pertinent observations that:

Figure 2.18
The usefulness of drapery: on board Cleopatra's barge. *Cleopatra* (1963). Production still.

To us, De Cuir's interiors look futuristic, prescient. Cleopatra's apartments are sparse but opulent, with expanses of open floor and cut-stone wall punctured by hints of deep aqua and pale orange. The camera glides past fabulous objects d'art and critically placed pieces of minimalist furniture. The whole reads more like an anticipation of Dubai than faux Ptolemy. This is a Middle Eastern ethos that modern viewers recognize, a context that helps free the story from its ancient-Egypt-only niche.[41]

With this salient point in mind, the queen's palace bedchamber, therefore, can be read as being more reminiscent of a Napoleonic boudoir than anything that an Egyptian noblewoman would have recognised. The double bed, in which Taylor-Cleopatra romps, dreams, rages and loves, is in itself pure Dorchester Hotel, 1963 (Figure 2.19).[42]

Bedrooms and bathrooms are always points of contention in epic films, the occasion when the reality of the past simply does not satisfy contemporary taste. Ancient homes, even palaces, rarely had dedicated sleeping and bathing spaces and beds, even for Egyptian queens, were simple affairs. With narrow wickerwork frames supporting thinly padded bed-rolls and hard carved wooden headrests, ancient Egyptian beds were intended for sleeping and little else. Taylor-Cleopatra

Figure 2.19
Drapes and stylish bedroom furniture – including a comfortable bed – befitting a
Hollywood queen. Cleopatra's handmaidens take advantage of their mistress's absence.
Studio publicity photograph taken on the *Cleopatra* set, 1962.

demands something more opulent of course: for her a bed is a place
where she makes sensual love to Burton-Antony, or at the least, where
she lies daydreaming about empire in the arms of Caesar. Cleopatra's
bed is therefore appropriately queen-size, lotus-embossed, curtained and
adorned with plump, comfy pillows (Figure 2.20). Semedar's boudoir in
Samson and Delilah shows us that Philistine taste in bedroom decor ran
to canopies, chiffon drapes, a bolster cushion and a springy mattress
(Figure 2.21); she also has a dressing table and a smart upholstered chair,
a feature shared by Cleopatra too (Figure 2.19).

Whatever the story and wherever the locale, in most epic films there
comes an obligatory halt in the plot for a lingering scene in which the
heroine, sometimes the hero, washes and anoints herself in preparation
for a feast, an orgy, or perhaps for some less public pleasure. Taylor-
Cleopatra's marbled bathroom (Figure 2.22) with its leonine water spout
has as its focus a round health-spa-type tub (lacking only in power-
driven water jets); in fact marketing for the movie advertised the sale of
the Cleopatra Whirlpool, Air Tub or Soaking Bathtub. Before the 1920s,
American bathrooms, previously severely utilitarian, took on the gleam
of marble, tile and chrome, and the tactile luxury of fuzzy towels and rugs
thanks largely to the popularity of movie bathroom scenes. The master
of this genre was Cecil B. DeMille who made the bathroom a delightful
resort for leisure and pleasure. By the 1930s, plumbing corporations,
which had never mentioned their wares in public, were taking full-page

Figure 2.20
Relaxing on a queen-size bed: 'There are never enough hours in the days of a queen, and her nights have too many . . .'. Elizabeth Taylor with Rex Harrison. *Cleopatra* (1963). Production still.

Figure 2.21
Stylish 1940s bedroom furniture with Philistine accents. Angela Lansbury and Henry Wilcoxon plot the demise of Victor Mature. *Samson and Delilah* (1949). Production still.

Figure 2.22
The obligatory bath-scene: Cleopatra's jacuzzi; asses milk optional. *Cleopatra* (1963).
Production still.

advertisements in newspapers and magazines displaying bathroom fixtures frankly modelled on DeMillian splendour. In films such as *The Sign
of the Cross*, in which Claudette Colbert's Poppaea luxuriates in a huge
sunken tub filled with ass's milk (Figure 2.23), bathing became an art
form: 'Bathing was shown as a ceremony rather than merely a sanitary
duty. Undressing was not just the removing of clothes, but a progressive
revelation of entrancing beauty, a study in diminishing draperies.'[43]
DeMille's Jazz Age films, including his ancient-world spectaculars, represented increasingly ostentatious and even outré levels of consumption
both as spectacle for visual appropriation and as a showcase that set
fashion trends in interior decorating. Furthermore, in DeMille's pictorial

Figure 2.23
Bathing as an art form. Poppaea's ass's milk bath. *The Sign of the Cross* (1932). Production still.

mise-en-scène the representation of consumer goods such as bathroom fixtures and of Art Deco interior designs signified modernity and were several years ahead of developments in advertising as etiquette manuals for a consumer culture.[44]

This idea of modernity, that the ancient past also contains traces of the fashionable present-day, is a very important element in each of the Cleopatra films: Claudette Colbert's Cleopatra lives in a splendid clean-line Art Deco palace, a masterpiece of screen design by art director Hans Dreier (Figure 2.24), and an *homage* in itself to the Egyptomania that was sweeping through Europe and America in the 1920s and 1930s following the discovery of the tomb of Tutankhamun.[45] Paul Roen describes *Cleopatra* as 'a Depression era extravaganza that begins with a virtual delirium of ancient Egyptian imagery: the opening montage includes idols, pyramids, sphinxes, palm trees and a great stone gate sliding open to reveal a naked woman brandishing a pair or Oriental lamps.'[46] As audiences first gawped in wonder at Cleopatra's vast shining palace and its chic, Manhattan-style Egyptianising fixtures and furnishings, they would have realised that the look was not at all dissimilar to the Art Deco movie theatres in which the film was originally shown.[47] The prototype for the Art Deco throne room can be seen in DeMille's 1923 version of *The Ten Commandments* in which a vast pharaonic sphinx-throne is set

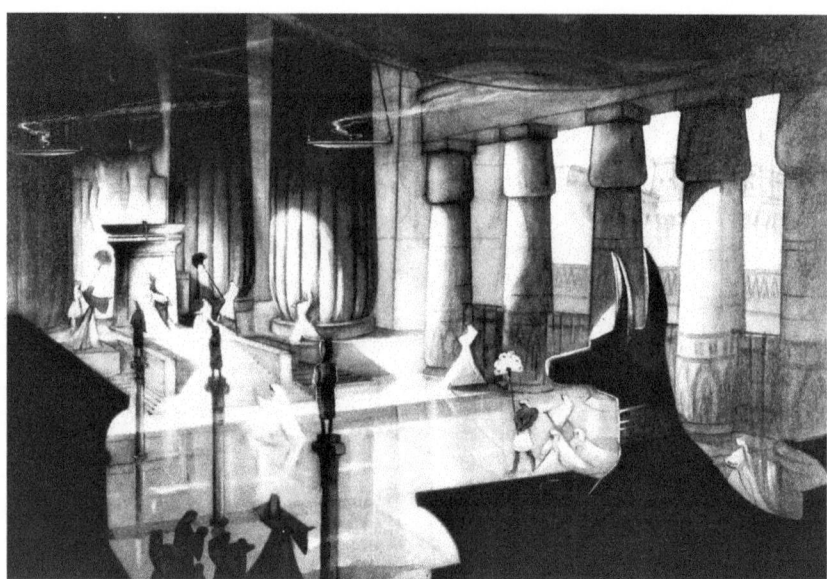

Figure 2.24
Cleopatra (1934), a masterpiece of screen design by Hans Dreier. Original concept art for
Cleopatra's palace. Pressbook.

between pillars, framing it like a cinema screen (Figure 2.25). In *Cleopatra*,
a vulva-like arch of soft ostrich plumes frames Colbert in seductive
mood, as she languorously reclines on board her love-boat (Figure 2.26);
it is reminiscent of the plush architectural features of the interior of the
Radio City Music Hall in New York. As Blanshard and Shahabubin
note, '*Cleopatra* combined Egypt, Rome and modern Art Deco to create
a luxury that Depression [era] filmgoers could both identify with, and
escape into.'[48]

However, in terms of historical veracity, the sets in DeMille's 1934
Cleopatra ignore the Hellenistic aspect entirely, as much, indeed, as the
script overlooks Cleopatra's Macedonian lineage.[49] Much of the film's
action takes place on a studio set representing a high and airy hall that
overlooks one of the palace courtyards (Figure 2.27). The set is decorated
with a lotus-pillar colonnade, pylon gateways, rooftop terraces and pediments, all of which are 1930s interpretations of New Kingdom Egyptian
temple architecture; an anachronistic metallic sheen is given to the set,
better suited to 1930s aeroplanes or military hardware than Hellenistic
palaces per se. The hall itself is hung in curtain swags with tasselled
boarders and large marble pediments, on top of which sit proud granite
statues of pharaonic lions with elegant Art Deco twists. The set is visually
extended by the use of a painted backcloth showing an Egyptian temple.
It is interesting to note that just as DeMille's Cleopatra is eternal Egypt,
so her palace is eternal Egyptian, and pharaonic Egyptian at that. There
is no call for a genuine Hellenistic Alexandria with its unique and fascinating mixture of Greek and Egyptian styles. A vision of eternal Egypt,

Figure 2.25
A prototype for Cleopatra's throne room in *The Ten Commandments* (1923). Production still.

Figure 2.26
Architecture of sensuality: Art Deco curves in ostrich plumes on Cleopatra's Love Boat. *Cleopatra* (1934). Production still.

Figure 2.27
The gleaming perfection of Egyptianising Art Deco 1: the palace. *Cleopatra* (1934). Studio
publicity shot.

filtered through the glorious clean lines of Art Deco, suffice (Figure 2.28).
As Ramírez notes, 'Again we find a hybrid Art Deco arising from an
opportune compromise between dramatised history, "entertainment",
and the more advanced tendencies of contemporary design, "modern-
ism." This formula, used again and again in Hollywood, made great
impact on American architecture of the time.'[50]

Gordon Edwards' 1917 *Cleopatra* was sold as much on the lavishness
of its sets as it was on the charms of Theda Bara:

> The mystic Land of the Pharaohs – Egypt – the Egypt of Cleopatra's
> time, luxuriously oriental and riotously extravagant, is wonderfully
> depicted in all its barbaric splendour . . . Watching *Cleopatra* is like
> having your personal guided tour to Egypt.

In actuality, Miss Bara's Cleopatra lives in a world of plush oriental
rugs and potted palms, a reflection of the late Edwardian taste for busy
and fussy interior design (Figure 2.29). Drapes, held open with fringed
tie-backs, frame picture windows and occasional tables are loaded
with flower arrangements and *objets d'art*: a canopic jar here, a brass
bowl there. The wall paintings of the palace are fake-Egyptian and the

Figure 2.28
The gleaming perfection of Egyptianising Art Deco 1: the throne. The flawless symmetry of design is augmented by the exquisite Art Deco lines of Colbert's costume. Cleopatra (1934). Studio publicity shot.

hieroglyphs are pure gobbledygook, but, alongside the cluttered Middle Eastern bric-a-brac, they do reflect the popular taste in Orientalism prevalent in interior design at the time.[51]

All three Cleopatra films boast monumental palaces and public spaces and, to varying degrees, other aspects of embellishment proper to the re-creation of antiquity – decorative and architectural flourishes that generate the pleasure of the gaze. Each of the films negotiates its way through the historical tensions between Roman, Greek and Egyptian identities which Cleopatra's real (historical) story tells and while working within the parameters laid down by epic film design (based as it is on Victorian academic painting and theatre design) – the demands that Cleopatra inhabits a fantastic, larger-than-life world that is at one and the same time distant and contemporary, alien and desirable. The production

Figure 2.29
The late Victorian fussiness of Cleopatra's place in 1917. Theda Bara as Cleopatra in a vast
peacock-feather robe. Studio publicity still.

designs of the twentieth century's three most conspicuous forays into
the world of Egypt's most famous queen revel in the notion of the set as
an embellishment, as artifice, and at the same time indulge themselves
in the looks of the eras from which they emerged.

Research and Realism

How were design decisions made? How was the period 'look' of a film
created? Each of the Hollywood studios employed teams of apprentice-
draughtsmen to work alongside the production designers in turning
out architectural plans, the numbers of which needed on any given
production could be prodigious. Edward Carfagno, the art director of
Ben-Hur (1925), recalled that there were 'stacks and stacks' of designs,
plans, and drawings made for the film: 'there were continuity sketches
that probably went up to the ceiling. We designed everything you saw
in the film and more, the props, the furniture, musical instruments that
were played . . . everything.'[52] It has been estimated that by the 1950s a
single production might require from 20,000 to 30,000 working sketches
which might include visualisations for mood and scale (Figure 2.30) and
more specific references for camera angles (Figure 2.31).

Figure 2.30
Concept art: the opening shot of *The Ten Commandments* (1956).

Figure 2.31
Shooting-aid sketch. *Ben-Hur* (1959).

A shooting-schedule for *Quo Vadis* (1951) gives a hint at the variety of sets needed in a single few weeks of filming, all of which demanded sketches, designs, plans, models and, finally, completed full-scale sets:

Int. Petronius' Inner Court and Terrace
Ext. Royal Balcony – Triumph
Int. Nero's Banquet Hall
Marcus' Table (Inside Set)
Banquet Hall (Outside Set)
Ext. Outer Court – Petronius' House
Int. Chilo's Shop
Ext. Quarry (Burning of Rome)
Int. Imperial Pavilion – 'Nero's Pavilion will follow the balance of Int. Petronius' Rome in order to kill this set for the prison sets.'
Int. Nero's Banqueting Hall – nite [*sic*] – podium section – Marcus' table.
Int. Petronius' House – Antium – day
Nero's Pavilion at Antium
Int. Nero's Pavilion – Imperial Tent – Day.
Int. Palace Throne Room – Day
Int. Entrance to Nero's Throne Room – Day
Int. Acte's quarters – Nero's Palace – day
Int. Women's wing – Acte's Quarters day
Prison – corridor and cells – nite [*sic*] (Marcus bribery). Afterwards Int. Prison[53]

Around 1947 a private scholar named Hugh Gray was hired by John Huston to research the 'appearance, customs, and eccentricities' of life in Nero's Rome in preparation for his new film version of *Quo Vadis*. When Huston was replaced as director by Mervyn LeRoy in December 1949, it seems that Gray's hard work had been in vain since, as Jon Solomon has noted, 'most of Gray's fact-filled notebooks went unread, for MGM had a film to shoot, not a lecture to give.'[54] Jennifer Cresswell has demonstrated, however, that Gray was still being consulted by MGM well into 1950 and she argues that Huston's production design team was not altered by LeRoy, while correspondence suggests that the designs based on Gray's research had been drawn up and were in place before LeRoy took over direction of the film.[55] Although there is little consensus as to the final role Gray played in the script-consultancy and design process of *Quo Vadis*, it is fair to say that the research he provided for the studio did indeed have an indelible impact on the look of the film. His research notebooks contain detailed suggestions for the design elements of various settings:

INT. PALACE THRONE ROOM – (B-L 9-2-48. Sc 31.)
GENERAL NOTES: The script refers to this as a 'magnificent chamber'. It might well have been. Within thirty years [of Nero's death] Domitian had built a palace of which the central hall assumed

to have been the Throne-room, was covered by a barrel vault, which had the widest span of any in Rome, the hall being 100 feet wide by 131 feet long ... The decoration of the room will basically be the same as in Petronius' house. But of course there will be a profusion and magnificence in keeping with Nero's character. What the good taste of Petronius chooses in moderation will be multiplied by Nero's passion and possession. His enthusiasm for everything Greek will be the predominating notes. If it were possible, we should reproduce the statuary of a Paxiteles [sic] and the paintings of a Protegenes [sic]. The throne itself will be a matter of choice. Either the official Sella Curulis, the chair of office of consul, praetors, all magistrates and the Emperor, with curved legs of carved ivory placed on a low dais; or, alternatively we might use something a little more comfortable to modern notions ...

Int. Palace – women's and Acte's quarters.

General notes: Here should be a feeling of luxury combined with delicate good taste. Mosaic or tiled floor, marble or porphyry walls with Greek frescoes, or mosaics. Delicate Greek statuary. Ivory and bronze carvings. Handmade ornaments. Ornate and delicate tables. On some of these, jewellery, polished hand mirrors and various sandal-wood or cedar boxes. Phials and jars for perfumes and oils and for the gilt hair powder that is overturned during the scene. There will be one or two delicately carved cabinets, couches with cushions and chairs and stools.

NOTE: It is possible that among the statuary in Acte's room there would be a bust of Nero.[56]

In order to enhance the authenticity desired in the final look of the film, producers often deemed it necessary to supplement library and museum research with close inspections of actual, historical, locations. Merian C. Cooper, producer of *The Last Days of Pompeii*, travelled alongside production designer Van Nest Polglase to the countryside around Vesuvius and, according to his account, did much of his own research on the streets of Pompeii itself (the fact that the screenplay compressed the forty-five or so years between the crucifixion of Christ and Pompeii's destruction for dramatic purposes mattered to few critics).[57] For *The King of Kings* (1927) Paramount representatives went much further by travelling to the Holy Land in order to observe, study and photograph its landscapes and architecture. The pre-production *Quo Vadis* crew spent many months in Rome in 1948 and 1949 ahead of filming there (see Text Box 2.5) and MGM made a virtue of sending the movie's stars there to take in the ambience of the city and be photographed amid the ruins (Figure 2.32).

From its inception, Hollywood filmmaking, working under the shadow of the studio system, crafted films which persuaded their audiences that they were witnessing real life. Realism was a style of filmmaking which created the illusion or effect of reality, of being a 'slice of

Figure 2.32.
Hollywood on the Tiber: Robert Taylor and Deborah Kerr are shown the ruins of the
Coliseum, June 1950. Studio publicity photograph for *Quo Vadis*.

life', and the directors of the Golden Age tried to show the surface of life
as closely as possible, so that the viewer accepted the film as a reality.
Notwithstanding the genre of the film, 'realism' remained the aim and
through the careful use of *mise-en-scène*, Hollywood purported to depict
reality. Thus, for instance, in a musical, street gangs might fight to the
death through the medium of song and dance, but the aesthetics of the
film convincingly tried to capture the look of New York's West Side;
the veracity of the narrative is enhanced through the detailed material
worlds which the characters inhabit. Whatever their backgrounds, art
directors always claimed to be aiming for realism.

Text Box 2.5   Hollywood on the Tiber: *Quo Vadis* in Rome

Report by Dora Wright on survey of possible film production in Italy, 23 January 1948

We visited the private studio of an architect named Brezini, who, besides designing the Via Dei Fori Imperiale [*sic*] (one of the most famous streets in Rome), various bridges, churches etc., had designs accepted by Mussolini for a New Rome. Brezini was Art Director on a silent version of QUO VADIS and has a great desire to work on this projected new version. He had many drawings and plans of Ancient Rome, and in fact this seems to be his hobby. He is undoubtedly a great artist, is modest in his fees (he is asking 70,000 lira a week) and as he is an authority on the period in question, we might do well to consider him. He is around 68.

Mr Cavazzuti has pointed out that the Colosseum was not built until some twelve years after the death of Nero. If it was decided to transfer the action now scripted in the Colosseum to, say, the Circus Maximus, we suggest considering the use of an unfinished Sports Arena in Mussolini's Forum for these scenes. We are having still photographs taken and despatched so that an impression can be given of its size and surroundings.

We are enclosing catalogues and photographs of existing models of Ancient Rome now on exhibition at the Mostra della Romanita [*sic*], and enquiries are being made to trace the makers or drawings of these, which might be useful to us for our scenes of burning Rome and also the model featured in Scene 64.

(Margaret Herrick Archive)

MGM production records, 6 September 1948

Valuable contacts:

Professor Giglioli and Professor Lugli – Both Giglioli and Lugli are of the University of Rome (Facolta [*sic*] di Archeologia) and specialists on Roman Topography, and who should be contacted for further details.

Signor G. Agosta, 12 Via Natale del Grande – Agosta is a student of Ancient Rome and also a film critic.

Signor Pietrangeli – One of the Directors of Museo di Roma.

Msgr. Belvedere – We visited the Catacombs of S. PRISCELLA. Belvedere, who discovered the Catacombs, gave us some very useful information.

(Margaret Herrick Archive)

Letter from Morgan Hudgins to Hedda Hopper, 31 May 1950

Greetings to you from Rome, the city which will never get over 1950, the year which had two such phenomena as 'Quo Vadis' and the Holy Year taking place at one and the same time . . . Italians have never seen anything like this film production and probably never will again. Like something from heaven, Hollywood has come along and offered them thousands of jobs which were non existing before. Everybody but everybody, it seems, is having something to do with the production.

    During the visit to St. Peter's Bob [Robert] Taylor created a mild furore among pilgrims who were there to visit the shrine, all of whom recognised him and pointed him out. Several of the Swiss guard requested his autographs.

(Margaret Herrick Archive: Hedda Hopper collection;
Morgan Hudgins No. 1185)

Variety, '*Quo Vadis* set to roll in Rome during April', 15 March 1950

The long awaited $5,000,000 production of Quo Vadis will start shooting sometime in April, and by May the Cine-Citta [*sic*] Studios will be humming, according to Henry Henigson, Metro unit production head. Mervyn Leroy [*sic*], the director, who has been in London for the past two weeks, has returned to Hollywood, but will be back in Rome April 8. William Horning, who designed the sets under the direction of Cedric Gibbons, Herschel McCoy, costume designer, and Courtney Haslam, wardrobe expert, will be the first of the technicians to arrive, with others following soon.

Time, 'Hollywood on the Tiber', 26 June 1950

By the time Producer Sam Zimbalist and Stars Deborah Kerr and Robert Taylor arrived, Nero's Rome was as lavish as the original. Some 3,000 Italian workmen were putting the last carefully touches on a mammoth reproduction of Nero's palace and a wooden replica of the Emperor's circus. A facsimile of the slimy, green-watered River Tiber had been dug, and for the single scene to be shot outside Cinecitta [*sic*], a section of the Appian Way had been repaved.

Look Magazine, 'The story behind *Quo Vadis*', 5 June 1951

First to go to Rome to look over the ground and survey the available facilities for making *Quo Vadis* were E. J. Mannix, MGM General Manager, and Henry Henigson, veteran Hollywood executive who had been engaged by the studio to serve as general manager of the project. For the most elaborate motion picture ever made it was necessary that the largest possible film-making space be obtained and Mannix and Henigson were fortunate in being able to lease the huge Cinecitta [*sic*] Studios ... Two years before starting date, three important Hollywood technicians arrived in Rome to assist Henigson in preparing for the production – William Horning, art director, Herschel McCoy, costume designer, and Hugh Hunt, set decorator. Each had spent months at the home studio drawing sketches and compiling data in connection with their respective assignments. Work began at once on the construction of the huge outdoor sets – a reproduction of the Circus of Nero, large enough to seat 30,000 people; the exterior of Nero's palace; a whole section of ancient Rome, presenting the streets, shops and houses as they appeared, according to careful historical research, two thousand years ago; a great bridge capable of supporting 50,000 people who were to flee across it in their escape from the burning city. To build these and more than 100 other sets, a staff of 500 skilled carpenters went to work, and for the next two years they were kept busy, their number frequently augmented by painters and other artisans.

In Golden Age Hollywood, a coherent narrative structure (that is to say clear storytelling) dominated the filmmaking process and screenplays adopting too much symbolism or too many metaphors which might put the narrative at jeopardy were not permitted; this helps explain why expressionistic forms of production design (such as developed in Germany and Eastern Europe) never developed in America. As we have seen with the case of *The Silver Chalice*, stylised settings were simply not the language of Hollywood films – although some concessions might be made for certain more 'arty' musicals (*An American in Paris*; dir. Minnelli, 1951) or horror/fantasies (*The House of Wax*; dir. de Toth, 1953). American film directors and production designers were not given enough artistic freedom by the studios to allow for the development of more idiosyncratic design concepts and decisions about the final look of a film always rested, in effect, with the head of the studio, a point made clear in Beverly Heisner's study of production design in the studio era:

American art directors never developed elaborate theories of film décor as did some of their European colleagues, especially the Russians and Germans, perhaps because of the overall emphasis by the Hollywood studios on 'realism'. Realism meant, in one form or another, a world that the audience recognised. This did not have to be the contemporary world around the audience, it could be one known from paintings, photographs, or even the frequently quoted Biblical world of Sunday School cards.[58]

In epic movies, the world of the past had to look real. Therefore the main question for any production designer of an epic had to be: how do we make the film sets look real? By the mid-1920s the problem had been solved: films must create the *illusion* of reality – and in press releases art directors began a confident campaign to convince audiences that what they were seeing was real, whether this was a Roman racing stadium or the Tower of Babel. Art directors often wrote about this aspect of their work with pride. Cedric Gibbons, who had conceived the look of the 1925 *Ben-Hur*, for instance, wrote:

One of the chief problems of the art department is to make something look real which is not. Because of the lack of time it is impossible, for instance, to reconstruct a 'medieval' castle using real stones and mortar! We must therefore use materials which will appear to be solid rock, and so construct a castle that, when fighting men, for instance, lunge against the wall, it does not 'give' but will maintain the illusion of solidity and antiquity.[59]

This helps explain why Hollywood publicity engaged in the rhetoric of numbers with such willingness: the more plaster, wood and nails which could be cited as being used in the artificial construction of reality the better. Citing the amounts of lumber needed in the building of a set not only drew attention to the cost of the production, but also rang true to the studios' rhetoric of exposure: making things 'real' in movies involved a lot of cheating.

Part of the process of cheating was accomplished simply through exaggeration techniques, a process explained by art director William Cameron Menzies:

In many cases authenticity is sacrificed, and architectural principles violated, all for the sake of the emotional response that is being sought. My own policy has been to be as accurate and as authentic as possible. However, in order to forcefully emphasise the locale I frequently exaggerate – I made my English subject more English than it would naturally be, and I over-Russianise Russia.[60]

Therefore the epic's penchant to over-Romanise Rome or over-Babylo-nise Babylon is part of the process of what might be termed 'exaggerated realism'. Antony Mann's *The Fall of the Roman Empire* famously saw the Roman Forum recreated at Las Matas near Madrid; at 400 × 230 metres (1,312 × 754 feet) this construction still holds the record for the largest outdoor film set and is popularly said to have been built on a bigger scale than the original. Studio publicity touted the numbers in support of this: 170,000 large pavement blocks, 22,000 feet of concrete to create the stairways and ramps, 24,000 pounds of nails, 33,000 gallons of paint and 230,000 roofing tiles. Yet the boast that the set over-Forumed the Forum Romanum is not true; it is the *mise-en-scène* which contrives to convince the viewer of the gigantic scale of the recreation. The crowded scenes of Commodus' entry into the Forum (Figure 2.33), or the last sequence in which the Empire is auctioned off to the highest bidder (Colour Plate 9), shows a peculiarity of screen design shrewdly identi-fied by Cedric Gibbons: 'The stage setting surrounds the actors. In the movies, once the scene if filmed, you might almost say that the actors surround the set . . . the people are always in the foreground, the sets are but backgrounds against which they play.' The presence of actors and movement is what helps give both verisimilitude and scale to the sets (see also Figure 2.34).[61]

Figure 2.33
Christopher Plummer as Commodus enters into the Roman Forum recreated at Las Matas
near Madrid. *The Fall of the Roman Empire* (1964). Production shot.

The producer of *The Fall of the Roman Empire*, Samuel Bronston, once
claimed that the Forum set was a three-dimensional representation of
the original, and that its temples and palaces and law courts were physically built in the round and not just as false edifices (see Text Box 2.6).
This assertion flies in the face of standard Hollywood practice and, true,
while the Forum set was not enhanced or extended by matte paintings
as was often the case in 1950s epics (see discussion below):

> one quick image detracts from the illusion: in a shot taken from the
> high ground near the Temple of Jupiter that shows the Roman citizens
> running towards Commodus, one can see between the edifices, a bare
> horizon, the flat Spanish plains of Las Matas, rather than a teeming
> ancient city.[62]

Nonetheless, the Forum Romanum as designed by John Moore and
Veniero Colasanti is a very fine work, as the actor Christopher Plummer
recalled:

> The sets were lavish beyond expectations and were inevitably to steal
> the picture. The two brilliant designers . . . had reconstructed the

Figure 2.34
The epic set given life by its population of extras. *Quo Vadis* (1951). Production still.

Roman Senate and large portions of Rome itself so faithfully that for decades after the film was forgotten, their massive set remained intact at Las Matas ... as a major tourist attraction. Roman scholars from everywhere came to marvel at its accuracy. Gore Vidal, whose book *Julian* had just come out, was a particular admirer.'[63]

The Rome set has the correct look and, indeed, the right *feel*. After all, the visual ambience of a film enhances its emotional dimensions, non-verbally enhancing the emotional dimensions and furthering the plot. Menzies, writing in 1930 about his own work, notes, 'in the case of pageantry such things as scale and pattern, figures, rich trappings against a high wall, through a huge arch are demanded', a concept well-captured in the historical details Moore and Colasanti employ in the Forum set. But there is more to this design than successful historical recreation.[64] As Martin Winkler recognises, the visualisation of Rome reflects the mood of the film:

Attentive and emotionally involved viewers – all those with a feeling for history – leave Mann's film with a feeling of sadness. The beauty and the greatness of Rome as a civilisation more than as an empire that the film has shown ... is lost ... [This] is a loss that affected all

Text Box 2.6   *The Fall of the Roman Empire*: Rome in Madrid

Figure 2.35
The vast Roman Forum set. *The Fall of the Roman Empire* (1964). Lobby card.

The souvenir brochure of *The Fall of the Roman Empire* gives considerable space and attention to the Forum Romanum set created by John Moore and Veniero Colasanti, based on research by Dr Will Durant (for a fuller excerpt, with discussions, see Winkler 2009: 136–44).

> In the autumn of 1960 producer Samuel Bronston contemplating a film of *The Fall of the Roman Empire* consulted with executive associate producer Michael Waszynski on the artistic and technical problems involved. Later, to his celebrated designers, John Moore and Veniero Colasanti, he posed the same question King Theodahad had uttered 1400 years earlier: could they re-create the Forum as it was at the height of its grandeur?
>
>   When they said they thought it could be done, Bronston made of the most dramatic decisions in film history – he authorised them to construct on the plains of Las Matas [near] Madrid, the Forum, as no living person had seen it since before Alaric swept over Rome fifteen centuries ago. He made clear it was not to be merely

another gigantic film set but a full scale reproduction that Commodus himself would recognise were he suddenly to come to life.

Moore and Colasanti . . . made 3000 sketches for the 27 structures that were the main features of the Forum. Construction began October 1, 1962 and as many as 1100 men worked for seven months to raise Ancient Rome . . . Moore and Colasanti . . . devised a man-made hill 95 feet high on which they built a temple 165 feet high. Thus the bronze equestrian figures on its peak were 260 feet above the stone-paved surface of the Forum itself, a considerable feat of architecture and engineering.

Every sculptor and skilled plaster worker in the Madrid area was invited to work on the adornment of the set . . . They moulded . . . some 350 individual statues . . . replicas of Greek statues and Roman sculptures copied from Grecian temples . . .

So much went into the re-creation – so much thought, devotion, and integrity – that when the last scene was shot and the last actor had left, Bronston was reluctant to order it demolished. It stands there, a Ninth Wonder of the Cinematic World, a place of pilgrimage not only for film people but for princes and commoners alike and for tourists abruptly stopping their cars to blink in awe at the Rome of Commodus shimmering in the sun of the Spain of today.

of civilised mankind in Europe and the West. *The Fall of the Roman Empire* shows it.[65]

Spending money and cutting costs

Epic sets were expensive to create and Hollywood never shied away from letting its public know just how much capital was being invested in creating, for their pleasure and edification, the look of antiquity. Massive outdoor sets, like those created for *Quo Vadis*, *The Ten Commandments* (1956), *Cleopatra* (1963) or *The Fall of the Roman Empire*, were carefully employed by budget-conscious directors who returned the narrative action to the same locale on several occasions throughout the film. In *The Ten Commandments*, for instance, the exodus of the Hebrews and, later, the rallying of pharaoh's chariots take place in front of the pylon-gates set, with its avenue of sphinxes in two extended scenes which were meant to capitalise on getting maximum use and attention out of the gargantuan set.

While in Mankiewicz's *Cleopatra* De Cuir's vast Alexandrian quayside set is used at regular intervals throughout the film, the even bigger Roman Forum set was featured only once, in the twenty-minute-long parade in which Cleopatra enters into the city with all the camp panoply of the Ptolemies on her famed sphinx-mobile (Figure 2.36). Clothed in gold and seated, statue-like, on a high throne, surrounded by throngs of cheering Romans, African dancers, Egyptian chorus girls and equine displays, Cleopatra's entrance into Rome was intended to be the film's

Figure 2.36
Ptolemaic *pompē,* Hollywood style: Cleopatra's sphinx mobile. *Cleopatra* (1963).
Production still.

main attraction and most important scene. According to Mankiewicz's
son, Tom, 'Johnny [De Cuir] . . . was told to build the Roman Forum
three times its size, as it was thought the real Roman Forum was not
impressive enough.'[66] During the shooting of the scene, which took
many days to complete, the set was filmed from every angle – including Cleopatra's point-of-view from atop the giant sphinx (Figure 2.37)
– giving the whole spectacle not only a sense of spatial depth (which
earned De Cuir Mankiewicz's acclamation as 'the city planner'), but
became a visual indicator of just how and why Twentieth Century Fox
had spent so much money on this one movie.

Producers were prepared to spend vast sums of money on studio sets
too if they thought they would be well-used. The final sequence of *The*

Figure 2.37
The view from the top: Cleopatra sees the Roman Forum from the sphinx mobile. *Cleopatra* (1963). Production still.

Robe, for instance, which lasts some twenty-five minutes, is a trial scene in which Marcus Gallio (Richard Burton) defends his new-found faith in Christianity and derides the tyranny of the Roman regime and its leader, the crazed emperor Caligula (Jay Robinson). The action takes place in 'the cold marble luxury of Caligula's palace', in a towering set which has at one end of the hall a high throne dais surmounted by a sculpture of the imperial eagle (Figure 2.38) and at the other a great portal which leads out of the palace and into the city; a long aisle runs down the middle of the hall. Camera-shots and edits ensure that the whole set is put to use and, when filled by the cast, the resulting *mise-en-scène* is impressive.

A similar scale is employed in the set of the Temple of Baal and Astarte in *The Prodigal* (ostensibly, the action plays out in Achaemenid-period Damascus, but has a strange visual affinity with China, to judge from the banners hanging against the wall (Figure 2.39)). The large, glossy 'marble' floor becomes the focus of the set and space is given in the *mise-en-scène* to that design element by constricting the crowd of extras up against the wall, at the very edge of the floor which is, clearly, the performance space. Why has this been done? The answer is simple: maximum space is needed to give focus to Lana Turner, the picture's star turn, in the role of Semira, the High Priestess of Astarte. In 1937 Lana Turner had made her first brief screen appearance in a contemporary psychological thriller, *They Won't Forget* (dir. LeRoy); she was costumed in a tight-fitting

Figure 2.38
Cold, cavernous and filled with corruption: Caligula's palace. *The Robe* (1953). Production
still.

Figure 2.39
The set serves the movie star: space is needed for Lana Turner to perform the 'Lana Turner
Walk'. *The Prodigal* (1955). Production still.

knitted top that showed every curve of her breasts. Because of this she has gone down in film history as Hollywood's first 'sweater girl'. The impact she made on the screen, filmed simply walking down a street, catapulted Turner into the sphere of the Hollywood elite. According to Turner herself the film's director, Mervyn LeRoy, recognised something special in the actress's look and demeanour. '"Just walk,' he [LeRoy] would tell me'; she later wrote, '"Walk from here to there . . ."' Of course it wasn't until the screening that I understood why.'[67] Prudish MGM knew they had an audience aphrodisiac on their hands, and they capitalised on it by making 'The Lana Turner Walk' part of Turner's selling power, demanding that she replicate that sexy stride in film after film, regardless of the plot, character or, for that matter, the time period of its setting. The *mise-en-scène* of *The Prodigal* conspires to give 'The Lana Turner Walk' the space it requires, emphasised as it is by a frame within the frame – the billowing curtain stretched between two poles. Here the soaring set, emphasised by its gigantic columns, serves one function: to give space to Turner's sexy sashay. The set is forced to serve the star performance, but undoubtedly, for MGM it was money well spent.

However, because of the crippling production costs forced upon studios by the lavish sets required for key moments in a film, it was considered prudent to scale back on costs whenever possible. Sometimes this meant that sets (or elements of the sets) might be reused by later productions. Indeed, in contradiction to the hullaballoo manufactured by Paramount around the supposed research-driven authenticity of the sets for *The Ten Commandments* of 1956, DeMille and his art directors happily recycled sets, props (and costumes) created for *The Egyptian* of 1954 (Figure 2.40); these were purchased en masse from Twentieth Century Fox at a bargain price and helped temper the ever-rising costs of DeMille's great vanity project.[68]

As we have seen, though, epic films demanded a wide variety of locations in order to tell a story, and while most of the sets which were required could be built on studio back-lots or on sound-stages, nevertheless full-scale sets could not be built for every scene encountered in a screenplay. An economical way of addressing the budgeting problem was to use textiles – drapes and curtains – to create a cheap but effective set.

Each of the production art departments had a division of employees in the drapery unit, working with textiles as varied as silk brocade and satin (used for set elements which appeared directly in front of the camera) to workable cotton and heavy calico or linen (which was mainly used as canvases for paint effects).[69] In very contained studio spaces, sets such as Delilah's tent (with its opulent double bed (Figure 2.41)) could be created out of hanging a variety of contrasting textiles coupled with a few well-chosen set dressings and props. Blanshard and Shahabudin have noted the rich iconographic potential of examining the *mise-en-scène* of tents in epic film, noting that tents 'provide a useful image of how consideration of even the smallest image can be rewarding' and

Figure 2.40
The elegant studio set of the Theban throne hall in *The Egyptian* (1954) was later reused (although repainted) in *The Ten Commandments* (1956). Production still from *The Egyptian*.

that 'students of the representation of antiquity in film need to pay attention to even the smallest details as sometimes these can be the most telling.'[70] Military campaign tents, for instance, such as that of Octavian in *Cleopatra* (1963) (Figure 2.42) is based on the concept of the 'war rooms' of twentieth-century campaigns, and, with its clean practical lines and lack of ornamentation, it speaks too of Octavian's pinched and pragmatic character. Roman military tents are usually depicted with an eagle-topped standard strategically placed (as here) alongside the tent-door – 'the placement', say Blanshard and Shahabudin, 'is inappropriate (do you pick it up as you head out of the door like an umbrella?), but few symbols are so identifiably Roman.'[71]

Drapery is also used as a device to separate on-screen space. When King David enters into his harem in order to greet his soon-to-be-bride, Bathsheba, for example, he does so by opening apart layers of softly draped, pastel-shaded chiffon – an allegory, it might be supposed, of the all-female world of the inner palace and of the chiffon garments David will remove from the body of his newest queen once the wedding ceremony is completed (Figure 2.43). The lavish *mise-en-scène* of the banquet on Cleopatra's barge (Figure 2.18) looks expensive thanks to the props and the costumes of the throng of extras, but cost comparatively little in terms of set construction; screens of fringed textiles and some painted

Figure 2.41
The economics of the drape 1: Delilah's tent, set made from textile hangings. *Samson and Delilah* (1949). Studio publicity photograph.

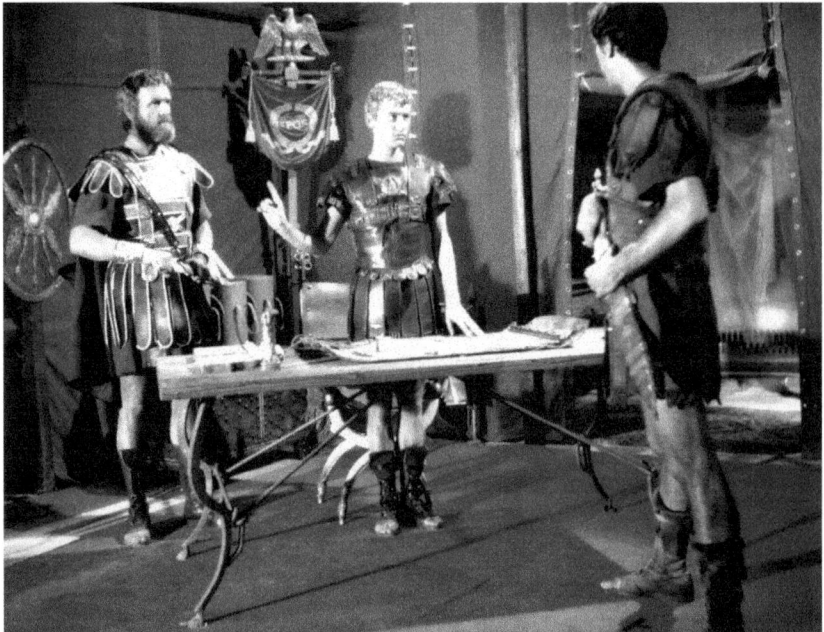

Figure 2.42
The economics of the drape 2: Octavian's campaign tent, set made from textile hangings. *Cleopatra* (1963). Production still.

Figure 2.43
The economics of the drape 3: King David's harem in Jerusalem, set made from textile
hangings. *David and Bathsheba* (1952). Studio publicity photograph.

fabric panels, coupled with effective lighting, do the bulk of the work. A
similar effect is achieved for Nero's study in *Quo Vadis*. Having gained
permission to use a scale model – the *Forma Urbis* – of Imperial Rome
which had originally been created for Mussolini to display in a Fascist
exhibition of 1937, the rest of the set is constructed simply from satin
drapery and a few rudimentary architectural elements (Figure 2.44). A
sense of depth is created by placing a heavy curtain at the rear of the
enclosed set.[72]

We noted at the beginning of this chapter the use of painted cyclo-
ramas – the vast painted canvas backdrops which gave an illusion of both
space and three-dimensional reality to the studio-based sets; these were
generally preferred over on-location filming since studio sets, expensive as they might be, nonetheless were more cost-effective than taking
whole film crews out of the studio and into the real world. When this
gigantean move *was* undertaken, however, the effect could be startling:
nothing quite compares with the vast colourful expanse captured by
DeMille's exodus scene filmed in the Egyptian desert (Colour Plate 5) or,
for that matter, the remarkable (and visionary) use of the scenery of the
American West employed for the 1965 epic *The Greatest Story Ever Told*.
The strength of the film is in the gorgeous cinematography by William
C. Mellor (who died on-set of a heart attack) and Loyal Griggs under the
direction of George Stevens. Griggs and Stevens had worked together
on the popular Western *Shane* (1953) and relished using the dramatic

Figure 2.44
The economics of the drape 3: a room in Nero's palace (with Mussolini's Forma Urbis added), set made from textile hangings. *Quo Vadis* (1951). Production still.

scenery of the movie Western to exploit the capabilities of widescreen technology, and so, when it came to filming the life of Jesus, instead of going to the places the events were supposed to have had taken place, or opting for conventional studio sets, the filmmakers decided to shoot most of the film in south Utah and north Arizona (Figure 2.45) and around the Colorado River, which became a substitute for the Jordan. Accurate or not, the chosen locales give the film a very distinct look and send out a clear message: America is Christ's country.

Technology brings the past to life

The work of the art department went hand in hand with technological developments in the film industry, the one complementing the other. In fact, some technologies relied on the crafts and skills of artists tradition-ally found working in the studio paint workshops.[73] The art of the glass shot or 'matte painting' was one which, for instance, employed the joint efforts of directors, production artists, cameramen and cinematogra-phers. Developed in the early silent era and employed by filmmakers until the dawn of the digital age, the matte process was one whereby a limited film set may be extended to whatever (or wherever) the director's imagination dictated with only the employment of an artist's brush. By placing a large plate of clear glass in front of the motion picture camera a matte artist would carefully paint in new scenery – an ornate palace ceiling, triumphal arches, towering temple edifices or

Figure 2.45
The Holy Land in the USA: south Utah and north Arizona stand in for Judaea. *The Greatest Story Ever Told* (1965). Production shot.

seascapes – which did not in fact exist in any physical form. An area of the glass was left clear and unpainted, through which the actors were filmed simultaneously with the matte art onto the original negative, producing an entirely convincing 'new' shot without the need for the production unit to leave the studio grounds. There were many technical variations of the matte process used in the pre-CGI (or computer-generated imagery) era and the processes utilised are exclusively old school 'photo-chemical', completely reliant on the artists' instinct and the cameraman's keen eye.

Ray Kellogg, Emil Kosa Jr, and Matthew Yuricich of the Twentieth Century Fox matte department were the undisputed masters of the genre and in the 1950s, due to the peculiar optics of the anamorphic lens used for the brand new widescreen process, they developed matte techniques into a genuine art form. For *Ben-Hur*, for instance, the mattes had to be painted partly 'squeezed' – which to the naked eye looked quite unnatural and distorted – to be eventually 'unsqueezed' during theatre projection and screened at the correct 2.40:1 ratio on the panoramic screen. In spite of this, Matthew Yuricich's painted mattes display many beautifully composed and rendered shots – including the majestic, show-stopping spectacle of the triumphal entry of Quintus Arrius into the city of Rome (Colour Plate 10).

Perhaps the most well-known of the technological developments directly related to epic film was the invention of widescreen. Originally pioneered in 1927 in France and embraced by Japanese directors in the late 1940s, many American filmmakers were daunted by widescreen's creative implications, arguing that the size and shape of the screen no longer approximated human physiognomy; audiences sitting close to the screen, it was argued, would need to repeatedly turn their heads to see the full width of the action. However, keen to challenge the growing appeal of television and to get paying customers back into the movie theatres, in 1953 Twentieth Century Fox decided to produce America's first widescreen movie, and used it to create an epic film, Koster's *The Robe*, which, it was thought, would benefit most from the new industrial wonder, CinemaScope (see Text Box 2.7).[74]

The CinemaScope process was a critical and audience success and *The Robe* was hailed as having successfully exploited the most important advance in cinema since *The Jazz Singer* (dir. Crosland) – America's first 'talkie' – of 1927. With a budget of four and a half million dollars, The Robe grossed thirty million dollars, easily justifying Fox's gamble on the CinemaScope process and encouraging exhibitors and cinema-owners to spend costly sums on refitting their movie houses with the huge curved screens and projection equipment needed for the process.[75] Most of the major studios quickly adopted CinemaScope for their new films, and those who didn't invented their own widescreen processes. Eventually, DeMille outdid them all with his VistaVision remake of *The Ten Commandments*.

The widescreen epics of the 1950s and 1960s promised the audience an involvement with the action unimagined with earlier movies. With its curved screen, CinemaScope thrust the audience into the midst of the action, and *The Robe* could thus imitate the physical recreation of ancient Rome in a way that a tourist visiting the ruins of the city could never experience. Audiences were encouraged to feel as if they were conceivably one of the 'cast of thousands' in the battle scenes or pageants; they were no longer 'voyeurs' of history but 'participants' in history. Monica Cyrino notes that with *The Robe*, 'once again Hollywood entrusted an epic spectacular about the splendours of . . . antiquity with the task of

Text Box 2.7 CinemaScope, Dimensional Movie Marvel, Is Coming!

Figure 2.46
CinemaScope advertisement. *The Robe* (1953). Pressbook.

From *The Robe* pressbook (1953):

With the premiere of THE ROBE in CinemaScope, the new dimensional marvel that does not require the use of special glasses, moviegoers will get their first look at a motion picture in an entirely new form . . . CinemaScope consists of an anamorphic lens which attached to a motion picture camera makes it possible for the camera to reach out to each side as the eye does and compass a wide angle screen on a narrow strip of 33mm film. When this film is projected through a compensating anamorphic lens attached to the theatre projection machine it spreads the image horizontally to its original form or to an aspect ratio of 2.55 to 1.

When the curtains open . . . you will know why THE ROBE had to wait for CinemaScope before it could fully encompass you in its power, spectacle and glory! Only CinemaScope is the anamorphic lens process of the newly made, curved Miracle Mirror Screen that achieves infinite depth and life-like reality without the use of glasses.

Only through CinemaScope with its matchless coordination of vision, colour and Stereophonic Sound could THE ROBE come alive.

When the curtains open . . . you will be encompassed in the vast and wondrous panorama . . . you will behold the awe-inspiring spectacle as the imperial might of Rome hurls its challenge against the Word of God.

showing off the enduring power, artistry, and prosperity of the film industry itself.' She further elucidates on the appeal of widescreen for the epic filmmaker:

Koster displays his lifelong passion for painting and his inspired artistic vision in the pictorial details of the film's design. *The Robe* opens with an impressive visual effect that announces its own cinematic innovation: the viewer watches the parting of heavy, red curtains to reveal a slowly widening panorama of the ancient Roman arena . . . [it is] self-descriptive of the new widescreen technology of CinemaScope. The dark red curtains, richly bordered with a classical motif, ambiguously evoke both the luxury of ancient Rome and the dark red robe of Christ.[76]

It is important to note, then, that by the early 1950s technological advances in film manufacture and projection dictated how the epic should conduct itself. But, sadly, part of that technological advance had a damaging effect not only on the epic, but on Hollywood film generally: afraid of disorientating the audience with close-ups, directors tended to position their cameras further away from the actors, arranging them in frieze-like rows across the screen. *The Robe* uses what was sometimes called 'washing line' composition throughout its three-hour duration; not since the silent-era had film staging been so self-consciously theatrical, although very slowly, throughout the decade, as confidence with the technology built, directors were able to contemplate less constrictive use

Plate 1

Hedy Lamarr, Henry Wilcoxon and George Saunders with extras in the Temple of Dagon setting. *Samson and Delilah* (1949). Production still.

Plate 2

Graphic design for *Solomon and Sheba* (1959) by Frank McCarthy. Horizontal poster design.

Plate 3

The rhetoric of spectacle: SEE! SEE! SEE! *Samson and Delilah* (1949). Lobby card.

Plate 4
The studio lighting rig and painted backcloth. *The Robe* (1953). Candid shot taken during filming.

Plate 5

Colour coordination and a cast of thousands. The exodus sequence from *The Ten Commandments* (1956). Production shot.

Plate 6

Arnold Friberg's painting of the construction of pharaoh's new city, based on a scene from *The Ten Commandments* (1956). Souvenir brochure.

Plate 7

Nero's palace. *The Silver Chalice* (1954). Set designers Boris Leven and Rolf Gerard. Production still.

Plate 8

Reproduction of an original set design for Cleopatra's barge by John De Cuir. *Cleopatra* (1963). Japanese souvenir brochure.

Plate 9

The Roman Forum recreated at Las Matas near Madrid. *The Fall of the Roman Empire* (1964). Production still.

Plate 10

Matthew Yuricich's matte painting of Rome. *Ben-Hur* (1959). Screen grab.

Plate 11

A limited colour palette used to maximum dramatic impact as the Nile turns to blood. *The Ten Commandments* (1956). Production shot.

Plate 12
The bright gold satin gown and turquoise jewellery worn by Gina Lollobrigida contrasts with the stone arch behind her. *Solomon and Sheba* (1959). Promotional portrait.

Plate 13

One of Travis Banton's costumes for Claudette Colbert: it reads silver-white on-screen but in reality was created from eau-de-nil satin.

Plate 14
Red and blue form the colour palette for *The Ten Commandments* (1956) and show opposition and rivalry.

Plate 15
Power through colour: Rameses' feather-motif cloak uses blue and red while his headcloth is red –
all show his dominance as the alpha-male of the story. *The Ten Commandments* (1956).
Studio portrait of Yul Brynner.

Plate 16

In a scene of the Sermon on the Mount only two individuals are dressed in white: Christ (seen from behind) and princess Salome (Rita Hayworth) – a proto-Christian. *Salome* (1954). French souvenir brochure.

of *mise-en-scène* (Wyler's 1959's *Ben-Hur*, for instance, is more confident in its employment of edits, close-ups and a visual depth of action).

When in 1949, after more than twenty years of filmmaking, DeMille released *Samson and Delilah*, he too used a biblical story to launch a new mode of film production – the use of colour film as a staple of the epic genre. During the 1930s and 1940s colour (the preserve of just one company, Technicolor) had been an option rather than a rule. By and large, colour had been reserved for fantasy movies such as *The Wizard of Oz* (dir. Fleming, 1939), in which the dreariness of Kansas gives way to the phantasmagorical colours of Oz, or of animated feature films such as Walt Disney's *Snow White and the Seven Dwarfs* (1937); musicals such as *Meet Me In St. Louis* (dir. Minnelli, 1944) could also receive colour treatments. Of course in 1939 *Gone with the Wind* (dir. Fleming) had bucked the trend and had been shot in colour and it was probably this film which convinced DeMille that the logical advance in epic filmmaking should be the use of Technicolor. This chimed well with DeMille's quest for historical verisimilitude, given that Technicolor's chief consultant, Natalie Kalmus, had explained in 1938 that colour film brought an 'enhanced realism' into being, which 'enables us to portray life and nature as it really is'.[77] For *Samson and Delilah*, George Barnes' Technicolor cinematography is lush and artfully lit, reminiscent of the paintings by Rembrandt which, indeed, served as his inspiration.

Like widescreen technology, colour differentiated movies from television and by the end of the 1950s more than half of Hollywood's output was in colour, leading to new products such as Eastmancolor (although it was only when colour TVs developed in the late 1960s that Hollywood abandoned black and white film). As we noted with the design of *The Silver Chalice*, colour coordination therefore became a major occupation of cinematographers, art directors, costume designers and technicians and in early colour epics much attention was paid to matching precise tones of salmon pinks, cherry reds, sea greens and pearl greys of the sets, the furniture and the costumes. Colour film stocks were less sensitive to light than black and white had been and therefore strong lighting was required to bring out the colours of the sets and costumes (see Colour Plate 2).[78] This accounts for the particular visual zing of colour we associate with epic production design in the early 1950s.[79]

The Temple of Dagon scene in *Samson and Delilah* (Colour Plate 1), for instance, shows a particularly effective use of colour palette being employed by the art department, with the stone pillars and platforms being relieved by the huge swags of orange fabric (as we have seen, it was a typical of DeMille to demand textile swathes in his sets – they also served the practical purpose of covering electric cables and joints as well as being very cost-efficient). By and large the colour scheme for the costumed stars and extras is composed of dark purples, burgundy, orange and, everywhere, the flash of gold armour. This allows Hedy Lamarr's blue peacock-feather cape to draw the eye, and its colour zings against the muted palette of the set and costumes which are arrayed behind Lamarr. The scene is crafted through a very elegant and effective use of Technicolor. By the mid-1950s the widescreen cinematic canvases were being more confidently painted with effective colour blocks: DeMille's great exodus scene from *The Ten Commandments*, for all its movement and chaos, is nonetheless a harmonious picture with a carefully controlled colour palette which is as judiciously utilised as that of any nineteenth-century artist (Colour Plate 5). The bright blood red river Nile – the first of the plagues on Egypt (Colour Plate 11) – works so well against the vivid contrast of the crisp white garments of the Egyptian courtiers and the sun bleached pillars of the temple.

Concluding Thought

In spite of the technological advances of the industry and the cinematic splendour of the widescreen epics, by the 1960s American taste in films was changing from the spectacular to the intimate. The change was brought about by both the developments of life in the USA in the postwar era and by the increasing dominance of television as the preferred form of entertainment. A gradual drifting of television-trained directors into the film industry, used to filming on location, saw the beginnings of the demise of studio recordings and with that the end of the studio art departments. By the 1970s, with the closing down of the old studio system, art directors had to look for work as independents or retire.

But at the height of the studio system the art departments were factories of brilliant, effervescent, creativity and no genre of filmmaking was served better by these remarkable artists than the epics. Lavishing money on sets, effects and technological wonders, the studios used ancient world epics as both showcases and champions of change. Through a curious combination of research and a flagrant disregard for what was discovered in the books and museum collections, Hollywood's great art directors rebuilt the Temple of Jerusalem, the Roman Colosseum and the gates of Thebes under the pretence of historical authenticity while maintaining a flair for contemporary design aesthetics. From plaster, plywood and painted canvas they brought a curious version of antiquity to life, one which nevertheless, satisfied cinema audiences' taste for the marbled, opulent vastness they wanted the ancient world to be.

Notes

1. Unsurprisingly, given that it breaks the illusion of reality, this photograph was withheld from circulation to publicity campaigners.
2. Isackes and Maness (2017: 2).
3. Margaret Herrick Archives: Henry-Grace papers; Scrapbook No. 1 – 1916–1951. I am grateful to Jennifer Creswell for this reference.
4. The invention of television changed these working habits. In 1948 a Supreme Court ruling stated that the Studios must divest themselves of interest in cinemas. From there on in, the power of the Studios began to diminish.
5. See in particular the study of studio styles by Heisner (1990).

6. *Life*, 7 August 1944. See further comment by Shiel (2015: 49).
7. Ramírez (2004: 21).
8. For the academic painters and their recreations of antiquity see Liversidge and Edwards (1996); Ash (1989, 1995 and 1999); Wood (1983). The Hollywood debt to the nineteenth-century artists is still felt today; see Landau (2000: 64–5). For the influence of Victorian theatre design on cinema art direction see Finkel (1996) and Mayer (1994); also, see comments by Becker (2013).
9. Ridley Scott, cited in Landau (2000: 28).
10. Rose (1974).
11. DeMille Presley and Vieira (2014: 224).
12. Higham (1973: 7).
13. On the use of tableaux in DeMille's films see Berthoieu (2009: 250–1).
14. Parker (1928: 245–6). See further Finkel (1996).
15. *Era*, 27 January 1906, cited in Richards (2009b: 203).
16. Mayer (1994: 20).
17. Davies and Annesley (2004).
18. Hanson (1972: 511); see further Drew (2001).
19. For a discussion of Frank Wortman and Walter L. Hall as the set designers for *Intolerance*, see Ramírez (2004: 116) and Hambley and Downing (1979: 102–3).
20. Becker (2013: 51).
21. Quoted in Grady Johnson, 'Moses and the Mormon Artist', *Instructor*, September 1954, cited in Swanson (2001: 31). On Friberg's work for DeMille see further Orrison (1999: 64–8).
22. Swanson (2001: 31).
23. See Hirsch (1978: 34–6) and Elley (1984: 117–18).
24. *The Silver Chalice* pressbook (1954).
25. http://www.tcm.com/this-month/article.html?id=1290764 | 309212 (accessed 23 February 2017).
26. Leslie Halliwell (1977: 828) described the film as '[p]o-faced biblical hokum ... with howling bad casting and direction ... [a] sea of boredom', while its leading man, Paul Newman, on hearing that the film was to receive its first TV broadcast (in 1966) took out an advert in one of the Hollywood trade papers apologising for his performance and requesting people not to watch the film. This backfired, and the broadcast received unusually high ratings. Newman called the film 'the worst motion picture produced during the 1950s' and once screened it for guests at his home, handing out pots, wooden spoons and whistles and encouraging the audience to offer noisy critiques.
27. http://www.dvdtalk.com/dvdsavant/s2842silv.html (accessed 23 February 2017).

Other recent reviews are more positive about the design:

From the gaudy feast of Nero (set inside what appears to be the Roman equivalent of DC Comics' Hall of Justice!), where everyone eats what appears to be silver food (actually looks quite strangely yummy) and scantily-clad, blue-skinned women (the kind Captain Kirk would so take his boots off for!) gyrate around to a poppy jazz score that is so out of time and place it almost goes the entire way around again and becomes perfectly scored, to the simple geometrical designs of Jerusalem that make this holy city an abstract wonder to behold as Newman's slave/artist Basil (a role originally turned down by James Dean) and the gorgeous Pier Angeli (James Dean's one-time lover) flee from Roman soldiers across the rooftops of this strange, exotic city, made even stranger and more exotic through staged architecture. Everywhere one looks, no matter the lack of charisma from Newman (who would have it in spades in future movies!) and the quite idiotic preening of co-star and Roman femme fatale Virginia Mayo, one is given a sight to behold indeed. (http://themost-beautifulfraudintheworld.blogspot.co.uk/2011/04/silver-chalice-or-paul-newman-holy.html (accessed 23 February 2017))

28. Roen (1994: 186).
29. Hirsch (1978: 36). Ramírez (2004: 130) suggests that the arches of the orgy scene were derived from the Palazzo della Città Italiana erected in Rome at the order of Mussolini: 'Fascist architecture, inspired by film, posthumously returns what it had once borrowed.'
30. MacDonald Fraser (1988).
31. Wyke (1997: 10).
32. Cary (1974: 91).
33. See further Barsacq (1970: 135): 'Films dealing with antiquity, whether Roman, Greek, Egyptian, or biblical . . . are merely pretexts for crowd scenes, for larger-than-life sets, for spectaculars.'
34. Tashiro (2004: 42).
35. See discussions in Grimal (1998: 86–104) and Green (1996: 127–41, 191–203).
36. *Cleopatra* Souvenir Brochure (1963: 16).
37. Quoted in Heisner (1990: 215–16).
38. For the architecture of the royal quarter see Foreman (1999).
39. IV Dynasty, reign of Khufu, *c*.2585 BCE. For details see Reisner and Smith (1955: 33–4), pls. 27–29; Lehner (1985).
40. XVIII Dynasty, reign of Tutankhamun, *c*.1347–1337 BCE. See Saleh and Sourouzain (1987: no. 180).
41. Ford and Mitchell (2009: 102).
42. A section of the 1963 souvenir brochure entitled 'The Designer's Contribution' includes fifteen full-colour illustrations of various sets used throughout the film. A section of *Life Magazine*, 20 May 1963, is devoted to the filming of *Cleopatra*. One particular segment is entitled 'Heroic Settings Designed for Larger-Than-Life Heroes' and includes good images of the Alexandrian set.
43. Essoe and Lee (1970: 32). Ramírez (2004: 211) suggests that it is possible to read the DeMillian Cleopatra's barge 'as a great bed rocked rhythmically by, if not her lovers, the waves.'
44. For an excellent discussion of the interplay between DeMille and twentieth-century consumerism in America see Higashi (1994: 142–75). On DeMille's bathroom scenes see Ramírez (2004: 209–10).
45. See in particular Ziegler (1994: 506–51).
46. Roen (1997: 33).
47. See Curl (2005: 212–20) and Montserrat (2000: 89); see also Ramírez (2004: 124–5).
48. Blanshard and Shahabudin (2011: 24).
49. The screenplay by Waldemar Young and Vincent Lawrence consciously underplays Cleopatra's ancestry and in DeMille's vision, Egyptian history begins and ends with Cleopatra; she has no past, since she has no ancestry, and, because of her lack of children, she is denied a posterity. See Llewellyn-Jones (2002b and 2013).
50. Ramírez (2004: 123).
51. *Cleopatra* brochure (British version, from the Dreamland Theatre, Chester), 1917.

52. Quoted in Ramírez (2004: 45).
53. Margaret Herrick Archives: John Huston papers MGM 1951 – shooting schedules f.762. I am grateful to Jennifer Creswell for this reference.
54. Solomon (2001: 217–18). See further Blanshard and Shahabudin (2011: 4).
55. Creswell, no date (accessed 25 February 2017).
56. Margaret Herrick Collection: Q93 Hugh Gray research volume 1. Turner/ MGM scripts. 15.
57. *Photoplay Studies*, I: 3 (October 1935).
58. Heisner (1990: 4).
59. Gibbons (1938: 46).
60. Quoted in Koszarski (1976: 245).
61. Heisner (1990: 3).
62. Martin (2007: 136).
63. Plummer (2010: 364).
64. Quoted in Koszarski (1976: 245). On the architectural veracity of *The Fall of the Roman Empire* see Junkelmann (2004: 271–82) and Winkler (2009: 215–20).
65. Winkler (2009: 220).
66. Quoted in Whitlock (2010: 161).
67. Turner (1983: 7). See John Little, *The Independent*, 14 July 1995, who, drawing on Turner's memoires, puts across the impact of her debut:

   > The movie was *They Won't Forget* . . . Lana Turner had only one small scene . . . All the aspiring starlet had to do was walk down the street. Wearing a sweater. A sweater so tight every curve is a come-on. Lana hadn't seen the rushes, so her appearance came as a shock: 'A girl came on screen. A Thing came on screen. She moved sinuously, undulating fore and aft. Mother and I scrooched in our seats. My mother said "My Lord". Someone in the audience whistled. There were gasps. Then the Thing was gone.' Lana ran from the picture palace, 'trying not to bounce'. It was her celluloid debut. She was 15. (http://www.independent.co.uk/life-style/ lana-1591575.html (accessed 7 March 2017))

68. Orrison (1999: 65). Elements of the Forum Romanum set for *The Fall of the Roman Empire* found their way into *A Funny Thing Happened on the Way to the Forum* (dir. Lester, 1966) and sections of the sets and many costume from the 1963 Cleopatra famously ended up in the classic British comic spoof, *Carry on Cleo* (dir. Thomas, 1964).
69. See Isackes and Maness (2017: xix).
70. Blanshard and Shahabudin (2011: 7), with full discussion of on-screen campaign tents at pp. 5–7.
71. Blanshard and Shahabudin (2011: 5).
72. For the *Forma Urbis*, see discussions by Wyke (1997: 140–1); Winkler (2001: 62); Cyrino (2005: 29).
73. This must include the collaboration of special effects artists who created miniature sets or, say, the silent *Ben-Hur* and DeMille's *Samson and Delilah*, for which Gordon Jennings' special effects department created some spectacular visuals, which still pass muster today. The big climax set in the Philistine Temple of Dagon is a triumph of convincing miniature high-speed photography and integrated live action. Less successful, perhaps, are the plague effects and the finger of God in DeMille's *The Ten Commandments* – although the parting of the Red Sea remains a miracle of 1950s filmmaking. See further Orrison (1999: 71–7); Forshey (1992: 136–42).
74. See discussion by Lev (2003: 115–25).

75. See Maltby (2003: 251–5).
76. Cyrino (2005: 47–8).
77. Quoted in Maltby (2003: 249).
78. The powerful lights needed to fill the studio space and especially to create the colourful richness of Technicolor film are evident in the vast lighting rig above Richard Burton's head. This setting is replicated in the closing shots of 2016's *Hail, Caesar!* (dir. Cohen and Cohen). The film's production designer, Jess Goncher, actually used a massive painted backing (depicting the city of Rome) that had been created for Wyler's *Ben-Hur* in 1959. The backing is used behind a courtyard set where a banquet is in progress. Gonchor chose to use the *Ben-Hur* original backcloth as a tribute to the artistry of Hollywood's Golden Age of filmmaking; see Isackes and Maness (2017: 298–9).
79. On the conceptual use of colour in film see Coates (2010).

CHAPTER 3

DESIGNER HISTORY: COSTUMES

What a costume designer does is a cross between magic and camouflage. We create the illusion of changing the actors into what they are not. We ask the public to believe that every time they see a performer on the screen he's become a different person.
Edith Head

Good costumes can make any film enjoyable, but great costumes can make a film iconic. The history of Hollywood has also been a history of amazing costume designers, the gifted artists who created memorable masterpieces. No one underestimates the impact which Marilyn Monroe's full-skirted white cocktail dress from *The Seven Year Itch* (dir. Wilder, 1955) has had on the iconography of female sexuality in contemporary society, or the way in which Humphrey Bogart's trench coat in *Casablanca* (dir. Curtiz, 1942) has added to the creation of a particular form of the he-man image. Images of costumes linger in the mind: the glimmering satin ball gown worn by Deborah Kerr in *The King and I*, John Travolta's white disco suit in *Saturday Night Fever* and Audrey Hepburn's little black dress in *Breakfast at Tiffany's* (dir. Edwards, 1961) all resonate beyond the screen, creating aspirational standards of sartorial expectations.

Epic costumes enjoy iconic status too. Elizabeth Taylor's 24-carat gold cape, designed to look like the wings of a falcon and intricately assembled from thin strips of gold leather and embellished with thousands of bugle beads and sequins, was one of the most expensive costumes ever made. The famous peacock dress worn by Hedy Lamarr's Delilah, Charlton Heston's striped woollen Moses-robe and Kirk Douglas' flat-top Spartacus hair style are all in their own ways icons of the epic genre.

Good directors understood the importance which the role of costume played in the overall success of an epic film production. Unsurprisingly, Cecil B. DeMille often fixated on the details of the costumes of his movies, demanding that his designers rework ideas until he was satisfied with the look which his movie stars – and especially the leading actresses – would wear on screen. DeMille had a very special relationship with women, both professionally and artistically, and he relied heavily on their intelligence and discrimination; he was a tough taskmaster, true, but if an actress pleased him and was prepared to work hard then in his eyes she could do no wrong. For their part, DeMille's women trusted his powerful presence and respected the absolute autocrat that he was. DeMille was certainly pleased with, and perhaps even a little overawed by, Claudette Colbert's rare ability to mix emotion, raw sex and playful irony alongside an innate comedy talent. He cast her as the Empress Poppaea in *The Sign of the Cross* in order to highlight her gifts as an actress and by way of paying homage to her skills, he commissioned the brilliant Mitchell Leisen to design her costumes. DeMille delighted in the publicity images which he had circulated of himself Svengali-like tweaking and teasing the final details of Colbert's sexy, revealing 'Roman'-style Leisen gowns (Figure 3.1).

Costumes, makeup and hair were classified by the Hollywood film industry as key components of the cinematic *mis-en-scène* and, as such, they were considered to perform an important function alongside sets, props, special effects and staging. Studios divided the Costume Department into three separate units of – Wardrobe, Hair and Makeup – each under the leadership of key designers. All three units were expected to work closely together in creating an overall design concept and to produce work which was harmoniously visualised and realised. The diverse elements that created 'the costume' needed careful technical attention. Film costumes needed to be well illuminated by the studio lighting rigs, framed correctly by the camera and even analysed for how the chemical processes of recording them on celluloid would make them appear. Equally important was the question of how costumes were edited into the film, how they developed character and contributed to telling a story (see Text Box 3.1). Edith Head, one of Hollywood's most noted costume designers, once wrote that, 'no matter how good a design might be, until you actually see something on the screen, you are still not sure.' The costumier's art was therefore as collaborative as any other aspect of Hollywood filmmaking.

But the costume departments of the Hollywood studios were also hierarchical, employing huge numbers of staff who were contracted in numerous tasks including research and purchasing or renting, manufac-

Figure 3.1
Cecil B. DeMille inspects the details of Claudette Colbert's costume for Poppaea. *The Sign of the Cross* (1932). Studio publicity photograph.

ture and construction, as well as styling and maintenance. Supporting labourers included seamstresses and beaders, embroiderers, fabric dyers, furriers, cutters, cobblers, pressers, menders, hair-combers and washers, stylists, wig-makers, manicurists, makeup artists, and work-room supervisors and cleaners. In the formative period of the studio system, as the film historian Elizabeth Nielson writes:

Text Box 3.1   The Costume Designer's Craft and the Problem of Spectacle

Deborah Nadoolman Landis, one of today's most acclaimed costume designers, comments on the art of costume design and on the difficulty of creating epic costumes (see Landis 2012d: 7–8):

> The role of the costume designer is really quite simple: costume designers design the people in the movie. Our contribution to the story is more profound than providing the clothes for a production. The word 'costume' works against us. The word is vulgar when what we do is incredibly refined. 'Costume' is invariably associated with Halloween, fancy dress, parade, theme park, Mardi Gras, carnival, and the clothes in fantasy and period films. To costume designers, 'a costume picture' [like an epic] means nothing more than our next project. Adding to the confusion by the industry and the public about our role is an uncertainty about the fundamental purpose of costume design. Film costuming serves two equal purposes: the first is to support the narrative by creating authentic characters (people); and the second is composition, to provide balance within the frame by using colour, texture, and silhouette.
>
> In addition to the creation of the authentic people in the movie, costume designers also help paint each 'frame' of film. If the dialogue is the melody of a movie, the colour provides the harmony, a satisfying visual cohesiveness or 'style'. It is imperative for the designers on a film to have a strong reference point from which to create a style . . . The choices for a designer abound . . . Some designers prefer the stark simplicity of the flat planes of solid colour fabric, while others prefer using multiple patterns and find it the key to layering character. Designers may alter their approach with the feel of the project and make adjustments to accommodate the style of the director . . .
>
> A successful costume must be subsumed by the story and be woven seamlessly into the narrative and visual tapestry of the movie . . . clothes [should] not get in the way of the writer's words. Even in the Hollywood style of the 1930s, which was considered realistic by the 1920s standards, motion pictures could not survive one glamorous entrance after another. Movies are not fashion shows that runway models perform with a blank stare . . . Costumes, like the characters they embody, must evolve within the context of the story and the arc of the character within it. Hollywood has suffered through the poor choice of spectacle over story again and again. From the early epics, which were top-heavy with gaudy sets and bejewelled extras, to today's super-hero special effects extravaganzas, Hollywood has always been tempted to show too much. Certainly, costume design has a place in cinema spectacle, but what the audience remembers

> and what stays forever, is a great movie regardless of the number of people (or what they are wearing) on screen. Whatever the budget, the best movies transport the audience. Suspension of disbelief is complete when the audience 'notices' nothing and is entirely immersed in the story . . . The subtleties of the costume design are well beyond the cut of a period sleeve; they reach into the very soul of the character.

The costume department was a favourite place for studio bosses to place 'girlfriends' and inept relatives for whom they could find no other job in the studios. This practice undermined serious union organisation and also contributed to the low regard in which the costumiers were held by their co-workers in other departments. Conditions and wages for the costumiers were among the worst in the picture industry.[1]

Costume Designers: Stitching Up the Past

In the early days of the film industry, studios had little room in the budget for an on-site costume designer to provide ensembles for the films, so actors generally raided their personal wardrobes to create a 'look' for their on-screen counterparts. In fact, actors played a large part in deciding what their characters would ultimately look like on-screen. But the silent-film era saw the first 'costume departments' being put together in the form of a communal dressing room, of sorts, from which actors could pick and choose what they wished to wear for particular scenes. Not only was this a cost-saving measure for the early studios, it also allowed for some creativity on the parts of performers looking to make an impression. In the case of Charlie Chaplin, it enabled the development of an iconic symbol of silent cinema. It was only with Biograph studio's movie *Judith of Bethulia* (1914) that D. W. Griffith decided to have the costumes for the leading characters specifically designed and created by an expert. Two years later, during the filming of *Intolerance*, Griffith took his attention to costuming detail one step further, hiring Clare West, the first 'studio designer', to craft costumes for not only the lead actors, but for all of the extras too. Whether he intended to or not, Griffith built the template for the costume departments of the later studio system.

Clare West was hired by Cecil B. DeMille in 1918 and she designed extravagant costumes for almost a dozen of his pictures. Her designs were extremely popular with the movie-going public and she dressed Gloria Swanson in *Why Change Your Wife?* and *Something to Think About* (both 1920) and Norma Talmadge in *Ashes of Vengeance*, *The Song of Love* (both 1923) and *Secrets* (1924). West was the first designer to have this kind of sartorial partnership with a filmmaker. *Photoplay* magazine of March 1925 declared that the costumes in *Intolerance* had swayed American fashion in the 1910s, and this became a defining characteristic of West's style over the next decade. She outdid French designers to become the favourite of her era's screen superstars and her costume designs, always pushing extremes, were important contributions to shifts in the wider fashion vanguard, both nationally and abroad.[2]

Movie marketing was already an established trade by the 1920s and costumes, it was realised, could be an effective way of selling a movie to potential fans. The exotic costumes or bold flapper looks worn by leading actresses could be marketed to a paying public eager to copy the on-screen modes. By the 1930s the studios were planning methodical campaigns in order to attract women to new film releases by placing eye-catching fashion images of the stars in fan-magazines and news-papers. For the marketing to work, the stars had to wear the best and most appealing fashions and so the studios hired the finest designers they could find. Therefore, by the early 1930s, sitting at the head of the costume departments were celebrity costume designers who almost commanded as much power, prestige, publicity and payment as the movie stars they dressed. Studios developed particular 'house styles' over the decades and each studio had a head designer who created the on-screen wardrobe of, chiefly, its female stars. At Paramount it was Travis Banton who dressed Marlene Dietrich, Carole Lombard, Mae West and Claudette Colbert. He had few rivals. Edith Head costumed the likes of Bette Davis, Barbara Stanwyck and Hedy Lamarr and would go on to win during her six decades of work, no less than eight Oscars. Paramount also boasted the extraordinary talents of Mitchell Leisen and Howard Greer.

RKO had Bernard Newman (of Ginger Rogers and Fred Astaire fame) working with costume director Walter Plunkett, the brilliant designer and history enthusiast who dressed Vivien Leigh and Olivia de Havilland in *Gone With the Wind*. Orry-Kelly too was committed to research and worked closely with Bette Davis at Warner Brothers in designing a series of dramatic costumes for her period dramas including *The Private Lives of Elizabeth and Essex* (dir. Curtiz, 1939) and *The Little Foxes* (dir. Wyler, 1941). MGM's two most valuable assets were the designer Adrian and his favourite responsibility, Greta Garbo; he costumed Joan Crawford, Norma Shearer and Katharine Hepburn too with his trademark sophistication.

Simply known as Irene, the woman who had started her career at RKO designing the on- and off-screen wardrobes of Rosalind Russell, Irene Dunn, Loretta Young and Ginger Rogers, later worked for seven glorious years at MGM before becoming one of the first Hollywood designers to have boutique salons in department stores throughout America. Charles LeMaire (Figure 3.2) had served his time as a costume designer since the 1920s working for a number of studios but was brought under contract to Twentieth Century Fox in 1944 and in his fifteen years as super-vising costume designer and head of the wardrobe department there

Figure 3.2
Costume designer Charles LeMaire is photographed consulting research material while
surrounded by his designs for *The Robe* (1953). Studio publicity photograph.

he assembled a very strong team of designers, but continued to work
designing for his favourite stars. Finally, Irene Sharaff's work at MGM
and Twentieth Century Fox costuming Gypsy Rose Lee, Deborah Kerr,
Rita Moreno, Judy Garland and Elizabeth Taylor is rightly regarded as a
high point in the history of film design. These individuals helped make
film costume design into an art form of surpassing brilliance.[3]

Yet, as we noted was the case with the production design departments in the preceding chapter, in Hollywood's Golden Age, the
Studios' factory-like environment forced costume designers and those
who were employed under their authority to work in certain restrictive ways. Often a designer was compelled to work on four or five
films simultaneously, producing dozens of sketches in a single day for
film genres as diverse as musicals, Westerns, social comedies and epics
and, because of the unending pressure on a designer's time, it must be
recognised that not all designers produced their own artworks – this
job was often given to a sketch artist who worked closely alongside the
designer, realising his or her idea onto paper through pencils, paints and
charcoals. Costume departments also kept padded mannequins in their
workshops with the measurements of the most prominent movie stars
of the studio so that dress patterns could be completed without having
to wait for an actress to appear for a fitting. This type of on-site assembly
line was needed simply to ensure that actors were costumed efficiently.
Indeed, a rigid separation of jobs helped maintain the industry-like

Figure 3.3.
An unnamed studio dresser checks Elizabeth Taylor's costume before the cameras roll.
Cleopatra. Candid shot, *c*.1962.

atmosphere; the costumiers who worked in the wardrobe department creating the garments, for instance, were formally differentiated from the costume crew (known as dressers – Figure 3.3) who worked the set and dressing rooms. It was the wardrobe workers and not the dressers who first formed a union (Motion Picture Costumers Local 705) in 1937 to protect their membership.

With several new films released each week, costume designers and their teams had to work to exacting standards. The first task was to 'break down' the script, reading it carefully to determine the setting, the period, the characters and the number of outfits needed in each scene. Creating an overall plan for the development of the costumes could be helpful. Irene Sharaff recalls that:

> For *Cleopatra*, in which I designed sixty costumes for Elizabeth Taylor alone, I started using a chart to keep things clear. It covered one wall of the small office, was useful for the colour plan, and served to tell at a glance which costumes and accessories had been shot, which were needed next, and which would be called for later.[4]

After creating a rough sketch for each costume, the designer (or a sketch artist) would produce a finished watercolour for approval by the producer, director and the movie star (Figure 3.4). If accepted, the costume was cut out in fabric – either calico or muslin – as a 'toile' or trial piece; this was used at the first fitting when an actor or actress would be required to turn up at the costume department to try on these rough

Figure 3.4
Reproduction of an original design by Irene Sharaff for Cleopatra (Elizabeth Taylor): a lotus-embroidered kaftan. *Cleopatra* (1963).

garments for shape and size (Figure 3.5). Charlton Heston recalls that for
The Ten Commandments:

> I had to undergo fittings for some fifteen or twenty costumes, from
> the intricate platelet armour I wore in my first scene as an Egyptian
> prince through the burlap rag of the brick pits and the Levite mantle
> of the Exodus. I go down firmly on record: of the many things I do
> preparing for a part, fitting wardrobe is the worst. It comes right

Figure 3.5
The agony of the fitting room: Charlton Heston tries on a calico toile of his charioteer
costume. Candid shot, c.1958.

before still-portrait sessions. Oddly, actresses seem to enjoy both.
Vive la différence![5]

The actress Myrna Loy would have disagreed. She too regarded the
business of wardrobe fittings as one of the most tedious chores of the
job:

> Each costume had to be tried on for endless camera tests, because
> no matter how good it may look in the fitting room, it's the eye of

the camera that has to be satisfied. Every detail has to be perfect in advance, so as not to hold up shooting or cause a need for reshoots . . . this required me to stand patiently and quietly for hours at a time.

There was no question of sitting around between scenes either. If there were waits while lights were adjusted or sets were changed, actors needed to remove their costumes and attend further fittings or were required to lean against stiff 'reclining boards' that were set up on the sound-stages – wrinkles in the costumes were not allowed.

Costume fittings could be fraught experiences, a time when egos clashed and tempers flared. Even the steeliest costume designers went to some fittings with trepidation, awaiting the mood of the movie star to dictate how events would transpire. Towards the end of her career, working with the notoriously difficult Faye Dunaway playing Joan Crawford on *Mommie Dearest* (dir. Perry, 1981) Irene Sharaff was asked by one of the wardrobe staff if she might enter the star's dressing room; 'Yes, you may enter Miss Dunaway's dressing room,' said Sharaff, 'but first you best throw a raw steak in to divert her attention.'[6] As Cyrino notes:

> The constant tension between Sharaff and Dunaway is the stuff of Hollywood legend: it started when Anne Bancroft quit the picture over the unsympathetic role; and then Dunaway stepped in, but demanded that Sharaff create an entirely new wardrobe for her. Sharaff refused. 'I didn't design the clothes for Anne Bancroft,' she told Dunaway, 'I designed them for Joan Crawford.'[7]

While a director and a producer may have been happy with the costume designs, there was no guarantee that the actor would be happy to wear the final costumes. Claudette Colbert, for instance, could prove to be a steely foe to designers and directors alike when it suited her, given that she believed that the protection of her star image relied on her complete control of the off-camera production process. Having studied fashion design as a girl, Colbert was very knowledgeable about the industry and her own wardrobe confirmed her to be a woman of exquisite taste (Figure 3.6). Yet she was very unsure about her own looks and was insecure about her beauty, obsessed with the idea that a tiny 'bump' on the right side of her nose – the result of a childhood accident – gave her a 'bad side'. Consequently she insisted on being shot from her left side (encouraging Mary Astor to quip that, 'The right side of [Colbert's] face was called The Dark Side of the Moon because nobody ever saw it').[8] Once one becomes aware of this fact it is impossible to watch her movies, even the very best of them, without trying to see that hated right profile (it really is not so different from her left side; the popular actress Norma Shearer had a far more drastically challenging profile than Colbert and she managed a successful screen career nonetheless). Colbert was determined to look perfect, and she thought that she knew

Figure 3.6
Like mother like daughter: ever the fashionable sophisticate, Claudette Colbert takes time
between shooting scenes to chat with her mother who was visiting the set. *Cleopatra*
(1934). Studio publicity still.

best about how to present her Kewpie-doll face with its widely spaced
eyes and apple cheeks: 'I have been in the Claudette Colbert business
longer than anybody,' she once said, with the pride of an entrepreneur.[9]

Colbert insisted too on working only alongside Travis Banton, the
one costume designer whom she truly trusted to create clothing which
flattered her (Figure 3.7). But this still did not rule out clashes between

Figure 3.7
Travis Banton with Claudette Colbert, together with one of his Cleopatra creations. Studio
publicity photograph from the *Cleopatra* pressbook (1934).

the designer and the star. For her role as Cleopatra, for instance, Colbert
asked Banton to create gowns which would bare as much of her bosom
as possible, focusing attention above her waist, which she considered
to be too thick, and drawing attention away from her neck which she
claimed was too short. Banton indulged her, as far as the censorship
regulations would allow. When she saw the sketches and prototype
garments she obtusely refused to accept any of the costume designs
he had created for her and flew into a rage when she realised that the
costume sketches had been rendered by another artist. With disapprov-
ing comments written all over the beautiful designs, Colbert departed
for home. Banton sent a second set of costume sketches for her approval,
with instructions that she had better either like them or slit her wrists.
The next day Banton waited and waited, only to have them returned
streaked with dried blood. Furious, Banton left the studio and went on a
drinking binge, not returning until several days later when studio head,
Adolph Zukor, called him personally and mediated the situation.

Colbert's rejection of the designs meant that Banton was obliged
to come up with another design concept and the delay that therefore
ensued in the wardrobe department cost the production many thousands of dollars (Text Box 3.2).[10] Yet if the star was profitable enough,
studios – and even autocratic directors like DeMille – turned a blind eye

Text Box 3.2   Costume Fittings as Blood Sport: Claudette Colbert's Cleopatra

By 1934 Claudette Colbert – all but a glorified ingénue when DeMille had cast her two years earlier in *The Sign of the Cross* – was one of Hollywood's most important assets, a genuine superstar. It was well known to costume designers that stars could be troublesome, but Colbert's behaviour during the production of *Cleopatra* can only be labelled 'unprofessional'. Her insistence on scrapping Banton's original designs necessitated a whole new wardrobe being made for *Cleopatra*; this brought chaos to the wardrobe department. A chronological outline of events (drawn from original production logs cited in Birchard (2004: 276–81) can be reconstructed thus:

9 March 1934: Costumer Victoria Williams resigns from the production, unhappy with what she perceived to be a lack of organisation in the costume department.

12 March 1934: First day of shooting. The daily production report notes that 'Costumes not ready'.

13 March 1934: Production report states: 'Costume delay owing to shoes not being ready'.

17 March 1934: Rehearsal with principals in the morning. After lunch, DeMille orders Colbert's headdress changed. A delay in filming of two hours and fifteen minutes.

23 March 1934: 'Delay owing to wardrobe not being ready'.

4 April 1934: Night shoot. Call at 7pm. 'Miss Colbert late on set. She was sent for at 7.10 and asked to come immediately when called, which was 7.40. She arrived at 8.10, not in costume'. Shooting wrapped at 5.20 am.

5 April 1934: 'There was a two and a half hour delay while the crown worn by Miss Colbert was changed'.

6 April 1934: 'There was a three-hour delay while Miss Colbert's costume was got ready'. The assistant director suggested that there might be an element of star temperament behind some of the delays, noting, 'the three hours delay of 4/6/34 was due to the fact that Miss Colbert did not fit [i.e. attend costume fittings] the night before, thus at 8.30 am of the 4/6/34 she found her costume unsatisfactory for her'.

7 April 1934: 'The company dismissed at 12.30 pm. Miss Colbert came back to the set at 1.40 reporting that she had sent back her costume as being unsatisfactory to her. The previous evening Mr DeMille released her from her final long shot in order that she might have a fitting. She gave 20 minutes of her time at the end of which she ok'd the costume. At 1.30 she sent it back as not being satisfactory, thus occasioning a two hour delay'.

10 April 1934: Colbert went home early, complaining of illness. She remained at home on April 11, 12, 13, and 14, putting the production three days behind schedule.

16 April 1934: Colbert returned to set.

20 April 1934: '84 mins lost owing to Miss Colbert not answering her calls on time'.

25 April 1934: 'Miss Colbert late back from lunch'.

2 May 1934: Principal photography completed. Colbert completes her work.

Figure 3.8
Four of Cleopatra's costumes are placed on dress mannequins padded to match Elizabeth Taylor's exact measurements. Second from the left is the lotus-embroidered kaftan seen in Figure 3.4. *Cleopatra* (1963). Wardrobe reference photograph, 1962.

to such tantrums and looked the other way when they pulled rank on employees lower down the studio power structure.

Once the first fitting had been completed the costume was cut out in the desired fabric – which could potentially be very costly – and was fitted to the dress-stands padded to the star's measurements (Figure 3.8). Once completed it was then finally fitted to the performer and the actor or actress was required to stand under studio lights approximating those used on the set; here the costume, hair and make-up was scrutinised by the director and designer from every angle. The necessary adjustments were made to costumes that passed the test, although many different looks might be tried out during these intense and stressful sessions; some costumes were dropped from the film, some needed reworking. It was only when the director, designer and the star were

Figure 3.9
A series of costume reference shots and makeup and hairstyle try-outs for Charlton Heston as prince Moses, alongside a reproduction of Arnold Friberg's conception sketch for Moses, Prince of Egypt. *The Ten Commandments* (1956).

happy with the final look (Figure 3.9) that the costume would be put aside ready to be used during the filming process itself (Figure 3.10) and in the myriad of photoshoots and advertisement campaigns needed to promote the film (Figure 3.11).

It was customary in the studios' wardrobe departments to assign different tasks to a set of designers: the principal female wardrobe was always assigned to a studio's head costume designer who carried out the studio 'look' and worked closely alongside the leading female stars, while male leads were costumed by another designer who specialised in the cut and construction of men's dress. Secondary male and female costumes were shared between other designers and yet more costumiers worked with the extras (the same division operated in the hair and make-up departments). For an epic film, given its scale, this method of partition was rigidly observed. DeMille appointed five designers to dress his cast in *Samson and Delilah* for instance, allotting Gile Steele and Elois Jenssen the responsibility for the male costumes and Dorothy Jeakins and Gwen Wakeling the daunting task of costuming the extras.[11] But he gave the glamour assignment to Edith Head, who was commissioned to dress Delilah and her sister, Semadar (Angela Lansbury). The task of costuming *The Ten Commandments* was given to Arnold Friberg (designing for Charlton Heston and Yul Brynner), Johnny Jensen (sup-

Figure 3.10
Elizabeth Taylor wearing the cerulean blue lotus-embroidered St Tropez-style tunic, designed by Irene Sharaff – see Figure 3.4. *Cleopatra* (1963). Production still.

porting actresses), Dorothy Jeakins (supporting actors), Edith Head (Anne Baxter and leading actresses) and Ralph Jester (extras). Regarding DeMille as an egotist or (as she bluntly put it in her memoirs), 'a freak trying to play God', Edith Head thought that DeMille's habit of over-staffing costume designers was 'a ploy for him to maintain complete control over the visualisation of his films; if he had several designers attempting to costume the film, then he became the unifying factor.'[12]

Many designers found this division of labour frustrating, perhaps none more keenly so than Irene Sharaff whose background as a suc-cessful Broadway costume designer had necessitated a 'one designer' approach to all productions, giving them a cohesive and integrated look. She noted that in Hollywood in the early 1950s:

There was an almost Victorian attitude in the separation of the design-ing of men's costumes from those of the women. Hardly any attention was given to integrating the costumes of stars with the others, and little thought was given to a degree of coherence in the look of a scene and of the production as a whole.[13]

Figure 3.11
Charlton Heston in the linen and leather charioteer costume seen in embryo in Figure 3.5.
Ben-Hur (1959). Pressbook.

The Production Code and Costume Design

From 1930 to 1966 Hollywood filmmaking was rigidly controlled by a set of morality regulations known as the Production Code, by which every film had to be submitted to a board of censors who worked in close conjunction with the Catholic Legion of Decency to keep a tight rein on Hollywood morality (Text Box 3.3); if it was felt that a film violated the Code, the producer was not allowed to release it to the cinemas until the required changes had been made.[14] Fearful of unintentionally crossing

Text Box 3.3   The Motion Picture Production Code

First published in March 1930, the Motion Picture Production Code (popularly known as the Hays Code after its creator, William H. Hays) was the first attempt at introducing film censorship in America by laying down a series of restrictive guidelines to film producers. The Code was founded on a basic concept: 'If motion pictures present stories that will affect lives for the better, they can become the most powerful force for the improvement of mankind.' The clear implication was that films were signally failing to achieve these moral aims.

The Code was based on three general principles:

- No picture shall be produced that will lower the moral standards of those who see it. Hence the sympathy of the audience should never be thrown to the side of crime, wrongdoing, evil or sin.
- Correct standards of life, subject only to the requirements of drama and entertainment, shall be presented.
- Law, natural or human, shall not be ridiculed, nor shall sympathy be created for its violation.

These were developed in a series of rules grouped under the self-explanatory headings Crimes Against the Law, Sex, Vulgarity, Obscenity, Profanity, Costume, Dances (i.e. suggestive movements), Religion, Locations (i.e. the bedroom), National Feelings, Titles and 'Repellent Subjects' (extremely graphic violence).

Although these guidelines were technically voluntary, in practice the major Hollywood studios used the Hays Code guidelines as a convenient means of staving off pressure groups and as a result, the Hays Code (and similar strictures laid down by the hugely influential Catholic Legion of Decency – see below) directly influenced the content of almost every American film made between 1930 and 1966, when the Motion Picture Association of America introduced classification certificates for each film produced by the studios.

So why did the studios agree to such Draconian self-censorship? There are several reasons. It kept Washington from exercising even more control over the studios; it quelled fears from religious groups threatening boycotts during economically unstable times; and, lastly, and perhaps most cynically, the Production Code was a sort of blueprint for screenwriters. Stories could move in only one direction – love ended in marriage, crime ended in punishment – a simple and efficient method for the studio system to streamline the story process and mass produce as many movies as possible.

The screenwriter Gene Fowler, commenting on the absurdity of the Hays Code, once wrote: 'Will Hays is my shepherd, I shall not want. He maketh me to lie down in clean postures.'

Catholic Influence on the Hays Code – The National Legion of Decency

In 1930 a Catholic priest, Father Daniel Lord, began writing a code that gave general guidelines for what was morally acceptable in films. His list banned glorifying criminal and gangster activity, adulterers, prostitutes, showing nudity, excessive violence, profanity, white slavery, illegal drugs, suggestive postures and overly sensual kissing in films. His code also asked films to promote morality and wholesome social institutions, and defend the government and religious institutions. Lord's code was difficult to enforce at first, so in November 1933, Catholic bishops appointed a committee to begin an outspoken campaign against immorality in movies. This led to the formation of the Catholic Legion of Decency in 1934. The religious affiliations of the Legion were directed within the membership of the Catholic Church, but also included Protestant and Jewish members. Though the group was originally called the Catholic Legion of Decency, Catholic was soon replaced by National because of its more widespread membership.

The Legion publicly listed film ratings declaring what was admissible for Catholics to watch. However, Catholics were not content with the outcome and enforcement of the code, and this contributed to the growing membership of the Legion, millions signing pledges to boycott movies that were offensive. The pledge was as follows:

> I condemn all indecent and immoral motion pictures, and those which glorify crime or criminals. I promise to do all that I can to strengthen public opinion against the production of indecent and immoral films, and to unite with all who protest against them. I acknowledge my obligation to form a right conscience about pictures that are dangerous to my moral life. I pledge myself to remain away from them. I promise, further, to stay away altogether from places of amusement which show them as a matter of policy.

In an attempt to work with the religious organisations, Will Hays appointed a Catholic, Joseph I. Breen, as director of his Production Code Administration. After 1934 no film could be viewed in any major US theatre without a seal of approval from the Production Code Administration. The Legion viewed every film made in Hollywood and released its ratings publicly, forbidding Catholics to attend any film that was condemned.

What the Legion Wanted Banned from Films: An Excerpt from the 'Don'ts and Be Carefuls' List

Resolved, that those things which are included in the following list shall not appear in pictures produced by the members of this Association, irrespective of the manner in which they are treated:

1. Pointed profanity – by either title or lip – this includes the words 'God', 'Lord', 'Jesus', 'Christ' (unless they be used reverently in connection

> with proper religious ceremonies), 'hell', 'damn', 'Gawd', and every other profane and vulgar expression however it may be spelled.
> 2. Any licentious or suggestive nudity – in fact or in silhouette; and any lecherous or licentious notice thereof by other characters in the picture.
> 3. The illegal traffic in drugs.
> 4. Any inference of sex perversion.
> 5. White slavery.
> 6. Miscegenation (sex relationships between the white and black races).
> 7. Sex hygiene and venereal diseases.
> 8. Scenes of actual childbirth – in fact or in silhouette.
> 9. Children's sex organs.
> 10. Ridicule of the clergy.
> 11. Offence to any nation, race, or creed.

the lines of acceptability, cautious directors even hired priests to serve as advisors on set or allowed priests to work on editorial boards for scripts. At the end of the production process, a film would be awarded a rating which, in reality, expressed its level of compliancy with the code. When it was released in 1963, for instance, *Cleopatra* was proclaimed 'morally unacceptable' by the Catholic Legion of Decency and was given an official 'B' rating ('morally objectionable in parts').[15]

Every aspect of production could potentially come into conflict with the Code but perhaps the most obvious bone of contention for the Code's operators and enforcers was the use of costume. Body-image was, after all, at the front-line of the Code's principal concerns. Each costume that appeared on-screen had to satisfy the rules of the Motion Picture Production Code and the costume departments of each of the Hollywood studios were bound by a series of rigid regulations:

General principles:
(1) The effect of nudity or semi-nudity upon the normal man or woman, and much more upon the young person, has been honestly recognised by all lawmakers and moralists.
(2) Hence the fact that the nude or semi-nude body may be *beautiful* does not make its use in films moral. For in addition to its beauty, the effects of the nude or semi-nude body on the normal individual must be taken into consideration.
(3) Nudity or semi-nudity used simply to put a punch into a picture comes under the head of immoral actions as treated above. It is immoral in its effect upon the average audience.
(4) Nudity or semi-nudity is sometimes apparently necessary for the plot. *Nudity is never permitted.* Semi-nudity may be permitted under conditions.

Particular principles:

(1) *The more intimate parts of the human body* are male and female organs and the breasts of a woman.

    (a) They should *never be uncovered*.

    (b) They should *not* be covered with *transparent* or *translucent* material.

    (c) They should not be clearly and unmistakably *outlined* by the garment.

(2) *The less intimate parts of the body*, the legs, arms, shoulders and back, are less certain of causing reactions on the part of the audience.

Hence:

    (a) Exposure *necessary for the plot* or action is permitted.

    (b) Exposure *for the sake of exposure* or the punch is wrong.

    (c) *Scenes of undressing* should be avoided. When necessary for the plot, they should be kept within the limits of decency. When not necessary for the plot, they are to be avoided, as their effect on the ordinary spectator is harmful.

    (d) *The manner or treatment of exposure* should not be suggestive or indecent.

    (e) The following is important in connection with *dancing costumes*:

        1. Dancing costumes cut to permit *grace* or freedom of movement, provided they remain within the limits of decency indicated are permissible.

        2. Dancing costumes cut to *permit indecent actions* or movements or to make possible during the dance indecent exposure, are wrong, especially when permitting:

            1. Movements of the breasts;

            2. Movements or sexual suggestions of the intimate parts of the body;

            3. Suggestion of nudity.[16]

In his lively and intimate memoire, *I Am Spartacus*, Kirk Douglas recalls the many fights he had with the studio censors during the creation of his Roman epic and notes how time-consuming, infuriating and creatively destructive the Production Code could be for artists of integrity. The correspondence focusing on costume issues which went back and forth between the production office and the censors, he says, 'seems laughable now', but during the *Spartacus* shoot, interference from the censors often caused costly delays. Some 'lowlights' (as Douglas calls them) of the costume offences identified in the script by the censors included:

Page 1: The costumes of the slaves will have to offer adequate covering.

Page 24: The loincloth costumes must prove adequate.

Page 72: Scenes of the men and women swimming in the nude will be unacceptable.

> Page 168: We cannot approve the reference to milk stains on Varinia's
> gown.
> Pages 200 and 201: This scene seems to suggest over-exposing Varinia
> while nursing her child.
> Page 210: It would be as well to avoid nursing action, in any event it
> will require most careful handling.[17]

For the studio costume designers the Code's regulations meant that they had to be especially inventive in their work. This applied especially to the costuming of actresses: the management of an actress's cleavage and the motion of her breasts as well as the amount of skin showing in the upper leg area was always of concern; the covering of her navel was always demanded, as Edith Head recalled:

> Censorship was kind of crazy in that period . . . the navel was some-
> thing you never showed. We used to stuff pearls in navels with glue.
> Sometimes we'd have a whole row of dancers with jewels in their
> navels. Even that kind of camouflage wouldn't always pass, so we
> finally had to put a band of gold or jewels around the waistline to
> hide the navel. I don't know why navels were so censorable, but they
> were. And why only women's navels? Male bellybuttons seemed to
> be okay. I could never understand the discrimination.[18]

In *Samson and Delilah*, therefore, Victor Mature was able to wear a short tunic or a skimpy loincloth which showed his chest, waist and even his thighs but Hedy Lamarr was not even permitted to reveal her navel. Consequently, Edith Head was forced to come up with novel ways of concealing the actress' navel and to restrict the appearance of pro-truding pelvic bones (Figure 3.12). With any focus on the pelvic area removed, attention naturally had to shift to the bust region. DeMille had set his mind on his Delilah being moulded on the 'classic temptress' look, and even the fastidious Edith Head admitted that DeMille had got his casting right: Lamarr looked like 'the all-time *femme fatale*' she wrote many years later.[19] Jacques Doniol-Valcroze considered Lamarr's Delilah a 'sophisticated vamp portrayed . . . with ravishing *froideur*, cal-culating femininity and the coquettishness of a petulant bimbo'.[20]

In casting Hedy Lamarr DeMille got Delilah's signature character right, but there was one glaring physical omission that Lamarr suffered: 'she is certainly a little bit stringy for the taste of those who like their Delilahs plump.'[21] Although there are no biblical descriptions of Delilah, within the tradition of classic biblical portraiture she had long been por-trayed as a voluptuous, big-bosomed woman. Indeed, 'the phenomenon of visualising a textual figure is almost indispensable while reading a narrative that contains references to love and sexuality. The stereotypic temptress is good-looking, quite young, saucy, inviting, ripe to overripe, seductively attired, with big breasts – a Playboy centrefold girl'.[22] It was an assessment borne out by many Old Masters: Rubens (who had deeply

Figure 3.12
Silver lamé costume by Edith Head for Hedy Lamarr as Delilah; the bellybutton is concealed, although legs and cleavage are revealed. *Samson and Delilah* (1949). Studio publicity photograph.

influenced DeMille's vision of Delilah), for example, depicted her with large naked breasts and exposed nipples squeezed into focus by her tight clothing.[25] Therefore, after consulting all the historical paintings of Delilah (as his usual research thoroughness demanded), one might have expected DeMille to choose an actress with similar proportions for this biblical story of 'first-degree fatal attraction'.[24] Certainly, the *Samson and Delilah* pre-production artwork commissioned from studio artist Dan Groesbeck showed a brawny athlete being eyed-up by a big-busted, slim-waisted siren. Yet, in the casting process DeMille chose the flat-chested Hedy Lamarr to star as his Delilah. Reviewers lamented Lamarr's lack of curves: 'All the revealing costuming lavished on her by [Edith] Head left me desiring her to put some clothes on! There was really nothing to see . . .'[25] and 'DeMille has allowed the strings of sex to sag.'[26] Edith Head's Oscar-winning intervention was required to make Lamarr more Rubenesque:

> For *Samson and Delilah*, we had sketched costumes with a voluptuous bust-line Hedy couldn't fill. 'I'm not a big bosomy woman', she said (she's slim actually); 'if you pad me I'll look ridiculous. I won't be able to act. I'll feel as if I'm carting balloons.' So her costumes were not padded; we achieved a voluptuous effect by line, by drapery, and nothing could have been lovelier than the Delilah I took to Mr. DeMille in a costume of mesh and beaten silver, so lovely he actually *smiled*![27]

As Lamarr's own agent confessed to her: 'When [DeMille] sells sex . . . people buy because he wraps it in fancy paper with pink ribbons.'[28] Somewhat ironically, the agent urged her to do the film because it would be a mixture of 'muscles, tits and sadism', or at least 'muscles and tits sugar-coated with religion'.[29]

Oddly, some reviewers were determined to see sex where none existed. For example, it was claimed that: 'C. B. DeMille's spectaculars . . . gave legions of puritanical voyeurists a good excuse to watch Delilah romping in the near-buff. For one ticket, the audience got both sermons *and* tits!'[30] Yet in the movie Delilah's body is never exposed or in a 'near-buff' state. But reviewers' willingness to seek for that particular brand of DeMillian sex does testify to the director's finesse for creating on-screen 'sexless sex' – as well as the skills of Edith Head and her beautiful costume designs.[31]

According to the Hollywood studios, women's dress in antiquity had to be timelessly graceful – that was a given – and the epics' virginal 'good girls', played mainly by English actresses, were often dressed in sophisticated gowns of restrained elegance. A deceptively simple looking 'Classical'-style gown of pink silk-jersey and white chiffon worn by Jean Simmons in *The Robe* for instance (Figure 3.13) actually has the highly complex cut of a contemporary Norman Hartnell creation – the young Queen Elizabeth II's favourite couturier. But the costumes of the queens and 'bad girls' of the epics – the Cleopatras, Bathshebas and Poppaeas, the Delilahs, Shebas and Nefretiris, played by fast-talking Americans or sultry Europeans, were expected to be contemporary, alluring and – importantly – diaphanous. In order to overcome the problem of the Code's restrictions on revealing the female body, many costume designers used *mousseline de soie*, a semi-transparent flesh-coloured silk to suggest nudity. When combined with transparent materials like gauze and chiffon, the *mousseline de soie* acted as a base: 'so long as there was

Figure 3.13
A complex cut for a deceptively simple costume. Jean Simmons as Diana. *The Robe* (1953).
Studio publicity photograph.

a covering, however thin', Irene Sharaff recalls, 'the studio could claim that the actress was fully clothed.'[32] Ralph Jester's costumes for Gina Lollobrigida in *Solomon and Sheba* capitalised on this trick and he used her olive skin, black hair and dark doe-eyes to give Sheba an appropriately erotic appearance (Figure 3.14). A review in the film magazine *Schermi* (20 January 1960) notes how 'La Lollo has a tête-à-tête with Solomon-Brynner, for which she wears a very transparent nocturnal combination, destined to become part of postwar erotic iconography.'

Figure 3.14
A flesh-coloured *mousseline de soie* and white chiffon confection for Gina Lollobrigida's
Queen of Sheba. *Solomon and Sheba* (1959). Studio publicity photograph.

Lollobrigida's costume is constructed with a Dior-like perfection out of
flesh-coloured *mousseline de soie* and white chiffon, artfully draped and
fixed in a way to both conceal and reveal the actress's body; the folds act
as a genital map, highlighting in particular the groin and suggesting the
line of the breasts which are, in fact, well corseted, uplifted, separated
and immovable. There is, however, no hint of a bellybutton.

The Studios were prepared to use epics, under the guise of historical authenticity, to push the Production Code to the limits. *Solomon*

Figure 3.15
Pushing at the Production Code: Lana Turner in a bead costume designed by Herschel
McCoy. *The Prodigal* (1955). Studio publicity photograph.

and Sheba's pressbook, for example, noted that 'all Miss Lollobrigida's
twenty-four separate costumes . . . were absolutely authentic and would
bring full approval from Biblical scholars and historical experts,' a familiar marketing tool that was employed too for *The Prodigal* which, with
its gowns for Lana Turner designed by Herschel McCoy, pushed against
the censorship regulations with some abandon (Figure 3.15). As Turner
herself recalls:

I was to play a creature called Samarra, the high priestess of Astarte, goddess of the flesh, who was the very temptress who incited the prodigal son of the Bible to leave his home . . . The costumes were atrocious. They were ornate concoctions dripping with heavy beads, and the material was so stiff that I felt I was wearing armour. 'Well', I thought, 'I may be trapped in this picture, but I'm going to make myself as sensuous, sexy, and gorgeous as possible . . . I wanted to show flesh. Afraid of losing her job, the wardrobe mistress refused to tamper with the costumes. 'Give me those scissors,' I said, and I proceeded to cut huge pieces out of the costumes . . . Actually I was quite pleased with my alterations. I revealed more than the Production Code allowed, and they had to airbrush my publicity stills before their release.[33]

In the 1956 version of *The Ten Commandments*, scantily clad women in translucent, clinging gowns became part of the marketing strategy, as the *New York Times* journalist Joseph Laitin, reporting from the set on the Paramount sound-stage, was quick to exploit:

Cecil B. DeMille had suddenly ordered the cameras to stop rolling as Nina Foch, playing pharaoh's daughter, emerged dripping wet from the 'Nile' bearing a blanket containing the infant Moses. With the dress clinging to her body, Miss Foch's personality came through as never before! The dress even looked flesh-coloured . . . The usual procedure is to test-dunk the material beforehand; in this case Miss [Edith] Head had deemed it unnecessary because the script merely said that Miss Foch would 'wade' into the river. 'How should I know', Edie later said, 'that Mr DeMille's idea of wading is what I call deep-sea diving?'[34]

The sheer clothing employed in the epics could be justified by the ancient settings and the need to visually portray moral temptation, but film-makers could hardly have been unaware of the added market appeal of such scenes. Defending his overtly sensual visualisation of the ancient world, DeMille argued that:

The men and women of the Bible [were] flesh and blood. Clothing them in what we think is reverence, we have too often stripped [them] of their humanity . . . People will not come to see a picture in which Biblical characters walk around looking and acting like Biblical characters . . . They were men and women. And that is how I portray them.[35]

History and Designer History

The notion of historicism contends that we should try to understand the past from its own perspective, and that we should attempt to totally eliminate our modern concepts of the past during the process of research. A historicist would therefore contend that the design of any historical film should be as authentic as possible. However, current issues in taste, perception and reception are always and unavoidably present whenever history is narrated, irrespective if it is academic scholarship or imaginative fiction. Historical investigation is a process of dialogue in which our present-day thinking encounters the thinking of the past. The present day cannot be denied or eliminated so that while describing the past, the author is simultaneously writing about his or her own world. This is very much the case with Hollywood's epics, where a variety of voices (director, designers, stars) converge, merge or clash over their retelling of history. The result, according to the film theorist Charles Tashiro, is not so much 'realist history' as 'designer history', a process through which:

> historical references become secondary to design, although they are never totally absent . . . Designer history . . . combines the apolitical focus of costume melodrama with the impersonal affect of the traditional History Film. The past becomes a movement of empty forms and exquisite objects . . . mannequins fighting over nothing beyond the quality of tailoring.[36]

The costume design of an epic film is particularly aware of the process of creating historical authenticity which at one and the same time appeals to contemporary taste. In fact, as Tashiro suggests, more than anything else, makeup, hairstyles and costumes in the typical epic are often adjusted to the period when the film was made to become the primary focus of Designer History. It is no surprise to see Cleopatra in high-heels (Figure 3.16).

As we have recognised, the construction of each of the on-screen costumes used in the making of epic films was a collaborative effort, involving chiefly the director and the costume designer together with the designers of hair and makeup; the results reflected the particular concepts of beauty and sexual magnetism which were popular at the time of filming. Costume designers were required to research the historical period of the film's location to give an aura of reality, but were then often free to interpret the ideals of feminine beauty embedded in their contextual culture, which she shared with the contemporary audience to whom they were trying to 'sell' their products. Hollywood's 'historical' costumes always make a fashionable statement, although at the time of a film's production, the contemporary aesthetic might be hard to spot because the audience themselves were so immersed in that 'look'. As Geoffrey Squire puts it:

> Every age remakes the visible world to suit itself and so has its own peculiar way of looking at the clothes which form its daily wear. The eyes of the beholders are so affected by their brains that they see not precisely what is before them, but what they wish to be there.[37]

Figure 3.16
Cleopatra in high-heels. *Cleopatra* (1963). Candid shot taken on set, 1962.

Epic costumes bridge the gap between past and present.[38] Hollywood's directors, designers, publicity managers and marketing experts understood that 'historical' films were actually devices used to exploit the notion of film glamour and the epic was primarily used to place top stars in fantastical situations, enabling their fans to see them acting in romantic or heroic ways while wearing revealing or flamboyant outfits. The star's personality or fashionable style could not, however, be subsumed beneath historical authenticity. Thus, as we have already gleaned in the case of Colbert's Cleopatra, the costumes had to suggest another time and another place, but not at the expense of losing what was unique and appealing about Colbert's own carefully manufactured Hollywood image. This was the standard Hollywood policy and this fact was never allowed to dampen the rhetoric of research which was integrated into the more commercial aspects of filmmaking. Publicity campaigns run prior to epic productions included cross-country lecture tours and the publishing of scholarly articles on the historical authenticity of the costumes employed in the film. Studios insisted on keeping the myth of historical research alive (see Text Box 3.4). In the pressbooks Charles LeMaire is credited as having worked with a curator at the Brooklyn Museum for two years in order to gather information for *The Egyptian* and for the 1959 *Ben-Hur* Elizabeth Haffenden is said to have 'spent more than a year in preliminary work before the first foot of film moved through the camera in Rome.'

As might be expected, the master rhetorician on the theme of veracity through costume was DeMille. In a short film called *Extra Girl*, used to advertise his 1935 medieval-era epic *The Crusades*, for instance, we are shown this important aspect of DeMille's idea of the marketability of historicity. The movie short, narrating a day in the life of an extra in *The Crusades*, is set on the Paramount sound-stages; DeMille is shown sitting on top of a studio camera crane directing the action on the studio floor from on high. He calls 'Cut!' and swoops down, *deus ex machina*-like, and focuses on the costume of the young female extra: 'What's that girl doing over there with a 1935 headdress!?', he bursts out angrily. 'You know, this isn't a fantasy, it's history! She looks as though she just walked out of a beauty salon!' Later in the film, lecturing less loudly but with equal bombast, he tells the girl that the 'art of the screen isn't just . . . looking . . . like a tomato-mouth-blonde. It's learning great art and to express that fire within.' With this kind of on-screen bombast, DeMille helped reconfirm his own myth as a devotee to, and high priest of, historical fact. In reality, of course, things were different, as John Cary notes wryly:

> When DeMille was ready to start directing, the research and documentation were put aside as cinematic licence cut sweeping arcs through all the historical data: Delilah, Cleopatra and Roman maidens at the time of Nero could all be seen wearing high heels with fashionable nineteen-thirties ankle straps, zippers on the sides of their costumes, and nature-aiding uplift bras.[39]

We have already ascertained that Edith Head's relationship with DeMille was strained and the fact is that much of the tension arising between them came from DeMille's reticence in treating her with the deference which she thought was her due, given her position as Paramount's Head Costume Designer. He would often demand that she make twenty or thirty designs for one costume and would have photostats made of

Text Box 3.4   Fitting for a Fabulous 'Prodigal'

Figure 3.17
Historical research runs riot. Costumes by Herschel McCoy for women of the Persian Empire on the
'Carousel of Love' in the brothel in Samaria, including Greek, Minoan, Egyptian and Japanese girls.
The costumes are pure Ziegfeld Follies. *The Prodigal* (1955). Studio publicity photograph.

MGM is spending more than $250,000 on a wardrobe for its current multi-million-dollar
production, 'The Prodigal'. This is the biggest wardrobe expenditure on this lot in twenty
years, some 3,600 hundred costumes are being created. The costumes for Lana Turner,
who plays the High Priestess of Baal and Astarte, the Syrian gods of fertility and creation,
cost $47,000. The costumes of Edmund Purdom who plays the title role of the Prodigal
cost $38,000.

Wardrobe for a motion picture, like a screenplay, starts with a basic conception or
theme. 'The Prodigal', based upon the parable told in Luke Chapter XV, takes place in Syria
and Palestine in the year 79 BC. This was after that territory was captured by Alexander
the Great and before the conquest of Rome. Greek and Persian influences dominated the
lives of the people in what was even then the crossroads of the world. Therefore the people
would be dressed in costumes which combined Greek and Persian elements.

Requisites

Wardrobe for a motion picture must be authentic yet theatrical. Authenticity for 'The Prodigal' wardrobe derives from the recent excavations in Persepolis, ancient capital of the Persian kings Cyrus and Darius. Thousands of almost life-size figures were uncovered. They represented citizens of all the nations of the known-world bringing tribute to Persia. The tribute bearers wore their native dress carved in miniature detail on the Persepolis figures. To take advantage of these newly excavated discoveries, every costume in 'The Prodigal', star and extra alike, is unique and especially designed and manufactured. Practically no advantage could be taken of the 650,000 costumes in MGM's seven wardrobe store buildings, all catalogued, sized, and hanging ready for use in two hours' notice.

Theatricality for 'The Prodigal' wardrobe was entrusted to Herschel McCoy, who designed costumes for 'Quo Vadis', 'Julius Caesar' and 'Joan of Arc'. McCoy spent weeks on research, weeks on discussions with Sam Kress, wardrobe department chief and with Richard Thorpe, the director. He then locked himself in a small room in the wardrobe building, with only a pencil and a sketchpad for company.

Materials

Once the patterns were judged workable, requisitions were made to the wardrobe stockroom which carries over half a million dollars' worth of fine woollens, silks, moirés, gold and silver metallic cloth, and embroidery. The required materials were screen-printed and dyed right at the studio. Special dyes were used to insure the proper colour for the sensitive eye of the camera and to prevent skin irritations.

Each costume was then cut. Fittings, three to every costume, were made first on the form and then on the star. The finished costume was then photographed carefully on coloured slides and on coloured motion picture film. The slides permitted minute inspection of each detail; the films showed how the costume moved, an important factor in the movies.

The approved costumes were taken to each star's dressing room. A special tent, large enough to accommodate a two-ring circus, was erected on the back lot to house the wardrobe for the extras.

Approximately one hundred people worked three months to create the wardrobe for this one motion picture. They will have succeeded in their purpose only if, when 'The Prodigal' is released, the audience is unaware of their labour. The wardrobe department has one aim – to make the costumes part of the whole effect of the movie. If the costumes are too striking, if they distract the audience from the story being told, then the wardrobe department has failed. The wardrobe department at MGM rarely fails. It has won more Academy Awards for its efforts than its opposite number in any other studio in Hollywood.

New York Times, 11 July 1954

the approved design which was then kept on file in his office. He used these as a point of reference to check on the completed costume. Head's memoirs, published long after DeMille's death, are a valuable source for understanding DeMille's methods of working and, despite his familiar rhetoric, for grasping his less than authentic approach to 'historic' costuming. It is interesting to compare the official language of DeMille's publicity machine with the private memoirs of Edith Head who recalls her experience of *Samson and Delilah* candidly:

> *Samson and Delilah* is not a picture of which I am proud . . . I never thought I did good work for DeMille . . . I always had to do what that conceited old goat wanted, whether it was correct or not. He never did an authentic picture in his entire career, and in my opinion that made him a damn liar as well as an egotist.[40]

One particular clash occurred over a cape worn by Hedy Lamarr in the last scene of the film, Samson's destruction of the temple of Dagon (Colour Plate 1). DeMille demanded something extraordinary for Delilah's last appearance and said that he wanted a costume with peacock feathers: 'For what reason, I don't know,' recalled Head. 'He never gave reasons.' DeMille remained fascinated by peacock feathers throughout his career and he used them liberally in his films; 'No peacock is safe around DeMille' became a running joke in Hollywood.[41]

Having no idea of what types of birds there were in 'Minoan' Philistia, Edith Head asked the research department to investigate. *Perhaps*, she was told by Henry Noerdlinger's team, there were peacocks – although that was nothing more than conjecture. However, knowing that DeMille would love the gaudy effect of peacock feathers, she designed a long, draping cape with the regal plumage, which DeMille liked very much (Figure 3.18). Nevertheless, Head's memoirs stress that she had the feeling that it was a historical anachronism and doubted that there were peacocks in Israel in the days of Samson and Delilah – whenever that was:

> I have always had the feeling that [the peacock cape] was entirely wrong. I doubt very much if there were any peacocks around or nearby in the days of Samson and Delilah. Nor would anyone, even Delilah, have worn the kind of cape that I designed – or any of the other costumes for that matter. I suppose that only scholars would know that the costumes were not historically correct, but it bothered me terribly. I was never able to find anything authentic to indicate what Samson and Delilah looked like, so I improvised. And I won an Oscar.[42]

Female Star-Image and the 'Period Look'

'Beauty was never a woman,' wrote Quentin Crisp, 'it was a man's idea of a woman.'[43] In Hollywood it was usually a Movie Mogul's idea of a fair-skinned American or European woman. In the studio era the moguls essentially crafted America's vision of female beauty through the promotion of the actresses they thought carried their ideal look. Epic movies, like all 'period films', were major vehicles for important and influential female stars, and (as we have now confirmed) the Hollywood star

Figure 3.18
Copy of Edith Head's costume design for Delilah's last scene in the Temple of Dagon.
Samson and Delilah (1949).

system allowed major actresses a say in how their film wardrobes would look.[44] Consequently, there was always an undeniable emphasis on both glamour and the contemporary fashionable silhouette in the costumes of Hollywood's ancient world. The original audiences of these films may not have been aware that the historical costumes reflected their own standards of style or ideas of beauty and taste because these realisations emerge with the passing of time, as tastes in fashion change with each generation, an idea supported by film historian Edward Maeder:

> Anachronisms are found in almost every motion picture that portrays another period. While presenting the illusion of an earlier time, these films rarely replicate the exact look of the prevailing time; instead

the costumes take elements from past styles and combine them with aspects of contemporary fashion. The excesses of Hollywood are the stuff of legend. Filmmakers went to great lengths to ensure that their films would be wondrous spectacles and that actors would look gorgeous ... Costumes must appeal to the audience in an aesthetic that they will understand ... Costumes for period films provide a fascinating source for understanding how each generation has looked at history, tempered by the contemporary fashion and convention, since the very beginning of film history.[45]

Let us, then, explore how female fashionable looks of the early- to mid-twentieth century were used to redefine the fashions of the ancient world, taking into account as we go the importance of makeup and hairstyles in the articulation of this concept, and noting, as Alicia Annas does, that 'as screen and fashion makeup became more interconnected, both studios and stars ended up locked into a modern makeup image no matter what the period of a film. Anything else ran the risk of alienating the fans.'[46]

The 1910s and 1920s

In period films of the 1910s and 1920s such as *Intolerance* and *The Ten Commandments*, the female costumes emphasise the straight tube-shaped silhouette that prevailed throughout much of the two decades. Estelle Taylor, cast by DeMille in the role of the Egyptian queen, is dressed like a flapper, with a chiffon skirt, beaded and fringed decorations and a feathered headdress, all of which were popular fashions at the time (Figure 3.19). The same shape, fabrics and details are worn by the priestesses of Ishtar in *Intolerance* suggesting that, regardless of the setting or the period, a generic ancient Oriental 'look' was all that was required (Figure 3.20).

There is no known costume designer for the 1917 *Cleopatra*, and it is possible that much of the costume design, hairstyling, and makeup may have been done by the performers themselves. Theda Bara's Cleopatra looks rather ample by modern standards (Figure 3.21), but in 1917 her Cleopatra-look was a wow with her fans. In the late 1910s, Europe and America were in the grip of a wave of exotic and erotic Orientalist fantasies such as the Ballet Russe's *Sheherazade*, Richard Strauss's opera *Salome* and the erotic dance-performances of Mata Hari and Little Egypt, and thus, with her hair set in contemporary ringlets and her eyelids shaded in heavy make-up, Bara's Cleopatra was crafted in the classic vamp mode and perfectly in accord with the times. Today one might think her costumes (and there were over fifty-five of them) rather amusing, but Hollywood publicity claimed that they were immaculately researched copies of Cleopatra's originals; in fact, it was said that Bara herself 'worked for months with a curator of Egyptology at the Metropolitan Museum in New York'[47] where she studied ancient items of clothing and

Figure 3.19
Flapper girls: Egyptian costumes for *The Ten Commandments* (1923) capitalise on the
Egyptomania seeping into America after the discovery of the tomb of Tutankhamun.
Production still.

Figure 3.20
The Babylonian Follies Bergère: the priestesses of Ishtar. *Intolerance* (1916). Production still.

Figure 3.21
Baubles, bangles and beads: one of many of Theda Bara's peek-a-boo costumes for
Cleopatra (1917). Studio publicity photograph.

jewellery and, more generally, the lifestyle of the ancient Egyptians.[48]
So imbued was Bara with a feeling for the period that she was quoted
as having declared that she 'felt the blood of the Ptolemies coursing
through [her] veins'.[49]

The publicity material mixed elements of historical authenticity
together with notions of eroticism, and in a *Motion Picture News* review

Figure 3.22
Theda Bara vamps with all her might as Cleopatra (1917); the sexual licence enjoyed by
early Hollywood is clearly on display in this next-to-naked costume. Production still.

of November 1917, the reader was encouraged to reflect on the reactions
of a man leaving a cinema where he has just witnessed Bara's Cleopatra
in full vamp:

> His mind will drift back to the first half of the picture where Miss Bara
> wore a different costume in every episode. Different pieces of costume
> rather; or better still different varieties of beads. His temperature will
> ascend with a jump when he recalls the easy way in which the siren
> captivated Caesar and Pharon and Antony ... He might suddenly
> realise that his mother back in Hohokus would shut her eyes once or
> twice for fear that the beads might break or slip, but then – mother
> never did understand Egyptian history after all.[50]

In fact, the suggestive peek-a-boo nature of Bara's costumes (Figure
3.22) – typical of the liberalities Hollywood made of the female body in
the age before the introduction of the Production Code – became a major
feature of film reviews. The film critic of the *New York Dramatic Mirror*,
for example, noted that, 'Those who like to see Theda Bara should not
fail to take advantage of the opportunity afforded in *Cleopatra*, for certainly you will never see *more* of her.'[51] The Fox publicity department
played up the effects of Bara's costumes and noted that, 'To match each
costume, the Siren of the Nile wears a complete set of jewels – fifty

dazzling sets of baubles.'[52] The use of baubles and beads, and in particular the employment of pearls, in Bara's costumes, places the film very much in its period: even though the Egyptians had developed skilled jewellery craftsmanship using gold and semi-precious stones, pearls were a rarity. But in 1917 (and throughout the 1920s) they were very much à la mode and were used extensively in costuming many silent movies set in antiquity.

1930s

When *The Sign of The Cross* was released in 1932, female fashions were on the change; the straight, drop-waist gowns of the 1920s were giving way to longer hemlines and more fitted forms promoted in Paris by designers such as Chanel and Patou. Meanwhile the first bias-cut evening gown was premiered at this time from the House of Madame Madeleine Vionnet; this revolutionary new technique in dress construction involved cutting across the grain of the fabric in order to let it drape and shape itself to the female body upon touch. These garments needed no complicated openings to allow the wearer to put them on or to slip them off since the cut and shape allowed the material to sit tight to the figure and then flare outwards near the base. The overall effect was sensual and elegant and Mitchell Leisen's gowns for Claudette Colbert as Poppaea (Figure 3.23) encapsulate the Vionnet-look to perfection. In spite of the designer's claims that 'Costume pictures . . . generally become as unconvincing and artificial as fancy-dress balls in a small college gym unless the gowns, hats, shoes [and] suits . . . are built and tailored exactly as they were in the days of the story,' Colbert's costumes slavishly follow the fashionable lines of the day, but are given additional elements of cinematic flare.[53] In a publicity article entitled *Modes of Ancient Rome*, prominently printed in the film's souvenir brochure, Leisen's designs (Figure 3.24) were placed alongside a substantial article in which he discussed the history of ancient Roman dress, arguing compellingly for the importance of historical research (see Text Box 3.5). Yet the costume designs themselves, in contrast to the historical minutiae of Leisen's research rhetoric, appear to have originated in a cutting-edge Parisian fashion house.

Evening gowns in the 1930s showed a preference for halter-necks, one-shouldered asymmetric necklines and thin shoulder-straps; the back was often fully exposed and a deep décolleté revealed even more flesh. Leisen capitalised on this look for Poppaea's costumes, recalling that, 'Making the costumes for Claudette was a real pleasure. She had just about the most beautiful figure I've ever seen. I slit her skirts right up to the hip to show her marvellous legs' (Figure 3.25).[54] Her clinging gold and silver lamé gowns (a fabric which was especially fashionable in 1930s high society) were designed to expose as much flesh as possible, confirming, in hindsight, Edith Head's recollection that in the pre-Code era, 'Our only rule was: will it stay on? If dresses fell off, we just shot [the

Figure 3.23
Mitchell Leisen's silver bondage-gown for Claudette Colbert as Poppaea exposes the
midriff, hips and much cleavage. The bellybutton is concealed. *The Sign of the Cross*
(1932). Studio publicity photograph.

scene] again.'[55] Poppaea's contemporary evening gowns are testament
to a particular DeMillian sexualised vision of history where bands of
lamé stand in for bodices (Figure 3.1) and beads, spangles and pearls
simultaneously conceal and highlight erogenous zones.

Colbert's makeup was the pure 1930s glamour formula, with thin,
plucked brows, heavy glamour lashes, dark shadow on the eyelids and
full, cupid-bow lips. She wore several wigs in her role as Poppaea, some
of which were elaborately curled and modelled on the contemporary
fashion trend, the Marcel Wave; her long dark wig with a fringe was not

MODES
• Of Ancient Rome •

Figure 3.24
Three of Mitchell Leisen's costume designs for *The Sign of the Cross* were published to
accompany his essay, 'Modes of Ancient Rome'. *The Sign of the Cross* souvenir brochure,
1932.

dressed in a fashionable style though, but it had been designed and set
by Hollywood stylist Antoine and quickly became something of a trend,
bringing about the fashion of the 'pageboy' cut. Colbert adopted the
look again for *Cleopatra*.

By 1934, films were mirroring and inspiring fashion trends in a kind
of osmosis from screen to street. The bias-cut *Cleopatra* gowns created
for Colbert by Travis Banton were immaculately cut garments, ravish-
ingly simple costumes on first glance that were carefully designed and
made to act as a 'second skin' for Colbert.[56] Perfectly in accord with
Art Deco fashion, the costumes were both pleasing interpretations of
a fabulous Egyptian antiquity and a stunning up-to-the-moment haute
couture, a bold and brilliant Banton melange of past and present. Walter
Plunkett once said that, 'The rest of us designers ... always watched
Banton carefully because he was always a couple of years ahead of the
fashion trend' – and if the historical authenticity of his costumes was
ever questioned, Paramount was there to protect his designs. Frank
Calvin, one of DeMille's research team, once defended the historical
truthfulness of Banton's work by arguing that, 'over six months were
spent in the research work on this picture, including a very careful study
of the costumes and headdresses of the period, and you can rest assured
they were correct. Quite often modern clothes-designers copy ancient
costumes and it is for that reason that you notice a similarity.'[57]

Colbert's Cleopatra-look both exploited the contemporary mode of
Egyptionisation in dress and accelerated its popularity overnight.[58] Yet

---

Text Box 3.5 *Modes of Ancient Rome*

From the earliest to the latest times the clothing of the ancient Romans was very simple, consisting ordinarily of two or three articles only besides the covering of the feet. These articles varied in material, style and name from age to age, it is true, but were practically unchanged during the Republic and Early Empire. The mild climate of Italy and the hardening effect of the physical exercise of the young made unnecessary the closely fitting garments to which we are accustomed, while contacts with Greeks on the south and perhaps Etruscans on the north gave the Romans a taste for the beautiful that found expression in the graceful arrangement of their loosely flowing robes. The clothing of men and women differed much less than in modern times.

The Romans in early times wore their hair and beards full, as did all uncivilised peoples. Varro tells us that professional barbers first came to Rome in the year 300 BC, but we know that the razor and shears were used by the Romans long before history begins. Pliny says that the Younger Scipio was the first of the Romans to shave every day, and the story may be true. People of wealth and position had the hair and beard kept in order at home by their own slaves, and these slaves, if skilful barbers, brought high prices in the market.

People of the middle classes went to the public barber shops, and made them gradually places of general resort for the idle and gossiping. Styles varied with the years of the persons concerned. The hair of children, boys and girls alike, was allowed to grow long and hang around the neck and shoulders. When a boy assumed the toga of manhood the long locks were cut off, sometimes with a good deal of formality, and under the Empire they were often made an offering to some deity.

Mitchell Leisen, *The Sign of the Cross* brochure, 1932

---

the silhouette of Colbert's costumes is not the straight, vertical line of the ancient Egypt of the 1920s, of course, but a figure-hugging 1930s cut that skims her hips and flares out elegantly below the knees to form a 'fish tail' trailing onto the floor. This contemporary treatment of the skirt, together with the halter necklines (one of Banton's hallmarks – Figure 3.26), was at the cutting edge of fashion in 1934. *The Billboard* noted the success of Banton's costumes and the effect they had on Colbert's performance, noting that 'Claudette Colbert *is* Cleopatra. She is ideally fitted for the part. She has been outfitted with abbreviated costumes that show off her beautiful body and make her the tantalising temptress she was supposed to have been.'[59]

Colbert's first scene as Cleopatra depicts her as a prisoner, barefooted, bound and abandoned in the vast expanses of the Egyptian desert. For this formative appearance Banton dressed her in velvet (Figure 3.27) – 'a ridiculous choice for the Egyptian climate'[60] – and yet as a costume it somehow makes sense: the soft velvet nap catches the light to emphasise

Figure 3.25
Slashed at the waist and at the thigh, Mitchell Leisen's costume for Claudette Colbert as
Poppaea is cut on the bias and made from gold lamé. *The Sign of the Cross* (1932). Studio
publicity shot.

each twist of Colbert's body and announces that she is wearing nothing
else. Like the famous black velvet gown in John Singer Sargent's famous
portrait, Madame X, Cleopatra's velvet shift plays on the paradox of
the sumptuous fabric and the naked flesh and anticipates the rest of
Cleopatra's wardrobe which the film showcases.

It has been noted that Cleopatra's body can be read as a sign: it
is desirable and yet forbidden. Banton employs an X-motif to both
embellish and cancel-out Cleopatra's sexuality. X-signs mark out her
waist, her breasts, her belly. X-sign-trim also criss-cross her torso and

Figure 3.26
Travis Banton's hallmark halter-neck top and bias-cut split skirt create a youthful looking
Cleopatra; note the strappy high-heels. *Cleopatra* (1934). Production still.

her hips in a gown she wears for her visit to the Roman senate (Figure
2.13); this elaborate mermaid-trained gown of beaded semi-transparent
chiffon makes her completely dependent on her handmaidens. Her final
costume (Figure 3.28), worn with a gold vulture crown (see Figure 2.28),
is an immaculately cut black satin couture gown of X-bands, mermaid-
cut train and a large, bold, beaded collar. Caroline Young notes that 'The
bold geometric Art Deco lines of the 1930s suited a film with an exotic
Oriental style, and Cleopatra's . . . revealing costumes were created in
shimmering lamé, with fishtails and extensive trains, and worn with
thick jewelled necklaces, which became known as the Cleopatra collar.'
For Maria Wyke the 1930s Hollywood Cleopatra 'came to be structured
along the lines of a figure who lived inside rather than outside the
borders of the United States. She was now glamorous . . . to be watched,
desired, consumed and even identified with'.[61] Indeed, following the
film's successful release the 'Cleopatra effect' could be seen in the fashion
houses promoting Egyptianising near nudity: Mainboucher designed
a gown with a bodice with thin straps just covering the bust, Lelong
slashed his décolletage down to the waist and Schiaparelli emphasised
the bust with daring asymmetrical cutting. Orientalism dominated
the fashions of 1935: Lanvin's dresses fell 'like majestic portières of an
Oriental palace', Schiaparelli's gowns were said to have converted her
models into eastern princesses and Alix made Egyptian-style dresses
with gold-bordered gauzes.[62]

Figure 3.27
A velvet bias-cut gown with a split skirt designed by Travis Banton for the opening
sequence of *Cleopatra* (1934). Studio publicity photograph.

Figure 3.28
Worn without the gold headdress and beaded collar that is used in the final scene of *Cleopatra* (see Figure 2.28), Claudette Colbert poses in a black satin bias-cut gown of intricate construction, a testament to the fact that Banton's designs functioned more as high fashion than as costumes. *Cleopatra* (1934). Studio publicity photograph used in the pressbook.

Cleopatra's headdresses and collars provided inspiration for fashionable accessories, as Shadowplay was quick to report:

> Already DeMille's 'Cleopatra' opus is starting fashion trends ... An Egyptian collar effect is seen ... And ... the winged bandeaus worn by Claudette Colbert promise to replace the tiara as an evening headdress ... Oriental jewellery is flashing into fashion in Paris. Byzantine necklaces of huge multi-coloured glass hemispheres and long pearl earrings recalling those worn by Cleopatra are giving an exotic touch.[63]

Cheaper ready-to-wear versions of Banton's gowns and accessories were mass-produced and were trumpeted in the Paramount *Cleopatra* press-book under the heading 'MODERN MERCHANDISING BUREAU': 'They are lavish, glamorous gowns with authentic details in jewels and trimming. From these we have made exciting adaptations in evening gowns and accessories. Our copies have all the allure of the original with exotic edges rubbed down and subdued into fashions that are definitely 1934 and wearable.'

Department stores, with their reasonably priced Hollywood knock-offs, proved so financially successful that the studio moguls waived their percentage of the sales. Women were the targets of a vigorous retail advertisement campaign as American department stores actively sought fashionable tie-ins with Hollywood films. As early as 1919 *Theatre* magazine was announcing that 'Los Angeles now fills the proud position Paris once occupied as the arbiter of fashion ... More women see DeMille's pictures than read fashion magazines ... five whole reels just crammed and jammed with beautiful creations.' Thereafter movie magazines published articles on how to recreate costumes through tips and sewing patterns. 'Are You a Screen Shopper?' *Motion Picture* asked. 'The modern woman is a screen shopper. You, being modern, are a screen shopper too.'[64] In 1932 Adrian had designed a costume for Joan Crawford which was so sought-after that over half-a-million inexpensive copies were sold in Macy's Department Store. Audiences were dazzled by Scarlett O'Hara's green sprig silk-chiffon barbecue dress in *Gone With The Wind* and this too was mass-produced in printed rayon and sold in department stores in their thousands; Vivien Leigh's hats, designed by John Frederics, were similarly cheaply replicated and sold in Sears Catalogue. This form of star-effect led to *Vogue* demonstrating an interest in film costumes:

> With ... personalities like these, with the movies ... a medium which can and does reach every nook and cranny of the world, you can see what stupendous potentialities the cinema has as an exploiter of fashion ... The movies are capable of shaping the tastes and prejudices of large parts of the world as regards not only ... decoration and beauty, but in showing women how a new mode actually looks in movement.[65]

By the mid-1930s the Hollywood brand had been born. Indeed, Charles Eckert's study of the relationship between merchandise companies, department stores, and screen fashions in Hollywood has revealed that from the 1930s the studios adopted an aggressive 'top-down' merchandising campaign in their promotion of commercial tie-ins while, simultaneously, among audiences, an adaptive process was at work which involved 'bottom-up' creativity, requiring a considerable degree of individual choice in the emulation of on-screen fashions.[66] As Melanie Hillmer commented:

> The clothes worn by immortal stars and . . . starlets serve as a pattern for our dreams and nightmares, and for things we have not yet dreamed. When we take clothes out of context, we slip into the role of Marlene Dietrich [or] Audrey Hepburn . . . speaking their sartorial language with our bodies. We are the copy, the variation, the improvisation, the parody.[67]

In 1939 MGM released a short promotional film entitled *Hollywood – Style Centre of the World*. It begins with a story about Mary, a pretty country girl who is asked out on a date by a clean-living boy-next-door type. Her proud father buys her a new 'outfit' from the 'Cinema Shop', a specialist concession within a local department store. The dress is one almost identical to that worn by Joan Crawford in her latest movie. As Mary admires herself in the mirror she morphs, for a second or two, into Crawford as a voice-over confirms:

> And so to this quiet little town, far from the metropolitan areas, the Hollywood influence reaches out to style and gown Mary, just as smartly as Joan Crawford is costumed for her role in [a] new film . . . The motion picture has annihilated space, blotted out the back woods . . . Today the girl from the country is just as modern and dresses just as smartly as her big city sister.

The historical period of a movie's setting was not a bar to its potential marketability as a 1933 *New York Times* article titled 'Lacquered Wigs Perform Wonders', confirms: 'What woman has not longed at some time to be a Cleopatra . . .? There is not one who would not like, for a brief space, to be someone else, or at least to alter her appearance so that she could play another role.' Confident of the popular appeal of Colbert as a fashion icon, Paramount released a huge merchandising campaign in collaboration with Macy's, which, at the time, was the 'most gigantic tie-up in cinema history'.[68] A studio press release sent to major American newspapers hoped to create a snowball effect on the marketability of the *Cleopatra* costumes:

> *Cleopatra* has gone to the ladies' heads! And to their feet – and into almost every article of apparel, judging by the growing vogue of

Cleopatra-styles, following the release of the Paramount picture of that name . . . A few of the highlights of the *Cleopatra* vogue are illustrated here in the two dresses designed by Travis Banton for Miss Colbert, and the *Cleopatra* hat and coiffure, the marked influence of Egyptian style and designs is evident in the sandals, jewelry and buckles selected to illustrate the new season's offerings.[69]

In the 1930s epics of DeMille, Rome and Egypt gave modern mass-produced objects a sheen of luxury, exoticism and exclusivity. It was precisely this combination of resonances that made antiquity so market-able in British and American mass culture in the 1920s and 1930s. Out of the darkness of the Depression era, Hollywood used the world of antiq-uity to provide a glamour and glitziness to dazzle and lift the spirits of a despondent population. The ancient world became aspirational.

1940s and 1950s

The first years after the Second World War might be regarded by fashion historians as a period of transition, a period of groping after the lines into which fashion would settle for an eight- or ten-year span. Only one epic encapsulates the fashionable look of the 1940s: *Samson and Delilah*. The year 1949, the date of its premiere, can be seen as continuing the transition. Fashion remained deliberately fluid, throwing out feelers in all directions. The basis was a figure-fitting sheath, but only in certain instances was this left in a simple, uncompromising form. In general, the narrow line was broken by a jutting sash, a hip bow, an apron skirt, a floating scarf or, for evening, draped complications at hip level. The designs Edith Head created for Delilah have an undeniable late 1940s silhouette – squared shoulders, fitted skirts, tight cropped bodices and uplift brassieres – which are all coupled with 1940s glamour makeup, elaborate rolled hairstyles and strappy platform sandals. The 1940s 'look' is well-captured in a surviving costume sketch for a Philistine noblewoman by Dorothy Jeakins, Head's co-designer (Figure 3.29).[70] Many of Hedy Lamarr's costumes are comprised of a tight-fitting skirt – usually slit open to the thigh – ending in a thin train, and a close-fitting bolero bodice, a kind of 'harem top' of popular American Orientalist fantasy. Head was quick to admit that, 'when you present someone in a bodice, you immediately have a costume that's not historically right.'[71] Added to this basic ensemble were jewelled headpieces which crowned Lamarr's raven-black hair, fine chiffon or gauze veils and masses of chunky costume jewellery.[72] Having nothing to do with the reality of Philistine-Minoan dress, Delilah's costumes are pure American-style *Arabian Nights* concoctions and the 'Delilah look' was copied by many manufacturers in 1949 and 1950. Russell's Department Store in New York commissioned the company Cabana to design a *Samson and Delilah*-style clothing range, including a golden dress with a single strap which retailed for a mere $19.95. The studio pressbook noted that 'there's a

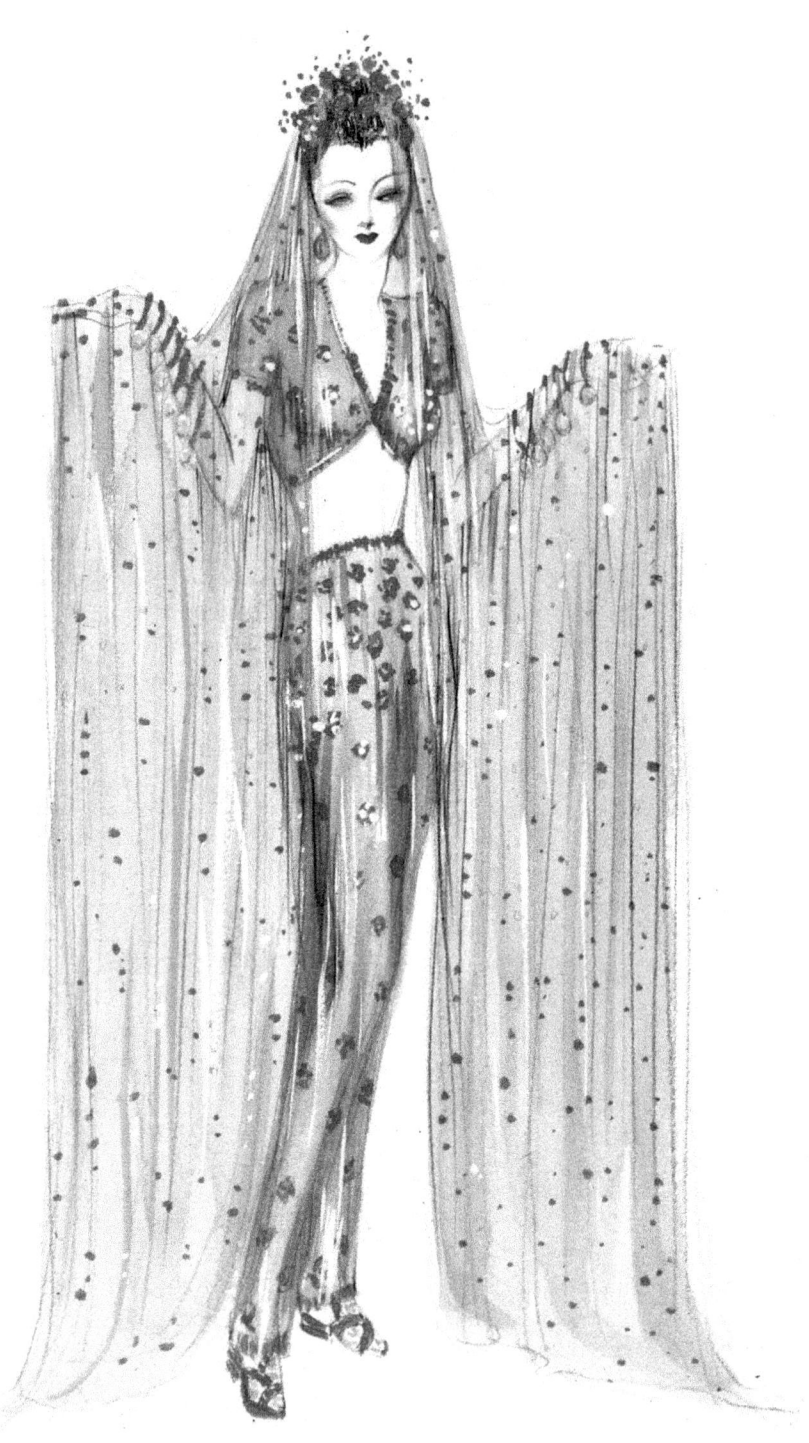

Figure 3.29
Costume sketch for a Philistine noblewoman by Dorothy Jeakins; note the 1940s padded shoulders. *Samson and Delilah* (1949).

ready-made public waiting for these arresting fashions' and advertised a variety of Delilah-inspired garments: a print patio-dress with a bolero and peep-blouse, a jersey side-draped evening gown, a one-shoulder patio dress with reversible wrap-around skirt, an organdie dance frock bound in velvet suggested by the trimming on Delilah's gown which also has a voluminous skirt. There were bejewelled headpieces and bejewelled wedged high-heeled sandals and, of course, a one-shoulder two-piece bathing suit to be worn with strappy beach sandals. And when in 1950 the New York *Saturday Evening Post* carried an advert for *Lucky Strikes* cigarettes, they used Hedy Lamarr to promote the product (Figure 3.30): 'Hedy Lamarr says, "A good cigarette is like a good movie – always enjoyable."'[73] The image shows Lamarr in Delilah's infamous peacock cape. Delilah advocated a chic and sophisticated lifestyle to the shoppers of New York's Seventh Avenue and London's Regent Street, an image far removed from the historical authenticity highlighted by DeMille's publicity machine, but one which, nonetheless, DeMille himself fostered with equal care.

The waistline was the defining feature of female fashion in the 1950s and early 1960s. A succession of style trends led by Christian Dior – the creator of the 'New Look' – and Cristóbal Balenciaga defined the changing silhouette of women's clothes through the 1950s and television joined fashion magazines and movies in disseminating clothing styles. The new silhouette had narrow shoulders, a tiny cinched waist, bust-emphasis and long slender skirts, draped, layered and flared. A trend for shoulder straps and a special feeling for the one-strap décolletage and the halter neck were used throughout the 1950s but the strapless look was firmly established early on in the decade. Throughout the postwar period, a tailored, feminine look was prized and accessories such as gloves and pearls were popular.

A red and gold pleated silk gown created by Edith Head for Anne Baxter as Nefretiri in *The Ten Commandments* (Figure 3.31) follows the classic silhouette of the era: the actress's waist is tightly clinched and the gown, though appearing to be flowing, is artfully cut and skilfully made on a foundation of corsetry. The ever-present 'lifted and separated' bosoms, carefully draped with pleats to give the shape are emphasised through the employment of an underwired, shaped bra. The contemporary 1950s 'bangs' (fringe), made popular by America's First Lady, Mimi Eisenhower, may distract from the ancient Egyptian fashion of plaited, artificial-looking wigs, but did not interfere with the illusion of historical accuracy that it presented to movie-goers in 1956.

The epitome of high-style, posture and the shape of the 1950s can be seen in Ralph Jester's costumes for Gina Lollobrigida in *Solomon and Sheba* (Colour Plate 12), which, it must be admitted, cannot be said to be based on any identifiable historical source. Lollobrigida's Queen of Sheba is entirely modelled on standard Western concepts of feminine beauty: her hour-glass figure is a perfect symbol of desirable 1950s womanhood. Her gold satin strapless evening gown which she

Figure 3.30
Cigarette advertisement employing an image of Hedy Lamarr in her peacock-feather Delilah costume. Magazine advertisement, 1950.

wears for her entry into Jerusalem emphasises her breasts and – with careful use of draping – her full, round hips, a look which did not go unnoticed by the reviewers: 'Gina Lollobrigida, the original Italian over-stuffed star, has the physical equipment to suggest a Little Egypt-type of charmer, but her way with a love-laden line or with a spontaneous show of emotion leaves something (other than the obvious) to be desired.'[74] The costume, nonetheless, is a triumph of couture and testifies to Jester's talent for creating costumes that mingled a 'historical

Figure 3.31
Red and gold pleated silk gown by Edith Head for Anne Baxter as Nefretiri. *The Ten Commandments* (1956). Studio portrait.

look' with the kind of Hollywood glamour the public expected to see on the screen.

It has been noted that in the mid-1950s something of a 'mammary fetish' had developed in the marketing of Hollywood's leading female stars. The excessive interest placed on the female physique of the period, exemplified by the likes of Jane Russell and Marilyn Monroe (and in Britain by Diana Dors), reduced them to playthings and objects of male desire – and was readily promoted by the Hollywood studios. Gina Lollobrigida herself admitted that her success in American cinema was largely due to 'the virtue of my physical attributes [and] now everyone is offering me parts where I open my mouth as little as possible and exhibit myself as much as possible.' In *Solomon and Sheba*, Lollobrigida's performance was decidedly wooden, yet her outstanding beauty and her regal disposition, aided and abetted by Jester's magnificent costumes, turned her, appropriately, into more of an icon than a flesh-and-blood woman. To this extent, it has been noted that this film marked Lollobrigida's detachment from the reality of what was required of a star at the transition of the 1950s and 1960s and her 'embalmment as a figure of Hollywood exotic'.[75]

We noted earlier that the marketing of epic movies often exploited fashion tie-ins and that in the 1950s and 1960s one of the chief beneficiaries of this two-way exploitation was Maidenform, the creator of America's most popular female 'foundation garments'. Also known as 'shapewear' or 'shaping underwear', Maidenform produced brassieres, girdles and corselettes which were predominantly designed to temporarily alter the wearer's body-shape to achieve a more fashionable figure; the chief function of the foundation garment was to enhance and exaggerate certain natural features in a way which was anything but 'natural'. As we have seen, Maidenform's 'dreams', 'fantasies' and 'reveries' advertisements encouraged America's female consumers to fantasise that they could become a Gina Lollogbrigida or, for that matter, a Queen of Sheba – actress, character and the couture of both were, after all, one and the same.

Throughout the 1950s and 1960s, studio pressbooks sold the marketability of epic costumes. The industry paid particular attention to its female fan-base because, it was reasoned, while men had the earning power, it was women who were more inclined to spend family income on what were seen as 'luxury goods'. In her ground-breaking study of female fandom in America, Jackie Stacey found that fans not only fantasised about stars but also fixated on their bodies and copied their makeup, hairstyles and dress sense. Female fans negotiated identities in which similarities and differences were highlighted in pleasurable fantasies: 'I preferred stars who were unlike everyday women', wrote one such fan, 'because I went to the cinema to escape into a world of fantasy, wealth and, above all, glamour . . . I could put myself into their place . . . and become everything I wasn't: beautiful, desirable and popular with the opposite sex.'[76] Moreover, Sumiko Higashi's study of stardom, fandom and consumption in the 1950s notes that 'stars and fans were thus both invested in a process of self-objectification and commodification in a shared beauty culture that required a practised consumption of goods.'[77] For that reason, nearly every Hollywood press kit – including those produced for epic movies – contained sheets of makeup and hairdressing tips, complete with advertising products for sale and with versions of the costumes worn by the female stars which were available off-the-rack in local department stores. *The Egyptian* pressbook published no less than four large-page spreads (printed on glossy pink paper) focusing on fashion tie-ins and trumpeted the marketability of the costume designs:

> A concurrence of archaeological discoveries, a great motion picture production, and world-wide renowned fashion arbiters has produced a powerful and rewarding force of an unprecedented merchandising campaign that will place *The Egyptian* to the fore as the most publicised and exploited picture ever produced, eclipsing even *The Robe*. 'The Egyptian' silhouette sweeps across the world as the big news in fashion from the great salons of Paris and New York to famed Seventh Avenue – control centre of the majority of style-conscious Americans – onward to California, Egypt's modern sun-worshipping counterpart!

Included in the campaign were Sally Victor 'Egyptian hats' (Nubian, Thebes and Sphinx), while society milliner Mr John of New York offered a series of hats and headdresses inspired by the film:

> His creations include 'Red Sea', a sculptured evening helmet of brilliant ostrich feathers; 'Theban', cocktail coif fashioned of ibis blue paradise feathers; 'Jet Lotus', an evening creation fashioned of pure silk jersey and covered with lotus blossoms of glittering jets; 'Royal Serpent'. . . and 'Midnight Luxor', a stunning starlight evening cap designed to make its wearer into a modern siren of the Nile.

Nettie Rossen marketed a fall collection of twelve dresses and coats, with Kingdom Red dominating the colour palette. Her designs included the Egyptian Lady, 'inspired by Gene Tierney's robes as Princess Beketamun' and a 'white moulded jersey evening dress inspired by the exotic Nefer, portrayed by Bella Darvi in the film'. There were, moreover, advertisements for 'Egyptian' lingerie by John Norman, exotic 'Egyptian' makeup ranges from Elizabeth Arden and 'Egyptian' jewellery from the Admark Company of Philadelphia; Harper's Bazaar advertised Egyptian coats in black, red and purple, and 'Egyptian' beachware was on sale 'for the winter southern vacation season'.

Salome too was marketed with an impressive pressbook fashion campaign (Figure 3.32) and exhibitors were encouraged to launch a '*Salome* Glamour Week' in which cooperation with local department stores was

'SALOME CORSAGE'

Top flower stylists of the Society of American Florists have designed a special "Salome Corsage," which Rita Hayworth is wearing in Still No. Exp. 13 (see right). This still, and the "Salome Corsage" itself, have been extensively publicized in the florist trade press and the Society of American Florists is recommending to all its local allied groups, the regional florists' associations throughout the country, ways in which they might tie in with special "Salome" promotions. Contact your local florists and arrange for "Salome Corsage" tie-ups along the following lines:

1) Plant Still No. Exp. 13 in conjunction with locally-written publicity stories on the "Salome Corsage," along with interviews of local florists specializing in the new bouquet.

2) Obtain a number of "Salome Corsages" for distribution as prizes on TV contest programs of local origin, and try for TV interviews with local florists who demonstrate how the corsage is made.

3) Supply florists with prints of Still No. Exp. 13 and other stills from the picture for use in special window displays built around the "Salome Corsage."

4) Go after newspaper co-op ads and florists' special mailings to their patrons.

5) If you plan a gala premiere (see page 15), one of the most effective stunts you might work is to send "Salome Corsages" to wives of your special guests.

6) Give away "Salome Corsages" to the first 50 women entering your theatre opening day. Announce the giveaway in advance, via a lobby 40" x 60", newspaper ad underline, etc.

7) Work with local florist in a stunt whereby theatre admits as a "guest" of the florist, any woman who arrives at the box office wearing a "Salome Corsage."

For any additional information about the "Salome Corsage," write direct to:

BOZELLE AND JACOBS, INC.
Miss Shirley Fisher
2 West 45th Street, New York City

GRIP-TUTH COMB

Rita Hayworth wears an ornamental jeweled Grip-Tuth comb in scenes for "Salome," and the manufacturers are publicizing the fact extensively, along with an endorsement by Columbia hair stylist Helen Hunt. Diadem, Inc., manufacturers of the Grip-Tuth combs, are taking two-page advertisements in three important beauty and novelty store trade publications:

- Modern Beauty Shop (*with a circulation of approximately 65,000 beauty shops*)
- Drug Topics (*which goes to approximately 60,000 drug store owners and managers*)
- Chain Store Age (*read by the managers of more than 20,000 chain and variety stores*)

In addition, the use of the Grip-Tuth comb in "Salome" has been announced by the manufacturer in its own special publication, which goes to all Grip-Tuth outlets in the country. Illustrated below is the manner in which Grip-Tuth treated the tie-up, making use of Still No. 324.

Go after local beauty shops, chain stores, drug and department stores. Try for cooperative newspaper advertising, window and counter displays using Still No. 324, special heralds, etc.

For additional information, write direct to:

DIADEM, INC.
Harold D. Baldridge, General Manager
Leominster, Massachusetts

Figure 3.32
The *Salome* pressbook of 1953 included several fashion campaign pages.

encouraged. Daily events such as a 'Salome Glamour Fashion Show', a 'Salome Cosmetics Demonstration' and even a 'Salome Glamour Cooking Exhibition' were heralded as a good way to 'get the campaign into every home in a manner limited only by the resources of the cooperating merchant's advertising programme.' To help with this, five of Jean Louis' original costume designs were mass produced and sent to stores and newspapers in the hope of stimulating box-office figures.

Throughout the 1950s Deborah Kerr, with her beautiful head of auburn hair and pale ivory skin, became the face of Lustre-Crème Shampoo and her flawless complexion saw her become to the go-to face of both Max Factor and Jergens Lotion (Figure 3.33). A campaign was launched to coincide with the release of *Quo Vadis* and has Kerr express her thanks to Jergens for keeping her skin supple and smooth during the filming of the Great Fire of Rome – only Jergens kept her hands 'as smooth as silk for those romantic close-ups'.[78]

1960s

When Mankiewicz's *Cleopatra* first went into production at Pinewood Studios in England in 1959, the theatre designer Oliver Messel was hired to design Elizabeth Taylor's costumes. He created a series of designs that reflected both ancient Egypt and late 1950s couture and, interestingly, also spoke of the queen's Greek heritage.[79] In one rare wardrobe test photograph, Taylor wears a Greek style *chitoniskos* (short belted tunic) and has her hair dressed in a Greek-style topknot (Figure 3.34).[80] From the few stills and costume-shots that survive, it would appear that Messel was keen to assimilate Cleopatra with the original Greek palace that had been designed and built for her by John De Cuir on the wet and windy Pinewood lot, but with the relocation of the shoot to the Cinecittà Studios in Rome, Messel was dismissed (or refused to sign a new contract – the evidence is sketchy)[81] and the task of creating Taylor's costumes was assigned instead to Irene Sharaff (Figure 3.35).[82] The rest of the costumes were designed by Italian designer Vittorio Nino Novarese and Hollywood's own Renié Conley;[83] Rex Harrison's outfits, however, also became the responsibility of Sharaff.[84] Her published memoirs for this period make an important contribution to understanding the decisions about the production of the 1963 film. In a typical piece of confident Hollywood rhetoric, Sharaff assures the reader that her designs for Cleopatra were based upon months of research in Egyptian museums, and draws attention to her use of the ancient literary and visual sources. When, for example, she designed Taylor's famous gold Isis gown (worn by Cleopatra for her lavish entry into Rome and, ultimately, for her suicide), she sensibly noted that:

> The bas-relief at Dendera . . . shows the elaborate crown and collar of an Egyptian goddess . . . [but] it did not mean that during her life [Cleopatra] dressed like that, except for sacred ceremonial occasions.

Figure 3.33
Deborah Kerr, the face of Jergens Lotion. Magazine advertisement tie-in to *Quo Vadis*
(1951).

The few photographs I found of sculpture and coins . . . suggest only
that she was plump, had a large nose, and that her hair was dressed
much like any other Roman matron of her times. The trade relations between the two countries must have carried continual mutual
influences. Cleopatra, as a Macedonian, as a ruler and as a woman,

Figure 3.34
Rare wardrobe test shot of Elizabeth Taylor in a costume designed by Oliver Messel for the Pinewood shoot of *Cleopatra*, c.1959.

was undoubtedly astute and surely delighted in anything novel from Rome or ports on the trade routes to add to her personal adornment. The script called for sixty changes of costume for Cleopatra, from a girl of seventeen to a woman of thirty-seven. One tends to think of

Figure 3.35
As formidable as she was gifted, the brilliant costume designer Irene Sharaff adjusts
Elizabeth Taylor's golden Isis robe in preparation for a photo shoot. Candid shot.

Cleopatra looking the same through her relatively short life, but of course the maturing had to be indicated. I found this was easiest to handle by dividing the costumes into three groups . . . All the ceremonial costumes were based on Egyptian tomb paintings; the second group were clothes such as a Roman woman of the upper classes might have worn; and the last group made use of one of the oldest garments, the *djellabah*.[85]

Yet there is little in the film to identify Sharaff's categorisation of dress-'types', nor is there much in the design of Cleopatra's wardrobe that suggests the clothing of a Greco-Roman noblewoman – the look is purely Egyptian, but with a reflection of early 1960s aesthetic, in particular the tightly clinched corseted waists and Christian Dior-style tailoring techniques, so perfectly suited to Elizabeth Taylor's voluptuous figure (Figure 3.36). Producer Walter Wanger's reminiscences for 26 July 1961 record that:

Figure 3.36
Green silk costume with snake motifs designed by Irene Sharaff and fitted to Taylor's bust
and clinched waist with the perfection of a Christian Dior couture evening gown. Candid
shot.

> Liz likes her clothes to fit skin tight . . . [so] she is on a diet again . . .
> One or two pounds can make all the difference, and Liz is always
> concerned about looking her best, naturally.[86]

Recalling the experience of costuming Elizabeth Taylor, Sharaff told
Time magazine in a 1973 interview that she had found the star's proportions challenging: 'She was five feet two and had difficult proportions:
high waist, large bosom, short arms, no behind but wide hips. I was

not awed by her.'[87] Taylor was indeed petite but very top-heavy and throughout the *Cleopatra* shoot her weight fluctuated alongside her moods. Sharaff needed to control Taylor's figure and found justification for squeezing her into corseted bodices and tight skirts from her naive analysis of ancient Egyptian sculptures which completely failed to take into account the ancient artistic requisites and preoccupations concerning the ideal female body.[88] Her memoirs note:

> I was lucky enough to find a photograph of a small headless statue in the Cairo Museum, whose dress gave me a clue to designing Cleopatra's costumes. The tight-fitting bodice showed fine lines of *tarunto* or, as it is more commonly called, quilting, one of the oldest forms of decoration.[89]

Taylor's very first appearance in the film, delivered in a rug before Julius Caesar, has her tumble out of the rolled up carpet wearing a flame-orange figure-hugging version of the 'Egyptian' dress, with so much bosom on display that she looks 'like a ripe fruit about to burst.'[90] In one of the film's intimate bedroom scenes Cleopatra refers to her own shape as a way of stressing the legitimisation of her rule: 'My hips are rounded and well apart. Such women they say have sons.' Thus her silhouette, as emphasised both by the script and by the immaculate tailoring of her costumes, is a signifier of her fertility and of her domestic role in the film as mother of Caesar's heir. Taylor's two-time husband, Richard Burton, never a stranger to hyperbole, wrote in *Vogue* in 1965 that Taylor's breasts 'were apocalyptic', and went on to say that 'they would topple empires down before they withered. Indeed, her body was a miracle of construction and the work of an engineer of genius . . . It was true art' (Figure 3.37).[91] If her fans never got to appreciate this miracle of genius engineering up close, they could nevertheless admire and emulate Taylor in their own ways. She was sublime at encapsulating iconic fashion though the decades, from the riding habit she wore as a child in *National Velvet* (dir. Brown, 1944) through the vision of postwar ideal young womanhood in *Father of the Bride* (dir. Minnelli, 1950). Under the banner of historical authenticity, for *Cleopatra* Sharaff was able to create a series of breath-taking costumes which nevertheless were completely chic to the tastes of 1963, displaying full, uplifted and separated breasts which set off minute clinched waistlines, two design features shared by the Italian love-goddess Sophia Loren in her costumes for *The Fall of the Roman Empire* (designed by Veniero Colasanti) in 1964 (Figure 3.38). In *Cleopatra*, though, more emphasis is given to the low cut of the décolletage, exposing much of Taylor's cleavage as possible: the black gown she wears to mourn the death of Caesar, for instance, is slashed to the waist and was used to secure press interest in the film when it was seen in *Vanity Fair* in 1961, two years before *Cleopatra*'s official release, in an iconic photograph by Bert Stern (Figure 3.39). *Look Magazine*, inspired by such titillating previews, published articles advising 'how to change

Figure 3.37
Revealing décolleté yellow silk-jersey costume with matching headdress worn by Elizabeth
Taylor for her first scene with Richard Burton on the *Cleopatra* set in 1962. Irene Sharaff
made a version of this gown for Taylor's subsequent wedding to Burton in March 1964.
'This marriage will last forever,' said the bride, while her husband added: 'Elizabeth Burton
and I are very, very happy.'

Figure 3.38
Sophia Loren in a well-boned and heavily constructed costume for *The Fall of the Roman Empire* (1964), designed by Veniero Colasanti. Candid shot.

American girls into Egyptian beauties' and recommended the appeal of the low-cut décolleté.[92]

The figure-hugging silhouette of Taylor's Cleopatra should be understood within the aesthetic context of the time. We have noted that Dior's New Look highlighted the female form with structured bodices and

Figure 3.39
The Cleopatra Look: Elizabeth Taylor in a *Cleopatra* costume slashed to the waist.
Magazine image, 1961.

fitted waistlines; throughout the 1950s voluminous skirts broke with
wartime austerity and provided women with an overtly feminine
appearance. Dior claimed that his collection 'affirms the natural graces
of Woman . . . Woman the stem, Woman the flower' – although that
'natural' woman nonetheless required a padded bra, a corseted waist,
and padded hips to create the correct image.[93] The immobility of the
New Look made women into an object of feminine perfection – it was
the uniform of the ideal American wife. The fashion historian Valerie

Steele has noted that throughout the 1950s and into the opening years of the following decade, women were the subjects of what she terms 'wife dressing':

> The first principle of wife dressing was complete femininity. A woman should be dressing to please her husband in order to help him with his career . . . fashion was part of the politics of the 1950s and early 1960s . . . the era of the feminine mystique was going back to strict gender roles so women were supposed to dress like women and men were supposed to dress like men.[94]

In the early 1960s the ideal model for this 'good housewife' look was Debbie Reynolds who, with her full skirts, her hair bangs and her pony-tail, embodied the 'girl-next-door' and was carefully marketed by Hollywood in that wholesome way. When in 1959 Taylor 'stole' Reynolds' husband, Eddie Fisher, and made him the fourth Mr Elizabeth Taylor, gossip columnists condemned Taylor as a home-wrecker who had rejected the norms of family life for a world of Hollywood depravity. Taylor's subsequent affair with Richard Burton and the shattering of her wedding vows to Eddie Fisher seemed to confirm this and in her costume designs for *Cleopatra*, Irene Sharaff exploited the hype, deliberately colliding the New Look swing-skirts of Debbie Reynolds with the tailored, figure-hugging sheaths of the mature, voluptuous, man-eating Taylor-Cleopatra.

Although both silhouettes highlighted the feminine form with a fitted bodice and clinched waist, the New Look extended the movement from waist to hip, while the sheath dress clung to the body, revealing its curves to the viewer. Taylor's sheath dresses 'permitted [the male] approach thanks to its more parsimonious occupation of space' confirming Cleopatra's costumes to be a sign of her sexual experience – and of Taylor's sex life too, of course. Taylor's costumes suggest both a traditional 1960s expectation for women to find husbands and they work too as a proto-feminist embrace of female sexuality on a woman's own terms. Cleopatra's highly sexualised position in the political and military world of men is emphasised through her sheath gowns which, however, simultaneously highlight her personal complexities and her political competence.

While the New Look silhouette created a particular kind of woman in the 1950s, Lee Wright has argued that the stiletto heel in the 1960s constructed another kind of femininity. When combined with the hourglass silhouette of the sheath dress and its associated undergarments, the shoe projected a particular message:

> The stiletto was used by some women to represent dissatisfaction with the conventional female image and replace it with that of a 'modern' woman who was more active and more economically independent than her predecessors. The paradox is that, in retrospect, it has been

labelled a 'shackling' instrument which renders women immovable and passive ... [But originally] the stiletto did *not* symbolise the housewife. From 1957 the stiletto was associated with glamour, with rebellion: it represented someone modern and up-to-date, and above all it represented someone who inhabited a world outside the home.[95]

Wright's analysis offers a historical framework for Sharaff's use of stiletto heels in Cleopatra's wardrobe. When combined with her use of the sheath silhouette, the message of the costume design is that both the actress Elizabeth Taylor and the character of Cleopatra physically align themselves with the sexual revolution of the 1960s, a brand of feminism which embraced the possibility that women might have it all: power, work, sex, independence, relationships, more sex, femininity and feminism.

With sixty-five costume changes, Taylor definitely took the film's fashion seriously (the budget for Taylor's costumes alone was $194,000, which calculates to roughly $1,440,000 today) – and so did the critics, for Irene Sharaff won an Oscar for Best Costume Design. A penchant for shimmery metallic fabrics, one-shouldered gowns, draping and heavy, ornate necklaces all combined to make Taylor's Cleopatra a 1960s fashion icon (who, given the revitalisation of 1960s fashion in TV series such as *Mad Men*, still resonates today). Thus in a *Photoplay* article of 1962, Taylor is quoted saying that:

> The day the picture is over, I'll come over in a truck and carry my entire wardrobe of sixty dresses off. You may call it a slight case of pilfering, but these gowns are too gorgeous to be left behind ... They'll make the most wonderful ball gowns and party dresses. This one I'm wearing now is pure 22 carat gold. All of them are precious. But what is more important, they're as modern as tomorrow. I think I'll set a new trend. Not only with the dresses but the hairdos and such – the Cleopatra look.[96]

No sooner said than done: the catwalks of all the major fashion houses for 1962 and 1963 were crammed with black-wigged models wearing variations on the Cleopatra theme as a new wave of Egyptomania swept over another generation of fashion lovers.

Capitalising on a contemporary 1960s trend towards more conspicuous eyes, Elizabeth Taylor's *Cleopatra* makeup incorporated the historical pharaonic fashion of brows and eyes thickly outlined with black kohl and heavily shadowed lids and sockets (Figure 3.40). Wanger's journal claims that the elaborate makeup creations were invented by Taylor herself:

> Elizabeth's makeup, conceived and designed by her, consists of one of the most glamorous eye-dos I have ever seen. To achieve the effect she wanted she stuck a lot of spangles on her lids, which created a

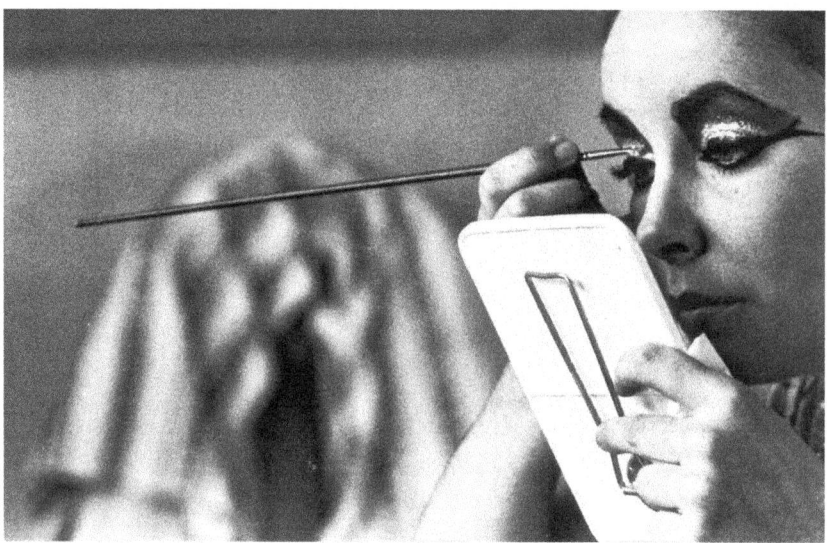

Figure 3.40
Elizabeth Taylor applying her own, complex, Cleopatra eye make-up. Candid shot, 1962.

wonderful appearance, but it took two hours just for her to put on her make-up.[97]

So much for historical authenticity or the boast of the film's academic research pedigree. What is interesting in such candid reports, though, is the apparent dichotomy between the official rhetoric, which stresses historical precision via painstaking research, and a rather slapdash attitude whereby the female star was allowed to design her own makeup without the aid of any 'specialist'.[98] In fact a scene in the film celebrates Taylor as her own makeup artist, and depicts Cleopatra trying out fancy eyeshadow designs on dummy heads (Figure 3.10 – see Text Box 3.6).

Much as the discovery of Tutankhamun's tomb in 1922 served as inspiration for the Art Deco movement, our image of Cleopatra from the 1963 film revived interest in the styles of ancient Egypt. Taylor's star power fuelled this. In the early 1960s the whole fascination or obsession with the look of the film was very much what caught the public's imagination not just with Elizabeth Taylor as Cleopatra, but with Elizabeth Taylor as Elizabeth Taylor. The persistent mythology of this powerful historical queen combined with the allure of the beautiful violet-eyed actress who personified her onscreen, make the figure of Cleopatra an enduring sartorial influence.

Costuming the Epic Hero (1): Tunics and Brylcreem

Men's costumes in epic movies had less of a need to be imbued with a fashionable flair than those of their female counterparts and while male movie stars could be style icons and some period films served as conduits for fashionable looks, unsurprisingly the tunics and togas of the ancient world failed to find popular market appeal. It has long been claimed that after Clark Gable removed his shirt to reveal a bare chest in a famous scene with Claudette Colbert in Frank Capra's 1934 master-piece *It Happened One Night*, American men abandoned the wearing of undershirts, so much so that undershirt sales declined by 75 per cent.[99] Nothing of that kind of impact (if the story is true) can be credited for epic costumes. Women in their droves were slavishly copying Elizabeth Taylor's black bobbed hairstyle and glittery eyeshadow but no man attempted to emulate Richard Burton's leopard skin armour or even his strappy knee-length sandals. This is not to say that movie tie-ins were not popularly marketed through male clothing. Alongside *Quo Vadis* underwear, for instance, a man might opt to wear Weldon's *Quo Vadis* pyjamas or a *Quo Vadis* rayon sports shirt (suitable for both dad and son), with 'up-to-the-minute adaptations of classical Roman themes'. 'Get on the chariot for a magnificent Roman holiday of SALES!' the pressbook exclaimed. Other items of a gentleman's wardrobe were less easy to tie into a movie; nevertheless, 'Aquascutum of London, England, makers of top-quality men's trench-coats and overcoats presents the *Salome* Aquascutum coat', heralded an advertisement in the 1953 *Salome* pressbook. A photograph of a bespectacled (and somewhat bemused) Sir Cedrick Hardwicke (the Emperor Tiberius) in a beige anorak and a dark trilby complemented the press copy.

The standard Hollywood 'ancient world' male costume consisted of a knee-length tunic over which might be thrown a wrap, a cloak or a toga. Open-toed sandals added to the antique look (Figure 3.42). For actors more used to tailored suits, cowboy chaps or denim jeans, the ancient-world look was not always flattering. Following his disastrous performance in *The Silver Chalice*, Paul Newman vowed never to act again 'in a cocktail dress' and lamented the on-screen appearance of his 'bony legs'.[100] Cast (brilliantly) in the role of the Emperor Commodus in *The Fall of the Roman Empire*, Christopher Plummer too recalled how the heavy fur cloaks he wore for the part had a habit of throwing him off-balance and that his knees were bare: 'the wind cruelly cut into them and turned them blue.'[101]

The problem of knees and spindly legs was also encountered by Irene Sharaff when she was commissioned to design Rex Harrison's Julius Caesar costumes in *Cleopatra*. 'The [original costumes I designed] were faithful reproductions of what was worn by a man of high-rank in Rome in 52 BC,' she recalled, 'but as Rex himself remarked, they made him look "like a right Charlie".'[102] Without his customary Savile Row tailoring, Harrison's figure was not impressive and the tunics with their short sleeves exposed all of his weak points, most noticeably his narrow shoulders, long thin arms and spindly legs, none of which were suitable for an on-screen image of Caesar. Sharaff went back to the drawing board and to the research volumes and discovered that according to Suetonius, Caesar had a distinctly avant-garde taste in

Text Box 3.6   The Cleo Craze

Figure 3.41
Magazine advertisement for *Cleopatra*-inspired makeup, 1963.

In the summer of 1962, *Cleopatra* was chic. The Cleopatra craze started before the film's actual release, with companies like Revlon leading the way with Cleopatra-inspired makeup colours and design. This is an advertisement run by Revlon in a series of leading women's magazines in 1962 and 1963:

REVLON solves the sweetest mystery in history with . . . **'THE CLEOPATRA LOOK'**
AN ENCHANTING NEW KIND OF SORCERY – 2,000 YEARS OLD!
Cleopatra herself would never have told! But now Revlon does! 2,000 years after Cleopatra used her beauty secrets to such outrageously unfair (but oh! so feminine) advantage, Revlon redistills them for you in a wonderfully wearable modern adaptation.
    Here is the look for you to wear now . . . a centuries'-old bewitchery brought brilliantly up-to-date.
    The magic begins with your 'Sphinx Eyes' Kit, the unique, new creative eye-make-up exclusively from Revlon. Add to it the provocative flattery of 'SPHINX PINK' – Revlon's new shade for lips and fingertips!
    Suddenly, you've spanned 2,000 years with fashion's favourite look – The Cleopatra Look.
THE CLEOPATRA LOOK – for lips, fingertips . . . and eyes!
SPHINX PINK – a vividly light, bright-at-night pink lipstick and nail enamel!
SPHINX EYES – 3 unique cosmetics blended for a totally new idea in make-up.
Desert Beige, Accent Shadow. . .
A new idea in shadow created to accent lids – not hide them! A shadow to brighten eyes – make them seem bigger!
Black or Brown Ash Cake Eyeliner
. . . a wonderfully new, non-flaking, long-lasting eyeliner for elongated, darkly outlined Cleopatra look.
Mist Grey, Khol Eyeshadow . . .
Smoky shadow inspired by the ancient Egyptians. Adds depth and drama – creates a new sculptured effect to set off the highlighting of *Desert Beige*.

dress and favoured wrist-length sleeves with fringes and a long tunic which was casually belted (leading to Sulla's warning: 'Beware that boy with the loose clothes!'). The Suetonius passage became the catalyst for the designer's approach to a new-look Caesar, and as she was to recall:

A sculptor made a [foam rubber] cast of [Harrison's] torso, then broadened the shoulders and increased the girth; he also made some 'symmetricals' to be added to the thighs and calves . . . All this gave Rex 'build' and was flexible enough for freedom of movement. Instead of the short tunic with pleated skirt generally worn under the military cuirass, I designed a leather jerkin with long sleeves. The greaves worn over the shins partly covered leather breeches. A cuirass worn by a military commander would have been elaborately decorated,

Figure 3.42
Togas, tunics and sandals: the ubiquitous male 'ancient world' look. Charles Laughton and
John Gavin in *Spartacus* (1960). Production still.

but for Rex I designed an outfit of dark polished leather, unadorned
except for the usual sculptured suggestion of a man's torso. Over
his shoulders he wore a heavy woollen cloak ... [All together] it
made him look quite startlingly dramatic ... His senatorial robe was
pleated and hung to the ground; the toga worn over it added bulk to
the silhouette.[103]

Sharaff's vision of Caesar aside (Figure 3.43), rich fabrics and ostentatious decoration were commonly used to indicate a character's wealth

Figure 3.43
Costume gives Rex Harrison's Caesar added imperial authority. *Cleopatra* (1963).
Production still.

and status. George Sanders as the Saran of Gaza in *Samson and Delilah*,
for instance, wears long tunics of green velvet alongside satin capes
lined with gold lamé. At one point in *Quo Vadis* Peter Ustinov's Nero
wears a floor-length pleated, beige silk tunic with elaborate detailing
in purple velvet, mauve silk and gold-thread embroidery around the
chest, side-seam and hem; a purple velvet mantle embroidered with
gold acanthus leaves completes the outfit and brings the right degree of
opulence to the emperor's portrayal.

By and large, in antiquity clothing was worn draped around the body without the need for excessive sewing or shaping (only Persian garments included sleeved tunics and coats and shaped trousers, styles which began to spill west during the later Roman empire). Created by rectangles of cloth of varying lengths and widths, the dress of Egyptians, Mesopotamians, Hebrews, Greeks and Romans were essentially wraparound garments; they were secured with pins, brooches, belts and sashes but rarely contained seams or sewn fastenings. This meant that in wearing their clothes, the peoples of antiquity must have been vigilant in adjusting, shifting and repositioning the fabrics which covered their bodies; ancient dress was in a constant state of flux and needed careful attention. Even a simple tunic had a proclivity to 'ride up' and expose the thighs, while the management of the multiple folds of a huge toga required both knowledge and a flair for fashion. Needless to say, film actors unused to wearing such awkward or cumbersome garments would look unnatural and uncomfortable on-screen trying to cope with a voluminous mantle worn over one shoulder or attempting to control the pleats of an Egyptian linen kilt. To combat this problem Hollywood costume designers created ancient costumes which were 'controlled' by foundation garments, stitched-in pleats and seams. Recently released images of original costumes (photographed for the auction catalogues of the Debbie Reynolds estate – see Text Box 3.7 below) show the lengths to which costume-makers went to make ancient dress 'workable' for actors. A ground-length tunic of taupe silk with delicate fleur-de-lis embroidery worn by Peter Ustinov's Nero, for instance, was 'controlled' with the help of an elastic belt sewn into an invisible waist seam, while for Charlton Heston's Ben-Hur a ceremonial tunic of beige wool with navy trim and copper bullion embroidery in checkerboard design had a distinct seam at the waist, placed there to lessen movement. The seam was covered by a wide leather belt.[104] Marlon Brando's 'Mark Antony' tunic of ivory wool (worn in *Julius Caesar*) incorporates not only a waist seam but also a waist-to-nape zip-fastener at the back (this was concealed beneath a leather cuirass).[105] An extraordinary orange silk and gold lamé-lined 'toga' created for George Relph in his role as Tiberius Caesar in *Ben-Hur* was carefully cut, pre-draped and sewn as one piece so that it did not need adjusting on the actor's body, but was simply allowed to hang from his shoulder.[106]

When a star actor was cast in a period film the studio faced a dilemma. The star's marketable image – his face, hairstyle and fashion sense – could not be sacrificed to history. In examining how Hollywood reconciled these two conflicting demands through the use of hair and makeup, one is able to appreciate how designers handled the task of combining stars' modern image with the ancient past. For Hollywood's leading actors the formula for makeup in epic films was simple: the minimum amount of makeup required by the lights and chemistry of the film stock was applied to give the actor a carefully manufactured 'no-makeup' look. In films with, say, Egyptian settings, the historical mode for applying thick lines of kohl and coloured shadow to the eyes and eyelids was therefore rejected since the use of male cosmetics would have given out the wrong 'message'. In terms of hairstyle, as Annas has observed, there were three workable options:

> First, modern and period hairstyles could be combined. The period features could be modified so that when viewed from the front, the hairline looked modern with the sides groomed tightly to the head, while in profile, the sides and back assumed a conservative period length [e.g. Victor Mature as Samson]. In the second option, a completely modern hairstyle could be used which supported the star's glamour hero image with no relation to history [e.g. Richard Burton as Marcus Gallio and as Antony]. Third, an authentic period style could be reproduced, but this option was rarely used except for character roles [e.g. Peter Ustinov's Nero] or historical likenesses [e.g. Jay Robinson as Caligula in *The Robe*].[107]

Kirk Douglas's role as the slave-cum-freedom-fighter Spartacus warrants, perhaps, a special note: for the role he wore a distinctly non-Roman but ultra-modern tough-guy flattop hairstyle, almost identical to the one he had sported in *Strangers When We Meet* (dir. Quine), a film he had made earlier in 1960 prior to shooting *Spartacus*. By the late 1950s the flattop was the most popular men's hairstyle in the United States and with its harsh lines and angles, a flattop suggested a solid work ethic, physical fitness and an intense, serious approach to life. In the early 1960s the hairstyle was very popular in the military, leading the Beatles, in their song *Come Together*, to satirise it as a symbol of social conservatism. As the slave-gladiator, Douglas wore his flattop alongside hair slicked back at the sides and one small section of the back crown drawn into a diminutive pony-tail, but otherwise period authenticity was sacrificed to serve the male lead's contemporary star image.

In epic movies facial hair (beards, moustaches, sideburns) could be added – conservatively – to help create a role, although the preference for clean shaven faces in the period 1920–65 meant that many actors were reluctant to be depicted in this way. A *New York Times* feature (24 October 1954) noted a sudden 'Bonanza in Beards' thanks to the popularity of the widescreen epics of the era:

> Beards – forked, waved, long, short, neat, shaggy, pointed, powdered, flowing and cuneiform – have suddenly jutted forth on the best Hollywood chins. The current rash of Biblical pictures . . . has prompted such upright, once clean cut leading men as Kirk Douglas, Gregory Peck, Robert Taylor . . . and Edmund Purdom to toss away their razors and let nature take its course, the outgrowth of which is the curliest box-office bonanza since Shirley Temple . . . What's behind this outcropping of beards? A push towards authenticity in Hollywood's all-out effort to stem the competition . . . The actor wears

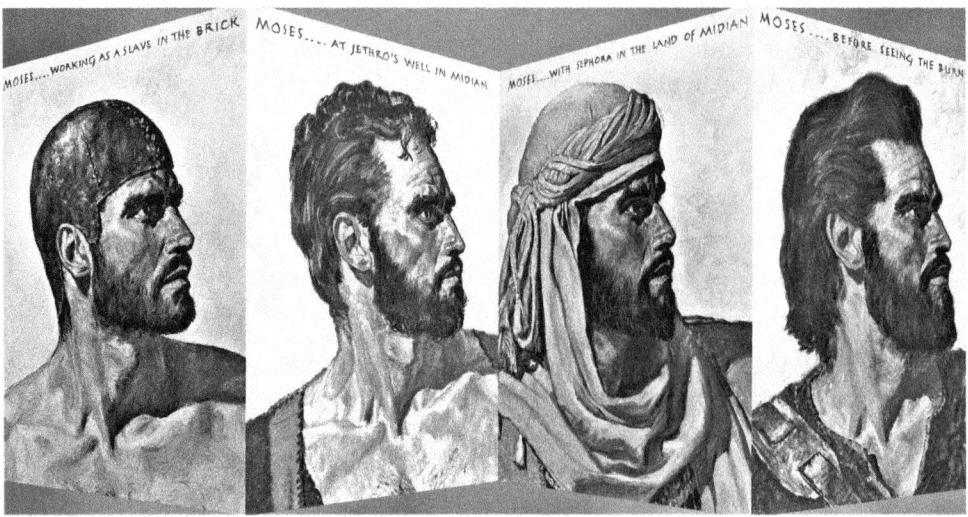

Figure 3.44
Some of Arnold Friberg's sketches suggesting the development of Moses' beard as worn by
Charlton Heston; *The Ten Commandments* (1956). Pressbook artwork.

a beard if the part calls for it – even if it means obscuring a celebrated
cleft chin or marring a quivering set of nostrils . . . Douglas . . . who
was bearded for 'Ulysses' speaks with pride about his growth: 'Raised
every knot in it myself, Man, what a beauty!' At Warner Brothers their
makeup ace, Gordon Bowe, is distressed [since] on 'Silver Chalice'
they have twelve important beards, all on principals, and all different.
To get them all ready by nine o'clock – and getting those experts over
there, when Metro and Twentieth and Paramount were fighting for
them too – took some doing!

Arnold Friberg, commissioned by DeMille to craft the look of the principal characters in *The Ten Commandments*, recalls the trouble he took in
designing for the bearded Charlton Heston (Figure 3.44):

I worked with DeMille on the 'Stages of Moses' for the makeup
department. Moses: Prince of Egypt; brick-pit slave; outlaw; shepherd; prophet-diviner; patriarch. [Henry Wilcoxon] had sketched a
beard on a photograph of Charlton Heston to convince DeMille that
he should play Moses because he looked like Moses when he had
a beard . . . And I believe that a tremendous religious leader like
Moses or Jesus should be presented as commanding and strong, not a
weakling or a victim.[108]

Hirsute chins aside, a defining feature of the fashionable male hairstyle
in America and Europe throughout the Golden Age of filmmaking was
the liberal use of Brylcreem. Keeping quiffs neatly in place since 1928,
Brylcreem was an iconic product of male hair styling with men of all

BRYLCREEM

grooms by Surface Tension

LET YOUR SCALP
BREATHE . . .
ENCOURAGE YOUR
HAIR TO LIVE . . .

In keeping your hair and scalp healthy,
Brylcreem's surface film of oil acts as a
filter, which prevents micro-organisms
from reaching down into the scalp. Massage
with Brylcreem also frees the mouths of the
follicles along which the hair grows, thus
facilitating the normal flow of sebum, the
scalp's natural oil. As a result, the hair is kept
free from dandruff and dryness and the scalp
has a chance to breathe—vitally important to
the growth of strong, healthy hair. Ask for
Brylcreem, the *healthy* hairdressing, in tubs 1/8,
2/6 and 4/6, or handy tubes 2/6.

Appearance counts for men at the centre of things—and
appearance depends so much on smart, healthy hair. That's
why men that people look to prefer Brylcreem, the perfect
hairdressing. Brylcreem gives the clean, smart look — the
lustrous, vital look that keeps a man perfectly set for the
day. With massage, Brylcreem guards the health of hair and
scalp, checks dryness, relieves dandruff. Use Brylcreem and
ensure a smart appearance all day, every day.

for smart, healthy hair

Figure 3.45
Brylcreem: the number one grooming choice for American men until the late 1960s.
Magazine advertisement, c.1952.

ages and classes using it to create the clean, smart hairstyle that was the
fashion at the time – and that not-a-hair-out-of-place look remained the
mode until the early 1970s; in fact, a brief history of Brylcreem is a brief
history of western masculinity in the twentieth century. By the 1950s
Brylcreem was most dominant product in men's hairstyling (Figure
3.45); it was used by film stars, business executives, sportsmen, blue-
collar labourers, popstars and Teddy Boys. Inevitably, then, Brylcreem
found its way into Hollywood's period films and, in fact, it might be
said that the epics of the 1950s are simply lengthy, costly Technicolor

Figure 3.46
God's anointed wears Brylcreem. The elegant and sophisticated Gregory Peck as King
David in *David and Bathsheba* (1952). Production still.

Brylcreem commercials. In his role as King David (Figure 3.46), for
instance, style-icon Gregory Peck, wearing his tunic-cloak-combo with
all the sophistication he brought to the grey flannel suit he wore in
Roman Holiday (dir. Wyler, 1953), has his thick dark hair immaculately
coiffured with a centre-parted quiff-pompadour and slicked-back sides
created with a lavish use of Brylcreem.[109]

No less a person than the French philosopher Roland Barthes once
noted that what defined Romans in Hollywood films was the use of the
quiff:

In Mankiewicz's *Julius Caesar* all the characters are wearing quiffs.
Some of them curly, some straggly, some tufted, some oily, all have

them well-combed, and the bald are not admitted, although there are plenty to be found in Roman history . . . What then is associated with these insistent quiffs? Quite simply, Roman-ness. We therefore see here the mainspring of the Spectacle – the sign – operating in the open. The frontal lock overwhelms one with evidence, no one can doubt that he is in ancient Rome: the actors speak, act, torment themselves, debate 'questions of universal import', without losing, thanks to this little flag displayed over their foreheads, any of their historical plausibility. Their general representatives can even expand in complete safety, cross the oceans and the centuries, and merge into the Yankee mugs of Hollywood extras: no matter, everyone is reassured, installed in the quiet certainty of a universe without duplicity, where Romans are Romans thanks to the most legible of signs: hair over the forehead.[110]

Costuming the Epic Hero (2): Armour and Beefcake

Beyond the tunic-toga combination, the defining feature of male epic costuming is, of course, armour, the historical veracity of which is open to debate. Some on-screen armour design is of the purely whimsical, if not fantastical, such as the *Aïda*-inspired falcon breastplates designed for Horemheb (Victor Mature) in *The Egyptian* and for Moses and Ramses in *The Ten Commandments*.[111] For Roman epics though, the muscle cuirass (generally worn by actors in the role of officers) or the leather *lorica segmentata* (worn by actors playing legionaries or ordinary soldiers) were often employed – with varying degrees of historical accuracy. Sometimes a simple leather or cloth jerkin or tunic, worn with an overlapping cape, was thought to suffice (Figure 3.47).

Interestingly there was a distinct shift in the conception, design and execution of Roman armour between the 1930s and the 1950s. DeMille's Art Deco Romans wear glittering military uniforms, embossed in soft leather and shimmering with gold lamé trim (Figure 3.48); in *The Sign of the Cross*, as Marcus Superbus, Fredric March wears a costume designed by Mitchell Leisen of malleable draped metallic cloth and a helmet comprising a felt skull cap draped in fine chain mail with adjustable metal headband and ear flaps with a laurel wreath motif (Figure 3.49).[112] By the 1950s, following developments in the taste for more physical bulk among American film stars, Roman armour had buffed-up too, emphasising girth, thickness and substance and suggesting in the muscled cuirass the physique of the man beneath the metal (Figure 3.50). A *Film Show Annual* article of 1951 entitled 'When in Rome' focuses on the physical efforts Robert Taylor was required to make in the recreation of a Roman military commander in *Quo Vadis*. He is cited as saying that:

As an American who grew up in the wide open spaces of the Mid West and who has entertained a fondness for the outdoor life, I've always taken pride in the ruggedness and athletic ability of the

Figure 3.47
Standard epic Roman fatigues: Richard Burton in *The Robe* (1953). Wardrobe test
photograph.

average American male, myself included. I figured that man for man,
probably we could match any other physical specimen of past or
present.

I'm still convinced that in the matter of physical prowess we can
hold our own in the world today. But I'm not so certain now about
some of those fellows who lived a few centuries ago. I am beginning
to wonder particularly about this superman who lived in Ancient

Figure 3.48
Art Deco Roman soldiers; *The Sign of the Cross* (1932). Production still.

Figure 3.49
Clad in shimmering silver metallic lamé and an Art Deco helmet, Fredric March kisses
Elissa Landi (with her permanent wave hairstyle). Both costumes are the work of Mitchell
Leisen; *The Sign of the Cross* (1932). Production shot.

Figure 3.50
Robert Taylor examines his costumes for *Quo Vadis* (1951). Publicity shot used in the pressbook.

Rome . . . For weeks I walked around in an armour plate that weighed almost as much as I did myself . . . I'm beginning to wonder if modern man isn't a bit puny after all? At any rate, after being an ancient Roman in the Twentieth Century, I'm just pleased that fate decreed I'd be one for the sake of *Quo Vadis* only.

A *Life* magazine pictorial survey of Hollywood's most popular male movie stars for 1954 makes the point that 'there is no one male movie star who sends all the girls [crazy].' The article acknowledges that women go to films to look at men as much as men go to view women and, what is more, the male image is no less as marketable a commodity than the female. 'Some like them tough', the article continues, 'some like them tender. Some like them wistful . . . others like them protective . . . Rippling muscles and a bare chest [or] a dimple in the chin', these are some of the things that, 'give some women shivers of delight'.[113]

Life's representation of the 1950s male star as an object of spectacle – and the attention it brings to the erotic status of male stars in Hollywood cinema – challenges, perhaps, Laura Mulvey's well-known and much-cited feminist essay which states that on-screen 'women are simultaneously looked at and displayed' while men 'are not the erotic object of the gaze'.[114] In fact the Hollywood studios conscientiously made it their business to sell the imagery of male stars both on- and off-screen as part of a product which appealed to both men and women. Pleasure was to be had in looking at actors but a particular pleasure came from looking at an actor showing off his body. *Photoplay* even commented in a piece on the actor Richard Egan that 'nobody discovered him until he took off his shirt in *Demetrius and the Gladiators*.'[115] It is not too far-fetched to label 1950s Hollywood as 'The Age of the Chest'.

The marketability of the epic actor's body – and the chest in particular – is central to the genre, as propounded by Babington and Evans in their brilliant study of the on-screen poetics of Victor Mature's roles in films such as *Samson and Delilah*, *The Robe* (Figure 3.51), *Demetrius and the Gladiators*, *The Egyptian* and *Hannibal*. These epics rarely fail to dress Mature without exposing parts of his body and especially so in the male-to-male combat scenes so beloved of the genre, where the rituals of a hyper-aggressive masculinity are brought to the fore. As the authors state:

> Whether bare-chested or besuited, [Victor] Mature's fleshy frame, 6 feet 2 inches, over 200 pounds with 15 inch biceps, fills the screen with an outsize form . . . Many scenes expose the Mature character to physical danger, showing off his muscular prowess . . . The epics rarely fail to dress Mature without exposing parts of his body . . .
>
> As an ego-ideal, Mature would have appealed to many 1950s men, not just as an obvious he-man but for more subtle qualities, particularly the way he displays emotion without suggesting weakness . . . As an object of desire, tall, massive and sensuously handsome, his box office popularity proves his appeal to many women and (however theorised) to many men, regardless of sexual orientation.[116]

Epic films are vehicles for foregrounding male bodies. In *Spartacus* the camera lingers on the spectacle of Kirk Douglas's body clad only in a loincloth and on the similar undress of his fellow gladiators so much so, in fact, that the naked torso becomes a costume in its own right. In

Figure 3.51
Epic beefcake: Victor Mature in *The Robe* (1953). Wardrobe test photograph.

the 1956 *The Ten Commandments* the melodramatic, painterly tableaux constructed by DeMille place the lead actors, Charlton Heston and Yul Brynner, squarely in the frame (DeMille avoids close-up in favour of medium shots) so that the audience's attention is riveted upon their bodies (Figure 3.52).

Both Moses and Ramses are presented as romantic heroes, although the (chaste, we imagine) romance between Moses and Nefretiri involves

Figure 3.52
The VistaVision-filling frames of Charlton Heston and Yul Brynner. *The Ten Commandments* (1956). Production still.

much bosom-heaving and honeyed-words: 'Your fragrance is like the wine of Babylon', he says to her. 'Oh Moses, Moses, you stubborn, splendid, adorable fool!' she coos back. Ramses is cut from a different cloth though: 'You are going to be mine', he snarls at Nefretiri:

> All mine, like my dog or my horse or my falcon . . . Only I will love you more and trust you less . . . You will be my wife; you will come to me whenever I call you. I will enjoy that very much. Whether you enjoy it or not is your own affair. But I think you will.

In fact, an interesting visual code of opposites is in operation throughout the film, highlighting the macho rivalry between the two alpha-males. As Steven Cohan has noticed:

> Moses/Heston . . . appears bare-chested at several key points in the first half of the film, although . . . never at the same time as Ramses/ Brynner . . . For instance, when Ramses is bare-chested in one scene . . . where he taunts Nefretiri . . . in the next scene, when he follows his father to Goshen, where Moses is working bare-chested, the Egyptian

appears fully clothed ... Moses strips to work ... following the Hollywood convention for showing off male beefcake.[117]

The pharaoh, Seti I, is perfectly right, it seems, when he calls the two princes 'crowing roosters'; throughout the four hours of the film, both actors huff, puff and blow out their chests to signify their virility and, it seems, to fill the VistaVision space of the screen, although it must be said that Brynner's posing and posturing is imbued with a much more self-mocking, tongue-in-cheek quality than Heston shows.

But yet another code is at work in the focus on the chests of Brynner and Heston, for the former movie star, made famous by his bald head (which he first shaved on the advice of Irene Sharaff when working together on the Broadway premiere of *The King and I*) has a hairless body while Charlton Heston's chest, belly and arms are hirsute. In the first half of *The Ten Commandments*, Heston is subjected to a state of undress comparable to that of Brynner in order to place their chests in visual juxtaposition. In the movie, all men of the Egyptian elite have shaved bodies, thereby visually reinforcing Egypt's association with Hollywood's traditional representations of 'Orientals' and Native Americans, whereas all the Hebrew men, even wicked Egyptophile Dathan (Edward G. Robinson) are hairy, shaggy even. Body hair therefore connotes the Hebrews' realness in contrast to the Egyptians' artifice; hair makes the Hebrews more honest and god-fearing. This means that every time Moses, as Prince of Egypt, takes off his tunic and displays his hairy chest, he reveals his true identity as a Hebrew (even though it is notable that his chest hair was subtly trimmed and his stomach hair shaved to give more artful symmetry to his pectorals), and therefore when Ramses has Moses brought into court in chains, wearing just a loincloth, his face unshaved too, there can be no denial of his true slavish identity. Once Moses accepts his Hebrew identity he becomes progressively more hairy (Figure 3.53). It should be noted that Charlton Heston's body takes on a different meaning from the bodies of his contemporaries, stars like William Holden, Kirk Douglas, Burt Lancaster and Marlon Brando, all of whom shaved their chests. This explains, argues Cohan, 'why they have not come to personify the epic genre as Heston has.'[118]

The association with the hirsuteness of the epic hero is played out again by Heston in *Ben-Hur*, where he spends a significant section of on-screen time as a galley slave wearing only a loincloth and displaying his hairy but scared, sweaty and dirty body. By matter of contrast, Messala's body is hairless and in a scene set within the Roman garrison's bath house it is oiled, gleaming and clad only a short, revealing towel. Stephen Boyd's body becomes a spectacle in itself. Yet the visual treatment of Boyd's hairless physique and of Heston's well-built bulk complete with a full chest of hair, are noteworthy signifiers in the changing cultural values regulating cinematic representations of the male body – and what, indeed, constitutes the notion of 'costume' – to determine its erotic value.

Figure 3.53
Hirsute heroes: John Derek and Charlton Heston show off their hairy chests, arms and legs.
They are joined by Henry Wilcoxon; *The Ten Commandments* (1956). Candid shot.

Colour

Colour was an important component in Hollywood costume design and
even before colour film was routinely used, costume designers had to
think carefully about how colour could be conveyed in black-and-white
projection and what the process of filming in black-and-white might do
to a costume design. Black-and-white film stock reproduces colour as
shades of grey which can be substantially different from colour stock
and from the way the human eye perceives colour. For instance, the

human eye sees some colours, like green, as brighter than others, like blue. Similarly, black-and-white film stock has its own sensitivities. For example, unlike the human eye, black-and-white stock tends to record blue as a lighter shade of grey than green.

It was important that designers knew how costumes would appear on a movie's film stock. Using white in a design helped in creating contrast, but pure white often produced undesirable tones in the filmed image and therefore costume designers used pink, yellow and pale blue to produce white or a light shade of grey. Famously, for Warner Brother's 1938 production of *Jezebel*, Orry-Kelly was tasked with creating a dress for Bette Davis whose bad girl chooses to arrive at a stylish 1860s cotillion ball in a bright red dress instead of the requested virginal white gown. One problem with panchromatic stock was that red often photographed as a dark grey or even black, so after experimenting with different colours, Kelly discovered that the perfect colour to represent a bright red on-screen was a rust-brown. The costume was created from this colour but was read as a vivid red in the projection process.[119] The true master of black-and-white costume design though was Travis Banton – even when the Technicolor revolution began to dominate the screen in the late 1930s, he continued to use a subdued palette of contrasting colours based around the black–white binary. He was also skilled in his technological grasp of black-and-white film stock as shown through the survival of one of his gowns for Claudette Colbert's Cleopatra: appearing on screen as shimmering silver, the intricately constructed bias-cut satin gown was actually mint green (Colour Plate 13).[120]

Because colour film stock came later, many filmmakers denied its right to exist as one separate medium, and conceived it as an addition to black-and-white. After the initial critical reception of bright Technicolor features, Hollywood toned down its colour scheme, and used colour only merely in ranges of grey, brown and dark blue, which created harmonious patterns but constrained colour's potential. The transition to colour film only became complete when filmmakers understood its creative potential beyond the realms of realism, and started treating it as a new artistic tool to empower their imagination. Colour brought to directors a number of artistic liberties to control audiences' emotions, and some of them stepped out of naturalism to engage with colour in a fantasy way, as in Fleming's *The Wizard of Oz* (1939). A colour costume can mould a specific mood or carry out certain symbols and emotions; for instance, red is associated with passion, anger and danger. Natalie Kalmus, who was credited as the 'colour supervisor' of virtually all Technicolor features made in Hollywood from 1934 to 1949, famously explained that for on-screen effect, colours mixed with white suggested youth, while with grey, it implied refinement and with black, dignity.[121] All colours, she argued, spoke their own language, and it was up to the director to play with their connotations and sharpen the meaning of a film.

By the early 1950s colour became a viable technology and contributed meaningfully to a film's style as directors stopped considering it as something superadded and used it to give an impulse to the drama and implicate it within the narrative. They had more control over lighting, exposure, choice of set and costumes. As the technology improved, they also had more control over the camera's movement, choosing if an angle would include or exclude a particular colour in the setting or costume, or minimise or emphasise a specific colour in the scene through long shot or close-ups. Colours also provided cues to read the face and body of actors and forge connections between characters through costumes.

To return to the 1956 version of *The Ten Commandments*, it is not just the bodies of the two male stars that visualise the difference between the Hebrew and Egyptian cultures, for colour too plays a key role is establishing the contrast between these two worlds. Noerdlinger noted that the bright sunlight of the on-location shoot in the Egyptian desert required the costume designers to come up with bright, contrasting hues to keep the actors from blending into the background.[122] But even the scenes shot on the studio sound-stages have a vivid Technicolor brilliance and depth of colour saturation which puts one in mind of the MGM musicals of the period. The cinematography privileged two colours in particular: a vivid red and a deep turquoise-blue and both of these colours were used extensively throughout the film's costume plot in a carefully controlled manner. For instance, when baby Moses is first lifted from the reed basket by Bithiah (Nina Foch) she sets aside the red Levite cloth which covered the baby, wrapping him instead in a soft royal blue blanket. From this point on, the red–blue binary signifies the oscillating fortunes of Moses in relation to Ramses' destiny, and vice versa (Colour Plate 14). If red dominates Moses' costumes, then blue is the chief signifier of Ramses' designs. Moreover, their emotional hold over Nefretiri is signified by colour switches in her costumes too: when she first greets Moses as the conqueror of Ethiopia she is dressed in brilliant red as a semiotic of both her passion and her loyalty towards Moses, the man she loves and desires, but in a later scene where Ramses stakes his claim on her as the heiress of the Egyptian throne, she is dressed in pale blue – signifying at best her lukewarm reception to his advances or at least anticipating her eventual fate. Later, when Moses returns from exile to the Egyptian court to demand freedom for his people, his shapeless Levite cloak reads as a dull red with white and black stripes (all other traces of colour are removed) but in stark contrast, Ramses' costume contains the chromatic elements of both protagonists in earlier scenes. Pharaoh's costume is a brilliant rainbow of colours (Colour Plate 15). His headdress is red with a golden uraeus jutting from its brow; a blue 'buzzard cape', as its designer Arnold Friberg called it, 'makes him look like a great bird of prey' and beneath it he wears a red embroidered kilt. Ramses' dazzling costuming incorporates the brightly coloured *mis-en-scène* of Egypt while Moses' drab red robe sets him apart from the land of his youth, alienating him from the pagan Egyptians. Steven Cohan has interpreted the colours employed in Ramses' costumes as having the same chromatic brilliance as the visualisation of the plagues

– when, to give an example, the blue sky of Egypt above the palace turns green before the devastating hailstorm or when the blue waters of the Nile turn the vivid colour of blood. Colour has the effect of equating Ramses' body with Egypt, to the point where, in this respect, he can rightly say, 'I am Egypt.'[123] And yet, for Ramses' final appearance, he is stripped of colour and, depicted lamenting the death of his son, his ill-fated first-born, both he and Nefretiri don simple blue-black robes, symbols of their united grief, shame, and loss.[124]

Concluding Thoughts

Sadly, by the mid-1960s the glory days of the great Hollywood costumiers was drawing to a close. In 1967, at the age of seventy and after forty-three years at Paramount, Edith Head's contract came to an end. She moved to Universal and continued to work under contract until her death in 1981 but Head's later career was the exception and not the rule. For most designers the security of working under a studio contract was over and with that haven went too the studio 'house styles' which had dominated the industry for half a century. With the demise of the studio costume designer, so too went the legend of Hollywood glamour, for during cinema's Golden Age, the costume departments – those thousands of seamstresses, cutters, fitters, milliners, wardrobe men and women, and dressers upon whose shoulders the great designers stood – had helped manufacture the Hollywood Dream. In no small way did costume designs promote and make epic movies some of the most lucrative box-office successes of their times.

The voluminous togas, the glinting metal armour, the gold lamé push-up bras and the gossamer veils all contributed to the success of these costly films. Despite the regular claims of historical dependability, when it came to designing the costumes for Hollywood's epics, designers were compelled to interpret the ideals of feminine beauty or masculine prowess embedded in the contextual culture of twentieth-century America. Designers had to straddle Hollywood's two major preoccupations and contradictions by pandering to marketable notions of historicity and 'selling' a glamour-product as part of a major marketing strategy. The historical heroes and heroines of epic movies always made a fashionable statement so that the result could never be historical realism but, by the nature of Hollywood itself, a 'designer history'.

Notes

1. Nielson (1990: 175). Accessing sources for costume in Golden Age Hollywood is fraught with difficulties, as Landis (2012a: 12) notes:

    Researching the history of motion picture costume design is particularly problematic. The paper trail inherent to conventional businesses does not exist in the movie industry. All of the major film studios have been bought and sold (especially over the last thirty-five years), becoming satellites of

Text Box 3.7   The Afterlife of Costumes: The Debbie Reynolds Auctions

Figure 3.54
Debbie Reynolds and two of Elizabeth Taylor's *Cleopatra* crowns.

In June 2011 the first of three auctions featuring vintage film costumes from the collection of the actress Debbie Reynolds (1932–2016) was held in Hollywood. Reynolds had amassed an enormous and important collection of Hollywood costumes and props dating from the silent era and the Golden Age with the intent of opening a museum of film costume. Reynolds recalled that 'It was inspired by shock.' When she heard that MGM was going to sell off its stock of costumes and props, she realised that her mission was to save as many of them as possible in one collection:

> My passion for collecting began in earnest when the studios broke up their inventories. In 1970 MGM announced it was going to auction off everything except their real estate. I was still under contract at MGM and knew this inventory well. These were the clothes that the studio wouldn't even lend us to wear to events or parties . . . After the auction, preserving as many of these costumes as possible became my obsession.

She formed the non-profit Hollywood Motion Picture Museum in 1972 and her collection grew with subsequent 20th Century Fox and Paramount studio sales. Fortunately, she was good friends with the President of Fox and was able to purchase many items prior to the auction, including twelve gowns worn by Marilyn Monroe: one was the famous subway dress from *The Seven Year Itch* which brought in $4.6 million at auction (Reynolds paid $200). Other Paramount acquisitions included costumes worn by Claudette Colbert in *Cleopatra*.

Reynolds continued to buy through the years and acquired such iconic items as Audrey Hepburn's *My Fair Lady* race-day gown for $100,000 (sold for $3.7 million). Other pieces came to her through donation: Harpo Marx gave her his top hat ($45,000 at auction) and when a costume worn in *Cleopatra* by Richard Burton came up for sale, Reynolds actually telephoned Elizabeth Taylor for the purchase money. She explained that she already had Taylor's Cleopatra costume and wanted to reunite it with one of Marc Antony's. 'I really need it because I have you already', Reynolds told her; 'So she sent me the money for the costume.' Richard Burton's tunic and cape sold for $85,000 and Taylor's headdress brought in $100,000.

The year 1993 saw the opening of the Debbie Reynolds Hollywood Hotel and Casino Resort in Las Vegas which included her prototype museum of costumes. A financial failure, it filed for bankruptcy in 1997 and was auctioned off to the World Wrestling Federation for only $10 million, less than what was owed to creditors. Reynolds placed her entire collection into storage where it remained.

An opportunity arose when she found 20,000 square feet of land in a development complex in central Hollywood and in 2001, the city gave her $50,000 for the creation of the museum. Troubled financially, in 2004 a new location was chosen in Pigeon Forge, Tennessee, near Dollywood. Much of the construction was completed when the project's real-estate developers claimed bankruptcy leaving Reynolds holding the bag. The museum project filed for bankruptcy protection in June 2009 forcing Reynolds to liquidate.

And so on 18 June 2011 the auction of Reynolds' important collection began. Auction estimates were exceeded by leaps and bounds: a test pair of the Ruby Slippers from the *The Wizard of Oz* sold for $510,000 and Judy Garland's blue and white gingham 'Dorothy test dress' sold for $910,000. Combined, their estimates were only $230,000. Marilyn Monroe's red sequined dress and feather headdress from *Gentlemen Prefer Blondes* fetched $1.2 million and her costumes from *There's No Business Like Show Business* and *River of No Return* together reached $1,010,000.

Other notable sales included $110,000 for Charlie Chaplin's bowler hat, $550,000 for Julie Andrew's *Sound of Music* jumper dress, $140,000 for her guitar and $320,000 for Charlton Heston's tunic and cape from *Ben-Hur*. Grace Kelly's chiffon evening gown from *The Swan* earned $110,000 and her coral knit dress from *To Catch a Thief* soared to $450,000. Other heavy hitters were Taylor, Ingrid Bergman and Barbra Streisand, whose gold velvet gown from *Hello Dolly* fetched $100,000.

Reynolds herself remained a star and a personality throughout the auction. She joked at the opening, 'I've been collecting for 45 years and I'm still 40.' When bidding for Greta Garbo's Camille couch slowed to $9,000, Reynolds yelled out 'I paid ten!' and it went for $11,000. She even went up to the buyer of Dorothy's dress and shoes and kissed him on the cheek.

In 2015, the Los Angeles City Council approved the construction of the Academy Museum of Motion Pictures, a $300 million museum that will celebrate the world of cinema. It is hoped that items from the former collection of Debbie Reynolds will be reunited and displayed there.

Figure 3.55
Richard Burton's armour from *Cleopatra*. the Debbie Reynolds collection.

large multinational conglomerates, and with each new acquisition paper records are jettisoned and archival information becomes more difficult to retrieve. Studios routinely discard ancillary design materials from the costume and art departments, including costume design illustrations now cherished by collectors. The Internet and specialty auction houses have become an active marketplace for movie memorabilia such as costume illustrations, costumes and props. But a wealth of prosaic paperwork – costume budgets, continuity photographs, costume change breakdowns and fabric swatch books – is dumped after a film has been released and the need for reshoots has ended. Not long after a movie has wrapped, its entire costume department disappears.

2. More scholarship is needed to track her invaluable progenitor role in fashion as well as her influence on other film designers. See further: https://wfpp. cdrs.columbia.edu/pioneer/ccp-clare-west/ (accessed 3 March 2017).

3. For the careers of the great costume designers see LeVine (1981: 160–245); Landis (2007 and 2012b); Jorgensen and Scoggins (2015).
4. Quoted in Landis (2012b: 26).
5. Quoted in Landis (2012b: 231).
6. http://www.imdb.com/name/nm0788695/bio?ref_=nm_dyk_qt_sm#quotes (accessed 22 May 2017).
7. Cyrino (Undated). I am grateful to Monica Cyrino for providing me with access to her unpublished paper.
8. Quoted in Ford and Mitchell (2009: 82).
9. Dick (2008: 87).
10. Bailey (1982: 281); Head and Calistro (1983: 25).
11. DeMille was always certain that his costumes demanded the work of several designers and that one or two designers would simply 'burn out' on one of his films. Dorothy Jeakins was also commissioned to design Delilah's costumes; see Annas, LaValley and Maeder (1987a: 118).
12. Head and Calistro (1983: 81).
13. Sharaff (1976: 66).
14. See Maltby (1993); Black (1994); Petley (2009).
15. The Legion issued ratings in order to attempt to give viewers an idea of the content of the films. It constructed a four-tier ratings system and began to review films, giving them one of the following four labels:
    A1 – Unobjectionable for general patronage
    A2 – Unobjectionable for adults
    B – Objectionable in part
    C – Condemned
16. The full text of the Code is available at: http://www.artsreformation.com/a001/hays-code.html (accessed 26 March 2017).
17. Douglas (2012: 142–3).
18. Head and Calistro (1983: 26); Dick (2008: 61).
19. Head and Ardmore (1960: 9).
20. Doniol-Valcroze (1989: 41–2).
21. Holt (1951: 251).
22. Brenner (1993: 231).
23. Brown (1983: 2).
24. Wurtzel (1998: 40).
25. Chabot (2000).
26. Harcourt-Smith (1951: 412).
27. Head and Ardmore (1960: 99–100).
28. Lamarr (1966: 173).
29. Lamarr (1966: 168–9).
30. Greenberg (1975: 8).
31. A term used by Kozlovic (2002).
32. Quoted in Stemp (2012: 23). Sharaff went on to note:

> In the 1940s the emphasis was on bosoms and the amount of cleavage permitted was left to the discretion of a man from the censorship office, whose okay was necessary for every dress and costume before it could be shot. [I was] on set when a censor was on the job, a small grey man, serious and stern at his job, he stood in front of Lana Turner's well-padded bosom, peering down her low-cut dress. Shaking his head, he turned to the designer standing anxiously beside him and said, 'You'd better cover the cleavage with net or tulle. It'll never pass the office.'

33. Turner (1983: 151).
34. Quoted in Landis (2007: 230).
35. DeMille (1960: 364–5).
36. Tashiro (1998: 95–6).
37. Squire (1972: 17–18).
38. On costume design and the contemporary image see in particular Annas et al. (1987a).
39. Cary (1974: 90).
40. Annas et al. (1987a).
41. Peacock feathers were a mark of DeMille's films: in *Male and Female* (1919), for example, as a Babylonian princess, Gloria Swanson wore a headdress of white peacock plumes (Figure OC.3) – a conceit Edith Head later used when she designed Swanson's costumes for *Sunset Boulevard*. Swanson, as Norma Desmond, wears an ermine-trimmed velvet wrap and suit and a hat decorated with a single white peacock feather. When, in 1970, Swanson returned to Paramount to narrate a documentary about early Hollywood, she asked costume designer Edith Head to remake the velvet and ermine suit Norma had worn to visit DeMille. But no one could find a white peacock feather to decorate the ermine toque that had been made for her. 'Imagine', a flabbergasted Swanson said, 'not a single white peacock feather in all Hollywood!' The cloak made for Lamarr is still on view in DeMille's estate in Los Angeles; it is made from 2,000 peacock plumes, allegedly gathered from peacocks that roamed freely on DeMille's ranch. See further Head and Calistro (1983: 84, 87–8); LeVine (1981: 17); Landis (2012a: 184–5).
42. Head and Calistro (1983: 85).
43. Crisp (1984: 17).
44. On the role of fashion and the star system see Davis (1993: 205–32).
45. Maeder (2012: 128–9, 131).
46. Annas (1987: 56).
47. Genini (1996: 39).
48. The idea that Bara, like other stars of early cinema, designed her own costumes is endorsed by her own memoirs of the filming of her 1918 movie, *Salome*:

    > I wanted to be a different Salome, so I ordered the wig-maker to send me a wig of tawny, blond hair. It was almost to be like a lion's mane, wild, unruly and weird. But the man had no imagination. He sent me one with Pickford curls. So I'm a brunette Salome after all. (Quoted in Golden, 1996: 167)

49. Wagenknecht (1962: 179). Bara claimed, 'It is not a mere theory in my mind. I have a positive knowledge that I am a reincarnation of Cleopatra. I live Cleopatra, I breathe Cleopatra, I *am* Cleopatra.' See Golden (1996: 130). The 1917 souvenir brochure accompanying *Cleopatra* contained an article asking, 'Is Theda Bara a Reincarnation of Cleopatra?' Several arguments in favour of the proposition were advanced:

    > (1) The character of Cleopatra and the character of Theda Bara are similar in many respects. (2) In appearance, so far as can be definitely ascertained, Miss Bara and the Siren of the Nile were similar. (3) Miss Bara's last name is similar to an Egyptian word meaning 'Soul of the Sun'. (4) The prophecy of Rhadmes fits Cleopatra as easily as Miss Bara.

50. *Motion Picture News*, 3 November 1917. See further, Wyke (1997: 89–90).
51. 27 October 1917.
52. *Cleopatra* pressbook 1917.
53. Quoted in Maeder (1987: 10).
54. Chierichetti (1995: 43). For the body-conscious Colbert, Leisen's costumes allowed her to highlight what she found most pleasing in her appearance – especially her beautiful legs (put to legendary effect in *It Happened One Night*, dir. Capra, 1934).
55. Quoted in Landis (2012c: 26).
56. One of Banton's original costume designs, together with a surviving lamé gown worn by Colbert, is illustrated in McConathy and Vreeland (1976: 146–7). See further Bailey (1982: 280–1); Annas et al. (1987a: 48–9); LeVine (1981: 141).
57. Quoted in Birchard (2004: 275).
58. On Egyptomania in the dress of the 1920s and 1930s see Ziegler (1994: 525–40) and Montserrat (2000: 85–7).
59. Blackford (1934).
60. Ford and Mitchell (2009: 83).
61. Wyke (1997: 90).
62. Robinson (1987: 20, 24).
63. Whitney (1934).
64. Donnell (1930).
65. Woolman Chase (1937: 76–7).
66. Eckert (1990).
67. Hillimer (1997: 12) (trans. Llewellyn-Jones).
68. Young (2012: 56).
69. *Ogden Standard Examiner*, 3 November 1934. See also *The Washington Post*, 5 November 1934:

> The most sensational hats in Hollywood this fall will be the adaptations from Cleopatra's headgears of gold, silver and bejeweled metal. Claudette Colbert is already wearing one of black wool, made like a skullcap, with iridescent feathers adorning the front . . . Leading jewellers of the world are turning the calendar back 2000 years for some of the ideas which Cleopatra made popular in her day . . . Details from the new jewelry trend are being borrowed from Cecil B. DeMille's production of *Cleopatra*.

70. See Annas et al. (1987a: 119).
71. Landis (2007: 184).
72. Part of Lamarr's marketability was her dark looks: 'a red-lipped, tawny-eyed, black haired girl' whose 'lush exciting beauty' started a 'brunette trend' among Hollywood actresses and their fans. Both Rita Hayworth and Joan Bennett were given Lamarr makeovers. Lamarr's dark hair was certainly used as part of Delilah's Oriental appeal. See further Berry (2000: 121).
73. Victor Mature's image as Samson was also used in retail marketing: Samson-sized cornflakes, for example, were mass-produced by Kellogg. See Higham (1978: 289).
74. *New York Times*, 26 December 1959.
75. Buckley (2000: 534).
76. Stacey (1993: 41).
77. Higashi (2014: 153).

78. On Deborah Kerr and female fandom see Massey (2000: 157–8).
79. In this respect, Messel's designs were in keeping with those he created for Vivien Leigh's Cleopatra in the 1945 *Caesar and Cleopatra*. Interestingly, British publicity rhetoric shared much in common with that of Hollywood. In a *Picture Post* report dated 15 December 1945, it was noted that:

> Envoys [were] sent to all the museums to check up the right way of putting a band of silk on one of Caesar's togas ... Miss Leigh's black wigs had to be plaited into 80 strands each night so that they were properly crinkled the next day ... 2,000 costumes were made ... they used a hundredweight of dyes ... more than 500 pieces of jewellery were used.

80. Several of the Messel creations are to be found at http://greene.xtn. net/~allant/cleocostumes.html.
81. The relationship between Messel and the American producers was obviously strained from the beginning of the project. See Wanger and Hyams (1963: 48). Wanger writes, 'Oliver Messel, the costume designer, is complaining about his position and authority.'
82. Wanger and Hyams (1963: 73). Wanger recalls:

> 29 April 1961: Irene Sharaff agreed to design Elizabeth's costumes ... I first approached Miss Sharaff, who is one of the top Broadway designers, to do the costumes for *Cleopatra* in 1958. Irene, who is tall, sharp eyed and candid [Tom Mankiewicz, the director's son, later labelled her as 'not very pleasant'], brushed it off with, 'It wouldn't be possible to do *Cleopatra* without making it look like *Aida*.'

The relationship between star designer and Hollywood star appears to have been very good. Wanger and Hyams (1963: 83): '12 June 1961: Brought Liz together with Irene Sharaff for the first time. An important meeting because I want them to like each other. Thank heavens, it came off well.' A report in *Life International*, 23 October 1961 has Sharaff calling Taylor a 'dreamboat'. Sharaff later went on to design Taylor's wedding outfit for her (first) marriage to Richard Burton.

83. An original design for a priestess by Renie Conley is illustrated in Annas et al. (1987b: 18).
84. Wanger and Hyams (1963: 93); Sharaff (1976: 112–13).
85. Sharaff (1976: 106).
86. Wanger and Hyams (1963: 85).
87. Jorgensen and Scoggins (2015: 275).
88. On the depiction of the clothed female body in Egyptian art see Robins (1993: 180–5).
89. Sharaff (1976: 106, 108).
90. Cyrino (2005: 155).
91. Quoted at: http://www.vogue.com/article/life-of-a-legend-vogue-looks-back-at-elizabeth-taylors-iconic-style (accessed 1 April 2017).
92. See Wyke and Montserrat (2011: 172).
93. Quoted in Cawthorne (1996: 114).
94. Steele (1989: 70).
95. Wright (2007: 203).
96. *Photoplay* (April 1962: 30).
97. Wanger and Hyams (1963: 139–40).

98. On the use of makeup in period films see Annas (1987: 63) noting, for example, that '*Spartacus* (1960) was quite simply a film about brown eyeshadow.'

99. The claim is rightly disputed: https://www.google.co.uk/?gfe_rd=cr&ei =bVPNV_3VAbLA8gf5lKLYCw&gws_rd=ssl#q=vest+it+happened+one+ night&*&spf=1 (accessed 4 April 2017).

100. Borden (2010: 24).

101. Plummer (2010: 365).

102. Sharaff (1976: 112).

103. Sharaff (1976: 113).

104. Profiles in History auction catalogue: *Debbie Reynolds: The Auction, June 18, 2011*: 132, 223. A cream wool tunic worn by Robert Taylor in *Quo Vadis* is constructed with a waist seam too; see Profiles in History auction catalogue: *Icons of Hollywood Auction, December 15–16, 2011*: 214. Catalogues are available at: https://profilesinhistory.com/auctions/debbie-reyn-olds-the-auction-part-i/ and http://www.moviepropcollectors.com/ magazine/2011/11/07/debbie-reynolds-the-auction-part-2-catalog-now-at-profiles-in-history (accessed 8 May 2017).

105. Profiles in History auction catalogue: *Debbie Reynolds: The Auction, June 18, 2011*: 156.

106. Profiles in History auction catalogue: *Debbie Reynolds: The Auction, June 18, 2011*: 225.

107. Annas (1987: 58).

108. Quoted in Orrison (1999: 66).

109. The pompadour was a fashion trend in the 1950s, especially among male rockabilly artists and actors. A variation of this was the duck's ass (or in Britain, 'duck's arse'), or simply the DA. This hairstyle was originally developed by Joe Cerello in 1940. Cerello's clients later included film celeb-rities like Elvis Presley and James Dean.

110. Barthes (2009: 15), with French adaptation by the author.

111. Orrison (1999: 62).

112. The helmet recently sold at a Bonham's auction for $9,375: http://www. bonhams.com/auctions/23477/lot/842/?category=list&length=10 (accessed 5 April 2017).

113. Cited in Cohan (1997: 164).

114. Mulvey (1975: 19–20).

115. Waterbury (1955: 62).

116. Babington and Evans (1993: 229, 234, 236).

117. Cohan (1997: 189).

118. Cohan (1997: 190).

119. LeVine (1981: 801).

120. Landis (2012a: 136–7).

121. Kalmus (1935).

122. Noerdlinger (1956: 130).

123. Cohan (1997: 148).

124. Orrison (1999: 66).

CHAPTER 4

MOVIE STARS: CASTING THE EPIC PAST

Cleopatra the queen holds great mystery, as does the Taylor and Burton affair. The fiasco of the film has ended up being an ongoing media sensation.
Amanda Triossi (1962)

A striking photograph of Sophia Loren shows her at a dressing-room mirror (Figure 4.1). She is in costume. She is, in fact, dressed and made-up for her role as Lucilla in *The Fall of the Roman Empire*; her hair, coiffed high on her head, is demurely veiled and ornamented only with a golden hair-pin; her gown is soberly elegant. She looks intently at her reflection and we seem to see her mind at work as the actress prepares for her role. And yet the photograph is, of course, a mirage, for there is no dressing room and there is no mirror. Sophia Loren holds onto a wooden frame surrounded by light bulbs (the semiotic shorthand par excellence for 'dressing room') and we see that it is supported on a trestle stand; it is not a mirror at all and there is no reflection of the actress. We see the 'real' Sophia Loren. Or do we? The photographer is playing with illusion and toys with the hackneyed image of 'an actor prepares' that was seen in so many fan magazines of the period.

The photograph places Loren's exquisitely beautiful face in a frame ('mirror') within a frame (photograph) and therefore her star image, encoded by those electric light bulbs, captures and dominates our gaze.

Figure 4.1
An actress prepares: Sophia Loren in costume as Lucilla in *The Fall of the Roman Empire*.
Studio publicity portrait.

And yet this is not the Sophia Loren that her fans know best; this is
not the smiling, sexy Sophia Loren of the magazine articles or of the
newspaper gossip columns (Figure 4.2). She is already in character, as
though she is just about to go to the set to film a scene (and in the movie
that sombre costume is worn in the scene where Lucilla sits at her
father's deathbed). In *The Fall of the Roman Empire*, Loren's performance
as Lucilla is that of stillness, restraint and intelligence, all of which
are anticipated here in this photographic image.[1] So what exactly are

Figure 4.2
A smiling Sophia. Publicity photograph, c.1963.

we looking at? A studio portrait of Sophia Loren or an off-set glimpse
of Lucilla? Actress and character, it would seem, have morphed and
merged into one. And yet we are aware of both the actress and the
role she plays, and we are cognisant of the artifice of the photograph
itself. This forces us to ask a question: can Sophia Loren ever cease to be
herself? How far can she ever embody the role of Lucilla when we, her
audience, still demand to see, and relish seeing, Sophia Loren? Is it possible for Sophia Loren to lose herself within the character of Lucilla or

must we think that Lucilla can only be filtered through the star-image of Sophia Loren?

From the beginning of film's history, movie actors have performed under what might be called the 'realistic imperative' – moulding their work to the strong illusion of reality which had been created by the film industry itself. We have been observing how in Hollywood epics a sense of 'realism' was achieved through sets, costumes and the endless marketing of the on-screen representation of antiquity as being 'accurate' and therefore 'real'. But as Robert Rosenstone has argued:

> The very use of an actor to 'be' someone will always be a kind of fiction. If the person is 'historical' the realistic film says what cannot truly be said: that this is how this person looked, moved and sounded. If the individual has been created to exemplify a group of historical people [like the Romans] . . . a double fiction is involved: this is how this sort of person (whom we have created) looked, moved and sounded.[2]

And yet, no matter how real movie acting is, or may seem, it depends nonetheless on skilful fakery. Sophia Loren is faking being Lucilla and the audience is complacent in their knowledge that Lucilla is a counterfeit image created by and through Sophia Loren whose stardom outshines any attempt at realism.

'Realism' dates, but stardom does not. In this chapter we will explore the concept of 'the Hollywood movie star' and question just what happens when a star collides with a historical character. What happens when a movie star performs a role in a film which, allegedly, represents the reality of the past? Movie stars have always held an intoxicating sway over their audiences – often representing far more than the roles they play. The casting of movie stars in epic films – like Rita Hayworth as Salome, Kirk Douglas as Spartacus and Victor Mature as Samson – helped shape the values and the contemporary consciousness, wishes and anxieties of the public who spent money at the box office to see them 'act out' the past. As George Custon notes:

> What is operating in biographical [epic] films is the star system speaking of itself through its own contained, controlled means, animating its own values through the figures of a parallel world of stars. Here we have a world where we see History as the Film Industry, great men and women as the star system.[3]

The glamour which was provided by the casting of Hollywood movie stars like Sophia Loren as Lucilla had to be outweighed against the inherent difficulties of casting movie stars in historical roles. It is impossible to think of the historical Cleopatra without visualising Elizabeth Taylor; she outlives history just as Charlton Heston outlives Moses and Kirk Douglas outlives Spartacus. Peter Ustinov will perpetually be seen

Figure 4.3
The 'polysemic star image': John Gavin as the young Julius Caesar poses with a bust of the
man he plays (although it is actually a portrait of the young Augustus). *Spartacus* (1960).
Studio publicity portrait. Pressbook.

in the guise of Nero, just as Nero will always be envisaged as Peter
Ustinov. Thus, as Sobchack persuasively puts it: 'While not embodying historical figures in any way that could be called "accurate" by
a historian's standards . . . the very presence of stars in the historical
epic mimetically represents not real historical figures but rather the
real significance of historical figures. Stars literally lend magnitude to
the representation [Figure 4.3].'[4] Richard Dyer perceptively refers to a
phenomenon he calls the 'polysemic star image' – the notion that the
movie-goer is drawn to resonant aspects of the impersonator (the star)

as well as the life interpreted (the character).[5] In this light, perhaps one admires Cleopatra VII of Egypt for her intelligence and statecraft but also because she is Elizabeth Taylor, the first actress to negotiate a million-dollar fee.

The use of an actor to 'be' any character, but especially a historical figure, will always be a kind of fiction – a film attempts to say what cannot ever truly be said: that this is how this person looked, moved and sounded. However, when famous movie stars appear in historical roles, they still tend to be more themselves than the historical individuals they present. There is, therefore, a risk of confusing historic figures with movie stars and although films might be promoted on this conceit, the result is rarely successful. The presence of the star pulls against the rhetoric of experiencing the 'reality' of the historical past, leading Pierre Sorlin to state that the potential to confuse historic figures with modem actors means that 'the star-system is the sore spot of filmed history.'[6] Perhaps Michael Wood summarises the issue of movie stars as historical figures most clearly when he states that 'here are familiar faces and figures rigged up again and again in strange costumes, as if to attend a revolving fancy dress ball ... It does reinforce the reflective, self-regarding quality in these films, the sense of the studio barely hidden in Egypt or Rome.'[7]

What Is a Movie Star?

There is a scene early on in George Cukor's 1954 movie *A Star Is Born* in which James Mason as Norman Maine walks into a nightclub, empty of patrons, and comes across the resident band of musicians rehearsing a number. Among them is Judy Garland (in her iconic role as Esther Blodgett/Vicki Lester – Figure 4.4) who tentatively and softly coos the opening bars of *The Man Who Got Away* to the strains of a solo piano; the on-screen orchestra joins in and is trebled in sound by an off-screen orchestra too, as Garland's performance of the song develops, swells and ultimately captivates. In this supposed rehearsal setting, Vicki Lester shows us that she is already a movie star of singular quality. Of course the audience already knows this – because that is what any screen appearance by Judy Garland guaranteed. For twenty-five years Garland had been charming audiences with her singular brand of star quality, singing and dancing her way into the hearts of millions of fans. What gave Garland her appeal? Hard work, undoubtedly; innate talent, certainly. But there was something else, something which Norman Maine/ James Mason attempts to put into words. Stumbling for the right turn of phrase, he declares simply that 'She's got that little extra *something* ...' (see Text Box 4.1).[8]

All movie stars (to varying degrees) have that *something* (Figure 4.5). Film historian Jeanine Basinger has spent a career analysing Hollywood films and thinking about the question of film stardom, and ultimately has recognised one key fact:

Figure 4.4
Icon of stardom with that certain *something*: Judy Garland as Esther Blodgett/Vicki Lester in
A Star is Born (1954). Studio publicity portrait.

The truth is nobody – either then or now – can define what a movie star
is . . . [But] it's clear that over the years, Hollywood collected a sensible
list of observations: A star has exceptional looks. Outstanding talent.
A distinctive voice that can be easily recognised and imitated. A set of
mannerisms. Palpable sexual appeal. Energy that comes down off the
screen. Glamour. Androgyny. Glowing health and radiance. Panache
. . . Charm. The good luck to be in the right place at the right time . . .
And of course *Something*.[9]

Text Box 4.1   Why Can't I Be a Movie Star?

It is difficult to see how a substantial segment of the American population can avoid hoping, however feebly, to be among the blessed whom the magic hand of Hollywood plucks from obscurity. Let us take an imaginary Fanny Jones in any town in the United States. Her talents may be dismal, her features ordinary, her intelligence uninspired. Yet how plausible is it for her to muse, 'It might happen to me.' And why not? Is Fanny Jones freckled? She knows how easily make-up experts hide the freckles of Joan Crawford or Myrna Loy. Is Fanny Jones astigmatic? She knows Norma Shearer has a squint. Does Fanny Jones lisp? She has read all about how words beginning with 'r' are cut out of Kay Francis' scripts. Is Fanny Jones short? They can photograph her on a box. Is she fat? They'll put her on a diet. Is she thin? They'll fatten her up. Can Fanny Jones act? Well, can Hedy Lamarr? They'll teach her. What fatal blemishes can the Fanny Joneses (or the John Joneses) actually admit that they'll bar them from the new Valhalla? They know that wizards will coat them, dress them, raise their eyebrows, straighten their teeth, lift their bust lines, lower their coiffures. Brilliant directors, writers, producers will dedicate themselves solely to the exploitation of their hidden talents.

The point is that these things do happen.

Leo C. Rosten, *Hollywood: The Movie Colony, the Movie Makers* (1940)

The studios were always on the lookout for hopefuls (Figure 4.6) who promised to deliver that extra *something* on-screen and the movie moguls of the Golden Age knew that their greatest assets were their stars. Movie stars had always had a central place in American film-making and for the studios they promised consistency and repetition, countering the uncertainties and shifting fortunes of filmmaking; they also brought with them legions of loyal fans who packed the movie theatres in order to see their latest performances and – as importantly – their latest looks (Figure 4.7). Over time the studios developed a system for creating and controlling star personas that would guarantee that movie-goers' attention was focused on the stars even between pictures. Publicity magazines, public appearances and news columns kept the star-image alive and vital. And yet the 'star system', as it has become known, was nothing short of a slave system – albeit a glamorous, highly paid one in which the slaves were better-known than their masters. As the actress Ann Rutherford recalled, 'We really were like slaves. You were chattels of the studios. They could buy and sell you.'[10] The actor Clive Brook described Hollywood as 'a chain gang [where] we lose the will to escape; the links of our chain are forged not of cruelties but of luxuries; we are pelted with orchids and roses; we are overpaid and underworked.'[11]

Figure 4.5
The saleability of stardom on the cover of *Life* magazine: John Wayne, Burton and Taylor, Rock Hudson, Katharine Hepburn, Sophia Loren, Ingrid Bergman, Ginger Rogers and Fred Astaire, Clark Gable, Judy Garland.

"DARLING, YOU'RE GOING PLACES!"
CRIES COLUMNIST HEDDA HOPPER

Figure 4.6
'Darling you're going places': gossip columnist knew how to make and break movie stars.
Magazine advertisement, c.1953.

During the Golden Age stars were associated with particular studio styles since actors were, after all, long-term employees. They were often under contract to a single studio for many years (usually seven years at a time) and worked forty weeks a year with twelve weeks unpaid vacation; they had little to no say in the roles they were assigned. Even personal names could be changed to those which the studios (often rightly) found more marketable: Cary Grant had been born Archie Leach; Joan Crawford was originally Lucille Fay Le Sueur; Rock Hudson was originally known as Roy Harold Scherer Jr and, infamously, John Wayne had been christened Marion Robert Morrison. Around these new

Figure 4.7
'More stars than there are in heaven': between the 1930s and 1950s MGM billed itself as
the studio which had the largest number of A-list movie stars under contract. The publicity
shot taken in 1949 includes such luminaries as Robert Taylor, Frank Sinatra, Katharine
Hepburn, Jennifer Jones, Ava Gardner, Judy Garland and Lassie.

names were woven on-screen and off-screen personas. Reporting on
stars' personal lives in fan magazines, newspaper articles and gossip
columns often allowed for multiple and contradictory interpretations
of their star personas. Photographs of long-time roommates and bosom
buddies Cary Grant and Randolph Scott, for instance, portrayed the
active, sporting lifestyle of two silver screen heartthrobs, but the images
of them cavorting poolside could also be interpreted in more decidedly
homoerotic ways (Figure 4.8).

In official press releases, the studios liked to encourage the belief
that movie stars were products of audience enthusiasm: 'I don't discover stars ... It's the public who ... makes them', Louis B. Mayer
once declared to gossip columnist Louella Parsons, although in a more
candid (private) conversation, his opinion was quite different:

> The idea of a star being born is bushwah! A star is created, carefully
> and cold-bloodedly, built up from nothing, from nobody ... Age,
> beauty, talent – least of all talent – has nothing to do with it ... We
> could make silk purses out of sows' ears every day of the week.[12]

The creation of star 'personas' – a form of typecasting – was central to the
Hollywood star system. Typecasting has often been seen to reflect a lack

Figure 4.8
Are they or aren't they? At home with Cary Grant and Randolph Scott. Studio publicity
photograph, c.1939.

of talent. Stage actors – those of the 'legitimate theatre' – often looked
down at the capabilities of their film colleagues. Sir Cedric Hardwicke,
for example, once stated that 'God felt sorry for Hollywood actors, so
he gave them a place in the sun and a swimming pool; all they had to
sacrifice was their talent.'[13]

Yet reading the concept of typecasting as a negative – 'Victor Mature
can't act, so he always played the same guy, and that's because that's the
only guy he *could* play' – undermines the central concept of star system,
since the studios saw things very differently. They knew that Victor

Mature, for instance, always played the same guy because that was the guy the public *wanted* him to play – and that guy *was* the performance. Indeed, Victor Mature was so good at playing 'that guy' that the public believed the image off-screen and on-screen. The *New York Times* raved about Mature's performance as Samson as 'a dashing and dauntless hunk of man whose hair is handsomely tonsured and whose face is as smooth as a baby's cheek' and it was this physical presence of the actor which led *Time Magazine* to confirm that Mature was 'the only actor in the world who could make Samson's strong-man exploits so believable.' But the Mature screen-persona belied a less than impressive reality, as Henry Wilcoxon recalled:

> Mature's niche was as the urban Film Noir protagonist. He wasn't known as an athlete. He wasn't known as the world's greatest actor [either]. So perhaps it was inevitable that DeMille and Mature would cross swords regularly. By that I mean between four and five times a day ... As the days progressed, DeMille slid into his 'disgust' mode and wanted less and less to do with his Samson ... Everyone motored out to the desert location with two Samsons: Victor Mature and [stunt-double Kay Bell]. The crew set up: lights ... camera ... and one ancient lion. He was so old his mane was falling out ... The point was lost on Mature, however; he flatly refused to get out of the studio limousine. No amount of coaxing, pleading or threats would get him to budge ... DeMille broadly hinted at the importance of the Samson-slays-lion scene. 'I never used stuffed animals in my pictures if it can be helped ... And I'll tell you why: they always look stuffed.' The fun-loving actor grinned. 'Look, C.B., there's only one Mature and I would hate to see him go this way.' [DeMille replied] 'I'm not going to press the matter, but I can assure you it will be perfectly safe. This lion was trained as a cub and fed on milk.' When DeMille departed, Mature mused to a friend, "I was raised on milk too, but I eat meat now!' As a last-ditch measure, DeMille discussed the problem with Hedy Lamarr, who volunteered to parade the aging beast past Mature's dressing room door. This she did ... Mature poked his head out of the dressing room and applauded. 'You're so beautiful, Hedy, I can see how any lion would follow you around.' He felt the attitude of the lion would change dramatically towards a male, particularly one attempting to apply an unfriendly headlock.[14]

Phil Koury recalled the outcome: 'What Mature finally took on in combat was an expertly stuffed specimen. DeMille was morbidly uncomfortable. He closed the set to all except a skeleton crew ... Once, when a workman let out an amused chuckle, DeMille raged, "If I hear another laugh, I'll clear the goddamn set!"'[15]

Candid reports of the 1940s and 1950s indicate that Victor Mature was the victim of numerous phobias and that his genial, charming personality was far too weak for DeMille's severe and stoical taste. When

Mature appeared in the Battle of the Jawbone in which Samson fights the Philistines, a great wind swept through the studio and he suddenly took fright at a particularly violent, machine-made gust and fled, hiding in terror in his dressing room. DeMille had him brought back like a naughty schoolboy who had run away from school. He picked up his megaphone and in a voice icy with disgust shouted in full hearing of the cast and crew:

> I have met a few men in my time. Some have been afraid of heights, some have been afraid of water, some have been afraid of fire, some have been afraid of closed spaces. Some have been afraid of open spaces – or themselves. But in my thirty-five years of picture-making experience, Mr Mature, I have not until now met a man who was 100 per cent yellow![16]

Although he guarded his he-man image closely and kept these tales of cowardice well-hidden, Mature was not interested in acting as a craft and was content to deliver the standard performance in film after film. Working next to Richard Burton and Jean Simmons in *The Robe* (Figure 4.9) meant, Mature recalled, 'having to give up golf'. But considering that his acting might pale into oblivion when next to British acting royalty, Mature was quick to realise that 'it meant knuckling down to business. I was up against excellent actors . . . to make [Demetrius] convincing I had to bring everything I had to the part.'[17] Ironically, Burton was unhappy about his performance in *The Robe*, describing it as 'poor' (he hated too the way he looked in the film, complaining about his appearance in tunics and armour), although he enjoyed the experience of working alongside fellow he-man Mature. Burton described one scene where overcome with religious zeal he 'screamed like a girl' while Mature simply stood still, staring heavenward with great conviction. When Burton questioned him about his technique, Victor Mature replied, 'I'm thinking of the money they're paying me.'[18]

Because of the tainted image of the Hollywood actor's talent, some actors suffered from severe self-doubt. When Robert Taylor was cast in *Quo Vadis* as Marcus Vinicius (Figure 4.10) he was forty years old and a heavy chain-smoker – hardly a match for the virile character he would play. He still had the good looks though that had propelled him to stardom in 1936 when he was cast as the romantic lead opposite Greta Garbo in *Camille* (dir. Cukor) and where he was marketed as 'The Man with the Perfect Profile' (Figure 4.11) and his role in *Quo Vadis* was meant to revive Taylor's flagging career – although Taylor had not been the first choice for the role of Vinicius, which had been written for the English actor Stewart Granger. When he refused to sign a long-term contract with MGM, Taylor was tested for the part and was given the role. Years later, Robert Taylor told Granger, 'Do you know what they did when they put me in *Quo Vadis*? They showed me your test and told me to play the part just like you!' Granger laughed and replied, 'If I was so

Figure 4.9
Richard Burton and Jean Simmons in *The Robe*. Studio publicity portrait used on a British magazine, 1953.

great, why didn't they use me? They chose you because you are a bloody fine actor. Just look at those [studio] arseholes . . . stunted, pot-bellied and bald . . . They were just jealous.' Like many of his contemporaries, Granger thought very highly of Taylor, recalling that:

> He was such a nice guy, but he had even more hang-ups than me . . . Bob Taylor was the easiest person to work with but had been entirely emasculated by the MGM brass who insisted that he was only a pretty

Figure 4.10
The all-American male in Roman fancy-dress: Robert Taylor. *Quo Vadis*. Studio publicity
portrait used on the cover of a British film magazine, 1951.

face. He was convinced that he wasn't a good actor and his calm
acceptance of this stigma infuriated me . . . [I often told him], 'Your
problem is that you are too bloody good-looking and it's fashionable
to say that good-looking guys can't act.'[19]

His *Quo Vadis* co-star, Deborah Kerr, agreed: 'Bob was good-natured
and un-fussy . . . I felt that he was a much better actor than he was given
credit for.'[20] Yet in spite of this kind of praise it has to be conceded that

Figure 4.11
The creation of Robert Taylor's star image operated around his clean-cut American wholesomeness. Studio publicity portrait, c.1936.

Robert Taylor's ability to play the Roman aristocrat was limited and that his performance suggested the American campus rather than Rome in its glory; his classical good looks did help overcome this disadvantage though.

While some movie stars were actors of limited talent (as Victor Mature was the first to admit, stating 'I'm no actor, and I have sixty-four pictures to prove it'), this did not affect their popularity or their box-office appeal (see Text Box 4.2). Talent is not needed for an actor to be star but having a charisma which fascinates and spellbinds is absolutely essential for stardom to flourish. Elizabeth Taylor, for instance, had the ability to

Text Box 4.2   The Critics' Choice?

Extracts from Bosley Crowther's reviews for the
New York Times

Because movie critics worked independent of the Hollywood studios, they often cut through the hyperbole and blarney of production rhetoric and of the fan magazines with sharp and short analyses of the finished movies. In an era when television was growing up and movies were still the major cultural force in American life, film critics were among the most influential voices in the country on the art and industry of motion pictures. Bosley Crowther, the film critic of the *New York Times* from 1940 to 1967, during the heyday of the epic, wrote as many as 200 film reviews and fifty longer Sunday articles each year. What appealed to him most were movies of social content – *Citizen Kane*, *The Grapes of Wrath* and *Gone with the Wind*, for example – but he also defended the epic genre when he saw good filmmaking at work: *The Ten Commandments*, *Ben-Hur* and *Cleopatra* all profited from his championship. But he could be ruthless in his criticism of bad direction, poor acting, and worthless plots and in that respect, epic films often found their way into his newspaper columns. Here are some examples of reviews good and bad.

Alexander the Great

Only a few performances are memorable in this multitudinous cast. Mr Rossen's choice of Fredric March and Richard Burton for the roles of Philip and Alexander, respectively, has paid handsome dividends.

Mr March is a tough, bearded, designing warrior consumed by lusts, preoccupied by wars and harried by suspicions. And he is hindered by jealousy of his son and hatred of his estranged wife, who, he feels, is pitting his brilliant son against him. Mr. March gives him natural attributes and imperfections.

As Alexander, Richard Burton contributes a serious and impassioned portrayal of a man inspired by but still repelled by his father. He is swayed but not ruled by his mother's will. He emerges, above all, as a dedicated chieftain who lends dimension to history. He does not seem out of place as a great military leader or as an ordinary man.

Claire Bloom's portrait of Alexander's beautiful mistress is marked by moments of fire and passion. As his sad and vengeful mother, Danielle Darrieux is effective in only a few brief scenes.

Barabbas

Now the man Barabbas, as played by Anthony Quinn, is but a great brute of a fellow who falls into and endures a succession of melodramatic adventures that are the raptures of a spectacle-maker's dreams. When he is captured in a fight with Roman soldiers (this is after he has seen Christ crucified, the evidence of the Resurrection and a girl stoned to death for worshiping

Him), he is put in the mine, where the labour is long and torturing. Barabbas endures this ordeal with spectacular agony.

Then, after the mine has exploded and he has dragged himself and a companion out with bursting strain, he goes through another strenuous period as a draft horse hitched to a plow. Finally, enrolled as a gladiator, he goes through the whole routine of training and fighting in the arena with a cast of thousands participating or looking on.

Mr Quinn is a sensational sufferer. He grunts and sweats and strains with more credible vengeance and exertion than any actor we can name.

Ben-Hur (1959)
For the performance of his characters, Mr Wyler has a cast that impressively delivers the qualities essential to their roles. Charlton Heston is excellent as Ben-Hur – strong, aggressive, proud and warm – and Stephen Boyd plays his nemesis, Messala, with those same qualities, inverted ideologically.

Jack Hawkins as the Roman admiral who fatefully makes Ben-Hur his foster son, Haya Harareet as the Jewish maiden who tenderly falls in love with him, Hugh Griffith as the sheik who puts him into the chariot race and Sam Jaffe as his loyal agent – these also stand out in a very large cast.

Cleopatra (1934)
Claudette Colbert, the Poppaea of *The Sign of the Cross*, is entrusted with the part of Cleopatra. She wears a dark wig and looks even more attractive than usual. She speaks her lines with the necessary confidence, whether they are concerned with love, hate or politics. When it is a matter of disposing of Pothinos with a javelin, she conducts herself with the coolness of a queen of the olden days. And when the chance is offered for a little comedy she acquits herself cleverly.

Julius Caesar is portrayed by Warren William, who shines in his role. There are moments when the dialogue is reminiscent of the Shakespearean speech and other occasions when it is so modern that one almost expects Mighty Caesar to have a typewriter and telephone at his elbow, as when he, while in Egypt, dictates a letter to the Roman Senators. Mr William is especially apt when it comes to delivering a brief line, such as 'Take it away,' when he wishes the body of the treacherous Pothinos removed from his sight.

Marc Antony . . . is interpreted by the English actor, Henry Wilcoxon, a fine figure of a man. His acting is excellent, especially in the more dramatic sequences.

David and Bathsheba
In Gregory Peck's delineation the producers have an authoritative performance. He is a man filled with anguish at the death of Jonathan and of Saul. He is a King willing to forego his regal rights for his love and he is the frail

vessel who movingly confesses his sins but one who also is strong enough to exclaim, 'Lift Thine hand from Thy people who suffer for my crimes.'

Unfortunately, however, the rest of the cast is entirely overshadowed by this role. Bathsheba, as portrayed by Susan Hayward, is a Titian-tressed charmer who seems closer to Hollywood than to the arid Jerusalem of the Bible. Raymond Massey, as the bearded Prophet Nathan, is little more than a voice of doom in the wilderness. Kieron Moore, as Uriah, Jayne Meadows, as the vengeful Michal, and James Robertson Justice, as David's aide, Abishai, merely make casual, brief appearances.

Demetrius and the Gladiators
They have got our old friend, Demetrius, still played by Victor Mature, as a prisoner of the Romans and a conscript at the gladiator school. This place, which has a strong resemblance to the training camp of the Chicago Bears, is presided over (of all people!) by the fellow who played Fatso in *From Here to Eternity*. And it isn't long before Demetrius is not only taking brutality but also finding pious reasons to dish it out, handsomely.

Likewise, his sacrosanct resistance to Susan Hayward, who plays the wife of Barry Jones' toddling Claudius, crumbles eventually before the snorting passion of Miss Hayward and a few strokes of circumstance. And it isn't until Michael Rennie, as Peter, comes around like a stern bill collector and taps him that he gets back upon the straight-and-narrow.

Meanwhile, Mr Ross, Mr Dunne and Director Delmer Davies have dropped in a vast lot of slamming and banging of gladiators, dancing by gauzy handmaidens, rolling around on the floor by assorted female entertainers and general raising of hob. Every so often, Jay Robinson, who didn't quite split his lungs playing the role of Caligula, the mad emperor in *The Robe*, makes a heroic effort to complete the job in the same role. If we never again see Mr Robinson, we'll be neither sorry nor surprised.

Esther and the King
Richard Egan, who looks about as Persian as an offensive back on the Baltimore Colts, is a sluggish, horse-operatic pretence ... The English-speaking acting of an Italo-American cast, under Mr Walsh's direction, is almost funny, it's so downright bad.

Helen of Troy
As Helen, Rossana Podesta is a bit of a dazzler, it is true, but her sense of emotional disturbance and her facial expressions are those of a chorus girl. Likewise, youthful Jack Sernas makes Paris a lively, handsome boy, but, again, his emotional projection is just a shade above nil. Sir Cedric Hardwicke as King Priam, Torin Thatcher as Ulysses, Niall MacGinnis as Menelaus, Stanley Baker as Achilles and many more make broad sweeps and eloquent gestures. But they are strictly two-dimensional – like the film.

Quo Vadis

To the credit of John Lee Mahin, S. N. Behrman and Sonya Levien, who wrote the script from the 1895 best-seller of Henryk Sienkiewicz, an apparent attempt to give the drama some literary quality was made, and at times the dialogue shows traces of pseudo-Shavian wit. Most competent in handling this dialogue is the Englishman, Leo Genn, who has the prize role of Petronius, the emperor's cynical goad. And because he is passably convincing, his fragile romance with a slave, played by Marina Berti, is the most touching thing in the film.

But the time that is given to Nero, whom Peter Ustinov plays in a manner to elevate Charles Laughton as a master of restraint in the role, which he portrayed in the DeMille picture, quickly runs into seeming hours. Mr Ustinov's mouthing and screaming, if halved, might be durable. As it is, they become the most monotonous and vexing things in the film. And this includes the solemn posturing of Robert Taylor as the soldier who falls in love with the beautiful Christian hostage, played by Deborah Kerr.

Unfortunately, the tracing of this romance through the fleshpots and the prison cells of Rome is done in a way that seems intended to spell it out for the most slow-witted minds. And Mr Taylor and Miss Kerr, in their performance, appear anything but inspired. 'Oh, Marcus,' cries the lady to the soldier, whom she has been resisting, when he starts to leave her life, 'you know I don't hate you!' And they come together for a rigidly dignified embrace.

Also the whole presentation of the impulse of Christianity is made in terms that are not only literal but frequently trite. The apostles Paul and Peter, whom Abraham Sofaer and Finlay Currie play, are comparatively dignified persons, and the sermon the latter gives to a secret gathering of Christians is well delivered, for all its trace of Scottish burr.

Solomon and Sheba

As the Queen of Sheba, Gina Lollobrigida, the original Italian over-stuffed star, has the physical equipment to suggest a Little Egypt type of charmer, but her way with a love-laden line or with a spontaneous show of emotion leaves something (other than the obvious) to be desired. And as Solomon, the Israelite ruler, Yul Brynner is as specious as that hair they have pasted (or he has grown) on his nude noggin. Neither it nor he suits the character.

George Sanders plays the heavy, the treacherous brother of the king, with standard expression and gestures; Marisa Pavan is a lovelorn Israelite girl and John Crawford, Laurence Naismith and several others strut and sweat under heavy robes.

Salome

In her dance performance, Miss Hayworth does give a lively show – more lively, at least, than the posturing that she does in the earlier parts of the film.

And the pop-eyed entrancement of Charles Laughton as Herod in watching her is a pretty fair indication of what her fans are expected to do. Like Miss Hayworth's, Mr Laughton's performance is not impressive in earlier phases of the film. Where he used to belch when he was sated, now he merely yawns. As for Stewart Granger as the Roman captain, Judith Anderson as Queen Herodias, Alan Badel as John the Baptist, Basil Sydney as Pontius Pilate and many more, they are simply supporting adornments for Miss Hayworth's expensive Salome.

Samson and Delilah
To play this romantic fiction Mr DeMille has used two people endowed with modern glamour much more than with Biblical style. Victor Mature as Samson is a dashing and dauntless hunk of man whose hair is handsomely tonsured and whose face is as smooth as a baby's cheek. And Hedy Lamarr as Delilah is a sleek and bejewelled siren whose charms have a strictly occidental and twentieth-century grace and clarity. As the woman of Timnath, Angela Lansbury is a plump and pouting doll, and George Sanders is stiff and haughty as Gaza's empirical Saran. Henry Wilcoxon, Olive Dearing and William Farnum are firm in lesser roles, and hundreds of other people swarm about in costumes.

Spartacus
Apparently, too many people, too many cooks had their ladles in this stew, and it comes out a romantic mish-mash of a strange episode in history. The performances are equally uneven. Mr Douglas sets his blunt, horse-opera style against the toga-clad precision of Mr Laughton and the Roman-nosed gentility of Mr Olivier. Tony Curtis as a former slave-boy minstrel contrasts in theatricality with the easy, accomplished clowning of a Romanised Mr Ustinov. Miss Simmons makes a very attractive slave-girl – from Britannia, she explains, which somewhat accounts for her polish and her accent, obviously. And John Ireland, John Gavin, John Dall, Nina Foch and Woody Strode make assorted American-looking gladiators, Roman senators, fancy ladies and such.

The Fall of the Roman Empire
Christopher Plummer plays Commodus for the reckless libertine he actually was, but he does it with howling histrionics rather than with subtle intimations of a mind diseased. And Stephen Boyd plays the soldier so bluntly and lumpishly that one senses no more than a sweating actor dressed up in an uncomfortable costume ... Meanwhile, Alec Guinness is pompous and full of hot air as the aging Marcus Aurelius, who is done away with in the first half; Sophia Loren is ornamental, without intelligence or sex, as Commodus's beautiful sister who, for some strange reason, loves the general; John Ireland looks like an unkempt Beatle as the leader of the northern tribes,

and Anthony Quayle gives a fair imitation of a punchy fighter as an aging gladiator. James Mason is completely baffling in a thoroughly enigmatic role that requires him to give a virtual oration on loyalty while his hand is being burned. Mel Ferrer is another enigma as a blind political spy.

The Greatest Story Ever Told

By staging the story of Jesus against the vast topography of the American Southwest and mingling the mystical countenance of Max von Sydow, the Swedish actor, with a sea of familiar faces of Hollywood stars, the producer-director George Stevens has made what surely is the world's most conglomerate Biblical picture in *The Greatest Story Ever Told* . . . Most shattering and distasteful of these intrusions are the appearances of Carroll Baker and John Wayne in the deeply solemn and generally fitting enactment of the scene of Jesus carrying the cross to Calvary. Suddenly, at a most affecting moment, the plump-cheeked Miss Baker appears as a woman of the streets (Veronica) to wipe the sweat from Jesus' face. And right at a point of piercing anguish, up pops the brawny Mr Wayne in the costume of a Roman centurion. Inevitably, viewers whisper, 'That's John Wayne!'

This sort of conscious intermingling of theatrical personalities with sincere dramatic intentions and occasional stunning effects is the ultimate evidence of distortion in Mr Stevens's clearly calculated way of handling his familiar material hyperbolically . . .

Fortunately, the political figures are played exceptionally well. Telly Savalas makes a hard-boiled Pontius Pilate, the most realistic character in the film. José Ferrer is excellent as Herod, materialistic and sinuous. Charlton Heston's John the Baptist is a bit too much of a muscular, Tarzan type. David McCallum's Judas Iscariot oozes a chilling treachery, but it is not made clear precisely why he does his fateful deed.

Many others – too many to mention – play their roles variously. Sidney Poitier's Simon of Cyrene, the African Jew who helps carry the cross, is the only Negro conspicuous in the picture and seems a last-minute symbolisation of racial brotherhood.

The Prodigal

What can be said about the actors in this sort of artificial frame? Mr Purdom performs with infinite patience and with his tongue in his cheek. That's fair. And Miss Turner plays with the dignity and the sense of high destiny you might expect of a heroine walking the last mile down the runway of Minsky's burlesque. She completes her priestly devotions by taking a high dive into a pool of fire, which gives you a pretty good idea of the lurid nature of this film.

Mr Calhern, in beaded robes and peaked hats, has the appearance and the manner of a grandee in the Ku Klux Klan, and Francis L. Sullivan sweats and grimaces as what we gather is his conniving friend. Walter Hampden as the bearded father of the hero, James Mitchell as his mute but agile pal and Audrey Dalton as the beautiful fiancé he tosses over for Samarra also serve. Joseph Wiseman as a straight Damascan con man puts it right on the plane of carnival.

The Robe

Richard Burton, the young English actor . . . is stalwart, spirited and stern as the arrogant Roman tribune who has command of the crucifixion of Christ and who eventually becomes a passionate convert through an obsession about the Saviour's robe. Jean Simmons is lovely and impassioned as the Roman maid who loves this headstrong man, Victor Mature is muscular and moody as the early converted Greek slave. Michael Rennie is solemn and transcendent as Simon Called Peter, whom they call 'the big fisherman'; Dean Jagger is full of piety as a humble convert and Jay Robinson is warped and shrill as Caligula. Several other actors comport themselves in minor roles according to the moods of the occasions that Director Henry Koster has decreed.

The Ten Commandments

Moses, as played by Charlton Heston, is a handsome and haughty young prince who warrants considerable attention as a heroic man of the ancient world. And Anne Baxter as the sensual princess and Yul Brynner as the rival, Ramses, are unquestionably apt and complementary to a lusty and melodramatic romance . . . The large cast of characters is very good, from Sir Cedric Hardwicke as a droll and urbane Pharaoh to Edward G. Robinson as a treacherous overlord. Yvonne DeCarlo as the Midianite shepherdess to whom Moses is wed is notably good in a severe role, as is John Derek as a reckless Joshua.

raise the stakes of her acting when she was given appropriately high-level cultural material to work with, most notably Edward Albee's *Who's Afraid of Virginia Woolf?* (dir. Nichols, 1966) or Tennessee Williams' *Cat On a Hot Tin Roof* (dir. Brooks, 1958) and *Suddenly Last Summer* (dir. Mankiewicz, 1959 – see Figure 4.12).[21] It is less often noted that her witty, capricious performance as Cleopatra provided an intelligent spark to a movie that is often lacking in coherency, as Bosley Crowther recognised in the *New York Times*:

Elizabeth Taylor's Cleopatra is a woman of force and dignity, fired by a fierce ambition to conquer and rule the world – at least, the world of the Mediterranean basin – through the union of Egypt and Rome. In her is impressively compacted the arrogance and pride of an ancient queen . . . She is likewise clever and passionate, able to lure Caesar to her bed with chic and voluptuous seductions and with the promise of

Figure 4.12
Iconic Taylor: *Suddenly Last Summer*. Studio publicity photograph, 1959.

a son. Yet she is powerless to avoid a howling tantrum when she is deserted temporarily by Antony.[22]

And yet Elizabeth Taylor was not a *reliably* good actress. She was, for instance, 'easily outclassed by elephants in *Elephant Walk*' (dir. Dieterle, 1955)[23] and in *A Little Night Music* (dir. Prince, 1977) she hit the nadir of her career, easily trumped by the classy and thoughtful co-star Diana Rigg. In any case, whether good or bad, it is not for acting that a star is a star, a point recalled by Irene Sharaff recounting the making of *Cleopatra*: 'When Elizabeth came on, everybody around the set – the stagehands, the cameramen, the wardrobe people – were absolutely hypnotised, and you felt it. The moment that camera started to buzz something happened between Elizabeth and that mechanical thing. Cukor said it once . . . It's the camera that chooses the star' (Figure 4.13).[24]

In his fascinating collection of movie reviews written in New York in the 1980s, Quentin Crisp often turned his attention to Classic Hollywood and on more than one occasion he discussed the notion of stardom and its relationship to acting ability:

> People – or rather critics – say that [stars] are discouraged from acting . . . That is true. A star acts only to the very slightest degree. She may wear her hair in a plait round her head to suggest she is a peasant or in a bun to tell us she is a schoolmistress, but nothing can ever be done to cheat the audience out of instant recognition . . . Her art is therefore not one of concealment, but of revelation. As the late Mr Cagney said, 'Technique consists of allowing nothing to come between you and your audience.'[25]

Perhaps, therefore, the question 'Can movie stars act?' should be replaced by another: 'Are movie stars believable on screen?' After all, as the director John Cromwell (who worked with some of America's most illustrious stars) has noted: 'All of [Hollywood's stars] could act, some, of course, better than others. But the point is, the audience believed in them. That's what movies call acting.'[26] Audiences responded to actors and actresses as 'types' (tough guy, all-American girl, exotic sex-symbol, boy next door) which they believed in and everything they knew about star 'types' they learned through accumulation, by going to movie after movie. Once stars were constructed as a 'type' the Hollywood factory manufactured products around them. As Ty Burr makes clear:

> A distinction can and should be made between stars and actors. All stars are actors one way or another; not all actors are stars. Great actors – the true craftsmen and women – transform themselves in role after role, and if the projects are successful and the actor is celebrated enough, that changeability becomes his or her persona, whether it's Lon Chaney in the silent era, Alec Guinness after World War II, Meryl Streep in the 1980s, or Cate Blanchett today. Stars, by contrast, don't hide themselves. On the contrary, the great movie stars each construct an image which is bigger than their individual films.[27]

When, therefore, DeMille cast Victor Mature as Samson, the first of his epic roles, he was aware of the potential success of the star's 'biblical' persona because he so embodied the American male ego-ideal he had brought to the screen in 1940s musicals, film noirs and Westerns simply by being 'Victor Mature'. His sheer physical bulk was his selling point, and by the 1950s his CinemaScope-proportioned fleshy frame made him the 'must have' star of the reinvigorated epic genre. In Mature's biblical epics, the actor gives his audience the 'Victor Mature performance' and,

Shown here are six numbered stills of Elizabeth Taylor as she appears as "Cleopatra" in the 20th Century-Fox Colour Epic, at the .... Cinema on ....

Here is your chance to win one of the fabulous prizes offered by this newspaper. All you have to do is to decide, from the list printed below, which description is most aptly applied to each of the photographs. For instance, if you feel that the description "Regal" most aptly fits photo number 4, place a figure 4 against the word "Regal" on the list. Carry on until you have selected what you think are the most apt descriptions for each of the six photographs.

Description						*Photo Number*
TENDER	...	...	...	...	...	....
PROUD	...	...	...	...	...	....
PASSIONATE	...	...	...	...	...	....
REGAL	...	...	...	...	...	....
LOVING	...	...	...	...	...	....
HAUGHTY	...	...	...	...	...	....
PLAYFUL	...	...	...	...	...	....
PENSIVE	...	...	...	...	...	....
SOPHISTICATED	...	...	...	...	...	....
GIRLISH	...	...	...	...	...	....

Figure 4.13
Not the most versatile actress . . . Nevertheless fans are invited to guess the mood of Cleopatra judging from Elizabeth Taylor's photographs. Pressbook publicity advertisement.

either wielding the jawbone of an ass or clutching gladiatorial tackle, the gigantism of his performances (which were far from subtle) seems perfectly aligned to the epics themselves. As Babington and Evans stress:

> Looking at Mature overdoing it may provoke derision but, whether in derision or admiration, our mixed response to his screen portrayals pushes us to move beyond mere empathy into an ... awareness of the artifice of all acting ... Mature and the Hollywood Biblical Epic, so well-suited to each other in so many ways, complement each other also in their crude ... appeals to their own deconstruction.[28]

Typecasting was discussed and planned for any newcomer right from the start of his or her career as part of the publicity build-up. The studios presented new hopefuls in a variety of different sorts of roles in the hope that the public would choose its favourite from those 'types'; in reality of course the public was selecting from a pre-selected menu, but the studios enjoyed promoting the illusion of stars being 'discovered' by the public.

Making and breaking stars

The case of the early career of Edmund Purdom is instructive in the way in which studios manufactured young hopefuls. In 1952, the young British actor appeared in small roles with Laurence Olivier and Vivien Leigh on Broadway in Shakespeare's *Antony and Cleopatra* and Shaw's *Caesar and Cleopatra*. His good looks in a tunic and a loincloth brought him to the attention of Hollywood and, cast in a small part in *Julius Caesar* at MGM, George Cukor recommended him to Charles Brackett for the bit-part role of Charles Lightoller in *Titanic* (1953). This, nevertheless, brought Purdom to the attention of executives at MGM who signed him to a contract worth $40,000 a year, serendipitously just at the point when Mario Lanza's short-lived career at MGM was brought to an abrupt end when he was fired from the lead role in a new version of the musical-operetta *The Student Prince* (dir. Thorpe, 1954). Purdom was cast in the part instead because he had the youthful good looks and, it was thought, the appropriate British theatrical pedigree – although he lip-synched to Lanza's extraordinary high-tenor singing voice. *The Student Prince* was a huge hit and Purdom was hailed as 'the most promising new star in Hollywood', with no less a person than Hedda Hopper calling him 'the most surprising and notable figure this year in Hollywood ... a fine actor in the great romantic tradition'.[29]

When Fox needed an actor at the last minute to replace Marlon Brando as the title character in *The Egyptian* (Figure 4.14), their most lavish production of 1954, Purdom was loaned out by MGM and was cast in the lead role of Sinuhe (and was chosen over John Derek, John Cassavetes and Cameron Mitchell for the role – see Text Box 4.3). MGM's head of production Dore Schary announced that the studio would build up

Figure 4.14
Hollywood new boy, Edmund Purdom cast as the lead in *The Egyptian* (1953). By the late 1950s he was making B-movies in Italy. Production still.

Purdom as a star and he was straight away was cast in three films: another MGM musical, *Athena*, the title role in the biblical epic *The Prodigal*, MGM's most lavish production of 1955, opposite Lana Turner (who had little time for him: 'They chose . . . Edmund Purdom, a young man with a remarkably high opinion of himself [to play the prodigal son]; his pomposity was hard enough to bear')[30] and the swashbuckler *The King's Thief* (1955), in a role originally meant for Stewart Granger. There was also some talk he would appear in the remake of *Ben-Hur*.

MGM was playing a traditional game in crafting the youthful Purdom in a series of character 'types': the musical hero, the epic hero and the adventure hero, waiting to see where fan loyalties would fall. Unfortunately *The Egyptian* was a box-office disappointment and Purdom garnished some less than favourable reviews: 'Edmund Purdom as the young Dr Sinuhe, specialist at opening skulls, is a handsome and earnest young actor who is obviously clutching at dramatic straws.'[31] A more recent assessment of Purdom's performance rightly concedes that this young, rather underwhelming if good looking actor was at the mercy of the studio system and struggled to bloom in the face of a confrontational director like Michael Curtiz:

Text Box 4.3   Hollywood's New Glamour Boy

Edmund Purdom, a 27-year old unknown, has snagged two big roles.
Hollywood's new crown prince is Edmund Purdom. Twenty months ago, an unknown living in a $30-a-month garage with his expectant wife, this British actor was facing desperation as an unemployed. Now, he is starring in two important films as a substitute in roles originally assigned to better-known actors. In MGM's *The Student Prince* he plays the hero and 'sings' with Mario Lanza's voice on the soundtrack. In *The Egyptian* at Twentieth Century Fox he replaced Marlon Brando in a spectacular part. After that, MGM has lined up three more important films for him, among them *Ben-Hur*. 'Just call me a lucky replacement,' says Purdom sardonically.

He aims to be a successful film lover using his own name.
Edmund Purdom won his first battle with Hollywood when he refused to be called 'Edmund York'. When warned that he might not be accepted as a film hero with his family name, Purdom pointed out that the greatest screen lover of the early movies had been Francis X. Bushman. Son of an English drama critic, Purdom spent a Spartan-like youth as a student in a Benedictine monastery. At 19 he went on stage; in 1951 he was in New York with the Oliviers in their two *Cleopatra* productions. Hollywood gave him small parts in *Titanic* and *Julius Caesar*, but a period of idleness threatened to force him home. Then came *The Student Prince*. 'During our abject misery', he says, 'an amazing number of people helped us. Now people ask us for money – a new experience!'

Life Magazine, November 1954.

I do feel for Purdom ... Watching him struggle to carry the huge, dead weight of *The Egyptian*, like a dachshund dragging a bus, does give you a sense of what the ancient Greeks meant about the experience of pity and terror. Although not top-billed, he's the film's central character, a philosophical physician seeking Truth, embroiled in your standard Hollywood historical-epic plot: loads of sin, sex and salvation in the days when Rome or Babylon was the world's entertainment capital. I do fault him, however, for a limited palette of expression. In the film's first half, playing an idealistic, love-struck youth, he slumps forward; as an older, embittered cynic in the second, he slumps back. Perhaps a sympathetic director could have helped Purdom expand his range of expression, by suggesting he slump to the right or the left, but the director here was Michael Curtiz, who was not known for his high opinion of actors, nor for theirs of him.[32]

If anything the reviews for *The Prodigal* were worse: 'Edmund Purdom brings all the dash of a rain-soaked undertaker to the role of the Prodigal.'[33] Both *Athena* and *The King's Thief* were also unmitigated flops.

Moreover, bad publicity focusing on his adulterous affair with Linda Christian (the wife of the popular actor Tyrone Power) lead to Purdom divorcing his wife in a bitter and public law suit, his ex-wife later suing him for child support. None of this impressed MGM who disliked the negative publicity Purdom was garnishing and thereafter they refused to offer him a second contract. Box-office poison and Hollywood anathema, Edmund Purdom left America for Europe where he undertook successive roles in Italian movies, including the title part in *Herod the Great* (dir. Tourjansky, 1959). In 1962 he was interviewed as saying, 'I couldn't stand Hollywood. The people, their status symbols and public image were too much. I walked out. Perhaps I should have been more patient,' which prompted the one-time adoring Hedda Hopper to write a stinging response:

> The truth is, he did his best to become a star here, but he didn't make the grade – even with Mario Lanza's voice; but he did walk out on his wife and family and start gallivanting around with Linda Christian. I'll bet he'll come hopping back if anyone crooked a finger.[34]

In contrast to Purdom's disastrous Hollywood career, one might cite the career of Ulster-born Stephen Boyd whose good looks and obvious talent saw him advance with ease through the Hollywood system. His remarkable performance as Messala in *Ben-Hur* (for which he won a Golden Globe for Best Actor, although he sadly missed out on an Oscar) was followed by Livius in *The Fall of the Roman Empire* – a role which, through the strength of Boyd's performance, bonds the film together. He had originally been cast as Antony opposite Taylor's Cleopatra until her sickness and lengthy recuperation saw Rouben Mamoulian hand over to Mankiewicz as director; Boyd was replaced by Burton. In 1966 he played the role of Nimrod in *The Bible: In the Beginning* ... He was happy to play in epic films and his tremendous talent meant that he brought both depth and reality to his on-screen characters. His contribution to the epic genre has largely gone unnoticed, but Stephen Boyd should be regarded as one of epic's brightest stars.[35]

Basinger characterises the inability of the Hollywood machine to sell an actor or an actress to the public as a 'malfunction', which means that in spite of the time and money lavished on a new hopeful, ultimately the adulation of the fans failed to materialise.[36] Some actors were able to escape the studio straightjacket and, by force of personality and some talent, managed to re-brand their image. After his disastrous debut in *The Silver Chalice*, Paul Newman had actually been approached to play the title role in the forthcoming *Ben-Hur* but his lifelong commitment to 'avoid frocks' led Newman to concentrate (except for Westerns) on modern characters, often those under emotional stress; he rarely played conventional romantic roles or comedies. He had famously lost out to James Dean when Elia Kazan screen tested them both for the lead in *East of Eden*, but in 1956, following Dean's death, the role of the boxer

Figure 4.15
Hollywood malfunction: the studios failed to find a niche for Haya Harareet, seen here as
Esther in *Ben-Hur* (1959). Staged publicity shot on set.

Rocky Graziano – earmarked for Dean – in *Somebody Up There Likes Me*
(dir. Wise) fell to him. That year, too, he starred as a brainwashed army
officer in the post-Korean war drama, *The Rack* (dir. Laven). Newman
found his niche in playing less than admirable characters and the studios
were happy to support and promote his many faceted and contradictory
persona which in many ways rendered the star image superficial – and
yet so famous was he for his dazzling looks and for having the bluest
eyes in the business that it is impossible to think of Newman as anything
other than a star.

   A good example of the malfunction process can be found in the case
of Haya Harareet, the beautiful Israeli actress brought to Hollywood by
William Wyler to become a rival to the Italian stars Gina Lollobrigida
and Sophia Loren. Casting her in the role of Esther in *Ben-Hur* (Figure
4.15), Wyler was keen too to capitalise on her essential Jewishness and
on her links to the recently formed state of Israel. And yet the marketing ploy chosen to promote the unknown actress was, from the start,
misconceived: '*Ben-Hur* Leading Lady is An Ex-Marine!', announced the
pressbook's marketing pages:

> Do you know of any feminine film star who received basic training in
> the Armed Forces? Haya Harareet, playing the feminine starring role
> opposite Charlton Heston in MGM's *Ben-Hur* has. Like other Israeli
> girls, Haya served in uniform for two years after she graduated from

BEN-HUR DRAPERY FABRICS

Some $200,000 has been invested in these fabrics by the Penco Fabrics, Inc., 271 Fifth Ave., New York 16, N. Y. They make excellent tie-ups for colorful window and counter displays. Contact your better interior decorating stores for displays of "Ben-Hur" designed drapes, slipcovers and upholstered furniture.

Display book illustrating line of Fabrics.

Figure 4.16
Haya Harareet providing a much-needed feminine touch to the marketing of *Ben-Hur*.
Pressbook advertisement.

high school in Tel Aviv. She carried a rifle in the Marines and went through basic training like any other soldier. It was after she left the service that she began her acting career.

Promoted as 'Hollywood's Newest Cinderella', Harareet who, it was reported, 'was born against a background of terror in Haifa', was given the full Hollywood glamour treatment and advertising tie-ins of her sporting the latest fashions or championing makeup styles, jewellery stores and other related women's products were used as part of the *Ben-Hur* campaign (Figure 4.16 – see Text Box 4.4). Reviews of her performance were enthusiastically positive:

Text Box 4.4   Promoting Haya Harareet

WOMEN'S PAGE STORIES
Some Practical Beauty Tips from a Beautiful Ex-Marine!

Hold on to you bonnet, but some of the sagest beauty advice to be heard in a long time comes from an ex-Marine! Her name is Haya Harareet, she plays the leading feminine role opposite Charlton Heston in Metro-Goldwyn-Mayor's *Ben-Hur*, and she has the distinction of having served two years in the Marine Corps of Israel.

Miss Harareet's story is a new twist on the classic Cinderella theme. Until *Ben-Hur* she made just two motion pictures (one in Israel and the other in Italy) and had appeared in several plays on the Tel Aviv stage. Then her career went into orbit in sudden and dramatic fashion when director William Wyler chose her for the role of Esther in the spectacular film.

It is safe to assume that the actress's dark beauty and flawless complexion had something to do with Mr Wyler's choice. However, Miss Harareet admits to no special rules for cosmetics, except for one maxim.

'The most important thing about makeup', she says, 'is to make up your own mind about it. While I was growing up in Israel and studying for the theatre, I never wore much makeup, perhaps nothing more than a light lipstick, sometimes not even that. Today I do wear more cosmetics, but still a very restrained amount. I don't think heavy make-up is right for me and I refuse to use it even if it is the vogue.'

Perhaps Miss Harareet's secret lies in the fact that she never permits cosmetics to obscure her naturalness. This could well be the very thing that fastened her in Wyler's mind.

As far as the specifics go, the actress is a soap-and-water girl.

'I don't use cream for cleansing or for lubricating the skin at night,' she says. 'It's a mystery to me how complexions can breathe when they are slathered. Happily I'm olive-skinned and rarely feel that my face is dry. When it does become so, I give it a coating of olive oil, which works wonders.'

A light foundation readies her skin for a touch of powder, next comes lipstick, then eye makeup.

'I would say it takes me about fifteen minutes to put on my face,' she estimates, 'and ten of them go into making up my eyes. To me, eyes are the most important facial feature and call for extra-special care and attention. First comes a subtle application of eye shadow, even in the daytime, followed by an eyeliner that's quite heavy around the outer part of the eye and lighter towards the nose. I mascara only the upper lashes. Possibly the most vital element of this whole process is patience.'

Not only does Miss Harareet keep her grooming simple, she also maintains an uncomplicated programme for figure-streaming.

'I walk everywhere,' she says. 'Old fashioned it may seem, I never ride if I can walk. I supposed I'm used to going places by foot-power because of my Marine training, but I really enjoy it. Walking is a wonderful way to keep in condition and isn't nearly as boring as a daily ritual of calisthenics.'

No dieting for this actress either. 'People tell me I'm lucky because I honestly don't enjoy rich foods. I never eat anything fried, much preferring boiled meats and steamed vegetables. And instead of reaching for a pastry at dinner, I'm more content with an apple or an orange.'

This is the kind of beauty-savvy that serves movie stars and women everywhere equally well.

Ben-Hur pressbook, 1959

Haya Harareet, an Israeli actress making her first appearance in an American film, emerges as a performer of stature. Her portrayal of Esther, the former slave and daughter of Simonides, steward of the House of Hur, is sensitive and revealing. Wyler presumably deserves considerate credit for taking a chance on an unknown. She has a striking appearance and represents a welcome departure from the standard Hollywood ingenue.[37]

So what was Haya Harareet's problem? She was a beautiful dark-haired, exotic woman who arrived in Hollywood surrounded by great hoopla and made her debut in the costliest, most ardently publicised movie of the time and had garnished good acting reviews. Everything should have proceeded without complication. The malfunction which occurred around Haya Harareet was threefold. First, selling a star by measuring her against established rivals, like the equally exotic Hedy Lamarr and Gina Lollobrigida, both of whom were familiar faces in the epic genre, was a miscalculation (and the fixation on Harareet's military past was a big mistake). Next, the role of Esther was dull, especially when set against Hollywood's penchant for ransacking Hebrew legends for stories involving temptresses, the biblical equivalent of the Victorian fallen-woman or the 1920s vamp. The temptress-type was a chance for fans to see Lamarr and Lollobrigida in revealing fancy dress. Derek Elley may be correct in suggesting that Esther's romance with Judah Ben-Hur is the catalyst for his conversion and that 'Esther is vitally important for her representation of the Judeo-Christian cause which Ben-Hur must ultimately embrace.'[38] Monica Cyrino's estimation of Harareet's performance as 'tentative and understated' is undercut by Jeff Rovin's opinion that 'she is not convincing as a character or an actress ... her performance is all too practised.' But this is not necessarily Harareet's fault; the fact is, Esther was a thankless role, poorly written and modelled solely on the morally upright virgin types of the Christian epics of the earlier 1950s.[39] When placed alongside the Italianate va-va-voom of La Lollo's colourful, pelvis-grinding, pagan queen in 1959's contending epic, *Solomon and Sheba*, Harareet's home-spun Esther faded into the shadows.

But what really damaged Harareet's chance of stardom was the indifference shown to her and to her on-screen character by Charlton Heston. When making *Ben-Hur*, Heston had commented that 'there is no place for a love story here' and he frequently downplayed (and continued to sideline) Esther's role in the story (in his autobiography, Haya Harareet is given similar short-shrift).[40] The audience does not much care about the entwined futures of Judah Ben-Hur and Esther; his relationship with Messala is more dynamic and interesting. Moreover, MGM's publicity machine found the casting of Heston and Harareet uninspiring and little attempt was made to build up publicity around any on-screen (or off-screen) chemistry that might have sparked between the two performers. In later life Harareet expressed her frustrations of working in the Hollywood system and being typecast as a product: 'I am not Esther of *Ben-Hur*', she once stated:

> I am an actress who played the part of Esther. But that doesn't mean I have to go on playing Esther for the rest of my life . . . MGM treated me as a father would have treated me. I was well taken care of. But I was not allowed to grow up. They could think of me only in terms of Biblical pictures. Other studios did not know me as a person, so they thought of me in the same way.[41]

Might some of the malfunctions found in the careers of Purdom and Harareet been rectified if these performers had been assigned better roles, or better publicity, or better managers? What if they had come along in different decades, or were not compared unfavourably to already established stars, or hadn't run into problems with co-stars, might they have become superstars then? It is, of course, impossible to know.

British 'types': Accents and Stiff-Upper-Lips

The political coding of epic movies was a particular feature of the 1950s when films were largely aimed at attacking, overtly and covertly, the Soviet Union and the House Un-American Activities Committee (HUAC). *The Ten Commandments* of 1956, for instance, can be read as a product of American Cold War ideology, highlighting and localising the foci of America's political, theological and economic conflicts by equating God's perspective with American interests, by the representation of 'true' Jews as proto-Christians and by the reclamation of the Middle East as legitimately within the American (Christian) sphere of influence.[42] But it has been suggested that another subtler anti-imperialist message was encoded in 1950s ancient world epics: rulers, especially Roman ones, should almost inevitably be played by British actors because 'the precisely enunciated [English] voice', argues Jeffrey Richards, 'recall[ed] the

Figure 4.17
Holding their cigarettes like Noel Coward socialites are the British-born actors Laurence Olivier and Peter Ustinov, with Tony Curtis in the centre. *Spartacus* (1960). Candid shot.

aristocratic Empire from which the United States had emancipated itself in 1776, and about which despite alliance in two world wars, it always entertained ambivalent feelings.'[43] To an American audience nothing said 'moral degeneracy' like an English accent. In Hollywood the decline of Rome was therefore set against a soundtrack of English accents. Thus were audiences treated to the elongated vowel-sounds of Ernest Thesiger's Tiberius in *The Robe*, Barry Jones as Claudius in *Demetrius and the Gladiators*, Maurice Evans as the Emperor Antoninus in *Androcles and the Lion*, Sir Cedric Hardwick's Tiberius in *Salome* and George Relph's Tiberius in *Ben-Hur*. In the same vein, Jay Robinson's screeching Caligula in *The Robe*, Sir Laurence Olivier's cold-hearted Crassus in *Spartacus* (Figure 4.17) and Alex Guinness's patient Emperor Marcus Aurelius in *The Fall of the Roman Empire* brought to the soundtrack the unmissable cadences of an impeccable English accent. In *Quo Vadis* Peter Ustinov as Nero delivers his lines with the clipped vocal panache of a Noel Coward caricature (see Text Box 4.5): 'My dear Marcus, what a proletarian observation! You must know that a woman has no past when she mates with a god' or – better yet – 'Tigellinus, the weeping vase!' (pronounced *vaahz*). Interestingly, this 'aural paradigm', as Maria Wyke has termed it,[44] was applied too to Egyptian pharaohs and other Oriental despots including Michael Winding as Akhnaton in *The Egyptian*, Jack Hawkins in *The Land of the Pharaohs*, Sir Cedric Hardwicke in *The Ten Commandments* and David Farrar in *Solomon and Sheba*; each delivers their lines with the

Text Box 4.5   Creating Nero

In his dazzlingly witty autobiography, *Dear Me* (1977: 224–6), Peter Ustinov had fun reminiscing about his casting as Nero in *Quo Vadis* and about the absurdities of creating an epic movie.

An exciting proposition came my way when I was twenty-eight years old. MGM were going to remake *Quo Vadis*, and I was a candidate for the role of Nero. Arthur Hornblower was to be the producer and I was tested by John Huston. I threw everything I knew into this test, and to my surprise John Huston did little to restrain me, encouraging me in confidential whispers to be even madder. Apparently the test was a success, but then the huge machine came to a halt, and the project was postponed for a year.

At the end of the year, the producer was Sam Zimbalist and the director Mervyn LeRoy. They also approved my test, but warned me in a wire that I might be found to be a little too young for the part. I cabled back that if they postponed again I might be too old, since Nero died at thirty-one. A second cable from them read 'Historical Research Has Proved You Correct STOP The Part Is Yours' . . .

I met Mervyn LeRoy for the first time some hours before we began to shoot . . . I spoke to him with unaccustomed earnestness about my role and asked him if he had any observations to make.

'Nero? Son of a bitch,' he declared.

I was inclined to agree with him.

'You know what he did to his mother?' he suddenly said, with decent Jewish concern, as though there was something one ought to do about it.

I replied that, yes, I did know what he did to his mother.

'Son of a bitch,' repeated Mervyn, almost angry.

I nodded my head. So far we were eye to eye. 'But is there any specific aspect of the man you wish me to bring out?' I asked.

To my surprise, Mervyn replied by doing a tap-dance routine.

'I used to be a hoofer,' he said.

I said, truthfully, that I didn't know that.

There was a long pause while I wondered uncomfortably if by some hideous chance he expected Nero to tap-dance.

'Nero', said Mervyn.

I pricked up my ears.

'The way I see him . . .'

'Yes?'

'He's a guy that plays with himself at nights.'

At the time I thought it a preposterous assessment, but a little later I was not so sure. It was a profundity at its most workaday level, and it led me to the eventual conviction that no nation can make Roman pictures as well as the Americans.

The Romans were pragmatic, a people of relaxed power with *nouveau-riche* lapses of taste . . . They too believed in the benefits of dressing for comfort, and the intrigues in their Senate matched anything in Washington, while their total belief in Roman know-how led to a few ugly surprises, as did the total belief in American know-how in Vietnam . . . what mattered . . . was a modus vivendi which was sometimes gracious, sometimes coarse, sometimes civilised and sometimes violent and cruel, and yet, ever, unmistakably Roman.

The inevitable vulgarities of the script contributed as much to its authenticity as its rare felicities. I felt then as I feel today, in spite of the carping of critical voices, that *Quo Vadis*, good or bad according to taste, was an extraordinary authentic film, and the nonsense Nero was sometimes made to speak was very much like the nonsense Nero probably did speak.

enunciated perfection of an Eton-trained politician. Farrar employed the same stiff-upper-lip accent as Xerxes in *The 300 Spartans* and George Saunders' distinctively languid upper-class English accent informed both the Saran of Gaza in *Samson and Delilah* and Adonijah in *Solomon and Sheba* while in 1967 his voice would make the animated character of Sheer Khan in Walt Disney's *The Jungle Book* (dir. Rutherman) into one of cinema's greatest and most memorable villains.

But there are other semiotics encountered in the use of the English accent in epics films. The first is age. It was common for older characters to be given English accents, while the younger characters speak in American tones. Senior Romans, like Charles Laughton as Gracchus and Peter Ustinov as Batiatus in *Spartacus* are played by British actors while their junior colleagues, such as John Gavin as the youthful Julius Caesar and John Dall's Glabrus, are played by Americans. In *Spartacus* the Englishness of the older men promotes their sense of gravitas and wisdom and imbues in them too a certain desirable British eccentricity and 'characterfulness'. The Scottish-born actor Finlay Currie, a large and imposing figure with a rich, deep voice and somewhat authoritarian demeanour, cornered the market in playing figures of religious and secular authorities like St Peter in *Quo Vadis*, King David in *Solomon and Sheba* and Balthazar, one of the Three Wise Men, in *Ben-Hur*, as well as an elderly senator in *The Fall of the Roman Empire*. His Scottish brogue, with its rolling lilt, brought a Presbyterian authoritarianism and, it must be admitted, puritanism to his white-haired venerable characters and acted as a neat counterbalance to another popular character actor, Hugh Griffith, whose Sheik Ilderim in *Ben-Hur* has the rounded vowels and playful musicality which betray his Welsh roots.

The 'aural paradigm' of Englishness is also encountered in the epic's female characters who tend to oscillate between villainous man-eaters and virginal good girls. Of the former it is Patricia Laffan's sumptuously decadent, scheming, malicious Empress Poppaea, sardonic and disdainful in her delivery (at times running close to overshadowing even Peter Ustinov) who dominates the bad-girl 'type'. At once sinister and alluring, a smile never more than a whisker away from a sneer, Laffan's commanding, imperious presence, suggesting innate superiority, is perfectly set off by her exquisitely enunciated English vowels, her languid, low voice and her double-entendre-heavy lines (Figure 4.18):

> *Poppaea*: [as Marcus enters] As usual your entrance is proud and aloof.
> *Vinicius*: I came proudly as fast as my hands and knees will carry me.
> *Poppaea*: And as always, sardonic and unassailable.
> *Vinicius*: So happily, so unassailable? I've never been so readily expertly vanquished in my life.
> *Poppaea*: I believe everything except the word vanquished.
> *Poppaea*: [Suggestively while taking wine] I should like to vanquish you Marcus.
> *Vinicius*: Like the spider who eats her mate when he is no longer a necessity?
> *Poppaea*: [Suggestively] Mmm . . . Hmmm . . . Something like that.

The virginal good girls get none of the good lines. The 'type' was best represented by Deborah Kerr and Jean Simmons, two British-born actresses who were blessed with beautiful looks and well-honed talent but who struggled against the studio system and Hollywood's insistence that they each should play off-screen and on the perfect English rose. 'I came over [to Hollywood] to act, but it turned out all I had to do was to be high-minded, long suffering, white-gloved and decorative,' lamented Kerr in a 1952 *Photoplay* interview. The flame-haired beauty was one of the most luminous stars of her time ('Deborah Kerr rhymes with star', the marketing agents stated) yet throughout her career which was, decidedly, brilliant Kerr fought the studio system's fixation with casting her as nuns, governesses, or society hostess-types and even after frolicking in the surf with Burt Lancaster in *From Here to Eternity* (dir. Zinnemann, 1953) in one of the postwar era's most iconic and sexy scenes, Kerr still had to fight off the restrictive label of her Englishness.[45] Hollywood's process of curtailing Deborah Kerr through her accent and her heritage had begun in the build-up to the release of *Quo Vadis* and her casting in the role of the Christian heroine Lygia. The pressbook provided a lengthy résumé of her British-born career, namedropping her training at Sadler's Wells Ballet, her appearance in open-air theatre in Regent's Park, her performance in the Playhouse Theatre in Oxford, her London stage performances next to Dame Edith Evans in Shaw and Shakespeare and, of course, the highlights of her British film career including *The Life and Death of Colonel Blimp* (dir. Powell and Pressberger,

Figure 4.18
The 'aural paradigm' of the English villainess is best represented by Patricia Laffan
(Poppaea), shown here with Robert Taylor. *Quo Vadis* (1951). Production shot.

1943) and *Black Narcissus* (dir. Powell and Pressberger, 1947). For *Quo Vadis* MGM's marketing executives concentrated on exploiting Kerr's British credentials by blending Lygia's demure decorum with Kerr's (supposed) upper-class refinement ('People always described me as ladylike,' she later reminisced, 'If only they knew').[46]

Monica Cyrino makes the point that, 'From the glamorous denizens of Nero's House of Women to the soprano voices of the Christian assembly, *Quo Vadis* exhibits a feminine world ... [of] luscious and appealing detail' and this is recognised too in the off-screen marketing ploys which were created around Kerr.[47] Beauty products, make-up, jewellery and fashion items were all part of the Deborah Kerr-*Quo Vadis* package, but in addition to the obvious marketability of her beauty, her Britishness too was used as a major sales product. Thus in pressbook advertisements she is shown drinking tea – the quintessential English obsession (Figure 4.19) – or, in a deliberately tongue-in-cheek nod at the transatlantic partnership of the romantic leads, she was photographed reading a copy of *The Times* alongside Robert Taylor (whom Kerr liked enormously) who was depicted scanning the *Los Angeles Examiner* (see Figure 1.6 earlier). Yet in spite of all the typecasting and the studio manufacturing, throughout her successful career Deborah Kerr embodied an on-screen essence that has rarely been matched and even as Lygia she produced a performance of refinement and delicacy of manner without seeming prissily virginal; Kerr's Lygia was vulnerable without being weak, sensual without being lewd, and beautiful without being anyone's toy – not even for Robert Taylor. In his discussion of *Quo Vadis*, Kerr's friend and biographer, Eric Braun, makes some interesting observations on Kerr's career and the nature of the Hollywood studio system:

> Kerr's performance as Lygia strikingly shows her ability to portray spirituality, contrasted with the outer convention of Hollywood-style beauty ... Lygia's costumes were particularly inappropriate ... Here was Hollywood inventiveness at its most out of place on the unworldly Christian heroine – the conventional glamour girl stamp which director Jack Clayton was to describe as 'ridiculously unsuitable' when imposed on Deborah Kerr. She had the unique combination of beauty and spiritual repose necessary to interpret the saintly early Christian, but at this period in her career she had to fight against costuming and makeup and rely on her inner resources to achieve conviction in the role. The two sides of the coin were never more at variance than in her portrayal of Lygia: only her instinctive truth in characterisation enabled her to overcome the initial disadvantages of presentation. This is not to denigrate the Technicolor camerawork of Robert Stevens, who achieved some stunningly beautiful shots of Kerr ... it was the fault of neither that the image in the camera was inappropriate to the occasion – the culprit was the Hollywood system, of which both star and cameraman were highly valuable components.[48]

50,000 Tea Posters Will Advertise "Quo Vadis"

TAKE TEA AND SEE MGM'S "QUO VADIS"

DEBORAH KERR

relaxes with TEA on the set of

MGM'S

"QUO VADIS"

Color by TECHNICOLOR

Miss Kerr is another famous
actress who drinks tea

RELAX ... EAT IN A RESTAURANT TODAY!

Two colors, size about 14" by 13". Tea Bureau will distribute 50,000 of them to grocery stores and restaurants. Check with them. This is a general tea promotion with no brands specified. If local places haven't posters in stock, a LIMITED quantity can be ordered direct from

MR. BILL TREADWELL, TEA BUREAU INC.
500 FIFTH AVENUE, NEW YORK 18, N. Y.

Figure 4.19
Deborah Kerr, everyone's favourite English rose, stops for afternoon tea. *Quo Vadis* (1951). Advertisement idea, pressbook.

Figure 4.20
With eyes fixed on heaven, Jean Simmons embodies female Christian virtues as Livinia in
Androcles and the Lion (1952). Studio publicity portrait.

Like Deborah Kerr, Jean Simmons' jaw-dropping beauty often obscured a formidable acting talent. Simmons was one of J. Arthur Rank's 'well-spoken young starlets' who, at the age of fourteen, had already made several movies before gaining critical attention for her portrayal of the young Estella in David Lean's film adaptation of the Charles Dickens novel *Great Expectations* (1946). She went on to appear predominantly in films made in Great Britain during and after the Second World War and she was nominated for the Academy Award for Best Supporting Actress for her role as Ophelia in *Hamlet* (dir. Olivier, 1948). Laurence Olivier urged the young actress to perfect her craft by acting on the British stage, but she chose a more romantic path and followed her future husband, the dashing British screen idol Stewart Granger, to Hollywood. Thereafter she found herself predominantly cast in the roles of well-spoken virgins. The first of these was in 1952 in *Androcles and the Lion* in the part of Lavinia (Figure 4.20) alongside Victor Mature followed the year later

Figure 4.21
A postwar erotic classic: Kirk Douglas kisses Jean Simmons. *Spartacus* (1960). Production
still retouched before distribution and any publication to conceal Simmons' breasts.

by *The Robe* in which she played Diana, virginal-martyr and (pure) love
interest of Richard Burton. In *Young Bess* (dir. Sidney, 1953), *The Egyptian*
and *Guys and Dolls* (dir. Mankiewicz, 1955) she continued to deliver the
same virginal performance (although as Sister Sarah Brown, for which
she won a Golden Globe, Simmons showed that she could play a girl
who knew how to let her hair down). Reflecting on her film roles in the
1950s, later in life she recalled that 'They were what I call "poker-up-the-
ass" parts. You know, those long-suffering, decorative ladies. I mean,
they're very, very, boring.'[49]
    Simmons' portrayal of Kirk Douglas's love interest, the British slave
woman Varinia, in *Spartacus* finally helped her break the mould. Varinia
is very sexual with Spartacus and is shown to be comfortable in her
own sexuality; indeed upon first meeting Spartacus, Varinia already
has the advantage over him in terms of sexual knowledge and experience. When they are finally married, she willingly reserves her sexual
expression solely for him, thereby maintaining the traditional structure
of gender relations of the film (and of the entire cultural outlook of the
early 1960s), yet her sexual power over Spartacus is never forgotten
throughout the film and is especially prominent in the scene where she
bathes naked in the river, exuding a free and unrestrained sensuality
(Figure 4.21). So rare was it to see a woman on screen who was not just

Figure 4.22
The prototype of barbarian masculinity and sex-appeal: Yul Brynner as the King of Siam.
The King and I (1956). British Newspaper cinema advertisement.

comfortable with, but revelled in, her sexuality that 'For men of a certain age, the memory of seeing Simmons naked from the back . . . ranks high among their early carnal thrills.'[50]

The Archaeology of Stardom

One night late in 1952 Cecil B. DeMille attended a theatre performance in New York City. It was of the new Broadway sensation, *The King and I*, starring veteran stage actress Gertrude Lawrence and a thirty-year-old newcomer, Yul Brynner, who was causing quite a critical stir in his role of the King of Siam (Figure 4.22). During the play's intermission DeMille went backstage to meet this golden boy and, shaking the actor firmly by the hand, he got straight to the point, asking, 'Mr Brynner, how'd you like to make a picture that your grandchildren will see in the theatres around the world?' Brynner replied, 'I think I'd like that.' 'Then you will play Ramses in the *Ten Commandments* for me', responded DeMille.[51] The deal was done. Brynner was the first actor to be cast in DeMille's new epic. DeMille later recalled, 'I went back to my seat in the theatre, Yul became the King of Siam once more and I did not see him again until we were ready for him to become the King of Egypt.'[52]

During that meeting with Yul Brynner, DeMille had gone into many details of the complex personality of Ramses. The old director left Brynner feeling very impressed and, for his part, DeMille was thrilled by the potential he saw in casting Brynner as Ramses: 'Yul Brynner is

Figure 4.23
Mutual respect: Yul Brynner dines with Cecil B. DeMille and discusses passages from the bible. Studio publicity photograph in preparation for *The Ten Commandments, c.*1955.

the most powerful personality I've ever seen,' he said, 'a cross between Douglas Fairbanks Jr, Apollo and Hercules . . . Along with great acting abilities, Yul has the pure knack of appealing to women at the same time he commands the respect of men.' During the process of working together on *The Ten Commandments* Brynner and DeMille shared a mutual feeling of admiration (Figure 4.23), and in later years Brynner recalled that 'the reason why I felt so close to Mr DeMille was that he thought like me, on a grand scale.'[53]

In 1956 both *The Ten Commandments* and the highly successful film version of *The King and I* (dir. Lang) were premiered to great acclaim.

'Yul Brynner is magnificent . . . an intelligent and not entirely cruel king but one caught in a cataclysmic moment of history,' said the *Hollywood Reporter* of his Ramses; 'It is Brynner who gives the movie its animal spark . . . He is every inch the Oriental king . . . He stalks around the palace like an impatient leopard. His eyes glower with rage . . . This is a rare bit of acting. Brynner is the king, and you don't forget it', wrote the *New York Herald* of his King of Siam. With the shared grandiloquence of these reviews, there can be little doubt that a sense of familiar repetition can be read into Brynner's two most noteworthy on-screen creations and while both are brilliantly realised and subtly differentiated (the Siamese king has more humour and the sadness and resignation of accumulated wisdom), in the on-screen look and the subsequent studio marketing of Yul Brynner there are significant overlaps. Brynner (who was still performing on Broadway during the filming of *The Ten Commandments*) kept his trademark bald head for the role of Ramses II and, as we have already explored, his naked torso, hairless and defined, was put to advantage in both roles. As one latter-day die-hard Brynner fan has enthused:

> Even as a ten-year-old, I knew 'the guy' who played [the] King [of Siam] was 'that same guy' who played Ramses in *The Ten Commandments*. My young mind concluded that, obviously, he was born to portray kings on screen. It was only natural – with his furrowed brow, piercing eyes, and physique that looked carved from granite. Yul Brynner became the walking shape of my childhood vision of 'the king'.[54]

When in 1959 Brynner played the lead in *Solomon and Sheba* with a full head of black hair (slicked back with Brylcreem), he somehow lost something of his natural persona and the admiration of the critics: 'As Solomon, the Israelite ruler, Yul Brynner is as specious as that hair they have pasted (or he has grown) on his nude noggin. Neither it nor he suits the character.'[55] He never appeared with hair again.

In his autobiography DeMille advised those who believed that Brynner, in any role, was still playing the King of Siam to watch *The King and I* back to back with *The Ten Commandments* in quick succession and

> see the differences in characterisation between the barbaric, puzzled, arrogantly defensive King of Siam and the no less arrogant but sophisticated, self-assured Pharaoh in *The Ten Commandments*. There are similarities in the two performances for Yul Brynner, after all, is only one man; but it is the subtle differences which show his great artistic competence.'[56]

The fact remains, however, that from the moment DeMille saw Brynner in *The King and I* on Broadway he knew that he had found one of a kind. Moreover, when he had witnessed Brynner's extraordinary performance on stage, DeMille's vision of Ramses II become suddenly fully formed:

Figure 4.24
Yul Brynner emerges from his sports car in front of a cinema marquee with an enormous cut-out figure of himself as Ramses. *The Ten Commandments* (1956). Studio publicity photograph.

in his swaggering, masterful, intelligent, exotic and highly sexual incarnation as the Siamese ruler, Brynner had created the blueprint for the Egyptian pharaoh (Figure 4.24). Whether DeMille had pictured his Ramses like this beforehand is impossible to say but what is certain is that for the part of Ramses DeMille did not so much cast Yul Brynner as cast Yul Brynner's King of Siam.

As we have already seen, in Hollywood filmmaking a star actor embodies a set of ideas, the value of which is often bound up in the fate of the character that the actor portrays. Greil Marcus notes, therefore, that 'when actors migrate from movie to movie, traces of their characters travel with them.'[57] But perhaps a better analogy for the symbiosis of the actor and the character played on-screen (and especially in the context of epic movies) is the notion of the movie star as an archaeological site. As an actor's career develops and he or she plays more on-screen roles, so too 'layers' of performance are built up, one on top of the other. The actor's past is constructed on separate levels, each one placed in time and space thereby providing a context for each performance. Those performances found in 'lower layers' of an actor's career are older than those found above them.

Context is everything to an archaeologist. Without it artefacts are just objects that provide little more than general information about their function or the people who made them. Likewise, context is imperative in the archaeology of stardom. Each stratum of an actor's career is created at a certain time and for a specific purpose and every new performance is based upon the experience of what is learned in past performances. Because of the restrictive world of the Hollywood studio system, traces of the layers of past performances always reveal the character 'types' expected of an actor, regardless of script or setting. The archaeology of stardom reveals old characters speaking through the mouths of new ones, and performing gestures that can be remembered from twenty years before.

If, for instance, we were to dig through the archaeological site of Victor Mature's epic career, the soil close to the surface would be his performance as the Carthaginian general in the little-remembered *Hannibal*; in the next level down we would find Horemheb from *The Egyptian* and then we would unearth a thick level of the slave-cum-fighter Demetrius (Figure 4.25) from both *Demetrius and the Gladiators* and *The Robe*. Underneath this is a thin layer of the Captain – from *Androcles and the Lion* – and finally, at the bedrock, at the lowest stratum of the site, is Samson. And it is Samson that informs the whole of Mature's career from 1949 onwards in terms of his casting, his performances, his marketing exploitation, his star-image and, ultimately, the loyalty of his fan base. But we can add another layer to the topsoil of Victor Mature's archaeological dig-site. In the 1966 film *After the Fox* (dir. De Sica), Mature played the role of Tony Powell, an over-the-hill matinee actor who, in spite of the fact he is in his late-fifties, is obsessed with creating the illusion that he is only in his mid-thirties. By boot-polishing his hair black and strapping himself into a corset, Tony Powell longs to be cast once more in the Hollywood strong-man roles he had played early in his career. Here Mature parodies himself as the one-time beefcake star and it is his Samson/Demetrius/Horemheb-image that allows him to function as a caricature of himself. His publicity image as a likeable (if not necessarily gifted) actor is perfectly captured in Mature's witty

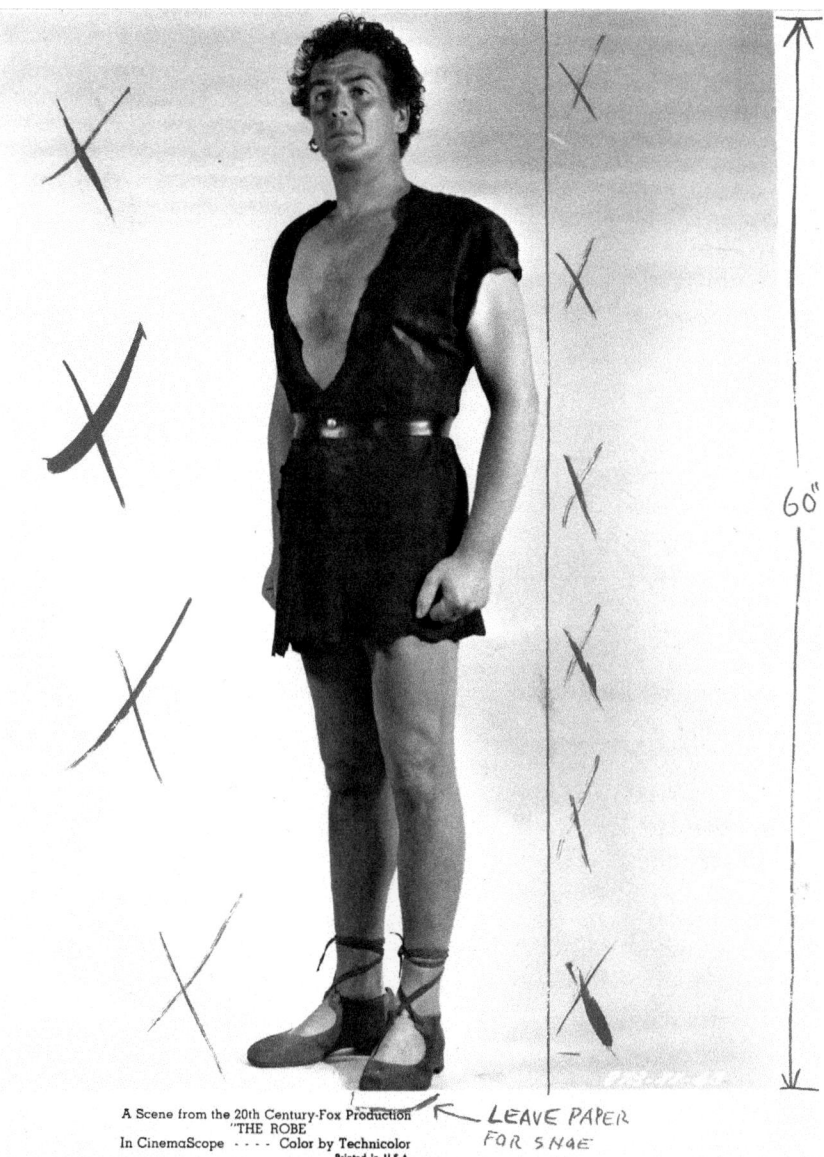

Figure 4.25
Epic beefcake: Victor Mature as Demetrius. *The Robe* (1953). Studio portrait with markings used by a newspaper editor in preparation for publication. Note the heeled closed-toe sandals for added height.

and willing self-mockery. The archaeology of stardom therefore exposes layers of a star's off-screen persona as much as it does a star's on-screen performances.

The archaeology of stardom can be practised on a number of actors who performed with some regularity in epic films (see Text Box 4.6), but perhaps the best, and in many ways the most complex, example of

Text Box 4.6   Movie Stars and Their On-screen Characters: An Epic Pedigree

Judith Anderson   Herodias (*Salome*), Memnet (*The Ten Commandments*)

Pier Angeli   Deborah (*The Silver Chalice*), Ildith (*Sodom and Gomorrah*)

Stanley Baker   Achilles (*Helen of Troy*), Astorath (*Sodom and Gomorrah*)

Ernest Borgnine   Strabo (*Demetrius and the Gladiators*), Lucius (*Barabbas*)

Stephen Boyd   Messala (*Ben-Hur*), Livius (*The Fall of the Roman Empire*), Nimrod (*The Bible: In the Beginning . . .*)

Yul Brynner   Ramses II (*The Ten Commandments*), Solomon (*Solomon and Sheba*)

Richard Burton   Marcellus Gallio (*The Robe*), Alexander (*Alexander the Great*), Antony (*Cleopatra*)

Claudette Colbert   Poppaea (*The Sign of the Cross*), Cleopatra (*Cleopatra*, 1934)

Joan Collins   Princess Nelifer (*The Land of the Pharaohs*), Esther (*Esther and the King*)

Finlay Currie   Peter (*Quo Vadis*), Balthasar (*Ben-Hur*), King David (*Solomon and Sheba*), Titus (*Cleopatra*, 1963)

Kirk Douglas   Ulysses (*Ulysses*), Spartacus (*Spartacus*)

Richard Egan   Dardanius (*Demetrius and the Gladiators*), King Ahasuerus (*Esther and the King*), King Leonidas (*The 300 Spartans*)

Nina Foch   Bithiah (*The Ten Commandments*), Helena (*Spartacus*)

Stewart Granger   Centurion Claudius (*Salome*), Lot (*Sodom and Gomorrah*)

Cedric Hardwicke   Tiberius Caesar (*Salome*), Priam (*Helen of Troy*), Pharaoh Sethi (*The Ten Commandments*)

Jack Hawkins   Pharaoh Khufu (*The Land of the Pharaohs*), Quintus Arrius (*Ben-Hur*)

Susan Hayward   Bathsheba (*David and Bathsheba*), Messalina (*Demetrius and the Gladiators*)

Charlton Heston   Moses (*The Ten Commandments*), Judah Ben-Hur (*Ben-Hur*), John the Baptist (*The Greatest Story Ever Told*)

Deborah Kerr   Lygia (*Quo Vadis*), Portia (*Julius Caesar*)

Charles Laughton   Nero (*The Sign of the Cross*), King Herod (*Salome*), Gracchus (*Spartacus*)

Victor Mature	Samson (*Samson and Delilah*), Captain (*Androcles and the Lion*), Demetrius (*The Robe* and *Demetrius and the Gladiators*), Horemheb (*The Egyptian*), Hannibal (*Hannibal*)
Roddy McDowall	Octavian (*Cleopatra*, 1963), Matthew (*The Greatest Story Ever Told*)
Debra Paget	Lucia (*Demetrius and the Gladiators*), Lilia (*The Ten Commandments*)
Edmund Purdom	Strato (*Julius Caesar*), Sinuhe (*The Egyptian*), Micah (*The Prodigal*), Herod (*Herod the Great*)
George Sanders	The Saran of Gaza (*Samson and Delilah*), Adonijah (*Solomon and Sheba*)
Martha Scott	Yochabel (*The Ten Commandments*), Miriam (*Ben-Hur*)
Jean Simmons	Lavinia (*Androcles and the Lion*), Diana (*The Robe*), Merit (*The Egyptian*), Varinia (*Spartacus*)
Woody Strode	Lion (*Androcles and the Lion*), Gladiator (*Demetrius and the Gladiators*), Moor (*The Silver Chalice*), King of Ethiopia (*The Ten Commandments*), Draba (*Spartacus*)
Peter Ustinov	Nero (*Quo Vadis*), Kaptah (*The Egyptian*), Batiatus (*Spartacus*)
Henry Wilcoxon	Antony (*Cleopatra*, 1934), Prince Ahtur (*Samson and Delilah*), Pentaur (*The Ten Commandments*)
The One Offs . . .	
Anne Baxter	Nefretiri (*The Ten Commandments*)
Marlon Brando	Antony (*Julius Caesar*)
Alec Guinness	Marcus Aurelius (*The Fall of the Roman Empire*)
Rita Hayworth	Salome (*Salome*)
Hedy Lamarr	Delilah (*Samson and Delilah*)
Angela Lansbury	Semadar (*Samson and Delilah*)
Gina Lollobrigida	Queen of Sheba (*Solomon and Sheba*)
Sophia Loren	Lucilla (*The Fall of the Roman Empire*)
Paul Newma	Basil (*The Silver Chalice*)
Jack Pallance	Simon the Magician (*The Silver Chalice*)
Christopher Plummer	Commodus (*The Fall of the Roman Empire*)
Anthony Quinn	Barabbas (*Barabbas*)
Omar Sharif	Sohamus (*The Fall of the Roman Empire*)
Robert Taylor	Marcus Vinicius (*Quo Vadis*)
Gene Tierney	Princess Baketamon (*The Egyptian*)
Lana Turner	Samara (*The Prodigal*)
Elizabeth Taylor	Cleopatra (*Cleopatra*)
John Wayne	Centurion (*The Greatest Story Ever Told*)
Michael Wilding	Akhnaten (*The Egyptian*)

Figure 4.26
Charlton Heston, the face of the Hollywood epic. Studio publicity portrait, 1956.

the star as an archaeological site is Charlton Heston, the one actor more than any other who is, and will always be, associated with the epic genre (Figure 4.26).[58] As a major Hollywood star, he appeared in a hundred films over the course of sixty years, rightfully making him one of the legendary figures of American cinema. A supporter of Democratic politicians and civil rights in the 1960s, Heston later became a Republican, founding a conservative political action committee and supporting Ronald Reagan in the White House. Heston's most notorious role in politics came as the five-term president of the National Rifle Association from 1998 to 2003.

As a young man, after enjoying a successful career on stage in weighty roles such as Macbeth and Mark Antony in both *Julius Caesar* and *Antony and Cleopatra*, Charlton Heston's big Hollywood break came when DeMille cast him as a circus manager in *The Greatest Show On Earth*, which was named by the Motion Picture Academy as the best picture of 1952. Thereafter he played a series of historical characters, Western heroes and American soldiers until DeMille began work on casting *The Ten Commandments*, selecting Heston for the lead as much for his looks as his reputation for acting ability. 'As I looked at these various paintings [assembled by his research assistant] one face kept suggesting itself to me,' DeMille wrote; 'That face was Heston's.'[59] DeMille commissioned a sketch artist to draw an impression of Heston wearing a long white beard and compared it to a statue of Moses by Michelangelo – the Moses of the public imagination. One final impetus persuaded DeMille that Heston was the man to play Moses – and that was Heston's broken nose (the result of a football accident). Charlton Heston's perfectly imperfect nose added the perfect biblical final touch, leading DeMille to comment, 'He looks like the Michelangelo statue . . . and [he] had the mental and spiritual qualities to play Moses – he has great honesty, respect for the truth, spiritual integrity and personal courage.'[60]

Heston immediately recognised the potential that the role would mean to his career. Writing in 1957 he commented:

> My role as Moses will always remain one of the creative peaks of my career. I hope to play many fine parts in my life . . . but surely films can never again offer me another part like Moses, not only in terms of its creative challenge for an actor . . . but also in the opportunity the part offered to attempt the portrayal of a man whose life had spiritual meaning to people of more varied faith than any other who ever lived.[61]

The Ten Commandments allowed the studios to create around Heston a public persona of both a religious high morality and an all-American masculinity, a patriarchal type of masculinity that was clearly not enamoured of corporate America and its many trappings. For his part, Heston was happy to project this double image since it suited him to do so. As we have noted, Heston represented a departure from the gray-flannel vision of masculinity personified by the likes of Cary Grant whose physical frame could not, anyway, contest with Heston's six-foot-two, 210-pound VistaVision build. Steven Cohan has suggested that, 'It was ultimately [Heston's] height more than anything else which forged his close identification with the epic genre that made him a star.' and, indeed, as the young Moses, Heston is costumed in just a loincloth so as to reveal his physique – a publicity stunt so transparent that *Time* magazine sneeringly labelled the film a 'Sexodus'.[62]

Heston was very conscious of the uniqueness of his looks and the way that his bony, angular face seemed to suggest another era: 'I don't look

like a modern man, and I'm seldom asked to play contemporary parts
. . . My appearance qualifies me for historic characterisations, going back
to the year one,' he wrote, adding:

> All the good modern parts go to Jack Lemmon or Cary Grant . . . You
> immediately believe in [Lemmon] as the junior executive of a corpora-
> tion and when people see me on horseback or in chainmail they seem
> to believe that I belong there.

Not that Heston was one to complain. He understood his unique
selling point, commenting:

> Not every star can play [a historical role] convincingly. I do not mean
> that as a judgement of anyone's acting ability. But can you picture
> Cary Grant in a toga or Elvis Presley in a suit of armour? It would be
> a complete contradiction of the public images they have worked so
> hard to establish.[63]

Besides, Heston was comfortable playing larger than life roles and all
which that entailed: 'I enjoy wearing costumes. I like portraying heroes
of antiquity whose values were grander and more spectacular than
those of today.'[64]

Following the triumphant release of *The Ten Commandments*, Charlton
Heston became a household name and he would remain equated with
the role of Moses throughout his life, and it is Moses, therefore, who
forms the bedrock of the archaeology of the actor. When he was next cast
as Ben-Hur the same moral loftiness and the same physical attributes he
had displayed in the DeMille epic were reactivated for Wyler's cameras.
His body was once more on exhibition – as he himself commented: 'My
costume consists largely of a damp rag [in the galley-slave sequences].'[65]
Heston well understood the importance of his physique in his films. 'I
have to make my living partly through my body,' he once told reporters;
'Your body is as much a part of what you do as your talent.'[66] Indeed,
Heston's body was so readily on display in *Ben-Hur* that he became
something of a homosexual icon, an image which was significantly
increased in the 1990s when the writer Gore Vidal publicly alleged that
he had written homosexual undertones into the scenes between Judah
and Messala – something which Heston vigorously and furiously denied
(Figure 4.27).[67]

Heston brought the same masculine physicality and moral upright-
ness to his next epics, *El Cid* (dir. Mann, 1961), the tale of the Christian
knight Rodrigo Diaz de Vivar who expelled the Moors from Spain, and
The Agony and the Ecstasy (dir. Reed, 1965) in which he performed as a
larger than life, angst-and-muscle-bound Michelangelo. He was back in
armour in 1965 for *The Warlord* (dir. Schaffner) playing a Norman knight
and in Victorian uniform as General Gordon in *Khartoum* in 1966 (dir.
Deardon). In 1965 Heston had also made a cameo appearance as John

Figure 4.27
'Once I had a secret love . . .': Stephen Boyd and Charlton Heston. *Ben-Hur* (1959). Studio publicity shot taken on set.

the Baptist in Stevens's *The Greatest Story Ever Told,* once more baring his chest as he waded waist-deep in the Colorado River to baptise Max von Sydow's Jesus. By this time Heston was recognised by millions throughout the world and his resonance in the epics of the 1950s and 1960s had become so deep that in 1978 one journalist even wrote that 'the standard Hollywood gag is that if God came to earth, most movie-goers wouldn't believe it unless he looked like Charlton Heston.'[68] Indeed, Heston's personal religious convictions added credibility to his epic characters and his upstanding personal life, which had helped him win the role of Moses, became his signature characteristic. Moses lies at the bottom of every Charlton Heston performance. Digging through the archaeological site that is Charlton Heston reveals a series of ethically upright hero 'types' and although the genres varied – epics, Westerns, science fiction,

CHARLTON HESTON: Actor, Father, Gun Collector, Outdoorsman, Life Member of the National Rifle Association.

"I've always spoken out on issues I feel strongly about. Voting, civil rights, defense, the environment. Also, the Bill of Rights.

"Why am I comfortable as a member of the NRA? Because I'm comfortable with the Bill of Rights. It says the right of the people to keep and bear arms shall not be infringed. That means, in this country, we get to choose. Americans exercise their right to own firearms for several reasons. For sport, for hunting, for collecting, for protection. They are all good reasons.

"I support the freedoms our Constitution guarantees. But democracy is fragile. It's threatened all the time from many quarters. Eternal vigilance is the price of liberty. The NRA helps maintain that vigil." **I'm the NRA.**

The NRA's lobbying organization, the Institute for Legislative Action, is the nation's largest and most influential protector of the Constitutional right to keep and bear arms. At every level of government and through grassroots efforts, the Institute guards against infringement upon the freedoms of law-abiding gun owners. If you would like to join the NRA or want more information about our programs and benefits, write J. Warren Cassidy, Executive Vice President, Box 37484, Dept. HE-1, Washington, D.C. 20013.

Paid for by the members of the National Rifle Association of America. © 1987

Figure 4.28
Republican ideologue and President of the NRA, Charlton Heston, 1997. Magazine advertisement.

to name a few – Moses' broad-shouldered brand of heroism informs them all. By the 1980s Heston had gained the position of Hollywood's 'elder statesman', a major moral and authoritative figure for the nation.

Yet by this time Heston had developed a new public persona as a Republican ideologue (Figure 4.28), a premonition of which was provided in his role as George Taylor in *Planet of the Apes* (dir. Schaffner, 1968) where, loincloth-clad and raging against American society, he seemed to reject the mixed-up values he had once held. In *Planet of the Apes* Heston's masculinity is explicit in the exposure of his hirsute musculature against which he is frequently seen holding a loaded rifle, which he also wields above his head in the manner of Moses brandishing his wooden staff. It was this image that was to be recalled again, notoriously, on 20 May 2000 at the 129th National Rifle Association convention when Heston declared that a potential Al Gore administration in Washington would take away his Second Amendment rights to bear arms. The journalist Army Archerd described the scene:

> [Charlton] Heston, in one of his most dramatic stances, with his chin jutted out, brandishing a gold-plated Colonial musket replica [rifle] above his head in a gesture that mimicked Moses when he lifted his staff to part the Red Sea, and in the same stentorian voice bellowed, 'I'll give up my gun when you take it from my cold, dead hands! I want to say those words again for everyone within the sound of my voice to hear and to heed, and especially you, Mr Gore, *from my cold dead hands*.[69]

This performance too must be seen as part of the same archaeological investigation of Heston's career because, for the Neoconservatives of America, Heston spoke with the authority of Moses, and it was widely thought that his authority had been handed to him from God. As Emile Raymond puts it:

> Heston embraced his identification with Moses and Christianity even ... with his dramatic video series *Charlton Heston Presents the Bible*. He enjoyed being associated with Moses not just because of the fame and the fortune the role brought him but because of the religious standards and traditions that the prophet represented.[70]

A 1996 poll revealed that Americans believed Charlton Heston to be one of the most significant and believable spokespersons in their country.[71] By that time, Heston's political outspokenness had become as much a part of his public persona as playing Moses. The archaeology of Charlton Heston forces us to dig very deep.

When Liz met Dick

A particularly intriguing form of movie stardom centres on the idea of a star's off-screen life finding resonance in the roles he or she plays on-screen, a matter, as it were, of life imitating art. The Hollywood studios often kept a careful look out for such naturally occurring phenomena in order to promote a blend between on-screen and off-screen worlds, but much of the time any kind of synergy came supported by some sort of marketing inventiveness. Theda Bara, as we have seen, was one of Hollywood's first sex symbols playing the notorious 'vamp' role in numerous pictures. She was promoted as a mysterious actress with an appropriately exotic background, the studio billing her as the

Figure 4.29
Cartoon lampooning *Cleopatra*. Left to right: Rex Harrison, Elizabeth Taylor, Joe
Mankiewicz, Richard Burton. *Cleopatra* (1963). Pressbook

Egyptian-born daughter of a French actress and an Italian sculptor. It
was claimed she had spent her early years in the Sahara Desert under
the shadow of the Sphinx, then moved to France to become a stage
actress. The studios called her the Serpent of the Nile and she was linked
to both mysticism and the occult – her very name was an anagram
for 'Arab Death', it was propounded. In reality, Bara had been born
Theodosia Burr Goodman in Cincinnati, Ohio; she had never visited
France, let alone Egypt, but she was willing to be manufactured into a
product and this compliancy thrust Bara into superstardom, the perfect
blend of on-screen and off-screen exotica.[72]

There is no better example of this extraordinary phenomenon than
the way in which the adulterous romance between the Elizabeth Taylor
(married to Eddie Fisher) and Richard Burton (wed to Sybil Burton) that
blossomed, flourished and exploded on the set of *Cleopatra* in early 1962
seemingly morphed into the historical world of Antony and Cleopatra
(Figure 4.29). As Ty Burr puts it, in the early 1960s, 'Elizabeth Taylor's

personal drama became more entertaining than her movies – because it appeared to be more truthful.'[73]

'I never wanted to be a queen! Cleopatra was a role, and I am an actor, so it was fun to play one, but it's not real. The real Cleopatra had an incredibly complicated life, and she had to be very, very canny to survive as long as she did.' Elizabeth Taylor was talking (in 2012) to Kim Kardashian who had, quite understandably, conflated Taylor and her on-screen portrayal.[74] The allure of Cleopatra for Hollywood had always lain in her legendary reputation for fabulousness, a facet of the Cleopatra tradition which has been sophisticatedly analysed by Lucy Hughes-Hallett: 'When Cleopatra becomes a movie, then frequently the movie becomes a kind of Cleopatra, deplorably, but thrillingly, spend-thrift.'[75] The historical Cleopatra VII is said to have enjoyed a lifestyle of excessive and fabulous wealth, an exotic opulence which we might now classify as 'conspicuous hyperconsumption', although in her own time this was labelled more succinctly (in Greek) as *tryphē* – a short word with a multivalent meaning: abundance, indulgence, the good life, too much of the good life and, of course, moral decline. Cleopatra VII was the personification of *tryphē* and so the alignment of Cleopatra to Elizabeth Taylor – a kind of superimposition, as it were – is reasonable. As Sally Riad has put, '[Cleopatra's] decadence was embodied by Taylor, with burgeoning accounts of her grotesquely excessive tastes and indulgent habits.'[76]

But the confusion of art and life acquired a new impetus when Elizabeth Taylor met Richard Burton. *Le scandale*, as Taylor and Burton later termed their affair, began when their work together on the *Cleopatra* set commenced in January 1962, after Mankiewicz had written enough patchy script material for them to start rehearsing and shooting.[77] 'For the first scene, there was no dialogue – we had to just look at each other,' Taylor recalled. 'And that was it – I was another notch.'[78] Walter Wanger, the much put-upon Producer of *Cleopatra*, recalled that very first scene of theirs in one of his many diary entries:

22 January 1962
Liz and Richard Burton played their first scene together. There comes a time during the making of a movie when the actors become the characters they play. This merger of real personality into the personality of the role has to take place if the performance is to be truly effective. This happened today.

The scene was written by JLM [Mankiewicz] so that the audience would be aware that Mark Antony and Cleopatra are attracted to one another, although they had little to say – the scene was Caesar's . . .

While other sections of the scene were being filmed, I noticed Liz and RB sitting next to each other on the sidelines, intently talking. Liz was radiant – elegant in a simple yellow silk gown. Burton was wearing a knee-length Roman toga that made him look handsome, arrogant and vigorous.

When they were called, they separated for a moment, then met on the set in their proper places. The cameras turned and the current was literally turned on. It was quiet, and you could almost feel the electricity between Liz and Burton.[79]

Mankiewicz already suspected that there was more going on than just electricity and this was confirmed when Burton triumphantly boasted of having sex with Elizabeth Taylor in the back of his Cadillac. A few days later (26 January 1962) the director confided in Wanger, who recalled:

Distressing news from JLM, who asked me to come to his room. 'I have been sitting on a volcano all alone for too long and I want to give you some facts you ought to know,' he said. 'Liz and Burton are not just *playing* Antony and Cleopatra!'[80]

From Mankiewicz's throw-away sentence, almost said in jest, a whole mythology was born.

No other actress ever embodied the myth of Cleopatra as Elizabeth Taylor came to do. By 1962 she was already Hollywood's bad girl – having stolen Eddie Fisher from Debbie Reynolds – she was one of movieland's greatest libertines: 'What do you expect me to do? Sleep *alone*?' she had once asked the gossip columnist Hedda Hoppa when reproached about the Fisher affair.[81] Taylor was also Cleopatra-like in her wealth and her power; already a wealthy woman, her million-dollar fee for *Cleopatra* had bought her an independence unknown and unobtainable to most women in the 1960s. In Richard Burton, Elizabeth Taylor met her Antony. Burton has received many biographical assessments and he is generally (probably correctly) presented as a man of tremendous talent but of weak will, too easily conquered by women, booze and pleasure (Figure 4.30). His Hollywood years are usually presented as a fall from grace, the period when he compromised his talent as a brilliant Shakespearean stage actor for the lure of movie stardom and the trashy lifestyle of Tinseltown; there may be some truth to this too, although in later years Elizabeth Taylor responded angrily to any such suggestions.[82] Whatever the reality of the dynamics which drove both Burton and Taylor, on the surface the Cleopatran echoes found in both persons are easy to spot, as Hughes-Hallett has elegantly elucidated:

She is a famous seductress, fabulously rich, on the loose (though actually married to Eddie Fisher) after the death of her Caesar, the charismatic film producer Mike Todd. Burton and Taylor's first meeting has a professional function (as did Antony and Cleopatra's at Tarsus), but passion seizes them, they drink, they swear, they brazenly flaunt their impropriety. They squander enormous sums on jewels and parties. She is jealous and passionate. In sex, her greed and energy are both prodigious and so are the pleasures she offers. He is feebly aware of the call of duty (in the shape of his wife). He tries to leave her and

Figure 4.30
Richard Burton relaxing on set during the filming of Cleopatra's grand entrance into Rome. Candid shot, 1962.

she stages hysterical demonstrations of her love for him, even faking a suicide attempt. They part temporarily. His British (cool, northern, commonsensical) friends attempt to separate him from the seductress of Hollywood – land of heat, luxury and loose morals – but her allure is too potent. They come together again. They fight, reunite, fight, reunite. Their union is glittering, public, shocking, hubristic. Finally, he is destroyed by it. Drunken, self-indulgent, his proper, honourable work on the English stage long neglected, he dies, a tragic might-have-been whose huge potential (so the story goes) has been dissipated on a love affair. But this Cleopatra is not destroyed with him. [For the rest of her life] . . . she traded on her Cleopatra-like reputation . . . What Taylor-Cleopatra enjoys, and offers, is excess.[83]

Figure 4.31
Elizabeth Taylor coifs Richard Burton's hair before the cameras roll. She wears furs (it
was her day off). Both are clearly happy. Joe Mankiewicz hovers at the side. Candid shot,
1962.

Yet these rich Cleopatran echoes found in Hughes-Hallett's reading of
the Taylor-Burton affair were, remarkably, already being highlighted
during the movie's production. Taylor herself had already identified
with Cleopatra before the Burton affair had begun. She felt that 'Mike
Todd . . . had been to her what Julius Caesar had been to Cleopatra.'[84]
Now Antony-Burton would take his place (Figure 4.31). According
to Wanger's diary (5 March 1962), the Cleopatran synergies were
ever-deepening:

> Today we filmed the bath scene. In it Germanicus has come from
> Rome to get Antony to return. Antony refuses to see him because he
> is so happy with Cleopatra – to hell with Rome, his wife and duty.
>   Cleopatra comes in to see Antony, who is in the bath with three
> handmaidens pouring water over him and sponging him down while
> he banters with them. When Cleopatra enters, the handmaids take off
> and Antony comes out of the bath looking very chic and masculine in
> a toga. They continue a beautiful love scene.

JLM's dialogue is right out of real life, with Cleopatra telling how she will feel if Antony leaves her. 'Love can stab the heart', she says. It was hard to tell whether Liz and Burton were reading lines or living the parts.[85]

And three days later:

8 March 1962
The papers today had a story that Burton would never marry Liz. He was quoted as saying he has no intention of divorcing Sybil.

The timing was perfect – we were filming the scene in which Cleopatra finds Antony has deserted her. She enters his bedroom, takes a dagger and stabs all his clothes. Then she slashes the drapes. She ends up cutting the bed to ribbons and collapses in sobs on it. It was a difficult, strenuous scene, but Liz did it all with only a few takes. She really went wild and lashed out in such a frenzy that she banged her hand. We had to send for Dr Pennington.[86]

The film's marketing and publicity executive, Jack Brodsky, writing home to America from Rome on 20 April 1962, was greedily excited by the potential the scandal offered the film's promotion:

To a man [everyone] is absolutely dying to see Cleo, thrilled by what they see here, excited by the gossip. The public may call Taylor names, but they can't wait to see her. Wanger made a good point about all the [slurs]: Ingrid Bergman was a saint to all her fans when she played Joan of Arc, and when she got into trouble she cracked and destroyed her image. Taylor is the exact opposite, that is her principal attraction, and why she's playing Cleopatra . . .[87]

Brodsky was correct; even if the affair was condemned by the Vatican (and its acceptance was by no means universal) the public devoured the stories of the infidelity with relish. Castigated, loathed, denounced by some, or venerated, treasured and idolised by others, Ian Lloyd reports an on-set incident which had a lasting effect on the Taylor-Cleopatra assimilation:

[Taylor] was due to film Cleopatra's entrance into Rome . . . This necessitated thousands of extras. The actress feared that she would be booed or even shot at, but the crowd, which had been primed to chant, 'Cleopatra! Cleopatra! Cleopatra!' eventually changed the wording to 'Liz! Liz! Liz!' Elizabeth was greatly moved by the display of affection from the Italian extras. 'The tears were pouring down my face', she later recalled. [Burton] stood by, clearly mesmerised by the effect his lover had on the crowd.[88]

By the spring of 1962 the rumours of the movie stars' adultery had gone worldwide, and Taylor-Burton innuendo was everywhere. The

Figure 4.32
Merv Griffin lampoons Taylor's Cleopatra, 1962. Studio production shot.

Perry Como Show ran a comic *Cleopatra* sketch in which a slave named Eddie kept getting in Mark Antony's way and the *Merv Griffin Show* followed this up with the host's own drag performance of Elizabeth Taylor as Cleopatra (Figure 4.32), while the popular musical entertainer Julie Prowse performed a review entitled 'I'm Cleo, the Nympho of the Nile' which included some risqué slurs about Taylor's vampish reputation:

She uses her pelvis just like Elvis . . .
There was not a man she couldn't get
That was Cleo's problem on and off the set.[89]

Life in Rome was a debauch and, having found better things to do with
her time, Taylor was not much committed to doing hard work. A memo
to Fox's President, Spyros Skouras, dated 23 June 1962, notes that a
great weight had been lifted from his mind when 'you were told that the
girl [i.e. Taylor] was officially finished (filming).'[90] A breakdown of her
working hours while in Rome follows:

ELIZABETH TAYLOR IN ITALY

Total production days (no Sundays & holidays)	226
Total days no call	48
Total days worked	121½
Of total days worked Miss Taylor was late on 99 days (or total 53 hours)	
Total days she did not work	56½
Absent because of her fault	34½
Illness	33½
Refused call	1
Cancelled because of	
Rain	3
Cold weather	1
Travel to Ischia	1
Mankiewicz illness	2
Days off per contract	3
Soundby call – not used	2
Saturdays on 6 day week	22
	56½

Taylor and Burton ate together, drank together, fought each other, made
loud and passionate love and shopped – how they shopped! Stories
of the reckless ways in which Taylor and Burton conducted their very
public affair were matched by the tales of the enormous amounts of
money squandered by, and spent on, Elizabeth Taylor. In Rome she
lived in a fourteen-room villa faced in pink marble; every evening the
cigarette holders, match books, candles, flowers and tablecloths were
changed to coordinate with her dress – she had brought three hundred
of them with her and threw each away after one wearing. In an attempt
to keep her, Fisher bought her an emerald necklace worth a quarter of a
million dollars; to win her back Burton bought her a necklace of Egyptian
scarabs 'going back to the time of Cleopatra'. Late at night, after bathing
by candlelight, she slept in nightgowns made by Dior.[91] The profligacy
continued in the post-*Cleopatra* years, of course: the Krupp diamond,
the Cartier-Burton diamond, the jet, the yacht, the furs, the Renoirs,
Monets and Van Goghs, the Persian carpets thrown out because the pet

dogs were never house-trained, the entourage of children, governesses, secretaries, hairdressers, nurses and Siamese cats in diamond-studded collars.

Of course, as with the historical Cleopatra, the real Elizabeth Taylor was a shrewd businesswoman and an adroit financial manager, but such dreary facts have nothing to do with the legend of Elizabeth Taylor and Richard Burton. His hangovers, her binging and even her fatness are read as audacious signs of abundance and this is the direct legacy of *Cleopatra* (see Text Box 4.7). Yet the reviews written at the time of the film's premiere were not necessarily kind and, as though getting revenge over the adulterous couple, they often used the Cleopatran imagery to highlight the discords between the historic nobility of Cleopatra and the brilliance of Antony and the pedestrian ordinariness of Taylor and Burton:

> Miss Taylor is a plump, young American matron in a number of Egyptian costumes and makeups. She needs do no more than walk around the throne room to turn Alexandria into Beverly Hills . . . The tedium is only occasionally lightened by the vulgarity of the display.[92]

> Antony and Cleopatra, it must be admitted, remain very much Mr Burton and Miss Taylor.[93]

A year after *le scandale* had broken in Rome, Walter Wanger was back in New York where he was writing up his *Cleopatra* diary entries for publication. He wrote one final entry, dated 7 March 1963, which he used as an opportunity to reflect on the year's events and in doing so he drew again on the familiar Cleopatran tropes:

> Elizabeth and Burton are now in London . . . Thanks to Elizabeth and *Cleopatra*, Burton has become a very big star. His salary has tripled in the past two years.
>
> As for Elizabeth, one thing is certain: she is made from far sterner stuff than the rest of us . . . During the year *Cleopatra* was in production I watched Liz mature as an actress as well as a woman . . . she has emerged as one of the most important stars in motion pictures today . . .
>
> The fact is that everyone everywhere is interested in Elizabeth. It is not a far stretch of the imagination to compare Elizabeth with Cleopatra. She has the intelligence and temperament of the Egyptian Queen – and she has the honesty and directness that characterise all great people . . .
>
> When Elizabeth and I began *Cleopatra* four years ago, we hoped it would be a great motion picture, one the world would be excited over. I feel we have achieved our goal. There will never be another motion picture like *Cleopatra*, just as there will never be another woman like her – or Elizabeth.[94]

Figure 4.33
Burton-Antony and Taylor-Cleopatra. *Cleopatra* (1963). Production still.

It is not difficult to believe in the collusion that occurred between
producers, publicists and actors in manufacturing a star image. The
construction of a star like Elizabeth Taylor is all about excess – excess of
meaning ascribed to her as an individual and to her pairing with Burton
as the ultimate Hollywood couple. This superfluity is mirrored in the
lifestyle of Taylor and Burton for if it were not excessive (mansions,
swimming pools, jets, diamonds, booze, parties) would we believe in
their star status? In Golden Age Hollywood excess had a positive value
for the studios and nothing signalled excess more than epic movies
themselves. It was fitting therefore that the financial excesses of *Cleopatra*
and the grotesque and unnecessary profligacy of its production should
be reflected by the baroque image-construction of its principal stars and
their off-screen lifestyle (Figure 4.33).

Text Box 4.7   *Cleopatra*: **The Fantastic Story That Shook the World – TWICE!**

Figure 4.34
Screenplay's *Cleopatra* issue, 1963.

For several years following the release of Cleopatra, the world remained fascinated by the Burton-Taylor affair. Countless newspapers and magazines ran stories of the stars' romance and their fabled lifestyle. Many of them used the familiar image of Elizabeth Taylor embodying the perceived excesses and sexuality of the historical Cleopatra as the central journalistic motif. In the summer of 1963 when the Cleomania was at its height, the popular movie magazine *Screenplay* issued a special glossy *Cleopatra* issue in which the rhetoric fixates on the Taylor-Cleopatra integration:

The *Cleopatra* Miracle

Two thousand years ago, the greatest love story of all time ended in the destruction of an Empire. Two years ago in Rome, it almost happened again. Here at last is the fantastic story of how history came close to repeating itself . . .

Strange are the ways of love. Centuries ago, queen Cleopatra and the great Roman senator and warrior Mark Antony fell hopelessly in love. Because of their mutual passion and devotion to each other, many thousands died, whole armadas were destroyed, cities went up in flame, an empire crumbled and the lovers both met deaths violently. Today, Elizabeth Taylor is madly in love with Richard Burton. Their mutual passion has broken up two homes, caused worldwide scandal, and may well wind up disastrously. Ah what price such overwhelming love!

Liz and Cleo: an amazing comparison

Both Elizabeth and Cleopatra were first touched by fame and fortune as young girls. Both women became objects of adoration which grew as they themselves grew from childhood into women of fantastic beauty. Cleopatra was still a teenager when she ascended the throne of Egypt. Elizabeth Taylor was a teenager when she won international recognition as the star of *International Velvet*.

Cleopatra declared herself the New Isis, stating that she was a reincarnation of the ancient Egyptian goddess; Elizabeth was created a goddess by millions of theatre-goers on every continent in the world who line up at the box office to see her films.

Cleopatra was honoured not only for her beauty but for her charm, her wit, her indefinite ability to enchant not only men but women. Elizabeth Taylor has these qualities, too.

Both these women have lived in worlds overpowered by giant and colossal events and places. Cleopatra reigned amid the vastness of ancient Egypt and the Roman Empire. Liz is the undisputed queen of motion pictures, the single most powerful and influential media of communication in the world today.

Both Cleopatra and Elizabeth have weathered tragedies in their lives. Each in her respective era struggled to overcome their many difficulties. Cleopatra was suddenly toppled from her rightful throne but, with the aid of her beauty, intellect and determination, regained it once again. Elizabeth Taylor was on the verge of death and came back fighting with a miraculous recovery made even more dramatic by her triumphant winning of the golden statuette named Oscar.

Cleopatra and Taylor have become synonymous in the minds of the public. The image of the Egyptian Queen will always be that of the actress despite what the history books might say.

In essence, both women loved well but not always too wisely. In essence, both women gained a great deal from life and love but had to give up as much in return. In her own time, Cleopatra was much-loved, but also much-maligned. In her time, here and now, Liz has reached public heights and public depths as far as world opinion is concerned. But, like her ancient counterpart, Elizabeth continues to live her life as she feels best – allowing no one and nothing to get in the way of the dictates of her own heart. Each woman had much happiness and also experienced much personal suffering – only time will tell how later life treats Elizabeth Taylor. We hope and pray the similarity between the two Queens ends with life – for in death, Cleopatra's end, despite its nobility, was much too violent.

Problems in Casting: Rita Hayworth's Salome

The Hollywood movie star as a construct has three components: the real person, the reel person (the on-screen character) and the star's persona. This latter persona exists independently of, but is a combination of, the former two – and when put together the result is a multi-faceted star-image. The machinery of Golden Age Hollywood looked to promote stars in a way that pushed their reel personas (their archaeology of performance, that is) and their created personas into the limelight while messy real-life problems like addiction, homosexuality, divorce and murder were circumspectly hidden away (unless, as in the case of Burton-Taylor, it could be harnessed for controlled marketing). Occasionally the Hollywood machine met with difficulties in the manufacturing process where the required result did not work. A good example of this misal-liance occurs with Rita Hayworth's one foray into epic filmmaking: her appearance in *Salome*.

When *Salome* opened in March 1953, the 'Spanish peasant girl' who had been born Margarita Carmen Cansino (dark-haired and low-browed) in 1918 in Brooklyn, New York, had been transformed by the Hollywood publicity machine into flame-haired beauty, Rita Hayworth', America's Love Goddess' – a term dreamed up by the press after she had become the most glamorous screen idol of the 1940s.[95] At the time she played princess Salome, the girl who, notoriously, danced for Herod and demanded the head of John the Baptist, Hayworth had given up her crown as the world's reigning movie queen, had divorced two husbands, had found a new love and had been crowned as a genuine princess (the wife of

Ali Khan); she had, though, lost the love of her prince charming and, returning from Europe, had re-entered Hollywood on a cloud of even greater celebrity. No wonder the press and the armies of fans clamoured for a view of her. Columbia Pictures, the studio that had financed, marketed and exhibited *Salome* happily capitalised on Hayworth's return and eulogised about the on-screen/off-screen resonances between the real-life princess-actress and the biblical character she portrayed:

> Probably never in the history of Hollywood has there been a more apt casting of a star than Rita Hayworth as Salome, that seductive princess whose dancing has held the imagination of the world, whose personality and temperament have absorbed the creative minds of writers and artists throughout time. Miss Hayworth is a renowned beauty, a dramatic actress of importance, a dancer of exceptional ability. She combines in her screen person all that is exciting, whether she is playing the good-bad girl as in *Gilda* . . . or [the] romantic young woman as in . . . *Cover Girl*.[96]

In the words of the glossy advertising brochure which accompanied the screening:

> Miss Hayworth is one of those rarities among Hollywood's reigning beauties: a top-flight dramatic actress, a top-flight dancer, a fabled woman of the world. There could be no possible alternative in the role of Salome, that proud, passionate, seductive princess whose graceful dancing steps left her impress on the world for all time.

At the age of thirty-three Rita Hayworth was far too old for the role of Herodias' teenage daughter, and in reality the part did not interest her at all; nevertheless much of *Salome*'s pre-premiere marketing focused on projecting the connections between the actress's obvious beauty (Figure 4.35) and dance talent and the legendary beauty and infamous dance moves of the biblical character she was contracted to play. Indeed, the whole concept of putting the Salome story on screen only worked because of its link to Hayworth. Based on the religious novella *The Good Tidings* by William Sidney, the script had been written by Jesse Lasky Jr, Harry Kleiner and Robert Ardrey for Hayworth's own company, Beckworth Productions, for a Columbia Pictures release. The autocratic and tyrannical studio head, Harry Cohn, urged them to write a vehicle for Hayworth, 'that has balls and is big'. Cohn, who had crafted Hayworth's early career, insisted that finding a vehicle to suit Hayworth's talents to promote her return to Hollywood and to capitalise on the popularity of the biblical epic was essential to Columbia Pictures' survival. Only Hayworth, he insisted, was capable of making the leap into epic pictures because only she had the guaranteed box-office pull.

To secure the picture's success, Academy Award Winner William Dieterle was appointed as director, in spite of his alleged communist

Figure 4.35
Rita Hayworth, Love Goddess, pin-up and forces' sweetheart, poses 'on her own bed in her own home' (as *Life* magazine put it), 1941.

sympathies which brought him to the attention of the McCarthy enquiry (although he was never blacklisted as such). With cinematography by Charles Lang, a music score by George Duning and Daniele Amfitheatrof, and Hayworth's costumes designed by Jean Louis, *Salome* was given Columbia Pictures' full attention and a lavish budget to match (and to recoup the cost, the elaborate costumes and monumental sets were reused in Columbia's 'B' pictures, *Serpent of the Nile* and *Slaves of Babylon*). Moreover, Cohn spared no expense in hiring Hayworth's on-screen co-stars, each of them considered by Hollywood to be acting royalty: Stewart Granger as Hayworth's love-interest, Centurion Claudius,

Charles Laughton as Herod, Dame Judith Anderson as Herodias and Sir Cedric Hardwicke in a cameo role as the Emperor Tiberius.

Of course, Hayworth had little room for manoeuvre in her acceptance of the role of Princess Salome. She had renewed her contract with Columbia for seven years and besides, her relationship with Cohn had always been fraught and had operated on one founding principle: Cohn had discovered and created Hayworth and felt that he owned her. His ownership of Hayworth operated on both a professional and a sexual level. Expecting intimate favours from actresses in exchange for picture contracts was part of the Cohn style and although similar allegations of sexual harassment could be made of many Hollywood producers of the time, Cohn's casting couch was considered the most notorious in Hollywood. But Hayworth managed to hold off his many advances decade after decade although her marriages (first to Edward Judson, then to Orson Wells and subsequently to Ali Khan) never stopped Cohn's endeavours.[97] Inevitably this unwholesome situation led to high tension between the actress and the producer and as Cohn's bullying increased, his grip on Hayworth's career became only tighter. Hayworth was Columbia's most valuable property and Cohn kept her under contract because she made the studio a lot of money. During the many years they worked together, each did their best to aggravate the other and make each other's lives miserable, yet in spite of their hostilities, the lengthy work relationship they shared produced financially lucrative and artistically acclaimed results.

As Cohn had anticipated, critics could not fail to see the clearly promoted synergies between Rita Hayworth and the character of the biblical Salome. As Bosley Crowther duly noted in his opening-night review:

> Considering the popular reputation of a girl named Salome, who had something to do with the unhinging of John the Baptist's head, and considering the wide-eyed admiration in which Rita Hayworth is held, it is not surprising to find the two young ladies brought together and exploited in a film . . . *Salome* . . . is a flamboyant Technicolored romance, based vaguely on a biblical tale wherein the highly regarded Miss Hayworth plays the legendary dancer at Herod's court . . . the climate is mainly saturated with the elegance of the heroine and the fascination of her. She is the object of all eyes.[98]

By and large the press regarded *Salome* as a colourful, entertaining, spectacle and if the movie was not profound, deep or cutting-edge it was at least, in the words of Orval Hopkins, 'a gee-whiz picture':

> Gee-whiz what sets; gosh, what costumes; holy smokes, what Technicolor . . . The panoramic shots in colour are tremendous; the scenes aboard a Roman galley, the slaves seating in their manacles, are startling; the acting, some of it at any rate, is of the scenery-chewing variety. Altogether, this is a whale of a spectacle.[99]

And yet beyond the thrill of the visuals, Hopkins expressed some doubt as to rationale of the storyline. 'The matter of the dance and the death of John the Baptist are out of sequence with the biblical account,' he puzzled, adding that ultimately, 'the picture is . . . a confused and muddy business'. Crowther saw something similar: 'In aggrandising the lady [Hayworth]', he noted, 'the gentlemen who wrote the script have taken considerable liberties with the biblical story of the fate of John the Baptist and also with later fables of Salome.'[100]

What gave rise to this critical consternation? As we have seen, it was perfectly acceptable for epic movies, especially biblical ones, to take liberties with their source materials so in what way, then, was the 1953 film more egregious in its miscalculation of the use of the plot line and in what way was Hayworth's princess out of step with the Salome tradition? By the turn of the twentieth century a Salome obsession was witnessed in her two most famous incarnations: Oscar Wilde's 1899 sublime, erotic and highly-charged one-act play, *Salomé*, and its brilliant and bold 1905 operatic adaptation by Richard Strauss. Both artists made the princess the focal point of the action and it was the perversion of lust and desire of Salome rather than Herodias' vengeance on John the Baptist that took centre stage in both renditions of the tradition. The kissing of John's severed head, which occurs in both stage accounts, testifies to the enduring notion of the virgin whore complex, a perversion of Salome's purity tainted by lustful desires. It was Wilde and Strauss who also introduced the world to the 'Dance of the Seven Veils', a phenomenon which quickly grew in popularity thanks to the performances of Maude Allen, billed as 'The Salomé Dancer' whose dance-show, *The Vision of Salomé*, took Europe by storm. It was the Dance of the Seven Veils that ushered the vampish Salome into the modern era and in 1908 it was Vitograph who first put her on dance show screen in a production entitled simply *Salome, or the Dance of the Seven Veils*. Thereafter, on-screen dancing Salomes were churned out with monotonous regularity, although most of them are forgettable until, that is, the great Theda Bara, Hollywood's silent-era sex-bomb cornered the Salome market in 1918 in the Fox production of *Salome*. Theda Bara gave the screen a Salome who, dressed in George Hopkins' bizarre concoctions of gauze veils, chiffon scarves and strategically strung ropes of pearls, was 'every minute the vampire, in manner, movement and expression'.[101] The 1910s was the age of the cinematic sex-kitten and bad girls were all the rage, but especially the bad girls of history – Bara's forte. *Variety*'s review of her performance noted that the 'scarcity of her attire . . . makes it most fascinating', and, indeed, it was in her peek-a-boo wickedness that Bara's Judean princess found lasting effect by inspiring a myriad of imitations – even some of a comic nature.[102] *Sadie Salome (Go Home)*, for instance, was a hit ragtime song written by Irving Berlin in 1919 for Fanny Brice to perform; it was directly inspired by Theda Bara's exotic screen cavortings but made funny by the relocation of a latter-day Salome in Brooklyn, New York City. It follows the story of a homely Jewish boy, Mose, upset to find that

Sadie, his sweetheart, has left home to take up a most unorthodox of all professions – stripping. Seeing her perform on the burlesque stage in the style of *Salome*, Mose is compelled to shout out from the auditorium, in a catchy, jaunty, tune:

> Don't do that dance, I tell you Sadie
> That's not a bus'ness for a lady!
> Most ev'rybody knows
> That I'm your loving Mose
> Oy! Oy! Oy! Oy!
> Where is your clothes?
> You better go and get your dresses
> Ev'ryone's got the op'ra glasses
> Oy! such a sad disgrace
> No one looks in your face
> Sadie Salome, go home!

By the 1920s Salome had secured herself a place not only on-screen but also in vaudeville and burlesque and 'Salome sets' were popularly performed by striptease artists throughout America and in Europe where cabarets and Music Hall competed with Cinemas for audiences. When the famous Russian actress Alla Nazimova came to film her straight adaptation of Wilde's play in 1923 (dir. Bryant), with costumes and sets based closely on the decadent drawings which Aubrey Beardsley had created for the published edition of Wilde's drama, she nevertheless could not resist the temptation to lampoon the excesses of the story. Her cast, allegedly all homosexuals and lesbians, were carefully chosen to pervert the stereotypes that had developed in the retelling of the Salome tradition over the previous half-century. However, in Nazimova's *Salome* the polarised image of Salome as killer and youthful entertainer was still realised. We should not forget that the silent-screen Salomes are the focal point, in 1950, of Billy Wilder's *Sunset Boulevard* and that Norma Desmond, in her gloomy old mansion, dreams of her screen comeback in the role of Salome.

It is easy to understand the critical consternation shown by reviewers to the Technicolor, WideScreen reworking of the old familiar story, given that in 1953 Rita Hayworth's Salome performs the Dance of the Seven Veils not to secure the execution of John the Baptist but in order to save his life. The *Salome* film-brochure provides a brief scenario:

> In the time of Christ, Galilee is ruled by licentious King Herod (Charles Laughton) and his scheming wife (Herodias), both of whom fear the preaching of the prophet John the Baptist (Alan Badel). Salome (Rita Hayworth), daughter of Herodias by her first marriage, is returned from Rome to Galilee by Tiberius (Sir Cedric Hardwicke), under the escort of Claudius (Stewart Granger), commander of the Roman legions in Galilee and a secret disciple of John the Baptist. When

Herod imprisons John, Claudius tries and fails to obtain assistance for him from Roman governor Pontius Pilate (Basil Sidney). Salome, convinced by Claudius of John's message, determines to ask his life for a boon after she dances the Dance of the Seven Veils for Herod. Salome's performance does excite the lustful king; Herodias, watching, wins Herod's consent for John's execution before the girl's sensuous dance is completed. When the Head of John the Baptist is brought into the hall, Salome denounces her mother as a murderess and, with Claudius, quits the palace. Aware of the enormity of his own crime, Herod seeks cringing comfort from his High Priest Ezra (Maurice Schwartz), who prays instead for John the Baptist.

The final scene is particularly crucial: Claudius and Salome, having fled the chaos and carnage of Herod's court are seen listening to Jesus preach the Sermon on the Mount. The camera moves in on them, showing Salome dressed all in white, her head modestly veiled, her eyes misty with tears. The final title appears: 'This was the Beginning'. We are left in no doubt that Salome was among the first of all Christians (Colour Plate 16).

For some critics, *Salome* was, 'a bizarre and even disquieting experience ... wholly fake; even its vulgarity strik[ing] one as lifeless.'[103] *Variety* even reported a London-based campaign which called for *Salome* to be withdrawn from cinemas because it was 'a shameful perversion of the Bible and a blot on Hollywood's record'.[104] In his masterful biography of Charles Laughton, Simon Callow declares *Salome* to be 'madly misconceived', largely because Harry Cohn had 'insisted that the star, Miss Hayworth, be (a) virginal, and (b) Christian.'[105]

There is little doubt that William Dieterle and Harry Cohn created a *Salome* that looked back to the Biblical silent movies of the 1910s and the early 1920s. It is inconceivable that Cohn was unaware of the Theda Bara version of the story, and if he knew of Nazimova's adaptation, then he probably knew too that it was a box-office flop that left the movie star bankrupt. The 1953 film, however, although informed by the Salome bad-girl tradition of the 1910s, instinctively moves away from it since both Bara's and Nazimova's Salomes were flapper-princesses-cum-vamps out for good times and murderous ends, and such blatant displays of on-screen degeneracy were no longer permissible (or wanted) in postwar Hollywood. The Hays Code insisted, after all, that 'No picture shall be produced that will lower the moral standards of those who see it. Hence the sympathy of the audience should never be thrown to the side of crime, wrongdoing, evil or sin' and that 'Correct standards of life ... shall be presented.' As we know, Hollywood's epic movies of the early 1950s were both timely and lucrative antidotes to the creative oppression of the Code, reflecting as they did America's postwar commitment to Christianity and moral rectitude.

In this climate of self-censorship and the promotion of wholesome American family values, Columbia Pictures could not afford to tamper with Rita Hayworth's lucrative box-office appeal which had been so carefully crafted during the 1940s. In spite of Hayworth's divorce from Eddie Judson, her marriage to Orson Wells (the press nicknamed the couple 'Beauty and the Brain'), the breakdown of that relationship, subsequent affairs with David Niven, Victor Mature and Howard Hughes (among others), and her marriage to the playboy prince Ali Khan, Rita's public image remained remarkably untarnished. The 1940s saw her reach superstardom with a string of screen hits and while Hayworth's romances were covered in the gossip columns, so were her war effort contributions, such as her charity work for the British War Relief Association of Southern California and her work at the Hollywood Canteen; she even toured with United Service Organisation (USO) to military hospitals and training camps.

During the Second World War Rita Hayworth's wholesome image was carefully utilised by the US government in a major publicity campaign, in which she became a much-loved household name bringing comfort to the boys at the front line of the war effort and inspiration to their wives and girlfriends at home. Regular mass exposure in magazines and newspapers and public appearances helped create her wartime role (alongside Betty Grable) as America's Sweetheart, every soldier's girlfriend. For her part, Hayworth enjoyed lucrative advertising contracts promoting a myriad of consumer products: household goods and products including toffee, cola, margarine and, of course, cosmetics. The employment of her image in these wholesome family-focused campaigns was matched in glossy fan-magazines such as *Silver Screen* and *Photoplay* which promoted Rita as the glamour girl, the most desired woman in the world, the 'American Love Goddess'.

As *Salome* went into pre-production it became clear that Rita Hayworth could not be moulded into a latter-day vamp. In spite of her glamour image and the romantic vicissitudes of her off-screen life, to have moulded Hayworth, at this junction of her career, to fit the expectations of a *femme-fatale* Salome would have been detrimental to Rita's carefully constructed and monitored star persona. As Alice Bach succinctly puts it, 'an out of control dominating sex goddess was the subject of horror films [and] hardly the domain of a box-office star like Rita, who was not the sort to be cast against audience sympathy.'[106] In the public consciousness Rita Hayworth could, seemingly, do no wrong. It figured that her Salome would have to follow suit. Thus in a piece of advance publicity published in March 1953, *Life* magazine ran an article entitled 'Salome, Nice Girl' (Figure 4.36).

The full-page image which accompanies the story is a telling testimony of the power of the Salome tradition: Hayworth, in veil number seven, the flesh-coloured body suit designed for her by Jean Louis, is shown shedding veil number six with obvious abandon. Her image is set against Aubrey Beardsley's striking black and white print depicting the gory climax of Oscar Wilde's play, as the princess takes the severed head of the Baptist into her hands, lifts it eye-level, and kisses

RITA HAYWORTH IS A WINSOME SALOME AGAINST BACKDROP OF DRAWING BY AUBREY BEARDSLEY SHOWING A LESS AMIABLE VIEW OF THE BIBLICAL DANCER

Salome, Nice Girl

RITA UNVEILS IN A WORTHY CAUSE

Most authorities since St. Mark have regarded Salome as at least a willing accessory in the killing of John the Baptist by her stepfather Herod. But the record is being set to rights by a new movie called *Salome*. Its heroine, played by Rita Hayworth, is seen to be a nice good-natured Idumaean girl who in history's most famous dance routine strips off six of her seven veils—the one above is No. 6—in an effort to save John, not to do him in.

Figure 4.36
'Salome, Nice Girl'. *Life* magazine, 1953.

its blood-dripping mouth. Hayworth's pose seems flippant in contrast to the cruel starkness of Beardsley's image; flinging her yellow veil into the air, she appears to cast off the weight of two millennia's-worth of the Salome tradition. She is setting the record straight, as the accompanying text duly emphasises:

> Most authorities since St Mark regarded Salome as at least a willing
> accessory in the killing of John the Baptist . . . but the record is being
> set straight by a new movie called *Salome*. Its heroine, played by Rita
> Hayworth [is a] nice . . . Idumean girl who . . . strips off her seven
> veils . . . in an effort to save John not to do him in.

This egregious overwriting of the ingrained Salome tradition was given
its most fluent articulation in a host of advance publicity articles gathered together in the *Salome* pressbook, all of which were intended for
mass distribution in newspapers and magazines. Typically, one such
article notes that Hayworth's Salome was simply 'a girl from Galilee',
although, unable to free itself completely of the old Salome stereotype, it
admits that she was also 'a tantalising princess whose dancing enthralled
a king and his court'. It continues by emphasising that Salome's life
story witnessed the momentous shift in civilisation from pagan idolatry
into Christian sanctity:

> Salome lived in an era when a new civilisation, a new way of life,
> was coming into being. Product of the past, Salome embodied in
> her person all the savagery, all the sensuous passion of the barbaric
> time which was to disappear. Alive to beauty and to love and to the
> promise before her, Salome today personifies the eternal contradic-
> tion, a disturbing, delightful embodiment of all that is good and
> bad in mankind . . . Long before filming began . . . Dieterle [was]
> discussing both the girl and her time with historians, research
> workers and religionists. Was she good? Was she bad? Was she
> both? Was Herodias, her mother, the evil genius behind those 26
> lines in Matthew and Mark? Neither . . . the Vulgate . . . or the King
> James Version provided the answers . . . Writers and artists [have
> all] differed in their interpretations; Salome was seductive, no ques-
> tion of that. But was Salome a victim of court intrigues, of maternal
> jealousies? Was Salome herself a figure of evil or was she the lover
> and the beloved, a woman who inspired and returned a soldier's
> passion?

For her part, and by emphasising the Salome-Claudius romance,
Hayworth 'gave numerous publicity interviews in which she portrayed
Salome as a nice girl who'd gotten a raw deal from love', thereby essen-
tially telling her own sorry story of failed romances.[107]

Virginal, (proto-) Christian, simply a 'girl from Galilee', a 'nice
Idumean girl' (whose Jewishness is completely overlooked both in the
movie and in its marketing), Rita Hayworth's 'Salome, nice girl' is, of
course, an abstraction masterminded by a Hollywood publicity campaign. And yet the construction was worth the effort: to bring the legendary biblical dance-seductress into the orbit of Hollywood's hottest
dancing Love Goddess was, for Harry Cohn, nonetheless a sure-fire
route to success.'

By 1953 cinema audiences had become familiar with Rita Hayworth in two on-screen reel personas. First, there was Hayworth the Hoofer, a superlatively gifted dancer with a string of musical box-office hits to her name including *The Strawberry Blonde* (dir. Walsh, 1941), *You'll Never Get Rich* (dir. Landfield, 1941), *You Were Never Lovelier* (dir. Seiter, 1942) and, most successfully, *Cover Girl* (dir. Vidor, 1942), in which she tripped the light fantastic with the likes of Fred Astaire and Gene Kelly. Then there was Hayworth the troubled femme fatale in *film noir* classics such as *Blood and Sand* (dir., Mamoulian, 1941), *Gilda* (dir. Vidor, 1946), *The Lady From Shanghai* (dir. Wells, 1947) and *Affair in Trinidad* (dir. Sherman, 1952). In this incarnation Hayworth played a series of women tormented by the trials of love; none were wicked, merely damaged. Even Gilda (Figure 4.37), Hayworth's most iconic role, 'wasn't really crooked, just a little out of line'.[108]

Both of Hayworth's public incarnations contained something of the real off-screen Rita – her natural beauty, her raw talent, her commitment to hard work, her friendliness and openness – although neither of them came close to expressing the deep insecurities and neuroses she experienced as a wife, a mother and a working woman. Hayworth, making reference to her most well-known femme fatale role, famously lamented: 'It's hard being Gilda for twenty-four hours at a time . . . Men may go to bed with Gilda, but they wake up with me.' It was hard being Rita Hayworth, one of Hollywood's most manufactured movie stars, and yet, nonetheless, as Adrienne McLean has perceptively observed, while 'there was an element of passivity in Hayworth's image', she also functioned as a woman who had overcome her 'type' as a Latino starlet, 'but also her own shyness, lack of confidence, domination by men, [and] diffidence' to prove that the postwar period was a time of social change and complexity.[109]

The synergy between Hayworth the Love Goddess and Hayworth the Hoofer explains why *Salome* went into production. In many respects the Dance of the Seven Veils sequence was the movie's only *raison d'être*. After all, the striptease had become central to the Salome tradition, and Columbia Pictures, like all other post-Wildean adapters, were happy to follow suit with that most beguiling of myths. Accordingly Dieterle hired the modern-dance choreographer Valerie Bettis to create Hayworth's dance, as the pressbook noted:

> In *Salome*, Miss Hayworth dances the Dance of the Seven Veils, the most expressive performance she has ever given on the screen. This dance, created for the film by Broadway choreographer Valerie Bettis, demanded the utmost in voluptuous movement, in bodily freedom . . . Rita in her dance must discard those veils without a hint of awkwardness which attends upon buttons and straps. Her dancing costume had to flow.

In many respects, however, Hayworth's Dance of the Seven Veils is an anticlimax, a safe affair that pales into insignificance besides the

Figure 4.37
Film noir icon: Rita Hayworth as Gilda. Studio publicity portrait, 1946.

memory of her 'Put the Blame on Mame' routine from *Gilda*. In that infamous dance number (choreographed by Jack Cole and probably the most famous striptease in all cinema), Hayworth struts, shimmies, tosses her red hair, wiggles her derriere, and slowly unpeels a pair of black satin evening-gloves (but nothing else) in the perfect illusion of erotic abandon; she teases the audience into 'imagining her revealing much more than her supple beckoning arms'. Gilda easily out-Salomes

Figure 4.38
Down to the last veil: Rita Hayworth as Salome. Studio publicity shot, 1953.

Salome. Bettis' choreography insisted upon Hayworth disrobing, veil
by veil, and although the routine is expertly constructed and excellently
performed, with Salome artfully removing each veil as the number
builds to its climax, the dance fails to entertain let alone arouse (Figure
4.38).[110] Hayworth is oddly, disconcertingly, wooden as a coquette and,
as Bach observes, 'in *Salome* the actress seems to be focusing on a choreographer's instructions. One can imagine her counting the steps rather
than the admiring glances from the men of the court.'[111]

Roland Barthes once noted that a striptease routine is based on a
single paradox: 'Woman is desexualised at the very moment when she

is stripped naked'; by the time the stripper lets slip her last item of her clothing she has regained, 'a perfectly chaste state of the flesh'. An effective striptease follows a law of diminishing returns so that the 'ritual' of disrobing, as Barthes sees it, makes the body 'more remote'.[112] But, as the *Gilda* dance routine shows, even the ritual might be imaginary; 'Put the Blame on Mame' exposes nothing of Hayworth's body other than two white arms, yet the illusion of complete sexual abandonment is tantamount to its success. The bodystocking worn by Hayworth as Salome at the climax of her dance may have caused a sensation in the American press, which alleged that no actress, had ever shown so much flesh, but in reality the girl-next-door in her Technicolor veils fails to ignite the passions. As Alice Bach wryly notes, 'Rita's dance compared with the other cinematic Salomes, whose task is to seduce Herod, is as salacious as the heroine of a hygiene film made for bored seventh graders.'[113] Having shed her garments, Salome's Dance of the Seven Veils ultimately renders Hayworth's sex appeal coldly redundant.

Thus, when Rita Hayworth dances as Salome, she is nonetheless both promoting and echoing her back catalogue of on-screen dance routines. She is a Gilda-want-to-be in biblical fancy dress. The casting of Rita Hayworth as Salome created more problems for the 1953 movie than it solved and her oddly virginal Salome says far more about 1950s America and the Hollywood star system than it does about the deep cultural resonances of the long-established Salome tradition. Columbia's marketing ambition to offer a synergy of Hayworth's on-screen personas turned out to be a garbled amalgam which, in the end, de-sexed the American Love Goddess. Salome, nice girl, ultimately wins out so that, as one reviewer put it, 'Salome was a good girl – just a wide-eyed cutie.'[114] Hayworth's star image was in conflict with the reimagining of Salome as a good girl and the archaeological strata of Hayworth the movie star were too deeply engrained with past performances to support a revisionist version of the old Salome story.

'Delicious Debauchery'

In Golden Age Hollywood a star's personal life was under the control of the studios as much as was his or her star persona. There was little room for resistance and even though a few leading stars like Bette Davis and Mary Pickford were able to take charge of their image construction (in which case their resistance became part of their persona), most stars colluded in the fabrication of themselves as a 'star' and actively participated in the manufacturing of themselves as representatives of 'normality'. Thus 'lavender marriages' – marriages of convenience in which one or both partners are gay – were not an unusual feature of the Hollywood lifestyle (and, sadly, continue to be so). Gay stars (the term 'gay' is of course anachronistic for the period of our study) were the most vulnerable in relation to the instability of the star image because they had to conceal their inner-lives while outwardly playing the accepted norm. We must recall that mainstream American attitudes towards homosexuals in the period of our study considered gay men, especially, to be 'the most despised minority in America'.[115] In 1947 the publication of *Sexuality in the Human Male* (known as the Kinsey Report) brought attention to homosexuality in American society and caused more of a backlash than understanding, with the *Washington Post* branding homosexuals 'sexual psychopaths'.[116] In a CBS poll taken in the early 1960s it was found that 'Americans consider homosexuality more harmful to society than adultery, abortion or prostitution . . . Two out of three Americans look upon homosexuals with disgust, discomfort or fear. One in ten says "hatred". The vast majority believes that homosexuality is an illness.'[117]

This double masquerade demanded of gay performers in Hollywood is best expressed through the life and career of Rock Hudson. With his six foot five inch frame, barrel chest, square jaw, low voice, thick hair and killer smile, Hudson was created to tantalise his female fans with his persistent bachelorhood (Figure 4.39). He played sensitive characters in touch with their emotions, and his outfits were always coordinated, whether he was wearing three-piece suits or a flannel work shirt and jeans. That Hudson played 'straight' roles on-screen is not exceptional, but the promotion of the 'real' Hudson, the non-acting Hudson, as a paragon of masculine heterosexuality was operated on an unprecedented level. And it was that deception, far more than the fact that Hudson liked to have promiscuous sex with men, that fuelled the public abhorrence and rejection that Rock Hudson experienced in 1984 when he admitted that he had AIDS.[118] He made it unequivocally clear that his entire Hollywood image had been a lie. If Rock Hudson could be gay, then who else might be? What other star images were predicated on falsehoods? Was all of Hollywood a lie?

The off-screen life of what might be termed 'deviant stardom' had no place in Hollywood. However, the performativity of deviance was welcome on-screen, especially in the epic where as a result of the strange and absurd calculations of the Production Code censors, ancient world movies, especially those with biblical themes, got away with more sex and violence than ordinary films. Cinematic images of antiquity, and in particular the Roman epics, enjoyed employing stereotypes of homosexual men and women as people who deviated from traditional gender roles. In the silent era and early 1930s, Hollywood cinema witnessed the 'pansy craze' – a very popular depiction of effete homosexual men, individuals who because of their mannerisms were always the butt of jokes and figures of derision. Limp-wristed and essentially emasculated, these pansy-type caricatures were churned out in movie after movie, but consistently they were presented as outré outsiders and somewhat sinister and threatening in their obvious sexual proclivities in spite of their camp – laughable – cavortings. In the same period, a more elegant 'lesbian chic' flourished in Jazz Age movies like *Blonde Venus* (dir. von Sternberg, 1932) and romances such as *Queen Christina* (dir. Mamoulian,

Figure 4.39
Inside the Hollywood closet: Rock Hudson. Studio publicity portrait, 1957.

1933) in which leading actresses like Marlene Dietrich and Greta Garbo allowed their stardom to project an alternative reading of sexuality.

Cashing in on the vogue for glamorous on-screen lesbianism, for *The Sign of the Cross*, Cecil B. DeMille cast Joyzelle Joyner, an avant-garde burlesque (and overtly bisexual) performer, in the role of Ancaria, the 'most wicked and talented woman in Rome' (Figure 4.40). At the request of Marcus Superbus, her most regular patron, she is shown performing the lesbian-overtoned 'Dance of the Naked Moon' as she caresses, kisses and paws at the Christian girl Mercia in an attempted lesbian seduction

ƆOYZELLE

Famous American dan-
seuse whose languorous
and sensual *pas de seul*,
performed by order of
Marcus Superbus in *The
Sign of the Cross*, was one
of the high lights of that
production.

Figure 4.40
Cabaret artiste and bisexual Joyzelle Joyner as Ancaria. *The Sign of the Cross* (1932).
Publicity shot.

– and then whips and lashes her when the ploy fails. The performance
mimics the style of a 1930s Weimar cabaret act or, possibly, a routine
from a New York fetish or drag club. Joyner intones, in the manner of
Marlene Dietrich, the verses of an erotic poem as her pelvis-grinding,
hip-bumping choreography reaches its crescendo:

Under the naked moon,
     I've found you.
We meet.
     I've seen you in my dreams.
In dreams indiscreet.
     With tortures so sweet.
I've loved you in dreams.
     Breathe upon me.
Draw me.
     Gently.
Touch my heart.
     Love will be warm.
In the gold of your hair.
     Feed from your lips.
We have been two,
     We shall be one.
Both throb . . .

Not surprisingly the censors leaped on the scene and demanded its dele-
tion on the grounds that it blatantly contravened the Production Code's
dictum that any form of 'sex perversion', including homosexuality, be
removed. Besides, the Code stated that, 'Dances with movements of the
breasts, excessive bodily movements while the feet remain stationary,
the so-called 'belly dance' – these dances are immoral, obscene and
hence altogether wrong.' 'What are you going to do about that dance?',
an angry Will Hays demanded of DeMille during a telephone conversation after seeing footage of Joyzelle Joyner's enthusiastic performance.
'Will, listen carefully to my words because you may want to quote
them,' said the unflappable director. 'Not a damn thing.' 'Not a damn
thing?' asked Hays, baffled. 'Not a damn thing,' DeMille repeated reso-
lutely. The dance remained. So too did Charles Laughton's particular
interpretation of the emperor Nero, the queerest character in a very
queer film.

Laughton's blonde Nero, chubby in skimpy clothing, is a disturbing
sight whether sprawled on cushions receiving a beauty treatment from
his handmaidens (hungover from the previous night's orgy – 'delicious
debauchery', he recalls whimsically) or more actively engaged in watching the spectacles of death in the arena, licking his fingers as the gladiators spill blood (Figure 4.41). In several scenes a half-naked male slave
(played by bodybuilder George Bruggeman) sits chained at Nero's feet.
Even if his pouty campness were not enough to give Nero away as gay,
the signs of his effeminacy are all around him. Interestingly, Laughton
himself was a closeted homosexual and it has been suggested that by
taking on the role of Nero, the actor was undergoing a type of public
therapy, as the *Sunday Times* critic James Agate suggested: 'As Nero, Mr
Laughton enjoys himself hugely, playing the emperor as the flaunting
extravagant queen he probably was.' 'His contemporaries', Laughton's

Figure 4.41
The pudgy white flesh of Charles Laughton's pansy Nero. *The Sign of the Cross* (1932).
Production stills.

most recent biographer has stated, 'knew exactly what he was up to.'[119]
In Richard Lindsay's assessment:

> In the role of Nero, Laughton got to play out his homosexuality on
> screen. Adding to his sense of queerness was his weight, and his per-
> ception of himself as ugly and unlovable in an industry that traded in
> beautiful people. Laughton wore these elements of his outsider status

Figure 4.42
Peter Ustinov's effete Nero. *Quo Vadis* (1951). Production shot.

like a crown of thorns, his supposed ugliness and perversity borne as
signs of his anointing as an artist.[120]

Taking his cue from Laughton, Peter Ustinov's Nero is also played as
a pansy poet (Figure 4.42), a flamboyant self-important homosexual
and an inflated narcissist bored with the conventions of morality. This
durable stereotype informed the on-screen image of the homosexual
male for much of the twentieth century and the postwar epic's treatment
of gay characters as monstrous perversions of normality was a hallmark
of the genre. In *The Ten Commandments* of 1956, for instance, Vincent
Price's Baka, the Egyptian overseer, is a mincing villain with a taste for

sadomasochism and in *The Robe*, Jay Robinson's Caligula quite literally screams his way through the action, his anger mixed with the frustration of knowing that, in comparison to Richard Burton's Marcus, he is impotent in action and authority. Stephen Boyd's performance of Messala, as we have seen, has a rich and brilliantly realised homoerotic subtext. In *Spartacus*, of course, we have, as Cyrino puts it, 'the most sexually tinged scene in the history of epic cinema', the so-called 'oysters and snails' bath scene (ultimately cut by the censors before the film's premiere) between General Crassus (Laurence Oliver, himself a bisexual philanderer) and the young slave boy Antoninus (the straight and over-sexed Tony Curtis).[121] The numerous Jesus films of the era routinely depict Herod Antipas as some kind of sexual deviant. In *Salome*, for instance, Charles Laughton plays the role, although it is difficult to believe that he is consumed with heterosexual lust for his stepdaughter and in the Dance of the Seven Veils sequence he squirms, twists, grins and salivates with too much enthusiasm to be credible. But why these repetitious images of deviance? Lindsay offers an answer:

> In general, the stereotype of the gay villain has represented American societal revulsion towards homosexuality and assumptions about the preferences of American religious film-goers to see perversity punished. In the end, however, the queer villains may have gotten the last laugh. Simply by existing, they introduced a queer element into what were otherwise considered to be moral films. It may be that budding gay boys or their adult brethren, living closeted in the cities and towns of America, were more likely to be introduced to the possibility of gay characters in homoerotic situations in [epic] films than in any other form of modern entertainment.[122]

Concluding thoughts

We have seen that in the Golden Age of Hollywood the great movie stars were constructed as bigger and more enduring than the individual films they appeared in. Each film, however, is connected by that movie star's persona so that, as I have advanced, the star becomes an archaeological site in which the strata of a career can be unearthed. Stars brought consistency to filmmaking and film-going and all film genres, even the epic with all of its focus on on-screen splendour and the cost of production, was nonetheless dominated by the star image.

Once cast in an epic role, a star was likely to play others too, since the studios were keen to capitalise on the distribution, marketing, exhibition and consumption potential that a familiar face brought to the genre. Some stars, like Charlton Heston, willingly donned the Roman armour or loincloths and considered themselves to be heightening the moral values of the American nation through their haughty, pseudo-classical performances; others, like Richard Burton, despised the genre, but donned the toga regardless – and took the money which the lucrative contract delivered; and some stars, like Paul Newman, feeling uncomfortable in the tunic-roles, rejected the epic altogether. Some stars, like Victor Mature, performed in multiple epics simply because they were told to do so.

Stars in classic Hollywood epics existed as marketing devices in order to encourage box-office success. As such the star was part of the same process that foregrounded the efforts taken in researching and constructing the sets and costumes; the star who was likened to the character from antiquity which he or she was playing, either in terms of looks, attitudes, interests, behaviour, even wealth, prestige and status had particular marketable appeal. So great was the value of such a star's visibility, that the manufacturing and marketing of the epic genre was willing to overwrite history to accommodate the star image, as Bosley Crowther's *New York Times* review of *Cleopatra* recognised:

> Elizabeth Taylor is not an ancient queen . . . in the quality of her thought – nor, indeed, in the modified high style of her exceedingly low-cut gowns, Mr Mankiewicz has wisely not attempted to present us with historical copies. He and the writers who have helped him have drawn their major dramatic episodes from Plutarch, Suetonius and others. But the minds of their characters work along lines more in accord with contemporary thought . . . Thus Miss Taylor's sultry sovereign . . . can [tell] Caesar that his knees are bony or, when they meet later in Rome, throw a wink at him . . .'

Notes

1. *New York Times*, 27 March 1964, was less fulsome in its praise: 'Sophia Loren is ornamental, without intelligence or sex.'
2. Rosenstone (1995: 68).
3. Custen (1992: 18).
4. Sobchack (1990: 36).
5. Dyer (1987 and 1998).
6. Sorlin (1990: 46).
7. Wood (1975: 182).
8. Richard Dyer (1987: 141–94) provides a brilliant analysis of the Garland 'product' and in particular the devotion of her gay fans. The knife-edge between tragedy and camp, he suggests, was one of her great on-screen/off-screen qualities. This is perfectly played out in *A Star Is Born*. The pathos of Garland singing *Over the Rainbow* during her declining years is part of that appeal too. Yet Garland could be refreshingly self-deprecating: when one fan begged her 'never to forget the rainbow', Garland replied: 'Why, honey, how could I ever forget the rainbow? I've got rainbows up my ass.' See further, important, studies on stardom in Dyer (1998 and 2002).
9. Basinger (2009: 4).
10. Cited in Basinger (2009: 131).
11. Quoted in Morley (2006: vii).
12. Quoted in McClelland (1985: 168).
13. Quoted in Morley (2006: vii).

14. Wilcoxon (1991: 71–2).
15. Koury (1959: 162–3).
16. Higham (1973: 287).
17. McKay (2013: 105).
18. Munn (2008: 78).
19. Alexander (2016: 272).
20. Capua (2010: 55).
21. On Taylor's performances see Smith (2012: 88–117).
22. 13 June 1963.
23. Dyer (1992: 113).
24. Quoted in Jorgensen and Scoggins (2015: 277).
25. Crisp (1984: 16).
26. Breakwell and Hammond (1990: 122).
27. Burr (2012: xxi–xxii).
28. Babington and Evans (1993: 232–3).
29. *New York Times*, 22 August 1954; *Chicago Daily Tribune*, 4 July 1954.
30. Turner (1982: 151).
31. *New York Times*, 25 August 1954.
32. http://grandoldmovies.wordpress.com/tag/edmond-purdom/ (accessed 10 May 2017).
33. *New York Times*, 14 May 1955.
34. *Chicago Daily Tribune*, 15 November 1962.
35. The only study of Boyd's life and career is Cushnan (2015).
36. Bassinger (2007: 103).
37. *Variety*, 17 November 1959.
38. Elley (1984: 134).
39. Cyrino (2005: 77–8); Rovin (1977: 116).
40. Heston (1995: 195–6).
41. http://www.imdb.com/name/nm0361823/bio?ref_=nm_dyk_qt_sm# quotes (accessed 14 May 2017).
42. Nadel (1993) and Wright (2003).
43. Richards (2008: 56). On British actors in Hollywood see Morley (2006).
44. Wyke (1997: 71). It has been noted that in order to complete this aural paradigm, the male heroic epic lead was usually played by an American actor. In his role of Marcus Vinicius, for instance, Nebraska-born Robert Taylor employed his own lugubrious 'sturdy, Midwestern cadences' (Cyrino 2005: 28) although in *Spartacus*, Tony Curtis' notorious Brooklyn accent ('I am Antoninus; I'm sing-ger of sawungs'), which impinged on all his roles, is distracting to the point of infuriation.
45. As Kerr recalled, 'For Karen Holmes [in *From Here to Eternity*], I studied voice for three months to get rid of my English accent. I changed my hair to blonde. I knew I could be sexy if I had to.' See Capua (2010: 65).
46. Quoted in Capua (2010: 54). Kerr's personal life was lively and her personality was completely different to the rather repressed, strait-laced women she so often had to portray. Twice married, she is believed to have had affairs with several of her leading men including Burt Lancaster and Stewart Granger as well as director Michael Powell. See further Braun (1977).
47. Cyrino (2005: 33).
48. Braun (1977: 126–7).
49. http://www.reelclassics.com/Actresses/Simmons/simmons-bio.htm (accessed 15 May 2017).
50. http://articles.latimes.com/2010/jan/23/local/la-me-jean-simmons23-2010jan23 (accessed 21 May 2017). See further Cyrino (2005: 110–11).

51. Capua (2006: 49).
52. DeMille (1960: 416).
53. Brynner (1989: 80–1).
54. http://blog.everlastingfootprint.com/2014/10/10/yul-brynner-the-king-and-me/ (accessed 22 May 2017).
55. *New York Times*, 26 December 1959.
56. DeMille (1960: 419).
57. Marcus (2011: 189).
58. See Heston (1962, 1976 and 1995); Rovin (1977); Heston and Isbouts (1998); Eliot (2016).
59. Quoted in Raymond (2006: 20).
60. Quoted in Raymond (2006: 21).
61. Quoted in Raymond (2006: 22).
62. Cohan (1997: 157–8).
63. *Hollywood Citizen News*, 28 March 1959.
64. *Hollywood Citizen News*, 22 March 1961.
65. *Charlton Heston Newsletter*, 14 August 1958. See further Cyrino (2005: 87).
66. Quoted in Raymond (2006: 35).
67. Gore Vidal's claims were published in the *Los Angeles Times*, 17 June 1996, and refuted by Heston in the same publication, 24 June 1996. See further Cyrino (2013a: 615–16) and the brilliant analysis of Lindsay (2015: 121–58).
68. *Saturday Evening Post*, 20 August 1976.
69. Quoted in Eliot (2016: 453), where the full speech is also given; see also comments by Raymond (2006: 257). A video clip is available: https://www.youtube.com/watch?v=ORYVCML8xeE (accessed 22 May 2017). See also: https://www.youtube.com/watch?v=UsdlO7Cl7LA and https://www.youtube.com/watch?v=DC2QaWmat7A (accessed 22 May 2017).
70. Raymond (2006: 287).
71. *O'Dwyer's PR Services Report*, July 1996: 20. Named alongside Heston are Oprah Winfrey, Michael Jordan, Billy Graham and Robert Redford.
72. See further Genini (1996) and Golden (1996).
73. Burr (2012: 173).
74. Brown (2012: 412).
75. Hughes-Hallett (1991: 284).
76. Riad (2014: 8).
77. For a reliable account of the affair and its aftermath see Kashner and Schoenberger (2010); for an evaluation of the affair and its relationship to the Taylor image see especially, and importantly, Cashmore (2016).
78. Kamp (2000: 146).
79. Wanger and Hyams (1963: 120).
80. Wanger and Hyams (1963: 121).
81. Kelly (1981: 107).
82. See especially Rubython (2011), who provides a good synthesis of earlier biographic explorations of Burton's life and career.
83. Hughes-Hallett (1991: 282–3).
84. Quoted in Kashner and Schoenberger (2010: 23).
85. Wanger and Hyams (1963: 134).
86. Wanger and Hyams (1963: 135).
87. Brodsky and Weiss (1963: 29).
88. Lloyd (2011: 79, 82).
89. Kelly (1981: 145, 164); Brodsky and Weiss (1963: 35, 39).
90. Chrissochoidis (2013: 128–9).
91. Kelly (1981: 133, 203).

92. *New Republic*, 13 June 1963.

93. *Sight and Sound*, July 1963.

94. Wanger and Hyams (1963: 182).

95. Hayworth has not been well-served by biographers, but there are some notable studies. For her life see Epstein and Morella (1983) and Leaming (1989). A lavish photographic biography is provided by Roberts-Frenzel (2001). A filmography and potted biography can be found in Ringgold (1974). A more interpretative account of the Hayworth life and legend is provided by McLean (2005).

96. *Salome* pressbook, 1953.

97. In fact, Judson was keen to pimp out his wife to Cohn. He saw his wife as an investment. According to Leaming (1989: 102), Harry Cohn 'developed an obsession' with the beautiful young Rita Hayworth. But in a rare, explicit show of strength, Hayworth refused her husband's order to sleep with 'the notoriously crude movie mogul'.

98. *New York Times*, 25 March 1953.

99. *Washington Post*, 8 April 1953.

100. *New York Times*, 25 March 1953.

101. *New York Times*, 7 October 1918. For Bara's *Salome* costumes see Golden (1996: 165–7).

102. Cited in Genini (1996: 47).

103. *Monthly Film Bulletin*, 1 January 1953.

104. *Variety*, 22 July 1953.

105. Callow (2012: 225).

106. Bach (1996: 117).

107. McLellan (2000: 122).

108. Bach (1996: 117).

109. McLean (2004: 63).

110. Bettis also choreographed Hayworth's *Affair in Trinidad* dances; see Billman (1996), s.v. 'Bettis, Valerie'.

111. Bach (1996: 117).

112. Barthes (2000: 84).

113. Bach (1996: 117).

114. *Manchester Guardian*, 18 July 1953.

115. Cited in Doty (2013: 280).

116. Lindsay (2015: 84).

117. Doty (2013: 280).

118. Hudson's announcement gave AIDS a public (and sympathetic) face and was one of several moments in the 1980s (one of which was Elizabeth Taylor' championing of Hudson, her long-term friend) that helped destigmatise the disease and those who suffered from it. It also gave a public face to homosexuality, one that was not stereotypical or the butt of crude humour. For an overview of Hudson's life see Mercer (2015), and for a thorough and explicitly refreshing account of his image construction see Hofler (2014). For homosexuality in Hollywood movies see, famously, Russo (1981). See also the dazzlingly erudite discussion of Hudson onscreen and off by Dyer (2002: 159–74).

119. Both cited by Lindsay (2015: 88).

120. Lindsay (2015: 88).

121. Cyrino (2013a: 617), with further discussion 618–19.

122. Lindsay (2016: 850–1).

WHY CLEOPATRA WINKS

She was the greatest of them all. You wouldn't know, you're too young. In one week she received 17,000 fan letters. Men bribed her hairdresser to get a lock of her hair. There was a maharajah who came all the way from India to beg one of her silk stockings.
    Later he strangled himself with it!
Max Von Mayerling (Erich von Stroheim), *Sunset Boulevard*, 1950

When Mankiewicz's Cleopatra enters Rome, she does so with considerable hullaballoo: trumpeters mounted twelve abreast on white stallions bedecked in blue and gold canter through a triumphal arch into the Forum and chariots pulled by plumed horses criss-cross the screen in a dazzling display of agility. A volley of arrows decorated with coloured streamers is fired by a cohort of Nubian archers as male slaves, dressed in pink loincloths, unfurl layers of shimmering silk to reveal a belly dancer wearing sequined nipple-tassels. Coloured smoke fills the Forum – first red, then bright yellow – and athletes scatter armfuls of glitter as a giant hollow pyramid opens to let loose dozens of white doves which take flight into the blue sky. African tribal dancers in beaded bikinis gyrate, stamp and shimmy, and girls wearing enormous golden birds' wings raise their arms in a hypnotic Busby Berkeley routine. The spectacle continues: more horsemen arrive pushing back the excited crowd. A hush descends over the Forum. There is the sound of a regular, deep, drum beat; cymbals clash; trumpets blare. Three hundred black slaves dressed in gold appear. They are pulling a giant mobile sphinx. It is as tall as the Senate House. And sitting there, enthroned on high, beneath the sphinx's chin, dressed in a pleated gold robe and wearing a tall golden crown, is Hollywood's most notorious film star, Elizabeth Taylor, pretending to be Cleopatra. Silence falls as the sphinx-mobile makes its way across the square. Antony looks flabbergasted;

Figure EC.1
Cleopatra winks. Screen grab.

Calpurnia, Octavia and the other Roman matrons are crestfallen; Octavian is dead-eyed; Caesar is wryly impressed. The sphinx comes to a halt and a red carpet bearing a golden cartouche of the Queen's name is rolled out. Cleopatra, mounted now on a golden palanquin is carried down the steps of the sphinx-mobile and is set down on the ground in front of Caesar. She approaches him. Her breasts heave beneath the low-cut décolleté of her shimmering, tight-fitting, gown. She bows low to Caesar. The crowd erupts in cheers and wild applause. The camera focuses on Elizabeth Taylor's face, her lilac eyes are outlined in heavy black eyeliner and her eyelids sparkle gold. Her mouth, beautiful in pale 'sphinx-pink' lipstick smiles sweetly. She catches Caesar's eye. And then a most extraordinary thing happens. Cleopatra winks (Figure EC.1).

As I read it, Cleopatra's wink is a sign of self-mockery. In that wink she communicates to Caesar what we know he already knows: that this spectacle is as shallow as it is colourful; that it is opium for the masses, the 'circus' part of the Roman concept of 'bread and circuses'. Cleopatra's spectacular Roman entry is a collusion: Caesar expects that his Cleopatra will be able to wow the (previously hostile) Roman crowd with some kind of Egyptian trickery – although he is not sure how. Now he knows. Cleopatra's wink says, 'See, I told you I could do it. But you already knew that. But did you *ever* think it would be like *this*!?' That wink puts me in mind of a story told about Liz Taylor's meeting with Princess Margaret, the sister of Queen Elizabeth II, in the mid-1960s: the Princess, herself no stranger to a certain opulence of lifestyle and its associated profligacy, once caught sight of Taylor wearing the Krupp diamond. 'That's the most vulgar thing I've ever seen,' Princess Margaret is reported to have said. 'Want to try it on?' asked Taylor. 'Oh, yes please,' said the Princess.[1]

With that wink, Cleopatra camps it up. Here I follow the reading of 'camp' propounded by the critic Philip Core who advances the idea that camp is 'the disguise that fails . . . the lie that tells the truth.'[2] This reading provides a route into understanding camp as being alive in a double sense, as embodying reality and pure artifice. In the way in which she was constructed by her Roman opponents, Cleopatra herself was camp and in her Hollywood renditions, especially her synergy with Elizabeth Taylor, that campness is covertly doubled. The camp Cleopatra is, therefore, an image of duplicity.

That wink stands as a metaphor for the epic film genre itself. Epic films are camp. They are more camp than the Hollywood musical by many leagues since that popular genre promotes upfront the artificiality of experiencing song and dance in an otherwise 'realistic' setting (the west side streets of New York City, the palace of the king of Siam or the cornfields of Oklahoma). The epic is po-faced in its humourless earnestness and refuses to acknowledge its own artificiality. However, the very sight of Lana Turner strutting around in *The Prodigal* with a ceremonial candlestick in both hands and a far-away look in her eyes is enough to cause a certain type of gay man (me, for instance) to collapse in a paroxysm of helpless laughter. The film also gives Turner a child protégé who is ordained to succeed her as High Priestess of Astarte. In one of the campier scenes, Lana gives the little girl lessons in the fine art of applying eyeliner. I just laugh. I do so because, as a gay man, I apply my own queer reading to the scene and to the whole epic genre, if truth be told. I read epics as queer camp, a kind of 'declaration of effeminate intent', as Andy Medhurst puts it, flowing 'like gin and poison through subcultural conversations'. For Medhurst camp is an aesthetic exclusively reserved for gay men, 'the domain of queens . . . a relationship between queens and their circumstances'.[3] I like the notion that camp is the property of queers. But I *know* (from experience) that camp has a broader appeal which expands well beyond any queer-encoded message.

We can *all* revel in Lana Turner's walk and her blonde bombshell look, with her torpedo bosoms shoved out (although perhaps only gay men will automatically link it to a quote by Golden Girl Blanche Devereaux – 'I always take a deep breath before I meet a man; it thrusts my breasts forward'). On one level, Lana Turner's act is corny. On another, it is knowing. Turner knows that her act works. The studios know that it works too, and that is why they created Lana Turner in the first place.

Epics are camp because, like Lana Turner, they are cunningly crafted to make the masses love them – in spite of their pretentions to lofty, worthy morality and their inflated budgets. Epics claim to tell us that we are observing the ancient past as it was lived. But we know that, *really*, epics are neither moral texts nor historical documents. Epic films were made by flesh-and-blood human beings with faults, foibles, lusts, lies and deliberate agendas. Morality was employed as a selling point or as political doctrine while the sets and costumes of antiquity were only spurious interpretations of modernity enabling audiences to buy into an idealised past. I am convinced that most cinemagoers in the Golden

Age were aware of this, but like Caesar with the winking Cleopatra, everyone went along with the show.

For me, Susan Sontag's wide-ranging appreciation of camp, stretching from the Hall of Mirrors at Versailles to the films of Marlene Dietrich, works best in this more embracing reading. All of what Sontag identifies as camp have one thing in common: they operate around the notion of the surface, of artifice, of theatricality, of style (often over substance) and of lavish decoration. As I have shown in this book, epic films are defined by their surface artificiality too: the hill of Golgotha created on a picturesque sound-stage, the city of Thebes made from a matte painting and the neo-fascist glossiness of Nero's palace. 'The love of the unnatural . . . of artifice, of exaggeration,' as Sontag puts it, is there too of course in the push-up bra worn underneath the Queen of Sheba's costume, the shiny Brylcreem slathered onto Robert Taylor's hair and in Elizabeth Taylor's glittery eye makeup. It is embedded in a publicity photograph of Claudette Colbert and Henry Wilcoxon sharing a cigarette off-camera during the shooting of *Cleopatra* (Figure EC.2). Colbert, with her bee-stung lips and her crescent-moon eyebrows, is in full glamour mode; she proffers her co-star a light. The photograph conveys the same essence that Colbert brought to her on-screen Cleopatra, a quick-witted, New York socialite in Egyptian fancy dress (with her hand on her hip, emphasising her waist, Colbert seems to echo the image of Mae West, the most fast-talking of all of Hollywood's 'fast-talking dames').

'The aesthetic of the epic is the spectacle of the artificial,' Richard Lindsay writes,[4] but the notion of artificiality can be expanded to images (and texts) off-camera too. This is why studio marketing liked to show the process of creating an epic in its publicity materials, chiefly in staged and controlled studio shots (Figure EC.3). The uncensored, de-glamorised workings of movie-making also found their way into the public consciousness through a myriad of candid phonographs that were never meant to form the official account of a movie's production but nevertheless add now to our awareness of the artificiality of putting the past onto the screen (Figure EC.4) – like the zips and seams concealed under a robe of pure spun gold.

We might also include here the artificiality and surface decoration of the studio research departments which churned out 'research' devoid of facts (or, if accurate, research which was by and large ignored) as well as 'research' which was only ever intended to be a marketing ploy but not a useful source for the movie-makers. Consider, for instance, the spurious factoids contained in a special *Cleopatra* edition of *Screenplay* magazine of 1963 in an article called 'A Hundred Facts about Cleopatra':

> Did you realise that in all of recorded history only two major wars have been fought for a woman? One was for Helen of Troy, the other was the Alexandrine War fought for Cleo . . .
> In real life Cleo's dresses were all bare to the waist . . .

Figure EC.2
Henry Wilcoxon and Claudette Colbert on the set of *Cleopatra*. Staged production promotion shot, 1934.

To lend even further authenticity to the film, 20ᵗʰ-Century Fox borrowed much of the furniture and props directly from art museums all over the country . . .

The 'lost' tomb of Alexander the Great was re-created to the exact specifications of descriptions found in history books. The tomb was made of crystal and resembles a huge Grecian vase . . .

Because of the vastness of scale, expenditure and labour needed in making them, the Hollywood epics of the Golden Age expose more than

Figure EC.3
Watching Hollywood at work: DeMille directs a scene from *The Sign of the Cross*. Staged
publicity promotion shot, 1931.

any other film genre the machine-like workings of the studio system,
from the manufacturing of movie star images to the crafting of peacock-
feather gowns and plaster-cast temple pillars. In their heyday, the way
epic films were presented to the public was as elaborate as the films
themselves and this book has exposed the showmanship, commitment,
craft and skill that went into bringing the ancient world to life on the
silver screen. On-screen antiquity was never the vision of one person
and even the most autocratic of movie directors, like DeMille, were
dependent on a team of experts whose talents ranged from cinematography and lighting to makeup application and hairstyling. For all the
talk of the auteur voice in Classic Hollywood, it must be said that epic
filmmaking was a holistic effort (Figure EC.5).

We might think the doyennes of the Hollywood epic to be the directors – the DeMilles, the LeRoys and the Mankiewiczes – or the movie
stars who lent their aura to the ancient-world characters they played
– the Bara-Colbert-Taylor Cleopatras and the Laughton-Ustinov Neros
– but for me the great (unsung heroes) of the epic genre are the thousands of studio employees who laboured off-set and on creating an

Figure EC.4
In between takes on the set of *Cleopatra*, 1962.

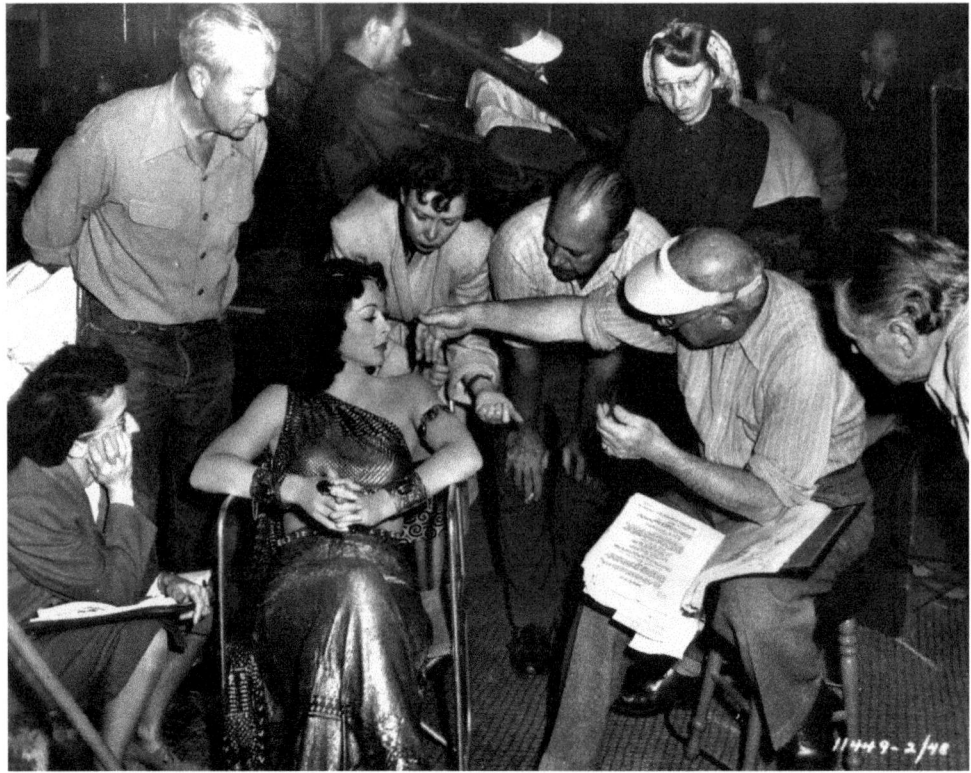

Figure EC.5
The machine at work: on the set of *Samson and Delilah*, DeMille instructs his labour force
on a detail of Hedy Lamarr's costume and makeup. Candid shot, 1949.

all-American vision of history. My heroes were those found supervising set construction, dying cloth, painting backdrops, moulding plaster cast statues, writing newspaper copy, rigging lights, embroidering chiffon gowns, beading headdresses, coining publicity stunts, printing posters, editing scripts, hammering nails, sawing wood, re-heeling shoes, polishing breastplates, applying makeup and dressing (oh so carefully) those precious commodities, the movie stars (Figure EC.6). All of this effort, all of this skill and energy and creativity, was there to underpin an empty piece of rhetoric which said that Hollywood was, in every way, committed to recreating the 'real world' of antiquity. We know that that commitment was strictly tailored to mass appeal. In every way, Hollywood had major designs on the past.

Notes

1. Kelly (1981: 200).
2. Core (1984: 7). See also Sontag (1966: 110).
3. Medhurst (1997: 276, 279).
4. Lindsay (2015: 17).

Figure EC.6
On the set of *Cleopatra*, an unknown dresser adjusts the crown of the Queen of Hollywood.
Candid shot, 1962.

BIBLIOGRAPHY

Affron, C. and Affron, M. J. (1995) *Sets in Motion. Art Direction and Film Narrative.* New Brunswick, NJ.

Alexander, L. (2016) *Reluctant Witness. Robert Taylor, Hollywood and Communism.* Albany, NY.

Ambrose, S. E. (1996) 'The Longest Day', in M. C. Carnes (ed.), *Past Imperfect. History According to the Movies.* New York, pp. 236–41.

Annas, A. (1987) 'The Photogenic Formula: Hairstyles and Makeup in Historical Films', in A. Annas, S. La Valley, E. Maeder and E. Jenssen (eds), *Hollywood and History. Costume Design in Film.* Los Angeles, pp. 52–77.

Annas, A., La Valley, S. and Maeder, E. (1987a) 'The Three Faces of Cleopatra', in A. Annas, S. La Valley, E. Maeder and E. Jenssen (eds), *Hollywood and History. Costume Design in Film.* Los Angeles, pp. 43–51.

Annas, A., La Valley, S., Maeder, E. and Jenssen, E. (eds) (1987b) *Hollywood and History. Costume Design in Film.* Los Angeles.

Ash, R. (1989) *Sir Lawrence Alma-Tadema.* London.

Ash, R. (1995) *Lord Leighton.* London.

Ash, R. (1999) *Victorian Masters and Their Art.* London.

Babington, B. and Evans, P. W. (1993) *Biblical Epics. Sacred Narrative in the Hollywood Cinema.* Manchester.

Bach, A. (1996) 'Calling the Shots: Directing Salome's Dance of Death', in *Samia* special edition 74, *Biblical Glamor and Hollywood Glitz*, pp. 103–26.

Bailey, M. J. (1982) *Those Glorious Glamour Years. Classic Hollywood Costume Design of the 1930s.* London.

Balio, T. (1993) *Grand Design. Hollywood as a Modern Business Enterprise, 1930–1939.* Berkeley.

Barbas, S. (2001) *Movie Crazy. Fan, Stars, and the Cult of Celebrity.* New York.

Barnes Tatum, W. (2004) *Jesus at the Movies.* Santa Rosa.

Barsacq, L. (1970) *Caligari's Cabinet and Other Grand Illusions. A History of Film Design.* New York.

Barthes, R. (1996) *Mythologies.* London.

Basinger, J. (1986) *The World War II Combat Film – Anatomy of a Genre.* New York.

Basinger, J. (1993) *A Woman's View. How Hollywood Spoke to Women 1930–1960.* London.

Basinger, J. (1999) *Silent Stars*. Middletown, CT.

Basinger, J. (2007) *The Star Machine*. New York.

Bassoff, L. (2000) *Mighty Movies. Movie Poster Art from Hollywood's Greatest Adventure Epics and Spectaculars*. Beverly Hills.

Becker, M. (2013) 'On Visual Cogency: the Emergence of an Antiquity of Moving Images', in P. Michelakis and M. Wyke (eds), *The Ancient World in Silent Cinema*. Cambridge, pp. 37–52.

Bernstein, M. and Studlar, G. (eds) (1997) *Visions of the East. Orientalism in Film*. London and New York.

Berry, S. (2000) *Screen Style. Fashion and Femininity in 1930s Hollywood*. London.

Berthoieu, P. (2009) *Hollywood Classique. Le temps des géants*. Paris.

Billman, L. E. (1996) *Film Choreographers and Dance Directors: A Heavily-illustrated Biographical Encyclopedia with a History and Filmographies, 1893 through 1995*. New York.

Birchard, R. S. (2004) *Cecil B. DeMille's Hollywood*. Lexington, KY.

Black, G. D. (1994) *Hollywood Censored: Morality Codes, Catholics, and the Movies*. New York.

Blackford, M. (1934) 'Motion Pictures: From the Box-Office Point-of-View – Cleopatra', *Billboard*, 46: 22.

Blanshard, A. and Shahabudin, K. (2011) *Classics on Screen*. London.

Block, A. B. and Wilson, L. A. (eds) (2010) *Blockbusters. A Decade-by-Decade Survey of Timeless Movies Including Untold Secrets of the Financial and Cultural Success*. New York.

Boggs, J. M. and Petrie, D. W. (1978) *The Art of Watching Films*. London.

Bondanella, P. (1987) *The Eternal City: Roman Images in the Modern World*. Chapel Hill, NC and London.

Borden, M. E. (2010) *Paul Newman*. Santa Barbara.

Braun, E. (1977) *Deborah Kerr*. London.

Breakwell, I. and Hammond, P. (eds) (1990) *Seeing in the Dark. A Compendium of Cinemagoing*. London.

Brenner, A. (1993) 'Afterword', in A. Brenner (ed.), *A Feminist Companion to Judges*. Sheffield, pp. 231–5.

Brodsky, J. and Weiss, N. (1963) *The Cleopatra Papers. A Private Correspondence*. New York.

Bronlow, K. (1979) *Hollywood. The Pioneers*. London.

Brown, C. (1983) *Rubens: Samson and Delilah*. London.

Brown, L. (2012) 'Kim Kardashian: Cleopatra with a K', *Harper's Bazaar*, 3591 (March): 405–12.

Brown, T. (2016) *Spectacle in 'Classical' Cinemas. Musicality and Historicity in the 1930s*. London.

Brynner, R. (1989) *Yul. The Man Who Would Be King. A Memoir of Father and Son*. New York.

Buckley, R. C. V. (2000) 'National Body: Gina Lollobrigida and the Cult of the Star in the 1950s', *Historical Journal of Film, Radio and Television*, 20 (4): 527–47.

Burgoyne, R. (ed.) (2010) *The Epic in World Culture*. London.

Burr, T. (2012) *Gods Like Us. On Movie Stardom and Modern Fame*. New York.

Butsch, R. (2001) 'American Movie Audiences of the 1930s', *International Labor and Working-Class History* 59 (Workers and Film: As Subject and Audience): 106–20.

Callow, S. (2012) *Charles Laughton. A Difficult Actor*. London.

Capua, M. (2006) *Yul Brynner. A Biography*. Jefferson, NC.

Capua, M. (2010) *Deborah Kerr. A Biography*. Jefferson, NC.

Carnes, M. C. (ed.) (1996) *Past Imperfect. History According to the Movies*. New York.

Cary, J. (1974) *Spectacular!* London.

Cashmore, E. (2016) *Elizabeth Taylor. A Private Life for Public Consumption*. London.

Casper, D. (2007) *Postwar Hollywood 1946–1962*. Oxford.

Cawthorne, N. (1996) *The New Look: Dior Revolution*. London.

Chabot, G. (2000) *Femme Fatale? I THINK NOT!*, http://www.epinions.com/mvie-review-10F6-168207C0-39648F88-prod5 (accessed 26 November 2016).

Chandler, C. (2004) *Nobody's Perfect. Billy Wilder: A Personal Biography*. New York.

Chierichetti, D. (1976) *Hollywood Costume Design*. London and New York.

Chierichetti, D. (1995) *Mitchell Leisen*. Los Angeles.

Chierichetti, D. (2003) *Edith Head. The Life and Times of Hollywood's Celebrated Costume Designer*. New York.

Chopra-Gant, M. (2008) *Cinema and History. The Telling of Stories*. London and New York.

Chrissochoidis, I. (ed.) (2013) *The Cleopatra Files*. Stanford.

Christie, I. (1991) 'Cecil B. DeMille: Grand Illusions', *Sight and Sound*, 1 (8): 18–21.

Coates, P. (2010) *Cinema and Colour. A Saturated Image*. London.

Cohan, S. (1997) *Masked Men. Masculinity and the Movies in the Fifties*. Bloomington, IN.

Collins, J. (1979) *Past Imperfect*. London.

Combs, R. (1997) 'The Choirmaster and the Slavedriver: Howard Hawks and *The Land of the Pharaohs*', *Film Comment*, 33: 42–9.

Coogan, M. D. (1999) *The Oxford History of the Biblical World*. Oxford.

Cooke, M. (2008) *A History of Film Music*. Cambridge.

Cooper, D. (1991) 'Who Killed Spartacus?' *CINEASTE*, 18: 18–27.

Core, P. (1984) 'Camp', *The Lie That Tells the Truth*. London.

Creswell, J. (n.d.) 'Quo Vadis? The Influence of Hugh Gray or Indiana Jen and the Raiders of the Lost Archive', https://independent.academia.edu/JenCreswell (accessed 25 February 2017).

Crisp, Q. (1984) *How to Go to the Movies*. New York.

Curl, J. S. (2005) *The Egyptian Revival*. London.

Cushnan, J. (2015) *Stephen Boyd. From Belfast to Hollywood*. Belfast.

Custen, G. (1992) *Bio/Pics. How Hollywood Constructed Public History*. New Brunswick, NJ.

Cyrino, M. S. (2004) 'Gladiator and Contemporary American Society', in M. Winkler (ed.), *Gladiator. Film and History*. Oxford, pp. 24–149.

Cyrino, M. S. (2005) *Big Screen Rome*. Oxford.

Cyrino, M. S. (2013a) 'Ancient Sexuality on Screen', in T. K. Hubbard (ed.), *A Companion to Greek and Roman Sexualities*. Oxford, pp. 613–28.

Cyrino, M. S. (2013b) *Screening Love and Sex in the Ancient World*. London.

Cyrino, M. S. (ed.) (n.d.) 'Designing Lizpatra (1963): The Vision and Influence of Irene Sharaff.' Unpublished conference paper.

Dance, R. (2008) *Glamour of the Gods. Photographs from the John Kobal Foundation*. Göttingen.

Davies, M. and Annesley, N. (eds) (2004) *The Price of Beauty. Edwin Long's 'Babylonian Marriage Market'*. London.

Davis, R. L. (1993) *The Glamour Factory. Inside Hollywood's Big Studio System*. Dallas.

DeMille, C. B. (1960) *Cecil B. DeMille. Autobiography*. London.

DeMille Presley, C. and Vieira, M. A. (2014) *Cecil B. DeMille. The Art of the Hollywood Epic*. Philadelphia.

Dening, G. (1998) 'Captain Bligh as a Mythic Cliché', in T. Barta (ed.), *Screening the Past. Film and the Representation of History*. London, pp. 19–44.

Dick, B. F. (2008) *Claudette Colbert. She Walked in Beauty*. Jackson, MS.

Doniol-Valcroze, J. (1989) 'Samson, Cecil and Delilah', *Wide Angle*, 11 (4): 32, 34–41.

Donnell, D. (1930) 'Are You a Screen Shopper?', *Motion Picture*, September, p. 70.

Doty, A. (2013) 'The Homosexual and the Single Girl', in L. M. E. Goolad, L. Kaganovsky and R. Rushing (eds), *Mad Men, Mad World. Sex, Politics, and Style in the 1960s*. Durham, NC and London, pp. 279–99.

Douglas, K. (2012) *I Am Spartacus! Making a Film, Breaking the Blacklist*. New York.

Drew, W. M. (2001) *D. W. Griffith's 'Intolerance' – Its Genesis and Its Vision*. Jefferson, NC.

Dunant, C. (1994) 'Olympian Dreamscapes: The Photographic Canvas. The Wide-screen Paintings of Leighton, Poynter and Alma-Tadema', in J. Bratton, J. Cook and C. Gledhill (eds), *Melodrama. Stage, Picture, Screen*. London.

Dyer, R. (1987) *Heavenly Bodies. Film Stars and Society*. London.

Dyer, R. (1992) *Only Entertainment*. London.

Dyer, R. (1998) *Stars*. London.

Dyer, R. (2002) *The Culture of Queers*. London and New York.

Eberson, J. (1925) 'A Description of the Capital Theatre, Chicago', *Architectural Forum*, 42 (6): 373–6.

Eckert, C. (1990) 'Carole Lombard in Macy's Window', in J. Gaines and C. Herzog (eds), *Fabrications: Costume and the Female Body*. London, pp. 100–21.

Eldridge, D. (2006) *Hollywood's History Films*. London.

Eliot, M. (2016) *Charlton Heston. Hollywood's Last Icon*. New York.

Elley, D. (1984) *The Epic Film*. London and New York.

Epstein, E. Z. and Morella, J. (1983) *Rita. The Life of Rita Hayworth*. London.

Essoe, G. and Lee, R. (1970) *DeMille: The Man and his Pictures*. New York.

Eyman, S. (2010) *Empire of Dreams. The Epic Life of Cecil B. DeMille*. New York.

Fahey, D. and Rich, L. (1988) *Masters of Starlight. Photographers in Hollywood*. London.

Finkel, A. (1996) *Romantic Stages. Set and Costume Design in Victorian England*. Jefferson, NC and London.

Finler, J. W. (2012) *Hollywood Movie Stills. Art and Technique in the Golden Age of the Studios*. London.

Fischer, L. (2003) *Designing Women. Cinema, Art Deco, and the Female Form*. New York.

Fischer, L. (ed.) (2015) *Art Direction and Production Design*. London.

Flanders, J. (2006) *Consuming Passions. Leisure and Pleasure in Victorian Britain*. London.

Ford, E. A. and Mitchell, D. C. (2009) *Royal Portraits in Hollywood. Filming the Lives of Queens*. Lexington, KY.

Foreman, L. (1999) *Cleopatra's Palace: In Search of a Legend*. London.

Forshey, G. E. (1992) *American Religious and Biblical Spectaculars*. Westport, CT.

Frost, D. (1997) *Billy Graham in Conversation*. Sandy Lane West, Oxford.

Genini, R. (1996) *Theda Bara. A Biography of the Silent Screen Vamp, with a Filmography*. Jefferson, NC and London.

Gibbons, C. (1938) 'The Art Director', in S. Watts (ed.), *Behind the Screen*. New York, pp. 42–50.

Golden, E. (1996) *Vamp. The Rise and Fall of Theda Bara*. New York.

Gomery, D. (2005) *The Hollywood Studio System. A History*. London.

Grace, P. (2009) *The Religious Film*. Oxford.

Gray, R. (2011) *Cinemas in Britain*. London.

Green, P. (1996) *Alexandria and Alexandrianism*. Malibu.

Greenberg, H. R. (1975) *The Movies On Your Mind*. New York.

Greenland, F. and Cartledge, P. (eds) (2009) *Responses to Oliver Stone's Alexander*. Madison, WI.

Grimal, N. (1998) *La gloire d'Alexandrie*. Paris.

Gunning, T. (1990) 'The Cinema of Attractions: Early Film, Its Spectators and the Avant-Guarde', in T. Elsaesser (ed.), *Early Cinema. Space, Frame, Narrative*. London.

Hall, S. (2002) 'Selling Religion: How to Market a Biblical Epic', *Film History*, 14 (2): 170–85.

Hall, S. and Neale, S. (2010) *Epics, Spectacles and Blockbusters: A Hollywood History*. Detroit.

Halliwell, L. (1977) *Halliwell's Film Guide to 8,000 English Language Films*. London.

Hambley, J. and Downing, P. (1979) *The Art of Hollywood*. London.

Hanson, B. (1972) 'D. W. Griffith. Some Sources'. *Art Bulletin* 54 (4): 493–515.

Harcourt-Smith, S. (1951) 'The Siegfried of Sex: Thoughts Inspired by Cecil B. DeMille's "Samson and Delilah"', *Sight and Sound*, 19 (10): 410–12, 424.

Hark, I. R. (1993) 'Animals or Romans. Looking at Masculinity in *Spartacus*', in S. Cohen and I. R. Hark (eds), *Screening the Male. Exploring Masculinities in Hollywood Cinema*. London, pp. 151–72.

Hark, I. R. (ed.) (2002) *Exhibition. The Film Reader*. London.

Harris, S. (1996) 'Spartacus', in M. C. Carnes (ed.), *Past Imperfect. History According to the Movies*. New York, pp. 40–3.

Head, E. and Ardmore, J. K. (1960) *The Dress Doctor*. Kingswood, VA.

Head, E. and Calistro, P. (1983) *Edith Head's Hollywood*. New York.

Heisner, B. (1990) *Hollywood Art. Art Direction in the Days of the Great Studios*. Jefferson, NC.

Heston, C. (1962) 'Mammoth Movies I Have Known', *Films and Filming*, April, pp. 5–7.

Heston, C. (1976) *The Actor's Life. Charlton Heston Journals 1956–1976*. London and New York.

Heston, C. (1995) *In the Arena: An Autobiography*. New York.

Heston, C. and Isbouts, J.-P. (1998) *Charlton Heston's Hollywood*. New York.

Higashi, S. (1994) *Cecil B. DeMille and American Culture: The Silent Era*. London.

Higashi, S. (2014) *Stars, Fans, and Consumption. Reading Photoplay*. London.

Higham, C. (1978) *Cecil B. DeMille*. New York.

Hillimer, M. (1997) *Film und Mode. Mode im Film*. Berlin.

Hirsch, F. (1978) *The Hollywood Epic*. London.

Hirsch, F. (1991) *Acting, Hollywood Style*. New York.

Hofler, R. (2014) *The Man Who Invented Rock Hudson. The Pretty Boys and Dirty Deals of Henry Willson*. New York.

Holston, K.R. (2013) *Movie Roadshows. A History and Filmography of Reserved-Seat Limited Screenings 1911–1973*. Jefferson, NC.

Holt, P. (1951) 'Samson and Delilah', in E. Anstey, R. Manvell, E. Lindgren, P. Rothaand G. Blumenthal (eds), *Shots in the Dark: A Collection of Reviewers' Opinions of Some of the Leading Films Released Between January 1949 and February 1951*. London, pp. 250–1.

Hozic, A. (2001) *Hollywood: Space, Power, and Fantasy in the American Economy*. Ithaca.

Huckvale, D. (2012) *Ancient Egypt in the Popular Imagination. Building a Fantasy in Film, Literature, Music and Art*. Jefferson, NC and London.

Hughes-Hallett, L. (1991) *Cleopatra. Histories, Dreams and Distortions*. London.

Hughes-Warrington, M. (2007) *History Goes to the Movies*. London.

Isackes, R. M. and Maness, K. L. (2017) *The Art of the Hollywood Backdrop*. New York.

Jorgensen, J. (2010) *Edith Head. The Fifty-Year Career of Hollywood's Greatest Costume Designer*. New York.

Jorgensen, J. and Scoggins, D. L. (2015) *Creating the Illusion. A Fashionable History of Hollywood Costume Designers*. Philadelphia and London.

Joshel, S. R., Malamud, M. and McGuire, D. T. (eds) (2001) *Imperial Projections. Ancient Rome in Modern Popular Culture*. Baltimore, MD and London.

Junkelmann, M. (2004) *Hollywoods Traum von Rom*. Mainz.

Kalmus, N. (1935) 'Color Consciousness', *Journal of the Society of Motion Picture Engineers*, 25: 135–47.

Kamp, D. (2000) 'When Liz Met Dick', in G. Carter (ed.), *Vanity Fair's Hollywood*. London. pp. 262–73.

Karnes, D. (1986) 'The Glamorous Crowd: Hollywood Movie Premieres Between the War', *American Quarterly*, 38 (4): 553–72.

Kashner, S. and Schoenberger, N. (2010) *Furious Love. Elizabeth Taylor. Richard Burton. The Marriage of the Century*. London.

Keenan, R. C. (2011) 'Film Noir', in P. C. DiMare (ed.), *Movies in American History*. Santa Barbara, pp. 951–5.

Kelly, K. (1981) *Elizabeth Taylor*. London.

Kelly, R. (2014) *Mark Antony and Popular Culture. Masculinity and the Construction of an Icon*. London.

Kernan, L. (2005) *Coming Attractions: Reading American Movie Trailers*. Austin.

Kerr, P. (ed.) (1986) *The Hollywood Film Industry*. London.

Keylin, A. and Bent, C. (eds) (1979) *The New York Times at the Movies*. New York.

Kinerk, M. D. (1998) 'Dream Palaces: The Motion Picture Playhouse in the Sunshine State', *Journal of Decorative and Propaganda Arts*, 23: 208–37.

Kinnard, R. and Davis, T. (1992) *Divine Images. A History of Jesus on the Screen*. New York.

Koszarski, R. (1976) *Hollywood Directors, 1914–1940*. Oxford.

Koury, P. (1959) *Yes, Mr. DeMille*. New York.

Kozlovic, A. K. (2002) 'The Whore of Babylon, Suggestibility, and the Art of Sexless Sex in Cecil B. DeMille's "Samson and Delilah" (1949)' in D. S. Claussen (ed.), *Sex, Religion, Media*. Lanham, MD, pp. 21–31.

Kydd, E. (2011) *The Critical Practice of Film. An Introduction*. London.

Lafornt-Couturier, H. (2013) *Peplum*. Lyon.

Lamarr, H. (1966) *Ecstasy and Me: My Life as a Woman*. New York.

Landau, D. (2000) *Gladiator: The Making of the Ridley Scott Epic*. London.

Landis, D. N. (2007) *Dressed. A Century of Hollywood Costume Design*. New York.

Landis, D. N. (ed.) (2012a) *Hollywood Costume*. London.

Landis, D. N. (2012b) *Hollywood Sketchbook. A Century of Costume Illustration*. New York.

Landis, D. N. (2012c) 'Setting the Scene: A Short History of Hollywood Costume Design 1912–2012', in D. N. Landis (ed.), *Hollywood Costume*. London, pp. 12–47.

Landis, D. N. (2012d) *FilmCraft: Costume Design*. London.

Lane Fox, R. (2004) *The Making of Alexander*. Oxford and London.

La Valley, S. (1987) 'Hollywood and Seventh Avenue: The Impact of Period Films in Fashion', in A. Annas, S. La Valley, E. Maeder and E. Jenssen (eds), *Hollywood and History: Costume Design in Film*. Los Angeles, pp. 78–96.

LaVine, W. R. (1981) *In a Glamorous Fashion. The Fabulous Years of Hollywood Costume Design*. London.

Leaming, B. (1989) *If This Was Happiness. A Biography of Rita Hayworth*. New York.

Lehner, M. (1985) *The Pyramid-Tomb of Hetep-heres and the Satellite Pyramid of Khufu*. Mainz.

Leib, K. (2011) 'The Ancient World in Film', in P. C. DiMare (ed.), *Movies in American History*. Santa Barbara, pp. 888–94.

Lev, P. (2003) *The Fifties. Transforming the Screen*. Berkeley.

Lindner, M. (2007) *Rom und seine Kaiser im Historienfilm*. Frankfurt.

Lindsay, R. A. (2015) *Biblical Epics. Camp Spectacle and Queer Style from the Silent Era to the Modern Day*. Santa Barbara.

Lindsay, R. A. (2016) 'Gay Villains in Biblical Epic Films', in R. Burnette-Bletsch (ed.), *The Bible in Motion. A Handbook of the Bible and Its Reception in Film*. Stuttgart, pp. 843–51.

Liversidge, M. and Edwards, C. (eds) (1996) *Imagining Rome. British Artists and Rome in the Nineteenth Century*. London.

Llewellyn-Jones, L. (2002a) 'The Queen of Sheba in Western Popular Culture 1850–2000', in St J. Simpson (ed.), *Queen of Sheba. Treasures from Ancient Yemen*. London, pp. 12–30.

Llewellyn-Jones, L. (2002b) 'Celluloid Cleopatras or Did the Greeks Ever Get to Egypt?', in D. Ogden (ed.), *The Hellenistic World. New Perspectives*. London, pp. 275–304.

Llewellyn-Jones, L. (2005) 'The Fashioning of Delilah. Costume Design, Historicism and Fantasy in Cecil B. DeMille's *Samson and Delilah* (1949)', in L. Cleland, M. Harlow and L. Llewellyn-Jones (eds), *The Clothed Body in the Ancient World*. Oxford, pp. 14–29.

Llewellyn-Jones, L. (2009) 'Hollywood's Ancient World', in A. Erskine (ed.), *A Companion to the Ancient World*. Oxford, pp. 564–79.

Llewellyn-Jones, L. (2013) 'An Almost All Greek Thing: Cleopatra VII and Hollywood Imagination', in K. P. Nikoloutsos (ed.), *Ancient Greek Women in Film*. Oxford, pp. 305–29.

Lloyd, I. (2011) *Elizabeth Taylor. Queen of the Silver Screen*. London.

Louvish, S. (2007) *Cecil B. DeMille and the Golden Calf*. London.

McArthur, C. (1998) '*Braveheart* and the Scottish Aesthetic Dementia', in T. Barta (ed.), *Screening the Past. Film and the Representation of History*. London, pp. 167–87.

McCarthy, T. (1997) *Howard Hawks. The Grey Fox of Hollywood*. New York.

McClean, A. L. (2004) *Being Rita Hayworth. Labor, Identity and Hollywood Stardom*. New Brunswick, NJ.

McClean, A. L. (ed.) (2017) *Behind the Silver Screen: A Modern History of Filmmaking. Costume, Makeup and Hair*. London.

McClelland, D. (1985) *Hollywood on Hollywood. Tinsel Town Talks*. Boston and London.

McConathy, D. and Vreeland, D. (1976) *Hollywood Costume. Glamour, Glitter, Romance*. New York.

McDonald, K. (ed.) (2011) *Americanization of History. Conflation of Time and Culture in Film and Television*. Newcastle upon Tyne.

MacDonald Fraser, G. (1988) *The Hollywood History of the World*. London.

McElwee, J. (2013) *Showmen, Sell It Hot! Movies as Merchandise in Golden Era Hollywood*. Pittsburgh.

McKay, J. (2013) *The Films of Victor Mature*. Jefferson, NC.

McLean, A. L. (2005) *Being Rita Hayworth. Labor, Identity and Hollywood Stardom*. New Brunswick.

McLellan, D. (2000) *The Girls: Sappho Goes to Hollywood*. New York.

Maeder, E. (1987) 'The Celluloid Image: Historical Dress in Film', in A. Annas, S. La Valley, E. Maeder and E. Jenssen (eds), *Hollywood and History. Costume Design in Film*. Los Angeles, pp. 9–42.

Maeder, E. (2012) 'Hollywood and History', in D. N. Landis (ed.), *Hollywood Costume*. London.

Malamud, M. (2009) *Ancient Rome and Modern America*. Oxford.

Malone, A. (2010) *Sacred Profanity. Spirituality at the Movies*. Santa Barbara.

Malone, P. (2012) *Screen Jesus. Portrayals of Christ in Television and Film*. Lanham, MD.

Maltby, R. (1993) 'The Production Code and the Hays Office', in T. Balio (ed.), *Grand Design: Hollywood as a Modern Business Enterprise, 1930–1939*. New York.

Maltby, R. (2003) *Hollywood Cinema*. Oxford.

Mann, A. (1977) 'Empire Demolition' in R. Koszarski (ed.), *Hollywood Directors 1941–1976*. New York, pp. 332–8.

Marcus, G. (2011) *The Doors: A Lifetime of Listening to Five Mean Years*. New York.

Marich, R. (2005) *Marketing to Moviegoers. A Handbook of Strategies and Tactics*. Carbondale, IL.

Martin, A. (2000) *Going to the Pictures Scottish Memories of Cinema*. Glasgow.

Martin, M. (2007) *The Magnificent Showman. The Epic Films of Samuel Bronston*. Albany, NY.

Martin, M. and Porter, M. (1987) *Video Movie Guide 1988*. New York.

Massey, A. (2000) *Hollywood Beyond the Screen: Design and Material Culture*. Oxford.

Matthijs, E. and Pomerance, M. (2006) *From Hobbits to Hollywood: Essays on Peter Jackson's Lord of the Rings*. Amsterdam.

Mayer, D. (1994) *Playing Out the Empire. Ben-Hur and Other Toga Plays and Films. A Critical Anthology*. Oxford.

Medhurst, A. (1997) 'Camp', in A. Medhurst and S. Munt (eds), *Lesbian and Gay Studies: A Critical Introduction*. London, pp. 274–93.

Medved, H. and Medved, M. (1984) *The Hollywood Hall of Shame. The Most Expensive Flops in Movie History*. New York.

Mercer, J. (2015) *Rock Hudson*. London.

Meyers, J. (ed.) (1999) *Sunset Boulevard by Billy Wilder. The Complete Screenplay, with an Introduction*. Berkeley.

Michaelakis, P. and Wyke, M. (eds) (2013) *The Ancient World in Silent Cinema*. Cambridge.

Montserrat, D. (2000) *Akhenaten: History, Fantasy and Ancient Egypt*. London.

Morcillo, M. G., Hanesworth, P. and Marchena, O. L. (eds) (2015) *Imagining Ancient Cities in Film. From Babylon to Cinecittà*. New York and London.

Mordden, E. (1988) *The Hollywood Studios. House Style in the Golden Age of Movies*. New York.

Morley, S. (2006) *The Brits in Hollywood. Tales from the Hollywood Raj*. London.

Mulvey, L. (1975) *Visual and Other Pleasures*. Bloomington, IN.

Munn, M. (1982) *The Stories Behind the Scenes of the Great Film Epics*. London.

Munn, M. (2008) *Richard Burton, Prince of Players*. London.

Mutti-Mewse, A. and Mutti-Mewse, H. (2014) *I Used to Be in Pictures. An Untold Story of Hollywood*. Woodbridge.

Nadel, A. (1993) 'God's Law and the Wide Screen: *The Ten Commandments* as Cold War Epic', *PMLA*, 108 (3): 415–30.

Naylor, D. (1988) *Picture Palaces: Views from Americas Past*. New York.

Nielson, E. (1990) 'Handmaids of the Glamour Culture. Costumiers in the Hollywood Studio System', in J. Gaines and C. Herzog (eds), *Fabrications: Costume and the Female Body*. London and New York, pp. 165–80.

Nisbet, G. (2007) *Ancient Greece in Film and Popular Culture*. Bristol.

Noerdlinger, H. S. (1956) *Moses and Egypt*: *The Documentation to the Motion Picture of 'The Ten Commandments'*. Los Angeles.

Orrison, K. (1999) *Written in Stone. Making Cecil B. DeMille's Epic 'The Ten Commandments'*. New York.

Park, W. (2003) *Hollywood. An Epic Production*. Portland, OR.

Parker, L. N. (1928) *Several of My Lives*. London.

Paul, J. (2013) *Film and the Classical Epic Tradition*. Oxford.

Paul, W. (2016) *When Movies Were Theatre: Architecture, Exhibition, and the Evolution of American Film*. New York.

Pepper, T. and Kobal, J. (1989) *The Man Who Shot Garbo: The Hollywood Photographs of Clarence Sinclair Bull*. London.

Perry, G. (ed.) (1989) *Dilys Powell: The Golden Screen. Fifty Years of Films*. London.

Petley, J. (2009) *Censorship. A Beginner's Guide*. London.

Plummer, C. (2010) *In Spite of Myself. A Memoir*. London.

Pomeroy, A. J. (2008) *Then It was Destroyed by the Volcano: The Ancient World in Film and on Television*. London.

Rambusch, H. W. (1930) 'The Decorations of the Theatre', in R. W Sexton (ed.), *American Theatres of Today*. New York, pp. 2–24.

Ramírez, J. A. (2004) *Architecture for the Screen. A Critical Study of Set Design in Hollywood's Golden Age*. Jefferson, NC and London.

Raymond, E. (2006) *From My Cold, Dead Hands. Charlton Heston and American Politics*. Lexington, KY.

Rebello, S. and Allen, R. (1988) *Reel Art. Great Posters from the Golden Age of the Silver Screen*. New York.

Reinhartz, A. (2013a) *Bible and Cinema: Fifty Key Films*. London.

Reinhartz, A. (2013b) *Bible and Cinema. An Introduction*. London.

Reisner, G. A. and Smith, W. S. (1955) *A History of the Giza Necropolis II*. Cambridge, MA.

Riad, S. (2014) 'Leadership in the Fluid Moral Economy of Conspicuous Consumption: Insights from the Moralizing Talks of Antony and Cleopatra', *Journal of Management History*, 20 (1): 5–43.

Richards, J. (2008) *Hollywood's Ancient Worlds*. London.

Richards, J. (2009a) *The Age of the Dream Palace: Cinema and Society in 1930s Britain*. London.

Richards, J. (2009b) *The Ancient World on the Victorian and Edwardian Stage*. London.

Ringgold, G. (1974) *The Films of Rita Hayworth. The Legend and Career of a Love Goddess*. Toronto.

Ringgold, G. and Bodeen, D. (1969) *The Films of Cecil B. DeMille*. New York.

Roberts, J. (2010) *The Complete History of American Film Criticism*. Santa Monica.

Roberts-Frenzel, C. (2001) *Rita Hayworth. A Photographic Retrospective*. New York.

Robinson, D. (1955) 'Spectacle', *Sight and Sound*, 250: 22–7, 55–6.

Robinson, J. (1987) *Fashion in the '30s*. London.

Roen, P. (1994) *High Camp. A Gay Guide to Camp and Cult Films. Volume 1*. San Francisco.

Roen, P. (1997) *High Camp. A Gay Guide to Camp and Cult Films. Volume 2*. San Francisco.

Rose, M. (1974) *The Doré Bible Illustrations*. New York.

Rosen, P. (2001) *Change Mummified: Cinema, Historicity, Theory*. London.

Rosenstone R. (1995) *Revisioning History: Film and the Construction of a New Past*. Princeton.

Rovin, J. (1977) *The Films of Charlton Heston*. Secaucus.

Royster, F. T. (2003) *Becoming Cleopatra. The Shifting Image of an Icon*. New York.

Rubython, T. (2011) *And God Created Burton*. London.

Russo, V. (1981) *The Celluloid Closet. Homosexuality in the Movies*. New York.

Saleh, M. and Sourouzain, H. (1987) *The Official Catalogue of the Cairo Museum*. Mainz.

Santas, C. (2008) *The Epic in Film. From Myth to Blockbuster*. Lanham, MD.

Santas, C., Wilson, J. M., Colavito, M. and Baker, D. (eds) (2014) *The Encyclopedia of Epic Films*. Lanham, MD.

Schatz, T. (1988) *Hollywood Filmmaking in the Studio Era. The Genius of the System*. Minneapolis.

Schickel, E. (1996) *D. W. Griffith. An American Life*. New York.

Scorsese, M. (1989) *Scorsese on Scorsese*. London.

Sennett, R. S. (1998) *Hollywood Hoopla. Creating Stars and Selling Movies in the Golden Age of Hollywood*. New York.

Server, L. (1987) *Screenwriter: Words Become Pictures*. Pittstown, NJ.

Sharaff, I. (1976) *Broadway and Hollywood. Costumes Designed By Irene Sharaff*. New York.

Shatz, T. (1988) *The Genius of the System. Hollywood Filmmaking in the Studio Era*. Minneapolis.

Shearer, S. M. (2010) *Beautiful: The Life of Hedy Lamarr*. New York.

Shepherd, D. J. (2013) *The Bible on Silent Film. Spectacle, Story and Scripture in the Early Cinema*. Cambridge.

Shiel, M. (2015) 'Classical Hollywood, 1928–1946', in L. Fischer (ed.), *Art Direction and Production Design*. London, pp. 48–72.

Sikov, E. (2000) *On Sunset Boulevard: The Life and Times of Billy Wilder*. London.

Simsolo, N. 2011) *Billy Wilder: Masters of Cinema*. London.

Slide, A. (2010) *Inside the Hollywood Fan Magazine. A History of Star Makers, Fabricators, and Gossip Mongers*. Jackson, MS.

Smith, G. A. (2004) *Epic Films. Cast, Credits and Commentary on Over 350 Historical Spectacle Movies*. Jefferson, MO and London.

Smith, S. (2012) *Elizabeth Taylor*. London.

Sobchack, V. (1990) 'Surge and Splendour. A Phenomenology of the Hollywood Historical Epic', *Representations*, 29: 24–49.

Solomon, J. (2001) *The Ancient World in Cinema*, 2nd edn. New Haven, CT and London.

Solomon, J. (2016) *Ben-Hur. The Original Blockbuster*. Edinburgh.

Sontag, S. (1966) 'Notes on Camp', in *Against Interpretations and Other Essays*. New York, pp. 275–92.

Sorlin, P. (1990) 'Historical Films as Tools for Historians', in J. E. O'Connor (ed.), *Image as Artefact. The Historical Analysis of Film and Television*. Malibu, pp. 43–68.

Squire, G. (1972) *Dress and Society*. London.

Stacey, J. (1993) *Star Gazing. Hollywood Cinema and Female Spectatorship*. London.

Staggs, S. (2002) *Close-up on Sunset Boulevard: Billy Wilder, Norma Desmond, and the Dark Hollywood Dream*. New York.

Staiger, J. (1985) *The Classical Hollywood Cinema: Film Styles and Mode of Production to 1960*. New York.

Steele, V. (1989) 'Dressing for Work', in C. B. Kidwell and V. Steele (eds), *Men and Women: Dressing the Part*. Washington, DC, pp. 64–91.

Stemp, S. (2012) *A to Z of Hollywood Style*. London.

Stubbs, J. (2013) *Historical Film. A Critical Introduction*. London.

Swanson, G. (1981) *Swanson on Swanson. An Autobiography*. London.

Swanson, V. G. (2001) 'The Book of Mormon Art of Arnold Friberg, "Painter of Scripture"', *Journal of Book of Mormon Studies*, 10 (1): 26–35, 79.

Tanitch, R. (2000) *Blockbusters! 70 Years of Best-Selling Movies*. London.

Tashiro, C. S. (1998) *Pretty Pictures. Production Design and the History Film*. Austin.

Tashiro, C. S. (2004) 'Film and History: Passing for the Past. Production Design and the Historical Film', *Cineaste*, 29 (2): 40–4.

Taylor, A. (1995) 'Review of *Braveheart*', *The Scotsman*, 4 September.

Thompson, F. (1996) *Lost Films. Important Movies That Disappeared*. New York.

Thorpe, M. F. (1939) *America at the Movies*. London.

Toplin, R. B. (2002) *Reel History. In Defence of Hollywood*. Kansas City.

Trent, P. (1982) *The Image Makers. Sixty Years of Hollywood Glamour*. London.

Turner, L. (1982) *Lana Turner. The Lady and the Truth*. New York.

Ustinov, P. (1977) *Dear Me*. London.

Vargas-Cooper, N. (2010) *Mad Men Unbuttoned. A Romp Through 1960s America*. New York.

Vermilye, J. and Ricci, M. (1993) *The Films of Elizabeth Taylor*. New York.

Vertrees, A. D. (1997) *Selznick's Vision. 'Gone With the Wind' and Hollywood Filmmaking*. Austin.

Vidal, G. (1992) *Screening History*. Cambridge, MA.

Vieira, M. A. (2013) *George Hurrell's Hollywood. Glamour Portraits 1925–1992*. Philadelphia and London.

Wagenknecht, E. (1962) *Movies in the Age of Innocence*. Norman, OK.

Wallen, G. A. (ed.) (2002) *Moviegoing in America*. Oxford.

Walsh, R. (2003) *Reading the Gospels in the Dark. Portrayals of Jesus in Film*. Harrisberg, PA.

Wanger, W. and Hyams, J. (1963) *My Life with Cleopatra*. London.

Waterbury, R. (1955) 'He Lost His Shirt and Became a Star', *Photoplay*, May, pp. 62–3, 121–2.

Webb, M. (ed.) (1986) *Hollywood. Legend and Reality*. London.

Wenzel, D. (2005) *Kleopatra im Film*. Remscheid.

White, H. (1988) 'Historiography and Historiophoty', *American Historical Review*, 93 (5): 1193–9.

Whitlock, K. (2010) *Designs on Film. A Century of Hollywood Art Direction*. New York.

Whitney, D. (1934) 'Designer's Say Shorter Skirts!', *Shadowplay*, 3: 16.

Wick Reeves, W. (2008) *Ballyhoo! Posters as Portraiture*. London.

Wilcoxon, H. (1991) *Lionheart in Hollywood. Life and Times with C. B. DeMille*. Metuchen, NJ and London.

Wills, D. (2013) *Hollywood in Kodachrome 1940–1945*. London.

Winkler, M. M. (1995) 'Cinema and the Fall of Rome', *Transactions of the American Philological Society*, 125: 135–54.

Winkler, M. M. (2001) *Classical Myth and Culture in the Cinema*. Oxford.

Winkler, M. M. (2004) *Gladiator. Film and History*. Oxford.

Winkler, M. M. (2007a) *Troy: From Homer's 'Iliad' to Hollywood Epic*. Oxford.

Winkler, M. M. (2007b) *Spartacus. Film and History*. Oxford.

Winkler, M. M. (2009) *The Fall of the Roman Empire*. Oxford.

Wood, C. (1983) *Olympian Dreamers. Victorian Classical Painters 1860–1914*. London.

Wood, M. (1975) *America in the Movies*. London.

Woolman Chase, E. (1937) 'Fashion: Sparks from the Paris Openings', *Vogue*, 89: 59–66.

Wright, L. (2007) 'Objectifying Gender. The Stiletto Heel', in M. Bernard (ed.), *Fashion Theory: A Reader*. London, pp. 197–207.

Wright, M. J. (2003) *Moses in America. The Cultural Uses of Biblical Narrative.* Oxford.

Wurtzel, E. (1998) *Bitch: In Praise of Difficult Women.* New York.

Wyke, M. (1994) 'Make Like Nero! The Appeal of a Cinematic Emperor', in J. Elsner and J. Masters (eds), *Reflections of Nero: Culture, History, and Representation.* London.

Wyke, M. (1997) *Projecting the Past. Ancient Rome, Cinema and History.* London and New York.

Wyke, M. (2002) *The Roman Mistress. Ancient and Modern Receptions.* Oxford.

Wyke, M. and Michelakis, P. (eds) (2013) *The Ancient World in Silent Cinema.* Cambridge.

Young, C. (2012) *Classic Hollywood Style.* London.

Ziegler, C. (1994) *Egyptomania. L'Égypte dans l'art occidental 1730–1930.* Paris.

INDEX